SPIRITUALITY, DIVERSION, AND DECADENCE

SUNY Series in Religion
Harold Coward, Editor

SPIRITUALITY, DIVERSION, AND DECADENCE

The Contemporary Predicament

Peter H. Van Ness

State University of New York Press

Published by
State University of New York Press, Albany

Production by Christine M. Lynch
Marketing by Bernadette LaManna

© 1992 State University of New York

For information, address the State University of New York Press,
State University Plaza, Albany, NY 12246

Library of Congress Cataloging-in-Publication Data
Van Ness, Peter H. (Peter Higbis), 1953-
    Spirituality, diversion, and decadence : the contemporary
predicament / Peter H. Van Ness,
        p. cn. — (SUNY series in religion)
    Includes bibliographical references and index.
    ISBN 0-7914-1205-9 (alk. paper). — ISBN 0-7914-1206-7 (pbk. :
alk. paper)
    1. Spirituality. 2. Civilization. Modern—20th century.
I. Title.   II. Series.
BL624.V34 1992
291.4—dc20   91-38672
                                                      CIP

10 9 8 7 6 5 4 3 2 1

To my parents

CONTENTS

PREFACE

Like other cultural artifacts, books have histories. This book was written during the last half dozen years while I taught philosophy of religion at Union Theological Seminary in New York City. Historians will surely associate this period in the city's life with the success and excess of Wall Street financiers, who, along with their counterparts in Tokyo, London, and elsewhere, came then to wield great power in a very public and almost flamboyant fashion. Just as surely will this era in world history be characterized by the movements toward democracy, especially in Eastern Europe and Latin America, which gave institutional form to the increasingly shared conviction that almost all persons should be empowered to participate in the governance of their own lives. These two developments are only apparently incompatible; indeed, their vivid simultaneity in the last decade has largely occasioned the writing of this book.

Citizens of the United States should be the last persons to be surprised that small numbers of persons can exercise inordinate powers in a democracy; constitutional rights and egalitarian laws insure that such an exercise of power is not direct and tyrannical, but they allow that it be indirect and persuasive. Hence as the world has become at least nominally more democratic, the leaders of powerful institutions—certainly governments and corporations, but also churches and professional organizations—have been led to seek novel means of social control. Their power resides in their ability to control the actions of others, and because direct coercion is outlawed, this power has come largely to consist of their ability to instill habitual patterns of behavior. Via advertising pitches and expert advice they achieve this control by inculcating habitual patterns of consumption in malleable populations. How one consumes products and services, and especially information and entertainment, is today a prime determinant of one's personal freedom and spiritual health. Pascal's notion of diversion and Nietzsche's idea of decadence have proved helpful to me in identifying and understanding contemporary types of spiritual pathology which make people vulnerable to manipulation by powerful institutions.

As I have become convinced that individual habits of consumption are vehicles of social control I became more convinced of the importance of spiritually disciplined practices as means for resisting such control. Some of the practices I discuss in the text I have pursued to one degree or another. I say this without presuming spiritual mastery of any of them. As I explored these practices, especially those rooted in my own Western Christian tradition, I became convinced that the ways in which they were described and justified were more a hindrance than an aid to their adoption. The primarily Platonic and Stoic notions enlisted for this task by Hellenistic philosophers seemed to me inadequate, and new philosophical resources seemed requisite. I have tried to furnish them by drawing upon key ideas from the formal, physical, and biological sciences. From this effort, and from the prior realization of the contemporary relevance of spiritually disciplined practices, *Spirituality, Diversion, and Decadence* was born.

Several parts of this book have appeared in print in other forms. I take this opportunity to thank the editors and publishers of the journals listed below for their permission to reprint the following materials:

> "Linguistic Self-Reference and Religious Language," *Union Seminary Quarterly Review* 41.2 (Summer 1987);
>
> "Nietzsche on Solitude: The Spiritual Discipline of the Godless," *Philosophy Today* 32.4 (Winter 1988);*
>
> "Apology, Speculation, and Philosophy's Fate," *Philosophy & Theology,* 5.1 (Fall 1990);
>
> "Pascal on Habit: Spiritual Discipline as the Practice of Paradox," *Philosophy Today,* 35.4 (Winter 1991).*

I also want to thank the many people who helped me to prepare and write this book. They, of course, are not responsible for any of its shortcomings: I have transformed their encouragement and insight in myriad ways. Among those I thank are Ewert Cousins, Ellen Davis, Elisabeth Koenig, Christian Miner, Richard Norris, Wayne Proudfoot, and Jennifer Rike. My colleagues on the Union faculty have consistently supported my work, and students in the Union and Columbia graduate programs have been helpful critics. I am especially grateful for conversations I have had in recent years with members of the "Spirituality Study Group" that Ewert Cousins has informally gathered at Columbia University in recent years.

* Copyright, 1988 and 1991 respectively, by De Paul University, all rights reserved; printed in the United States of America by Croatian Franciscan Press, 4851 S. Drexel Blvd., Chicago, Illinois, 60615.

I also wish to thank Union Theological Seminary and the American Academy of Religion for research grants that partially funded my research. I thank Leah Robinson for the book's index. Finally, I thank my editors, Bill Eastman and Harold Coward, and the staff at the State University of New York Press for their help in the book's publication.

Peter H. Van Ness
August 15, 1991

Introduction: On Praxis and Pleroma

This essay is intended to be a contribution to the contemporary philosophy of religion. In it I shall examine regimens of behavior which purport to promote human well-being, and which both agents and observers regard as distinctively religious or spiritual. Religious behaviors, therefore, are a more central concern than religious doctrines, and spiritual well-being is assumed to depend upon more than the truth of one's intellectual convictions. Yet just because the manner of reflection is philosophical, attention will especially be given to the nature of participants' descriptions of their religious practices and to their reasons for adopting them.

Only one of the two most common kinds of rationales will be examined. The example of prayer shows the relevant distinction. Prayer to God in its various forms is certainly regarded as religious behavior by persons who pray and by persons who observe them, even by observers who are not themselves religious. If asked why they do it, praying persons might answer by saying, "I pray because I am commanded to do so by God" or "I pray because my ancestors have done so before me and it is my sacred duty to conform to their example." These are theological rationales for prayer, emergent from and authoritative for some particular religious tradition. To the religious skeptic they seem more motivations than reasons. They are not my primary concern.

A different sort of answer might be given to this same inquiry about prayer. For instance, one might claim that prayer is warranted because it consistently directs one's attention away from quotidian concerns and entertains the most exalted thoughts—perhaps about God—of which the human mind is capable. In this instance prayer not only posits God's existence as an extraordinary being, but it also claims to discover distinctive, and perhaps, unique, dimensions of what it means to be human. This second rationale is philosophical in that its adequacy is not intentionally or logically restricted to a particular religious tradition. Admittedly, even this second rationale is not free of presuppositions which may make it irrelevant to certain persons, religious or otherwise; however, it moves toward that variety of generality characteristic of Western philosophy, and it is this sort of description and justification that will be investigated in the pages that follow.

Scholarly treatments of topics like prayer and fasting, and meditation and solitude, have most often been undertaken by historians and theologians. My work is philosophical, but still related to these more familiar efforts. In it I shall often locate the practices discussed in historical contexts, especially those emergent from the Western Christian tradition in which I have been reared and educated. I shall enlist the aid of social historians like Peter Brown; I have especially learned much from the historical theologian Margaret Miles, who, in a series of books, beginning with *Fullness of Life: Historical Foundations for a New Asceticism,* has urged a retrieval of some traditional Christian practices for the purposes of breaking unhealthy patterns of behavior typical of contemporary life.[1] I shall sometimes appeal to non-Western materials for which I provide little historical commentary. This practice exposes my historical limitations, but the risk involved is worthwhile, I think, because, at least, it signals a receptive awareness to new pluralistic realities. At best, it makes claims to philosophical generality more plausible.

In a similar manner I appreciate the work of theologians like Karl Rahner who make spiritual discipline an integral part of their confessional projects. I shall be especially attentive to those theologians who testify that religious reflection should not be conducted in abstraction from the social contexts and struggles which inevitably condition such reflection. Most instructive in this regard are Latin American discussions of the "spirituality of liberation," a phrase coined by Gustavo Gutiérrez and adopted by other liberation theologians who similarly reflect upon religious practices in their spiritual as well as in their political meaning.[2] While I shall deal with the social and political implications of the material I discuss, most of my theological views will remain implicit. Acknowledgements of my own confessional beliefs which, admittedly, influence the course of the essay, will be less prominent that would be desirable in a theological project. A philosophical approach has different priorities.

Then what recommends a philosophical approach to this material? What does it offer that historical or theological treatments do not? Some think it has little more to offer. Søren Kierkegaard dramatically expressed this doubt when he wrote: "to prove with reasons that to pray is a bliss that 'passes all understanding'... What a priceless anticlimax!"[3] Describing and justifying a regimen of religious behavior with philosophical resources may seem a superfluity, yet when the philosophical materials invoked are experienced as so objectionable as to discourage adoption of the regimen, then it becomes not only anticlimactic but antithetic as well. A major thesis argued in succeeding chapters says that this, indeed, has come to be the case for some classic philosophical rationales for a spiritually disciplined life. Hence philosophical reflection upon religious regimens can be uniquely helpful in removing such intellectual barriers.

Some religious teachers say that any philosophical belief erects a barrier to the fullest sort of spiritual life. The Zen Buddhist monk, Shunryu Suzuki, was one such teacher: "By enlightenment I mean believing in nothing. . . . It is on this original truth that our activity, our thinking, and our practice should be based."[4] This thought is recorded in a recently popular manual of Zen Buddhist meditation; there Suzuki encourages the development of a mind empty of privileged doctrines and open to spontaneous experience. Such teachings have had influence in the West. For instance, Thomas Merton came to urge a type of "contemplative prayer" not directly informed by Biblical language and theological doctrine: "We should let ourselves be brought naked and defenseless into the center of that dread where we stand alone before God in our nothingness, without explanation, without theories."[5]

In some respects I am sympathetic to this nonprescriptive orientation, though, naturally, as a philosopher, I regard Suzuki's categorical statements more as helpful hyperbole than inviolate rule. It is not desirable (nor possible!) for beliefs about prayer and like activities to be entirely eradicated; rather, in my view, they are to be kept fluid and vital by intellectual criticism and imaginative rethinking so that they might be aids rather than obstacles to their associated activities. Here is a more constructive agenda for the philosophical treatment of this material: to provide metaphorical redescriptions and conceptual reformulations of the ways that regimens of religious behavior are described and justified, with a special emphasis on making such language continuous with the most adequate general explanations of the world and so relevant to the full expanse of human experience. David Ray Griffin has written that a philosophical approach to this topic characteristically examines "the ways various theories about the nature of reality. . . support or fail to support spiritual discipline."[6] Although stated in terms less qualified than my own, it is this sort of project that I shall undertake in the pages that follow, recognizing that implicit in this effort is a judgment that such behavior is not so misguided as to devaluate rethinking, nor so sacrosanct as to prohibit reformulation.

The effort of redescription and reformulation will eventually be directed toward the notion of spiritual discipline itself. As a prefiguring of that engagement consider the terms 'praxis' and 'pleroma'. They are learned borrowings from ancient Greek (both are listed in the Oxford English Dictionary!); they are roughly translatable as 'practice' and 'fullness' respectively. They are convenient rubrics under which to offer these introductory remarks because together they specify the topic soon to be examined, i.e., practices which promote spiritual fullness, or, even more succinctly, pleromatic praxis. Yet the very compression of this formula creates difficulties; it masks ambiguities which any satisfactory philosophical rethinking of these matters must resolve. Some etymological digression will be helpful.

'Praxis' was traditionally used as an antonym for 'theory'; it generally meant human action construed in accordance with a specific reflective interest. In the later Hellenistic period the word was used to describe religious behavior: the New Testament collection of writings about the apostolic labors of Peter and Paul acquired the title of 'ΠΡΑΞΕΙΣ ΑΠΟΣΤΛΩΝ' (*The Acts of the Apostles*). A second-century Middle Platonist, Albinus, expressly defined the term to mean "the active operation of the reasonable soul working through the instrumentality of the body."[7] This conception of praxis as the embodied action of a spiritual agent is aptly descriptive of the regimens of behavior that are the object of study here; however its usage would be anachronistic in a contemporary theological context where 'praxis' is immediately suggestive of Karl Marx's notion of revolutionary praxis. For instance, Gutiérrez employs this term with its Marxist connotations and make it a central category in his conception of the spirituality of liberation.

In Marx's celebrated *Theses on Feuerbach* 'revolutionäre Praxis' is construed to be the collection of human activities effective for the politically progressive transformation of the social and economic order; it is contrasted with merely "abstrakten Denken" that keeps that the extant state of affairs undisturbed.[8] Certainly this association is desirable to the extent that it reminds one that religious practices are ethically suspect when motivated solely by personal projects of salvation undertaken in flight from a suffering world. On the other hand, a reduction of the value of such practices to their tangible political utility is equally questionable. A counter to this threat is the Aristotelian notion of praxis as moral activity having no goal or function extrinsic to itself, and which achieves social value through its realization of some intrinsic goodness (*Nicomachean Ethics* 1140b).

Resolution of this ambiguity in the meaning of praxis as it applies to religious regimens will be a goal of this essay; it will entail a response to Marxist and other critics who contend that practices described as spiritual disciplines are, in fact, impediments rather than aids to worldly human flourishing.

'Pleroma' harbors a similarly fundamental ambiguity. 'Pleroma' and its cognates were often used in Hellenistic religious thought to identify a condition of human well-being consisting of more than purely human happiness. This human fullness was often realized as the influx of something sacred. This usage is exemplified by the author of the New Testament letter to the Colossians who writes that in Christ "the whole fullness (πλήρωμα) of deity dwells bodily, and you have come to fullness of life (πεπληρωμένοι) in him" (Col. 2:9–10).[9] In the second century of the Christian era the term received a technical religious meaning in the speculations of Gnostic thinkers like the Alexandrian Valentinus. For him the Pleroma was a hierarchical assembly of personified divine attributes that collectively constituted a primordial realm of being. Pregnant within the natures and relations of these constituent beings (or Aeons) were conflicts which precipitated the Gnostic drama of salvation and prefigured the radical cosmic dualism for which the Gnostics were infamous. Spiritual fullness for Valentinians meant being reawakened and restored to one's proper place in the primordial perfection of the world. Yet the Gnostic Pleroma was an emblem of fecundity and extravagance not only in a strictly ontological sense, but also in looser imaginative sense. Upon describing one version of the worlds come forth from the Gnostic Pleroma, Irenaeus, Bishop of Lyons and contemporary of Valentinus, writes that "Everyday one of them (the Valentinians) invent something new, and none of them is considered perfect unless he is productive in this way."[10] Though intended as a disparagement by an orthodox Christian opponent, this remark correctly highlights the Gnostic appreciation of imaginative creativity as a mark of spiritual well-being.

In Gnostic spirituality, then, fullness of life is at once a more satisfactory relation with what is real and also a more vibrant way of imagining what is possible. This ambiguity becomes an issue for this project when it is asked whether the rethinking of spiritual discipline is a redescription which substitutes lively for stale metaphors, or whether it also involves a reformulation which seeks compatibility of religious language with scientific and philosophical accounts of the way the world actually is. Some critics of Western religion, who, unlike Marxists, for instance, persist in pursuing a spiritual variety of fullness of life—and this includes many feminists like Margaret Miles, and especially her Harvard colleague, Elisabeth Schüssler Fiorenza—argue that unless imagination informs the rethinking of traditional religious doctrines and practices, their retrieval will comprise only a more subtle accommodation with an unjust history and society.[11] Hence resolution of the ambiguity of whether spiritual fullness is an ontological or imaginative achievement will be a task of this essay, and will entail a response to critics who contend that contemporary spirituality demands an imaginative freedom from prevailing conceptions of scientific rationality.

In the course of this brief examination of 'pleromatic praxis' two quite different tasks have emerged. First, the task of resolving an ambiguity attached to a general notion; and second, the task of defending an interpretation of a general notion having once recognized that its possible meanings can be bearers of conflicting convictions. Actually these two tasks reflect the dual character of the Western tradition of philosophy of religion which has historically included both evaluative and explanatory elements. In the last few pages I have sought to respond to the query as to why someone with an interest in religious practices like prayer should attend to what a philosopher may have to say on this subject. Briefly summarized, I have responded that a critical philosophical examination of the language used to describe and justify such practices can remove impediments to their adoption, and that a constructive philosophical rethinking of such descriptions and justifications can relate them helpfully to a broader realm of nonreligious activities and aspirations. Now the question deserves to be answered from the opposite point of view, saying why philosophers of religion should attend to practices as well as doctrines. My response is intimated by the two tasks mentioned above: a philosophical investigation of descriptions and justifications of religious practices very quickly confronts crucial issues that comprise the philosophy of religion in its traditional evaluative and explanatory forms, i.e, in its historical occurrences as apology and speculation.

Apology and speculation are forms of intellectual discourse which have fallen into disfavor with many recent thinkers. Karl Barth and his heirs have excoriated theological apologetics as an implicit renunciation of the true dogmatic task of correcting the Christian Church's proclamation of Word of God. Barth's task is not now my own. More relevant here is the judgment of the later Ludwig Wittgenstein and his followers that philosophical apologetics is a misguided effort to make philosophers the arbiters of a forms of life and language which have their own distinctive integrity. The disenchantment with speculation has even earlier origins. Immanuel Kant identified in the faculty of theoretical reason a consistent tendency to transgress reason's legitimate bounds: in theological arguments which posit supersensible realities he found a paradigmatic case of illegitimate speculation. Kant's influence and other factors have led many philosophers and theologians to accept a popular equation of speculation with not very well informed guesses.

In my view a philosophy of religion that is deliberately absented of all elements of apology and speculation becomes trivial for its irrelevance to questions of truth and value. Conversely, a genuinely significant project in the philosophy of religion that professes no apologetic or speculative dimensions is, in my mind, guilty of dissimulation. Certainly philosophers may choose to pursue a descriptive agenda in their reflections upon religion—and redescriptions of familiar religious practices will figure prominently in this essay—but this does not mean that they are free from apologetic and speculative commitments, but only that they have laid them aside in preference to descriptive tasks. Merold Westphal is quite frank in making this acknowledgement when he presents a "descriptive philosophy of religion" in his recent book *God, Guilt, and Death: An Existential Phenomenology of Religion.*[12] The essay which follows addresses descriptive, evaluative, and explanatory issues. Since the latter two have become so controversial I will briefly identify the traditional meanings of apology and speculation as dimensions of the philosophy of religion and will indicate the ways in which they figure in the project undertaken here.

Since at least the beginning of the Christian era an apology in the religious sense has been understood to be a rational defense of religious beliefs and practices. The most celebrated apology in antiquity was Socrates' defense before an Athenian jury; there he responded to several charges, among them an accusation by Miletus of disbelief in the state gods. Charging Socrates with impiety was not entirely unfounded. Greek philosophers since Xenophanes of Colophon had criticized tenets of Greek Olympian religion. Socrates himself was especially adamant in offering the philosopher as an authoritative guide to basic beliefs, and, in doing so, he challenged the attribution of this office to Homer whose mythological narratives were primary repositories of Olympian religion. Apology, though literally meaning defense, is inseparable from criticism as the opposite which engenders it. Thus apology may be understood to be argumentative discourse expressing either religious or irreligious sentiments.

Christian writers developed their own tradition of apologetics: the speech at the Areopagus attributed to Paul is something of a Scriptural prototype (Acts 17:16–34). The *Apologiae* of Justin Martyr are more self-consciously philosophical examples of this variety of literature, and they combine defense of Christianity with criticisms of Greek religion. Clement of Alexandria's *Protrepticus* was a second-century apologetic work which contained a much more extended and detailed denunciation of popular Greek religion. It also suggested themes developed elsewhere, specifically, in the *Stromata*, which constituted a very early Christian appropriation of Greek philosophical ideas for the purposes of describing and justifying Christian beliefs and practices. Included in this effort is the first systematic defense of nonliturgical Christian practices devoted to promoting spiritual fullness. In the first part of this essay I shall explicate central aspects of Clement's rationale for Christian spiritual life (Chapter 1.B); subsequently I shall argue that it is a philosophical case deficient in several important respects (Chapter 2.A). Hence this essay is an exercise in irreligious apologetics—in philosophical argumentation designed to gainsay traditional religious claims.

Yet my conclusions on this issue are not entirely negative (Chapter 2.B). Also, Clement's treatment of the philosophical problems associated with spiritual life was redirected in subsequent tradition. Blaise Pascal lived and articulated a particularly momentous transformation. His aims were similar to Clement's: his celebrated *Pensées* being the fragments of a projected *Apology for the Christian Religion*. His interests were similarly practical: he is famous for his contention that religious belief is more a matter of habit than of rational proof. Pascal was able to rethink the challenge of spiritually disciplined practices because he combined deep intellectual insights, for example, into probability theory and the process of scientific experimentation, with personal experience of a wide variety of social roles: inventor and entrepreneur, prose stylist and religious polemicist, family benefactor and spiritual adept. His Wager argument and his diagnosis of diversion (*divertissement*) are the two most prominent fruits of this achievement. In the next section of this book I indicate the enduring significance of Pascal's predicament (Chapter 1.A); I conclude the first part by claiming there is need for yet further reformulation in light of the same sorts of intellectual and social changes that advanced Pascal beyond early Christian rationales such as provided by Clement, Augustine, and medieval piety (Chapter 2.C).

The apologetic concerns of the book reappear in its third part. Friedrich Nietzsche's discussion of "ascetic ideals" in *On the Genealogy of Morals* is a very significant philosophical treatment of this topic, and his ideas are invoked as corroboration for my own criticisms of traditional asceticism (Chapter 6.A). Nietzsche, while insisting upon the importance of a spiritually disciplined life, is far more vigorous than I in his criticisms of Christianity and the other religions he discusses. Thus the following part of the book seeks to counter Nietzsche's harsher criticisms while at the same time learning from them (Chapter 6.B). This response culminates in a proposal for a novel and multifarious philosophical conception of what a contemporary spiritual discipline should be (Chapter 7.A-C).

The greatest recommendation for religious apologetics is that religious persons learn from their critics while bearing witness to the truths they believe most deeply. In recent Christian theology Karl Marx has led many theologians to recognize that traditional conceptions of salvation must include liberation from oppressive social and economic conditions. Claims that alienation and exploitation are inevitable consequences of capitalist modes of production gives the Marxist construal of social liberation its distinctive character. From Nietzsche I hope to have learned how decadence and resentment are structural concomitants of contemporary modes of consumption. These lessons I deploy in order to restore meaning and efficacy to transformed versions of traditional religious practices.

What intervenes between the first and third parts of the book is a speculative interlude in which alternative notions are suggested for doing the philosophical work which I believe Clement's Platonic and Stoic borrowings no longer do well (Chapters 3–5). Speculation in the ancient world consisted of the rational revision of religious cosmologies and anthropologies. The use of the Logos theme in the first verses of John's Gospel established a Biblical precedent for speculation as a variety of Christian discourse. Yet it was not until Boethius in the sixth century that the meaning of the term was fixed: in *De Trinitate* (2) he used 'speculativa' for the sort of knowledge Aristotle called theoretical, i.e., that knowledge whose end is truth rather than action, and which can be characterized by its degree of abstraction from matter and motion (*Metaphysics* 993b20 and 1026a15). References to speculation in *De Consolatione Philosophiae* (4.1 and 5.2) reveal a distinctively Neoplatonic construal; they occur in the context of Lady Philosophy's disquisition on God, evil, and freedom (quite a revision of the Adamic myth and the Exodus stories!), and they show speculation to be identified with intellectual ascent to a realm of ideality, knowledge, and peace.

Apology was said to take two distinct forms because its argumentative nature implicitly posits a critical counterpart to an intellectual defense. Speculation also adopts two forms, but does so for quite different reasons. Speculation is a venture of inquiry rather than argument; it seeks the broadest possible premises and the most fecund concepts for an area of knowledge. Argument in the form of logical deduction plays only the subsidiary role of testing the implications and applications of candidate premises. Here too Socrates provides the classical paradigm with his dialogical inquiries into the essential definitions of virtue, justice, and love. Speculation has adopted two characteristic forms for the historical reason that religion was traditionally thought to provide the broadest cosmological premises while now natural science does so for most educated persons. Hence it is possible to distinguish between a religious speculation which revises religious conceptions of the world and humanity in light of human rationality, and a scientific speculation which revises scientific cosmologies and anthropologies in light of human religiosity—in light of those aspects of self and world that have been traditionally called religious. The medieval appropriation of Aristotle's natural philosophy by Thomas Aquinas and other Scholastic theologians is perhaps the best example of the former sort of speculation. Alfred North Whitehead's inclusion of God in the categoreal scheme of his philosophy of organism is one of the most influential ventures of the sort of speculation I have called scientific.

The technique Whitehead calls "philosophical generalization" plays a role in the middle part of the essay. In the first chapter of *Process and Reality,* where he presents a conception of speculative philosophy, Whitehead defines philosophical generalization as "the utilization of specific notions, applying to a restricted group of facts, for the divination of the generic notions which apply to all facts."[13] The first part of this essay identifies notions which by way of a process of philosophical generalization have historically been used to describe and justify religious practices. Since I criticize the Platonic and Stoic heritage that has informed much Western thinking about spiritual life, yet continue to ascribe value to at least some spiritually disciplined practices, I feel obliged to sketch alternatives to the options I have opposed. The central speculative task undertaken here will be (1) the identification of such alternative notions, culled from twentieth-century mathematical, physical, and biological sciences; (2) their philosophical generalization as what I shall call categoreal themes; and (3) their deployment in the description and justification of selected forms of Western and Eastern spiritual disciplines.

My acknowledgement of a debt to Whitehead should not lead the reader to expect a contribution to "Process Thought." Whitehead exemplifies well, but not exclusively, the sort of speculation I have called scientific. Albert Einstein's choice of expressing his boldest generalities in a theistic idiom is a more anecdotal variety of this intellectual attitude; it is an attitude evident in Niels Bohr's recollection that Einstein expressed dissatisfaction with the Copenhagen interpretation of quantum physics by doubting "whether God plays dice with the universe."[14] Also relevant are the reflections of the sort Hermann Weyl provides in his book entitled *Symmetry*.[15] He describes this book as an attempt to to do three things: to identify a general but vague notion—symmetry as the state of being well-proportioned; to investigate a concrete embodiment of that notion—bilateral symmetry in nature and art; and then to articulate the relations between its empirical varieties with a precision and generality made possible by recent advances in mathematics and science. Whitehead carries the process of generalization further than Weyl, as shall I with specific regard to symmetry; but still a very similar process is evident in reflective scientists like Einstein, Weyl, and others.

My own constructive efforts shall seek to be of this scientific variety, though I recognize that residual influences of religious cosmologies are undoubtedly present. I seek to learn from the more speculative writings of important scientific thinkers while entertaining little sympathy for the view that twentieth-century science gives rational credibility to religious claims, e.g., that quantum physics supports Eastern mysticism or that modern cosmology confirms part of the Biblical creation story. I regard arguments to this effect as fallacious, being only a thinly veiled version of an *argumentum ad ignorantium*: that a rigorously mechanical determinism was once judged incompatible with theistic doctrines of providence and is now itself deemed irreconcilable with quantum physics does not count as natural scientific support for the presence of divine agency in the order of nature.

Attention to contemporary science is warranted because new metaphors and concepts have emerged from this quarter in recent years. Thus it offers a font of resources to be used for an invigorating redescription of ancient practices. Also, valuable new thinking in the sciences seems to have been generated by, and to generate in turn, a more stable and extensive community of discourse than, for instance, is the case in the humanities. Most scientific research has become a pluralistic endeavor in the sense that it receives contributions from scientists throughout the world and commands the respect of educated persons in likewise diverse places. Its most fundamental notions purport to inform human experience in its individual variety and its social diversity, and thereby promise, when used in thinking anew about religious practices, to make these practices continuous with many nonreligious and non-Western phenomena. Thus an attentiveness to science as both a source of novelty and regularity promises to help achieve the philosophical tasks undertaken in this essay.

I recognize that the generality sought in the constructive program outlined here will sound chimerical to historicist heirs of Wittgenstein and Nietzsche. My initial response to this challenge is to profess that my path to generality is more pragmatic than Platonistic. General concepts and truths, as I understand them, are less Platonic recollections accessible to the privileged few, than they are Peircian anticipations of what will increasingly be confirmed by a process of self-corrective reasoning that benefits from the contributions of diverse participants. This pragmatic optimism about the value of uninhibited intellectual conversation is a rational variety of faith; it is a presupposition of this essay and a prelude to the style of philosophical inquiry and argument characteristic of this essay.

Subject matter labelled spiritual may seem to be a topic of study ill-suited to rational inquiry. This is not the view of an increasing community of scholars in the field of religious studies for whom spirituality is an area of renewed investigation. 'Spirituality' is a notoriously vague term; its scholarly meaning comes from reports of inner experiences offered as personal counterparts to religious doctrines and institutions. Derivatively, it also denominates the academic discipline which studies this domain of religious phenomena.[16] The word is not entirely suited for its intended purpose because an ontological opposition of spirituality and materiality promoted its initial usage in this context; now most scholars in the field de-emphasize this dualism. I share this new sensibility, and partially militate against this connotation by preferring an adjectival to a substantive form of the term. Introducing a complete neologism to serve the same purpose seems artificial to me, and disingenuous insofar as it is a ploy to conceal a Platonic heritage.

Thus far I have taken 'spiritual' to be roughly synonymous with 'religious'. Robert Neville has cautioned against this conflation. He describes his book *Soldier, Sage, Saint* as "a philosophic study of some aspects of spiritual development, construing the field of spiritual development in a broad way without essential connection with organized religion."[17] I shall heed this advice because, as will become evident in the essay's third part, philosophers from Epicurus to Nietzsche have recommended forms of spiritual self-mastery while vigorously condemning received forms of religion. 'Spiritual' and 'religious' are labels that overlap. Some instances of spiritual discipline have long and intimate associations with organized religion; others do not.

In its philosophical conception Neville's book is similar to this essay; however, its typological interest and its basic categories are different. Neville understands the goal of the spiritual life to be perfection and its hallmark an absolute quality of self-relation: " 'Spiritual' will be used to refer to those aspects of life particularly involved in one's relating to oneself absolutely."[18] I have invoked fullness as the desideratum of spiritual seekers and shall use 'spiritual' to convey an accent on wholeness rather than absoluteness. Paul Ricoeur's account of the archaic meaning of cultic practices informs this preference. In *The Symbolism of Evil* he writes that ritual action, as conjoined with a counterpart myth, indicates "the intimate accord of the man of cult and myth with the whole of being; it signifies an indivisible plenitude, in which the supernatural, the natural, and the psychological are not yet torn apart"; he quickly adds that "this intuition of a cosmic whole, from which man is not separated, and this undivided plenitude, anterior to the division into supernatural, natural, and human, are not *given,* but simply *aimed at."*[19] Ricoeur concludes that it is only in intention that wholeness and fullness are restored, and the restoration is always partly symbolical. I believe that spiritually disciplined practices are likewise marked by this intentional and symbolical character. Hence I seek a philosophical rethinking of spiritual discipline based upon what might be called a semiotics of plentitude. This task is different from, but not incompatible with, the one undertaken by Whiteheadians like Neville, Griffin, and others who seek to furnish spiritual discipline with a metaphysics of freedom.

Summarily stated, the spiritual aspect of human existence is here hypothesized to have an outer and inner complexion. Facing outward, human existence is spiritual insofar as it intentionally engages reality as a maximally inclusive whole and makes the cosmos an intentional object of thought and feeling. Facing inward, life has a spiritual dimension to the extent that it is experienced as the project of one's most vital and enduring self, and it is structured by experiences of sudden transformation and subsequent slow development. An integration of these inner and outer characterizations is achieved by equating the spiritual dimension of life with the existential task of discovering one's truest self in the context of reality apprehended as a cosmic totality. It is the quest for attaining an optimal relationship between what one truly is and everything that is; it is a quest that can be promoted by apt regimens of disciplined behavior.

A definition of spiritual life which includes reference to an enduring self and cosmic totality will be received cautiously by many philosophers. This is so because such notions figure prominently among the ideas that Immanuel Kant treated under the rubric of 'transcendental illusion'.[20] When reified in Platonic fashion as the individual soul and transcendent God, Kant believed that these notions transgress the limits of possible experience and are therefore rationally insupportable. Yet he also said that they are the product of "a natural and unavoidable dialectic of pure reason," such that when nondogmatically entertained, they are capable of legitimately serving as "regulatory ideals."[21] For instance, they can enliven the study of nature, and provide transition and support for the comprehension of moral ideas. It is primarily as imaginative ideals of this sort that truest selves and cosmic wholes are philosophically presupposed in this conception of spiritual discipline.

How people define 'spiritual' is often pregnant with the main features of what they think is most admirable in human existence and action. It can germinally contain their own imaginative ideals. As used here the word 'spiritual' is applicable to human selves which are neither Aristotelian substantial souls nor Kantian transcendental egos; they are more Peircian bundles of habits—the agents for repertoires of behaviors. A human being is spiritual when he or she encounters the world as a whole and experiences the self—in its truest sense—as both intentionally related to that totality and yet also a part of it. Spiritual selfhood is thus something defined with reference to a totality of which it is a part, and as Bertrand Russell has especially taught, it is thereby something rife with paradox.[22] Spiritual adepts have frequently reported the experience of being intimately part of the world yet also transcendent to it—the definition of spiritual life offered here stresses this paradoxical profession.

A corollary to the accent on wholeness says that anything which purports to be maximally inclusive will be continually enlarged by each new description of it; therefore it has a complexity requiring multiple levels of description, none of which singly or collectively exhaust the reality so posited. The world encountered by the spiritual agent has this sort of complexity, and, in a mediated way, so does the spiritual agent because he or she is defined in terms of this world. Accordingly, spiritual fullness is something that involves an extravagance of well-being that is physical, mental, social and more. Spiritually disciplined practices, or simply spiritual disciplines, are intended to promote this sense of spiritual well-being amidst a wondrously complex reality.

Finally, to discipline one's behavior for the sake of a spiritual fullness involves, at least implicitly, and often explicitly, a description of oneself as a being having a complexity resistant to reductive description and so capable of indescribably ample well-being. This description is a sort of creative act: to proclaim oneself complex is to make oneself a being who is at least more complex than beings alike in every respect except that they do not predicate complexity of themselves. A spiritually disciplined life is very much about creative self-transformations of which reflective acts of self-description are an abstract intimation.[23]

Of course, spiritual and religious self-descriptions may be resisted altogether; one may think it more satisfactory to explain such behavior by appeal to principles given in a quite different language of description. Psychotic fantasies, often religious in subject matter, deserve an attentive but ultimately disbelieving interpretation. I posit without argument that this same skeptical approach is not appropriate for all religious and spiritual self-descriptions. (To support this point explicitly would inevitably involve my own religious self-descriptions and lead to theological issues I choose not to pursue here.) In addition, I assume that spiritual agents at their best contend forthrightly with the problematic aspects of human existence, and I grant that they sometimes engage in regimens of disciplined behavior that promotes genuine human vitality. My assumptions about contemporary society are less generous, believing as I do that spiritually disciplined practices are most often undertaken in antagonism with persons, institutions, and other social forces which seek to induce behavior that is predictable and controllable, and in some cases, addictive and deadly. This is the political drama of the spiritual life. It is also a personal drama in which habitual behaviors vie with one another to constitute the self through life-affirming self-control or through myopic and deadly selfishness. Together these political and personal struggles contribute to the predicament which each generation of spiritual aspirants confronts. I turn next to the example of Blaise Pascal for insight into the nature of this spiritual predicament in the early modern period.

I

The Philosophical Problem

CHAPTER 1

A Historical Perspective

PASCAL'S PREDICAMENT

A problem is something proposed for examination and solution. A problem becomes a puzzle when examination proceeds in a spirit of childlike fascination such that a solution becomes as much the opportunity for exercising the mind as for achieving a definite result. So highly did Bertrand Russell estimate conceptual and linguistic puzzles that he said logic's proper method was to assemble and analyze as many kindred puzzles as possible, and then to seek a systematic explanation of both their capacity to elicit bewilderment and their underlying nature. Certainly Russell's own efforts to explain the Liar ('I am lying') and related paradoxes proved as philosophically valuable for the questions raised as for the answers offered.

Problems that elicit an urgency of feeling in addition to a playfulness of intellect I shall call predicaments. A predicament is a human situation fraught with danger and pathos. Here intellectual constructs are immersed in feeling, and the problem beset human being is embedded in a context of social relations. While Russell was surely right that engagement with intellectual puzzles can yield insightful logical theories, his teacher, Alfred North Whitehead, was also correct in saying that general ideas which fail to take on an emotional pattern of memorable intensity remain ineffective for shaping personal and communal histories. Feeling and social relationships matter. Whitehead said that it is when predicaments are overcome, and not merely when puzzles are solved, that civilization advances.[1] Human life is itself an abiding predicament in the sense that people are always faced with decisions they hope will result in circumstances conducive to their happiness. When such decisions are made amidst memories of a wondrous childhood and intimations of an impending death, they constitute the most general of adult human predicaments. It is with this reality that reflection here must begin if it is to be faithful simultaneously to the generality of the philosophical ideal and the urgency of the religious quest.

19

The life and writings of Blaise Pascal portray a dramatic spiritual predicament. They portray a person contending mightily with sin and death; they also show a man who dares to think honestly about the resources that human beings bring to this confrontation. Upon reflection, Pascal discovered "the greatness and wretchedness of man."[2] His problem was thereby compounded. The question "What shall I do?" became linked to the more basic query "Who am I?". The predicament was intensified. Pascal consciously addressed this predicament in thought and action, yet his extraordinary efforts did as much to deepen as resolve the problem, at least for others besides himself. His famous "night of fire" conversion and his unfinished *Apology for the Christian Religion* have elicited very diverse interpretations. While most interpreters agree that what Pascal examines is "man in nature (l'homme dans la nature)," this phrase itself is rife with paradox.[3] Pascal understood human nature as at once good by creation, yet sinful by Adam's fall; he saw the natural world as the realm of the infinite, and of the abyss as well; finally, he confessed God to be hidden and at the same time the only thing knowledge of which can provide happiness. That the human situation is characterized by these contradictory features is what makes it puzzling. That sin and godlessness bring death makes a remedy urgent. Part of Pascal's enduring appeal is that he made the spiritual problems besetting him yet more puzzling and their resolution more urgent; and he did so with intellectual incisiveness and elegance.

Interpreters of Pascal have frequently found in him a precursor of their own problems and preoccupations. In addition to wide acclamation as a forerunner of existentialism, Pascal has had several other laudatory titles bestowed upon him. The Marxist Lucien Goldmann has proclaimed Pascal "the first modern man" whose masterpiece, the *Pensées,* illustrates the transition from rational to dialectical thought;[4] the Freudian Charles Baudouin sees him as a "passionate pilgrim" whose ascetic temperament represented "a sort of impressively transposed anorexia" and whose multifarious achievements reveal a distinctly modern strategy of sublimation;[5] and the semiologist Louis Marin finds in Pascal the prototype of the self-conscious fashioner of self-referential texts whose critical intent is "to deconstruct the ideology of presence and its reproduction."[6] Surely French intellectuals are especially prone to this sort of tendentious interpretation, yet I do think that there is something about Pascal's life and writings which makes them especially capable of mirroring the contemporary concerns of his readers. Forewarned by the example of predecessors in this sort of undertaking, I shall try to make the case for the enduring significance of Pascal's predicament with a minimum of philosophical cant.

Pascal was a mathematician, physicist, and inventor; a philosopher, theologian, and prose stylist; and even an educator, entrepreneur, and philanthropist. He was accorded great eminence by the social and intellectual elites of his time; he was "admired not merely in all of France but in all of Europe" according to a contemporary observer.[7] Among his greatest intellectual achievements was his formulation of the basic principles of probability theory in a series of epistolary exchanges with his countryman Pierre de Fermat; later, drawing upon the probabilistic ideas he helped make rigorous, he formulated a celebrated argument for the prudential character of theistic belief. In his thinking about both science and religion Pascal helped to transform an Aristotelian language of metaphysical necessity into the newer idiom of subjective probability. His wide experience and intellectual acuity enabled him to portray human predicaments and practices in novel ways.

By devising of a workable calculating machine and inaugurating an intracity bus service Pascal showed further evidence of an innovative and progressive character. Still he was hardly free from retrograde impulses. His advocacy of the Jansenist cause, with its revival of traditional Augustinian themes, is perhaps the most renowned expression of this conservatism, and the consequences of these views for his conception of disciplined spiritual life is the traditional aspect of his religiosity that will be of most concern here. To philosophers of religion Pascal presents both an innovative diagnosis of the ills of the human condition and a very traditional remedy for them. He has generally been more persuasive in his diagnosis than in his cure, and this has attracted the interest of thinkers convinced by alternative remedies, or convinced there is no remedy at all. He, like Kierkegaard, is a favorite Christian thinker of non-Christians.

Again, like Kierkegaard, Pascal is attractive to twentieth-century sensibilities because he acknowledged that people must live with contradictions; or as Goldmann says, he was a dialectical thinker. Pascal wrote eloquently about the greatness and wretchedness of human life, and while it is fair to say that he contrasted the "wretchedness of man without God" and the "happiness of man with God," it is improper to ascribe to him a traditional theological dualism.[8] Even within the experience of wretchedness there is a possibility of greatness: "Man's greatness comes from knowing he is wretched: a tree does not know it is wretched. Thus it is wretched to know that one is wretched, but there is greatness in knowing one is wretched."[9] In this passage reflective self-knowledge is said to give dignity to human wretchedness. Elsewhere Pascal suggests that it can flaw rare experiences of happiness: he envies the faithful who live "so unconcernedly (avec tant de négligence)";[10] he recommends unreflective devotional acts that "will make you believe and make you more docile (vous fera croire et vous abêtira)";[11] and he implies regarding a man's self-knowledge "that it is better for him not to know himself if he wants to be happy (qu'il lui meilleur de s'ignorer pour être heureux)."[12] Rational self-consciousness, says Pascal, both redeems our wretchedness and pollutes our happiness. Pascal realized viscerally that his extraordinary intelligence could not alone remedy his spiritual ills, yet he was equally convinced that faith should not entirely eclipse reason. He decried "two excesses: to exclude reason, to admit nothing but reason."[13]

Reason, then, is both a blessing and a burden to those confronting the spiritual predicament that Pascal describes; it is emblematic of the contradictions which are the consequences of the loss of an original fullness of life and which are also impediments to its reattainment. Certainly Pascal's own acute rational powers intensified his serious bouts of existential and theological deliberation. The results of these deliberations are evident in the several experiences of Christian religious conversion that punctuated his life. The second and most notable conversion occurred in 1654; it is commemorated in the famous memorial he inscribed on a scrap of paper and kept inside the lining of his clothes. In this short text one finds many of the philosophical and stylistic elements that previous Christian thinkers used in their descriptions of encounters with God. A central line of *The Memorial* reads simply "Fire," suggesting that the encounter with God involves a spiritualized apprehension of light and heat. A repeated theme is that the Pascal feels "cut off (séparé)" from the God revealed in Jesus Christ; he yearns to overcome such isolation: "Let me never be cut off from him!"[14] The desire to be joined with God is so important for Pascal because he understands salvation as an appropriation of the spiritual self-sufficiency of God. In *The Mystery of Jesus,* another intensely passionate religious text, he writes, "But he (Jesus Christ) healed himself and will heal me all the more surely. I must add my wounds to his, and join myself to him and he will save me in saving himself."[15] The way to effect this communion with Christ is also indicated in *The Memorial*; a sentence fragment reads: "Total submission to Jesus Christ and my director."[16] This reference to his spiritual director at the Abbey of Port-Royal, Monsieur Singlin, shows that Pascal sought relief from his spiritual predicament, and from the deliberations it necessitated, in the surety of God's grace and in the stability afforded by a subordinate position in a hierarchical system of authority. Such avowals of obedience are the most traditional part of Pascal's spiritual remedy.

Pascal's life subsequent to his 1654 conversion is a subject of historical controversy. A hagiographical tradition indebted to his pious sisters Jacqueline and Gilberte claims that Pascal's last years were ones of solitary retirement at the Jansenist Abbey of Port-Royal des Champs. According to one story he broke cleanly and abruptly with his worldly ways of research, debate, and enterprise after a momentous incident at the Bridge of Neuilly. The story goes that Pascal and some companions were riding in a carriage drawn by several teams of horses when, due to faulty bits, the lead horses veered erratically off the bridge and toward the waters below. At the last moment, just before the carriage followed the horses to destruction, the leather reins broke, and the carriage and its occupants were spared harm. According to Gilberte, Pascal interpreted his deliverance from peril as a divine warning to mend his ways and pursue a solitary mode of life. Yet Pascal's modern biographers, such as Jean Mesnard, dispute this account, contending that Pascal did not immediately and permanently retire to Port-Royal after his conversion.[17] While his greatest religious works were written subsequent to 1654, specifically *The Provincial Letters* and the unfinished *Pensées,* he also wrote then *The Mind of the Geometrician (De l'Esprit Géométrique)* and his essay on cycloids. Furthermore, while he gave to the poor with increased generosity after this date, his charitable venture of establishing an intracity bus service in 1662 was as socially transformative in its implications as was his earlier invention of a calculating machine. Though influential and not entirely baseless, Gilberte's biographical account of Pascal's later years is historically inaccurate and theologically unsophisticated. Until the onset of his final illness in March of 1659 Pascal engaged in only intermittent periods of devotional solitude, and his restriction of scholarly activities and other forms of public life fell far short of categorical renunciation.

Another story, this one preserved by Gilberte's daughter, Marguerite Périer, contributed to Pascal's reputation as an ascetic. She records that Pascal was converted by a sermon delivered by Monsieur Singlin at Port-Royal de Paris on the day of the Conception of the Virgin Mary. She further surmises that the example of the Virgin Mary commended in the sermon prompted a conversion experience which included a pronounced depreciation of human sexuality.[18] As revealed in the *Pensées,* Pascal's personal piety did include an express commitment to traditional Augustinian values: "True religion teaches us our duties, our weaknesses, pride and concupiscence, and the remedies, humility and mortification."[19] He several times identifies bodily passions as enemies that must be destroyed by Christ.[20] Indeed, he contributed himself to the literature of self-denial with his theme of the self's hatefulness ("Le moi est haïssable").[21] Thus family recollections and Pascal's own statements led a lineage of pious commentators to accord him an ascetic and saintly status. Now, while it seems true that Pascal gave up his own indefinite marriage plans upon his 1654 conversion, his advice to others was far less categorical. In a series of letters written in the autumn of 1656 to the Duc of Roannez and his sister, the latter of whom was then contemplating spiritual retirement as a nun at Port-Royal, Pascal encouraged a sense of Christian vocation but refrained from explicit abjurations. Of ascetic austerity he wrote very sensibly: "For it is neither austerity toward the flesh nor tribulation of the spirit but rather the good impulses of the heart which have merit and which relieve bodily and mental suffering."[22] So, like his solitariness, Pascal's ascetic nature has been much exaggerated.

It is precisely upon the basis of the hagiographical traditions inaugurated by Gilberte and others that Friedrich Nietzsche called Pascal "the most instructive victim of Christianity."[23] He essentially accepted Gilberte's portrayal of her brother but interpreted Pascal's change of life quite oppositely. Nietzsche bewailed Pascal's fate of becoming the sort of man for whom Christian faith "resembles in a gruesome manner a continual suicide of reason."[24] Furthermore, he saw Pascal as destined to this demise, his self-hatred and morbid humility being no aberration, but instead, the true character of Christian spirituality which most Christians concealed from themselves with delusions of monkish love and learning. According to Nietzsche, Pascal attained a tragic greatness because he endured the horrible truth of Christianity once he had judged it to be the only alternative to the banalities of commerce, academic scholarship, and polite society. Nietzsche, of course, proposed a radically non-Christian alternative—his philosophy of the will to power—yet he continued to respect Pascal as "the admirable logician of Christianity."[25]

My task in the remainder of this chapter is to present a more adequate interpretation of Pascal's predicament than did either Gilberte or Nietzsche. I am convinced that Pascal's predicament is as fraught with meaning as these commentators claim, yet I believe that meaning is different from what either supposes. From the vantage point of the late twentieth century Pascal's predicament appears multiform: he was a mathematical physicist whose knowledge of the natural world seemed to alienate him from nature; he was a prose stylist whose most public communications seemed to accompany his increasing retirement to a strict religious community; and he was a philosopher whose self-knowledge seemed to depreciate his sense of worth as a human being. A radical depreciation of nature, society, and self seems to inform Pascal's deliberations about what one should do when bemired in sin and confronted by death. Supernatural revelation, submission to external authority, and self-mortification seem to be the hallmarks of his conception of a spiritually disciplined response to this situation. A philosophical argument for spiritual discipline motivated solely by the experienced disutility of knowledge of self, society, and the world amounts to little more than a rationalization of despair. Individual quotations from Pascal's writings can be cited which suggest this sort of rationale.

Yet a quite different case can also be made. Readers of Pascal must not shy away from the contradictions and complexities of his thought; to do so misses his creativity. Just as Pascal's attitude toward human reason was complex and ambivalent—reason being capable of partially redeeming human wretchedness and partially polluting human happiness—so too must the other central categories of his thought be given polyvalent characterizations. God is not absent from nature, but is hidden there; society is not abandoned, but becomes an arena of redemptive mission; and while the self may be hateable, it is also the thinking agent which reflects God's majesty. Pascal's spiritual remedy, like the predicament he articulated, is especially profound because it both recalls traditional elements and suggests a more novel point of view. I believe that the progressive elements are especially manifest in his famous Wager argument, in his notion of diversion, and in his modification of the epistemological foundationalism of Aristotle and Descartes. They provide a subtle intellectual counterpoise to his severe Jansenist piety.

Pascal believed that it is an irreducible part of the human predicament that momentous decisions cannot be avoided. Neither listless boredom nor strategies of diversion are successful evasions; they merely conceal one's choices, mostly from oneself. In fact, Pascal says, even apparently insignificant actions are responses to the twin perils of sin and death. Since people thereby act and endure the consequences of their actions, and since their actions are always attendant with risk, Pascal construes these actions as implicit wagers—wagers not on the outcome of some contrived game, but on the outcome of the contest between God and the Devil for the allegiance of the human soul. It is characteristic of Pascal's penetrating and paradoxical mind that he accused his aristocratic friends of seeking to flee their greatest responsibilities by pursuing games of table and field, yet he then used ideas formulated by reflection upon games of chance in order to justify the choice that Christians make when they believe in the God who promises eternal life. A game of dice for Pascal is both a symbol betokening wretchedness and trope recommending salvation.

It is also characteristic of Pascal that his subtle insight into the behavior of his contemporaries gains its full meaning in the context of Augustinian theology. Any genuine remedy to the "wretchedness of man" must overcome both spiritual boredom and addictive passions. All passions, even diverting ones, are expressions of the concupiscence which mars human nature after Adam's fall. It blinds the eyes and distracts the mind, and for the resulting want of information, bad decisions become automatic. "We run heedlessly into the abyss after putting something in front of us to stop us seeing it."[26] A spiritually disciplined life, or something so simple as the experience of solitude, eradicates diversions and makes one struggle with boredom. It restricts a person to the momentous alternatives of thinking or not thinking, especially, of thinking or not thinking about God.

This is the proper context for Pascal's famous argument known as "The Wager."[27] It is addressed to persons no longer absorbed by diversions, but who are still calculating rationalists shaped by the gaming mentality. It speaks in the voice of someone convinced of the uselessness of proofs for God's existence yet insistent that thought be given to God as that which is most formidable and most valuable in human life. The Wager argument offers a new way of thinking about God. Nicholas Rescher provides this summary: "What is at issue is the pragmatic validation of a praxis in terms of its potential benefits, which in turn engenders an oblique, indirect validation of belief in the existence of God as a presuppositional precondition for this praxis"; he concludes: "a shift from cognition to praxis is the pivot of the Wager argument."[28]

From theory to praxis, from evidence to prudence, and from necessity to probability—the Wager argument initiates each of these innovative transitions. Pascal believed that by properly employing these new resources one can rationally recommend belief in God. God's existence may not be rationally proved but it can be responsibly presupposed. Still he knew that it could not effect faith, and faith

in Jesus Christ he thought was the only genuine way out of the
predicament posed by sin and death. To this recognition of the
limitation of reason he had a most traditional response:

> Get it into your head that, if you are unable to believe, it is
> because of your passions, since reason impels you to believe
> and yet you cannot do so. Concentrate then not on convincing
> yourself by multiplying proofs of God's existence but by
> diminishing your passions.[29]

The passage concludes with a recommendation to accept church
discipline and profess God's glory. The new and the old are ever
combined in Pascal's thought.

Spiritually disciplined practices figure in two ways in the
acquisition of a saving faith in Jesus Christ. First, they combat
diversions; they counter the trivializing and benumbing effects of
activities which engage the mind only so much as to prevent it from
being engaged by the profound concerns of life and death, and sin
and salvation. Second, spiritual discipline quiets "the passions." They
allow the dictates of reason to become effective in action by
suppressing competing impulses. Pascal's psychology is clearly
Platonic in the sense that a rational part of the soul is given the task
of mastering its appetitive and spirited complements. Yet there is
also an Aristotelian element here because Pascal talks about habit
as the empowering force in Christian conversion:

> Proofs only convince the mind; habit (la coutume) provides
> the strongest proofs and those that are most believed. It
> inclines the automaton, which leads the mind unconsciously
> along with it.... It is, then, habit that convinces us and
> makes so many Christians.[30]

Spiritually disciplined practices thus serve to break bad habits and
establish new ones. They are the preparation and implementation
of reason, making rational reflection about God both possible and
effective. They combine with reason in the fixation of faith. For a good
Augustinian like Pascal, they also depend upon the presence of God's
grace, being ultimately a work of the Holy Spirit rather than an
individual achievement. Hence in Pascal's view faith is attained
through the interconnected operations of habituation, ratiocination,
and inspiration.[31]

Opting to trust God and accept church discipline serves a social function according to Pascal. It makes the Christian a "fixed point" by which others can note the progress of secular society toward depravity.[32] When portrayed as a proto-existentialist Pascal is too often abstracted from the social realities of his time. Pascal scrutinized diverting pastimes as a member of an elite stratum of French society. He was the son of a successful lawyer who enjoyed considerable wealth and, at most times, court favor. Hence laboring to provide food and shelter did not occupy the minds of persons like him. With few of the demands of quotidian occupations, persons like Pascal were more likely to ward off thoughts of death with "some novel and agreeable passion which keeps them busy, like gambling, hunting, some absorbing show, in short by what is called diversion (divertisse-ment)."[33] Pascal perceived his social peers to be consumed with a desire for power in their occupations or for diversion in their recreations. Each pursuit achieves the same end: "Being unable to cure death, wretchedness, and ignorance, men have decided in order to be happy, not to think about such things."[34]

Pascal reduced the most respected social pursuits to more humble categories. Art became for him a type of diversion for the upper classes; Pascal never took much pride in his own literary gifts. Scientific research, like the *beaux-arts* confined to the upper classes in the seventeenth century, took on for him no more significance than other forms of practical work. In a letter to Pierre de Fermat, Pascal presented his last recorded thoughts on the labors of mathematicians: "For to speak to you frankly about geometry, I consider it to be so unprofitable that I make little distinction between a man who is merely a geometrician and a skillful artisan."[35] For Pascal, the social options of his day seemed few: marriage and career, bachelorhood and diversion, or submission to the church. For Pascal, the quest for spiritual discipline begins with a recognition of a diseased and atrophied community life.

Pascal understood that one of the most distressing aspects of the human predicament is that when people try to resolve it they frequently compound its harm. Certainly *divertissement* is portrayed by him as such an illusory source of relief. The counterpart of *divertissement* as a mode of practice is the theoretical orientation now called foundationalism. Pascal, like Descartes, used the metaphor of the foundations of an edifice to convey the role of first principles in a scientific exposition of knowledge. Unlike Descartes, Pascal understood methodological prescriptions for securing first principles as strategies for attaining happiness apart from God, or at least, apart from revealed truth. Just as people seek comfort and safety in a well-constructed domicile so too do they seek a more rarefied sort of security from a rigorous system of cosmological knowledge; yet in Pascal's view the disquietude caused by the unpredictable destructiveness of nature and the inevitable demise of human life was not reparable by a purely intellectual conversion.[36] He rejected the strategy of a rationally theistic foundationalism inaugurated by Plato and reformulated by Descartes. He instead affirmed elements of Socratic skepticism which emphasized the intermediate status of the agent of knowledge as neither fully ignorant nor fully informed; he combined this Socratic skepticism with the modified Platonism of his Augustinian theology.

An expert geometrician himself, Pascal followed Plato and Aristotle in believing that rigorous knowledge should conform to the axiomatic form of presentation which had proved so effective in the development of geometry. Items of knowledge were most certainly connected by logical deduction. On this point he seemed to harbor little doubt. This fact is ironic because Augustine accepted some Academic arguments for the inefficacy of logic which cited logical paradoxes as evidence. (See *Contra Academicos* 3.29.) Pascal directed his skepticism toward the sets of first principles, or in geometrical parlance, the axioms, from which theorems were logically deduced. Theorems derived from axioms have the rules of inference to vouch for their truth, while the axioms themselves were said to have a character of "self-evidence"—they are so evidently true that one cannot clearly conceive them to be false. Pascal correctly surmised that the development of the mathematical and physical sciences since antiquity required first principles sufficiently informative so as to make claims of self-evidence implausible; furthermore, his sense of the depth of human fallibility made him judge to be unpromising Descartes' methodological route to basic truths. Pascal came to believe that first principles gained their cogency by the heart, not the mind, by intuition and not logical evidence, ultimately, by faith and not reason. Herein lies Pascal's famous dichotomy of faith and reason, and his motivations for giving faith priority even to the point of elevating devotional life to a status superior to scientific research. Pascal's theological objections to Cartesian rationalism may not themselves have been particularly progressive, but they forced him to adopt a more practical strategy for solving his predicament, and this I think was fortuitous.

An example of an area of mathematical research which lacks unproblematic axioms is analysis or calculus. This mathematical topic was pioneered by Pierre de Fermat and by Pascal himself—elements of his essay on cycloids proved influential in Leibnitz's formulation of basic principles of integral calculus.[37] This area of mathematics touched upon problems of the infinitesimal and the infinite, and helped provide metaphors for Pascal's description of human life as the experience of dwelling suspended between "two abysses of infinity and nothingness."[38] Knowledge has no worldly foundation and human beings have no secure natural abode. "What is man in nature? A nothing compared to the infinite, a whole compared to the nothing, a middle point between all and nothing, infinitely remote from an understanding of the extremes; the end of things and their principles are inevitably hidden from him in impenetrable secrecy."[39] Pascal eloquently says that the human predicament cannot be adequately addressed without attentiveness to the natural world; yet he is equally eloquent in saying that nature cannot be reduced to an object of human intellectual mastery and technological control. The natural world in its beauty and terror points him to God, and reminds him of the necessity that grace and habit aid reason in the spiritual life.

Many aspects of Pascal's predicament which were once germane to a select company of privileged individuals like himself are now characteristic of the middle classes of developed nations. A more productive and less regimented economy allows many people to enjoy the breadth of occupational and recreational experience Pascal enjoyed. Their predicament is in many cases intensified by experiences of the insufficiency of several different paths to self-fulfillment. Also, advances in education and communication have enabled many people to bring sophisticated tools of analysis and multiple points of view to an understanding of the spiritual challenge of their death and their ineradicable shortcomings. As was the case for Pascal their predicament is deepened by sensitivity to complexities and inconsistencies in their situation.

Pascal's insight that people divert themselves from contending with the most important issues in their lives was especially prescient of today's consumerist culture. An immense variety of diverting consumer products and services are available today, and they are available to persons of relatively modest means. Hunting is now supplemented by other survivalist pursuits and various forms of commercialized thrill seeking; alcoholism occurs now as only one manifestation of the abuse of an expanding list of licit and illicit drugs; debauchery is pandered to by the traditional prostitutes and pornographers, and by new dating services and high-tech means of sexual titillation; and finally, gambling, Pascal's favored example, is now cultivated alike by government lotteries, corporate casinos, and organized crime. This list only includes correlates to the diversions Pascal mentions; it is sufficient to indicate that much of contemporary culture is devoted to creating a life of *divertissement.*

In the intellectual realm Pascal's views likewise signalled many broader developments. His rejection of self-evident epistemological foundations has increasingly found favor with recent philosophers, though his resort to faith as an alternative source of certainty has not proved nearly as portentous. Likewise Pascal's appreciation of the value of restating traditional intellectual conundrums in terms of practice and probability has proved prescient, though his interest in traditional theological perplexities has not been widely shared. For philosophers of religion Pascal's legacy includes the strategy of conceiving God's relation to the human predicament in a new way. As Rescher notes, it is a relation couched more in practical than theoretical terms. This point of view, I believe, holds great promise and will be adopted in the chapters that follow. I admit that Pascal's own practical approach conceives human interests and benefits in an entirely otherworldly way; thus it cannot be too easily identified with the pragmatism of William James, who was indebted to Pascal for parts of his own philosophy of religion, nor with the emphasis on praxis in Marxist thought and recent Christian theology. Still an important shift commences with him: spiritual life self-reflectively locates its origins in a practical predicament. Also, Pascal's example of bringing new scientific ideas to bear upon traditional theological problems will be emulated here. Indeed, the second part of this essay is concerned with the use of some increasingly important scientific notions for understanding practical regimens of religious behavior.

On the other hand, the way Pascal drew upon many Platonic and Augustinian resources is vulnerable to the criticism that they too compounded the difficulties he confronted; the next two chapters will expound these early Christian resources and offer a critical evaluation of them. Nietzsche's appreciative criticism of Pascal, briefly mentioned above, foreshadows the philosophical continuation of the project endeavored here. Nietzsche's negation of traditional ascetic ideals is something with which any sympathetic treatment of spiritual discipline must contend. Also, Nietzsche's way of rejecting religion while insisting upon spiritual self-mastery is a continuation of the philosophical rethinking of this issue begun by Pascal himself and which I shall carry forward in the subsequent chapters of this essay.

CLEMENT'S RATIONALE

That Pascal gave a traditional response to his novel articulation of the human spiritual predicament does not immediately imply that his response was inadequate. If one concludes that the nature and consequences of Pascal's 1654 conversion do not provide a model for contemporaries who share the main features of his predicament, then a case should be made to this end. It should be argued that the practices he recommends, and the philosophical notions which undergird them, suffer from significant deficiencies. I shall try to make such a case. In order to do so the relevant philosophical notions and religious practices must be identified. It is not difficult to locate works containing these precedents; indeed, it is more difficult to choose from among the plethora of available materials. Historical and heuristic considerations will guide my choice.

Pascal was a partisan of the theological views of Cornelis Jansen, a Dutch Roman Catholic theologian who crusaded for a traditional conception of personal holiness and against what he perceived to be the licentious theological innovations of certain Jesuits. Jansen's views were published posthumously in a book entitled *Augustinus*. As the title suggests, Jansen found Augustine's doctrine of election, with its strong affirmation of grace's efficacy and irresistibility, to be a useful theological tool for enforcing a comparably adamantine Christian moral code.

In some ways these theoretical and practical manifestations of rigor were not well matched, as theological views intended to motivate disciplined behavior would more naturally seem to presuppose some appreciation for individual moral exertion. On the other hand, the philosophical conceptions of God and human nature in Augustine's thought unequivocally provided resources for a severe religious ethic such as was advocated by Jansen. This second set of ideas, though, owes less to Augustine's retrieval of Paul than to his version of a Christian Platonism. Of course, Augustine was not the first Christian thinker to appropriate elements of Greek philosophy for the purpose of articulating a conception of disciplined Christian behavior. Clement of Alexandria, writing in the latter part of the second century, is arguably the first in this lineage. He preceded Augustine in drawing upon the resources of the Platonic tradition, but he did not anticipate Augustine's doctrine of election; he quite freely confessed spiritual achievement to be a joint product of God's grace and human effort. While Clement drew upon the earlier writings of Justin Martyr, he more self-consciously justified his borrowings from Greek philosophy and gave more sustained attention to religious practices than did Justin. In large part these traits emerged from Clement's efforts to overcome the bias of orthodox Christians against philosophy and to counter Gnostic use of philosophy for authorizing extremely ascetic practices.

There are also heuristic reasons for turning to Clement's writings as a source for early Christian conceptions of the spiritual life. These writings are more ample than Justin's, but less extensive than Augustine's. Also, they more directly address the issues of interest here. Of Clement's several extant writings, one, *Paedagogus,* is devoted to practical prescriptions for Christian behavior, and a second, the *Stromata,* contains a chapter which philosophically describes and justifies Christian spiritual life. This latter text has pagan parallels in both Middle Platonism and Neoplatonism, e.g., respectively, the second book of Apuleius' *De dogmate Platonis* and the first book of Plotinus' *Enneades* (1.4). Greek philosophers like these Platonists were quite critical of Olympian religion and much inclined to understand philosophy as concerned with the discovery and pursuit of a way of life leading to happiness. So were the Stoics, to whose views Clement's probable teacher, Pantaenus, was attracted before his conversion to Christianity. These parallels suggest that Clement is historically close to the origin of a philosophical conception of spiritual discipline which has informed Christian practice until the era of Pascal. Indeed, Clement's rationale for spiritual discipline will be summarized in this chapter because it is representative of the tradition of spirituality inherited by Pascal. The themes that Pascal presents imagistically in his mystical writings, e.g., *The Memorial* and *The Mystery of Jesus,* Clement first articulated discursively in the texts cited above. In a discursive format these themes are also more available for philosophical evaluation.

In the seventh book of the *Stromata* Clement describes the beliefs and practices of the Christian "gnostic (γνωστικόν)".[40] He deliberately tries to wrest this term from the Alexandrian followers of Valentinus. When employing the term in the presentation of apostolic teaching, he invokes other Greek philosophical conceptions. Clement's attempt is epitomized by his special way of identifying the Platonic theme of "assimilation to God (ὁμοίωσις θεῷ)" with, first, the Genesis affirmation that Adam was made in the "image and likeness of God" (Gen. 1.26) and, subsequently, with Paul's call to be imitators of Christ, the second Adam (I Cor. 11.1).[41] Christian Gnostics, like the heretical Valentinians, made similar claims. What distinguishes Clement from Valentinus is the strenuous effort he makes to have knowledge of a transcendent God distinct, but continuous with, a less sophisticated faith in Christ; also, he sought to make the experiential preconditions for each sort of divine encounter, likewise, distinct but continuous. That meant integrating a plan for ascetic self-discipline with a regimen of moderate social behavior; in more philosophical terms, it meant articulating compatible paths of salvation consisting of the extirpation of the passions ($\dot{\alpha}\pi\dot{\alpha}\theta\epsilon\iota\alpha$, adapted from Stoic ethics) and their moderation ($\mu\epsilon\tau\rho\iota o\pi\dot{\alpha}\theta\epsilon\iota\alpha$, more characteristic of Aristotelian ethics). Contrary to the more extreme Gnostics, each path is affirmed as a legitimate way of coming to see and know God, and while the final vision—when Christians no longer "see in a mirror dimly but. . .face to face" (I Cor. 13.12)—is reserved in both cases until after death, Clement was sufficiently elitist to claim that Christians following an ascetic life more fully anticipate this vision before death than do other Christians.

Clement and Gnostics like Valentinus draw upon some of the same Greek resources—Orphic, Pythagorean, and especially, Platonic, Peripatetic, and Stoic materials. The task of identifying the classical sources Clement used in describing and justifying spiritual practices is a complex one. It will be simplified here by selecting for investigation three notions of special importance, all of which can be gleaned from the seventh book on spiritual life in the *Stromata*. Giving them names, they are the themes of suprasensual vision, unencumbered causality, and static hierarchy. These notions, or categoreal themes, are the result of a history of philosophical thinking that Clement inherits. It was customary in older scholarship, such as Charles Bigg's classic volume, *The Christian Platonists of Alexandria*, to understand Clement as rather directly appropriating materials from Plato, Aristotle, and Chrysippus. More recent research, e.g., Salvatore Lilla's *Clement of Alexandria: A Study in Christian Platonism and Gnosticism*, holds that the synthesis of second-century Middle Platonism constitutes the proper philosophical source for most of Clement's philosophical ideas.[42] Granting this historical point, I shall sometimes speak of Clement's intellectual heritage in an abbreviated fashion that neglects to mention these Middle Platonic intermediaries. That my interests here are more philosophical than historical motivates this usage.

One intermediary I cannot fail to mention is Philo of Alexandria. In his *Philosophy of the Church Fathers* Harry Wolfson provocatively presents the history of Christian philosophy as beginning with Philo.[43] This overstates the case, but it does well to emphasize that a major factor in Clement's intellectual environment was the Hellenistic

Judaism of Alexandria for which Philo's writings provide ample representation. Each of the themes denominated above are prefigured in Philo's writings. For instance, in the tract *De vita contemplativa* Philo describes a Jewish community devoted to the study of Torah and a disciplined communal way of life. There he employs the theme of suprasensual vision to condemn traditional Egyptian religion, with its animal images of deities, and to recommend the exegetical practices of the "Therapeutae." The Egyptians, Philo writes, "have lost the use of the most vital of senses, sight"; the true import of this judgment is clarified by subsequent remarks: "And by this I do not mean the sight of the body but of the soul, the sight which alone gives a knowledge of truth and falsehood."[44] In a more affirmative tone Philo observes that by means of the allegorical interpretation of sacred scripture—"by looking through the words as through mirrors"—the Therapeutae were able "to discern the inward and hidden through the outward and visible."[45] These brief quotations suggest the central features of the theme of suprasensual vision: (1) visual perception is a model for all types of human knowledge, and (2) a vision somehow unmediated by sensual materiality is paradigmatic of the highest sort of wisdom, including sacred wisdom.

The theme of suprasensual vision posits that the goal of the Christian life is to attain a vision of God that transcends perception with the eyes and becomes a more intimate sort of communion. In the seventh chapter of the *Stromata,* Clement writes:

> Counted as holy among the holy, and translated absolutely and entirely to another sphere, they (gnostic souls) keep on always moving to higher and yet higher regions, until they no longer greet the divine vision in or by means of mirrors, but for loving hearts feast for ever on the uncloying, never-ending sight, radiant in its transparent clearness, while throughout the endless ages they taste a never-wearying delight, and thus continue, all alike honored with an identity of preeminence.[46]

The dualism of visible and intelligible spheres shows definite Platonic influence, as does the intermixture of language of love and ascent. In a subsequent part of the same passage Clement explicitly invokes Platonic language in labelling this vision a "gnostic assimilation" (γνωστικῆς ἐξομοιώσεως). The language here suggests that the object perceived is not strictly sensible and that the encounter itself is not strictly ocular. In a later passage Clement is more explicit in stressing the intellectual and suprasensual character of this vision: "When he (the Christian gnostic) gets hold of a scientific principle, he believes that he sees the Lord, while he directs his eyes to the unseen; and if he fancies that he sees what he is unwilling to see, he chides the faculty of vision whenever he is conscious of a feeling of pleasure at the visual impression; since he desires to see and hear nothing but what beseems him."[47] The true Christian gnostic experiences a seeing which is not seeing—a knowing which is not knowing. Indeed, at the conclusion of the chapter of the *Stromata* which deals with issues of faith and knowledge Clement affirms the central tenets of a negative or apophatic theology. (See *Stromata* 5.11–12.) Part of his motivation at this juncture is pastoral; he is consistently concerned with reconciling the faith of uneducated Christians with the knowledge of more sophisticated pagan converts. A trusting knowing of what God is not integrates elements of faith and knowledge.

A second pastoral reality helps explain Clement's fondness for the language of suprasensual vision. This language expresses the paradoxical experience of Christians who receive divine grace in the sacrament of baptism. One is saved by dying and rising with Christ, yet one still needs to pursue a fuller communion with God. Clement is rather frankly a synergist, believing that while God's grace is necessary for salvation, human effort is also required for attaining the higher stages of spiritual life. For this effort both philosophy and spiritual disciplines like devotional prayer and physical austerities are important. Practical regimens of behavior which moderate or extirpate the passions are crucial because they make possible a vision of God untainted by sensuality: they, along with God's grace, are antidotes to a human sinfulness that corrupts affective dispositions in the direction of inordinate sensual attachments. Philosophy is a different sort of schooling in the apprehension of transcendent realities. Clement believed that philosophy served a comparable function for the ancient Greeks as the Mosaic Law served for the Jews—it restrained sin and prepared adherents for the reception of the Gospel of Christ. For individual development, too, philosophy serves as a propaedeutic; it brings the student beyond the stage of understanding attainable in the liberal arts, and then readies that pupil to receive the deepest mysteries revealed by Christ. Philosophy, like spiritually disciplined practices, is only partially successful: the pious Christian attains a vision of God in this life, but one still tainted by sensual impairments. This intermediary situation is the condition of the baptized Christian during mortal life.

It is in this context of pastoral concerns that Clement's employment of the philosophically pregnant theme of suprasensual vision should be understood. As the goal of the spiritual life this vision bears the philosophical influence of Plato's contrast between human knowledge of the visible and intelligible worlds. Like many ancient Greek philosophers, Plato based his empirical epistemology upon the paradigm of visual perception. Then when speaking of geometrical knowledge in the *Republic,* Plato identifies it as knowledge of the intelligible rather than the visible world, because while geometers employ images, they do so only as illustrations, the actual objects of study being immaterial. Socrates is portrayed as saying, "The very things which they mold and draw, these things they treat in their turn as only images, but what they really seek is to get sight of those realities which can only be seen with the mind" (ἃ οὐκ ἂν ἄλλως ἴδοι τις ἢ τῇ διανοίᾳ).[48] Dialectical reasoning, the other mode of genuine knowledge, does not proceed deductively from first principles, but from these principles it ascends yet higher to the one first principle "making no use whatever of any object of sense but only of pure ideas moving on through ideas to ideas and ending with ideas."[49] Such passages are the philosophical inspiration for Clement's adoption of the theme of suprasensual vision.

Two stages of philosophical generalization are evident in the history recounted here. First, Plato uses the notion of geometrical knowledge, with its idealized objects and its axiomatic structure, in order to explain the character of all reliable knowledge. Then, Clement and the tradition he appropriates uses the Platonic conception of knowledge for explaining the character of the human encounter with God. With each generalization there is a correlative valuation: knowledge which is not conformable to the geometrical pattern is depreciated as are encounters with God not conformable to the Platonic vision. This philosophically informed description of experiencing God implies that a vision of God is valuable not only for strictly soteriological reasons, but also because as a mode of knowledge it represents the highest achievement of a human being, at least, according to Platonic philosophy. It also underlies Clement's rationale for specific spiritual disciplines, for instance, chastity. Restraint on sexual desire promotes that passionless state of being which is a prerequisite for an suprasensual vision of God. Clement is careful to allow that this virtue may consist of modest sexual intercourse among marriage partners or of celibacy by religious adepts: he shuns a radically world-denying ethic.[50]

Pascal was an intellectual heir of this twofold generalization. He believed that genuinely reliable knowledge is presentable in the axiomatic form characteristic of geometry, and he confessed that God can be apprehended as spiritualized light and heat. He likewise drew the conclusion that quelling human passion was a prerequisite for the fruition of the spiritual life. Hence Pascal's conversion experience, and the practical changes in behavior it effected, was not simply a manifestation of his own peculiar psychology; it was also the expression of a long tradition of reflection upon the nature and meaning of a spiritually disciplined life.

The second categoreal theme was introduced indirectly when reference was made to the passionless state of being which is a prerequisite for the vision of God. This anthropological version of the theme of unencumbered causality is based upon a theological counterpart which is logically and temporally prior. The latter version says that God is a First Cause so powerful as to create and rule the entire world, and it also says that God is so transcendent to this created realm as to be immune from any reciprocal action by creation. Thus the Christian gnostic who acts in a passionless way is imitating the divine model of agency. Christians are called to glorify God's creative power as it is physically manifest in the natural world. Yet they are also called to know God as a causal power of another sort: "Being ruler therefore of himself and of all that belongs to him the gnostic makes a genuine approach to truth, having a firm hold of divine science, for the name science would fitly be given to the knowledge and firm hold of intellectual objects; its function in regard to divine things is to investigate what is the First Cause ($\pi\varrho\tilde{\omega}\tau\text{o}\nu$ $\alpha\,\iota\tau\iota\alpha\nu$). . . that through which all things were made and without which nothing has been made."[51] Clement here portrays God as a First Cause in the sense of being the ultimate source of the world's intelligibility; this philosophical conception complements the more anthropomorphic picture of God as a personified agent who creates and rules the physical world.

Henry Chadwick believes that Clement's doctrine of creation is the central and distinctive feature of Clement's thought: his affirmation of the goodness of God's creation distinguishes him from the world-fleeing Gnostics and his affirmation of a natural knowledge of divine providence distinguished him from the naturalistic hedonism of many pagans.[52] Certainly Clement's portrayal of God as a personified agent of creation is congenial with the Biblical account of creation; on the other hand, his attribution to God of the title of First Cause is characteristic of Greek philosophical foundationalism.

Since God is unitary, truths emerging from philosophical inquiry and Biblical revelation cannot be in conflict: Clement was one the first Christians to enunciate this maxim (*Stromata* 1.20). A second implication of this twofold portrayal of God as cause is that the Christian should partially come to share both God's knowledge and God's rulership. This point is made succinctly in the passage quoted above where Clement intimately links self-mastery and knowledge of God.

The Christian gnostic knows that God as First Cause is "exempt by nature from all need"; and he concludes, therefore, that a Christian of the intellectual sort should strive to become a person "having his resources in himself and being independent of others."[53] The ideal of autarky, or self-sufficiency, affirmed here by Clement is a major part of his strategy for countering threats to the Christian's well-being coming from extrinsic forces, whether they be bodily virulence or social oppression. The ideal is not one of quietistic solitude, but of dispositional freedom—the freedom to interpret any practical vicissitude as incapable of violating one's deepest sense of well-being. In the language I am recommending the Christian gnostic is enjoined by Clement to become an unencumbered cause like God: through the process of assimilation to God the theological and anthropological aspects of the theme of unencumbered causality become conjoined.

For Clement, self-sufficiency does not preclude potency: the impartation of divine wisdom is itself effected without change or diminution in God—the causal agent (*Stromata*, 7.7 (47)). Indeed, to the Greek philosophical mind, power and independence are mutually implicatory, so that by assimilation to God the gnostic comes to share both a divine self-sufficiency and a divine potency. The Christian gnostic becomes a vehicle of a new creation, both through the manifestation of God's grace in deportment and through the teaching of the Christian message. "Paedagogus" was for Clement both an office of Christ and a responsibility of the Christian gnostic; in some respects it is a prototype of the vocation of spiritual director of which Pascal's Monsieur Singlin was a lay practitioner.

The moment of initial assimilation to this creative career is the regeneration that occurs in baptism; its fulfillment consists of the "face to face" vision of God in the afterlife. Between these two moments lies the Christian life as the domain of spiritually disciplined behavior—as the arena of spiritual creativity. This creativity is described by means of an anthropological specification of the theme of the unencumbered cause; it takes the specific form of the already mentioned passionless human agent. "In being assimilated to God, the gnostic is making and fashioning himself and also forming those who hear him, while, so far as may be, he assimilates to that which is by nature free from passion ($\dot{\alpha}\pi\alpha\theta\dot{\epsilon}\varsigma$) that which has been subdued by training to a passionless state ($\dot{\alpha}\pi\dot{\alpha}\theta\epsilon\iota\alpha\nu$): and this he effects by undisturbed intercourse and communion with the Lord."[54] Passions for the Stoics included not only sexual desire, but any impulse that fell within the four categories of appetite, pleasure, fear, and distress. For Stoics like Chrysippus passions were impulses ungoverned by reason and so subject to inconsistency and mutability. Later Stoics, like Posidonius, who returned to a Platonic tripartite division of the soul, specifically associated passions with the irrational dimensions of human nature. Clement is clearly following the later Stoics on this point, but because he does not embrace a Gnostic condemnation of human sexuality it is important to preserve some connotation of consistency in his interpretation of passionlessness. The passions are to be extinguished so that attention can be consistently reserved for God, so that in knowing God one might be transformed and become capable of transforming others.

The absence of passion here does not signify an ascetic quietism, nor is it designed to warrant practices of severe mortification. Clement was a presbyter and teacher, a public figure and a leader. The ideal is the Stoic one of being a philosopher and at the same time a public agent of action. Marcus Aurelius, for many years a Roman emperor and Clement's elder contemporary, combined these personae most dramatically. He wrote: "To be a philosopher is to keep unsullied and unscathed the divine spirit within him, so that it may transcend all pleasure and all pain, taking nothing in hand without purpose and nothing falsely or with dissimulation—depend not on another's actions or inactions, accept each and every dispensation as coming form the same Source."[55] Yet he also urged one to act with promptitude and deliberation, befitting a "being who is virile and mature, a statesman, a Roman, and a ruler."[56] Clement appropriates this Stoic ethical ideal while rejecting Stoic materialistic pantheism; instead, he makes the passionless state a prerequisite for encountering a transcendent God.

A practical implication of this employment of the theme of unencumbered causality, or passionless agency, is, of course, the discipline of sexual continence. A life of poverty is equally recommended. Sociologists say that the exchange of commodities, even as gifts, establishes mutual obligations; they are actions which presume and perpetuate interdependence. Early Egyptian hermits established solitary residences as an alternative to village life; poverty was a consequence of solitude, of the disinclination to engage in customary patterns of social exchange. It was not a primary goal, nor simply an antidote to greed. This is likewise true for later Benedictine monks—the monastery was not a place where economic activities and relationships were suspended, but a place where they were transformed in a way that made human economic ties less obstructive of a life of prayer and worship.

In the *Paedagogus* Clement gives very precise instruction about what manner of dress and deportment is fitting for the Christian. He does not commend a radical poverty as did Francis of Assisi at a later date. He wanted to serve the pastoral needs of rich Alexandrians rather than dismiss them from the Christian community because of their wealth. Thus in his *Quis Dives Salvetur* he interprets in a figurative way Jesus' saying that "it is easier for a camel to go through the eye of a needle than for a rich man to enter the Kingdom of God" (Mt. 19.24). For him, the import of the saying was "to banish from the soul its opinions about riches, its attachment to them, its excessive desire, its morbid excitement over them, its anxious cares, the thorns of our earthly existence which choke the seed of the true life."[57] Christian poverty is constituted more properly by the absence of these passions, than by a dearth of actual possessions. Neither individuals nor the Church can do without some material wealth. Clement recognized this reality, yet still he encouraged Christians to adopt a simple lifestyle that had a personal efficacy of destroying passions and an symbolic efficacy of calling others to the Christian Gospel. The "poor in spirit" are, in practice, unencumbered causes doing God's will.

Again Clement inherits the product of a two-step process of philosophical generalization. The exemplars of unencumbered causes in Greek antiquity were the supposedly eternal heavenly bodies— the stars eternal for their material composition and the planets eternal for their uniform motion. The power they exerted on human life was deemed immense, with the physical influence of the sun and moon being especially prominent. Various astrological theories about the direct influence of the stars on human behavior described a second variety of influence. Aristotle's conception of God as given in Book XII of the *Metaphysics* represents a first stage of philosophical generalization in which the causality of heavenly bodies is systematized and rationalized. God is portrayed as an unencumbered cause in the sense of being a source of motion which is itself not moved by anything else: "The first principle and primary reality is immovable ($\dot{\alpha}\varkappa\acute{\iota}\nu\eta\pi o\nu$) both essentially and accidently, but excites ($\varkappa\iota\nuo\hat{\upsilon}\nu$) the primary form of motion which is one and eternal."[58] Whereas Aristotle's portrayal of God in the *Metaphysics* as a self-contemplative being suggests some degree of personification, in the final books of the *Physics* it is clear that Aristotle's God is a logical rather than a personal construct. The personification of the idea of God inherited from Plato and Aristotle occurred in subsequent Hellenistic philosophy: the famous hymn to Zeus by the Stoic Cleanthes is a fine example of how God became portrayed as both an anthropomorphic deity and as an apotheosis of reason. This theological admixture was part of Clement's intellectual background and suited his own task of reconciling philosophical and Biblical notions of deity. It also facilitated a further generalization of the idea of an unencumbered cause so as to make it applicable to human agents as well as to a unique divine agency.

The Stoic ideal of passionlessness had social roots in the Cynic valuation of autarky. The deliberately unconventional behavior of Diogenes of Sinope and his followers (such as defecating in public, for which they earned the title 'Dogs' or, in Greek, 'κυνικοί') was not emulated by Stoics, but his point that the natural human endowment of reason was sufficient for a life of virtue did influence Stoic thinkers. It is likely that this Cynic ideal emerged from reflections upon social phenomena, and especially upon the life and death of Socrates. Plato and Aristotle similarly believed that Socrates embodied the ideal of the self-sufficiency of philosophical wisdom. Hence the theme of unencumbered causality is indebted to both social and cosmic sources, and expresses an ancient Greek ambivalence toward the involvement of the most sublime causal agents in the world where creative power is exercised.

Pascal's periods of retreat at the Abbey of Port-Royal, and his castigations of many social activities as *divertissement,* show that he was strongly attracted to the ideal of spiritual self-sufficiency. His conviction that Christ could heal him because Christ alone has the power to heal himself is evidence that Pascal subscribed to theological expressions of the theme of unencumbered causality. Clement first formulated notions like unencumbered causality that Pascal took for granted as part of his spiritual heritage and that he relied upon especially in times of spiritual crisis. Pascal's conservative response to crisis contrasts sharply with the innovative character of his most productive labors. Clement's rationale for the spiritual life was innovative in its time, but it was not so germane to Pascal's circumstances.

Clement's employment of the theme of unencumbered causality becomes part of a rationale for Christian spiritual life because it is descriptive of the type of human agency that is appropriate for the vision of God. Such a state of detachment is valuable both because it is constitutive of virtuous human behavior and because it is a precondition for the direct vision of God. Another precondition for the vision is a stable social environment, a reality which Clement understood in terms of the notion of a static hierarchy. This principle of order which Christ teaches is manifest alike in individuals, the church, and the cosmos: "He (Christ) is the source of Providence both for the individual and the community and for the universe at large."[59] The multiple levels upon which the hierarchical principle of order operates makes some of Clement's language ambiguous as to whether he is speaking of actual life in the church community or the afterlife of the saved community cosmically conceived. The distinction between the visible and invisible church was not known to Clement. This ambiguity is present in the following passage where Clement identifies power, goodness, and safety with relations of strict dominance by Christ the High Priest:

> Being then the power of the Father, he (Christ) easily prevails over whomsoever he will, not leaving even the smallest atom of his government uncared for: else the universe of his creation would have been no longer good. And I think the greatest power is shown where there is an inspection of all the parts, proceeding with minute accuracy even to the smallest, while all gaze on the supreme Administrator of the universe, as he pilots all in safety according to the Father's will, rank being subordinated to rank under different leaders, till in the end the great High Priest ($\dot{\alpha}\varrho\chi\iota\epsilon\varrho\acute{\epsilon}\alpha$) is reached. For on one original principle, which works in accordance with the Father's will, depend the first and second and third gradations; and then at the extreme end of the visible world there is the blessed ordinance of angels; and so even down to ourselves, ranks below ranks are appointed, all saving and being saved by the initiation and through the instrumentality of the One.[60]

Clearly the hierarchical relationship of God, Christ, angels, and human beings makes salvation possible; it provides the world structure which enables Christians to travel to God.[61] Yet the theme of the static hierarchy also directly informs Clement's understanding of the contemplation of God. Clement thus writes:

> It (knowledge of God) easily transplants a man to that divine and holy state which is akin to the soul, and by a light of its own carries him through the mystic stages, till it restores him to the crowning abode of rest, having taught the pure in heart to look upon God face to face with understanding and absolute certainty. For herein lies the perfection of the gnostic soul, that having transcended all purifications and modes of ritual, it should be with the Lord where he is, in immediate subordination to him.[62]

Here the soul has transcended ordinary bodily existence. Especially important for the present discussion is that the goal of ascent is at once called rest and immediate subordination. Subordination within the divine hierarchy brings stability and security. A system of subordination to God is the enabling condition for salvation and it also contributes to the very experience of salvation itself. In God one is "absolutely secure from all vicissitude."[63] Subordination satisfies the deep desire to endure. Hierarchy is the condition for endurance and a philosophical tool for articulating the meaning of the importance of obedience as an religious virtue. As noted previously Clement's thinking about obedience takes two forms: the moral rectitude of the faithful Christian and the passionless vision of the Christian gnostic.

Clement's use of the categoreal theme of static hierarchy has religious roots in both Jewish apocalypticism and Gnostic versions of Plato's legacy, and all of these religious themes reflect ancient social reality. Patriarchal family relationships in both Hebraic and Greek contexts provided ample social data from which generalizations about social order might conveniently follow. In the ancient Greek world women and children usually had little status or power in the family; hence the stability of family relationships was most directly determined by the degree to which women and children were effectively subordinated to the male head of the household.[64] This authoritarian social structure was also evident in the militaries of the ancient Greek city-states. An apparent advantage of rule according to strict relations of hierarchical dominance was that new children or conquered peoples could readily be incorporated into the extant social structure by occupying the lowest positions of social status and power. Hence it was a principle of rule that seemed to preserve stability amidst an increase in numerical complexity. Of course, Athenian democratic traditions, as, for instance, articulated in Pericles' Funeral Oration, provided an alternative to complete authoritarianism, but it is important to recall that Greek democratic governments were limited in their distribution of power and brief in their tenure of ruling. They were relatively rare exceptions to the authoritarian principle of order summarized by the theme of static hierarchy.

The ideal of the static hierarchy in Greek thinking did not have its sole manifestation in social relationships. Consider the characteristic prominence of post and lintel constructions in Greek public architecture. Columns in buildings like the Parthenon were constructed of multiple segments piled one on top of the other. Gravitational force of the huge masses and the frictional resistance of the segments' tangent surfaces effectively kept the columns erect and capable of supporting the roofing materials. Fluting, shaping and spacing of the columns combined to accentuate the aesthetic sense of ascent. This combination of massive presence and vertical ascent gives an apt visual epitome of the theme of the static hierarchy.

The philosophical integration of the sociological and architectonic motifs of static hierarchy was achieved first by Plato. In the *Republic* personal and social justice is said to involve respectively the proper subordination of inferior parts of the soul to the faculty of reason and of inferior classes to philosopher kings. This ordering is for Plato the worldly imitation of an ontological hierarchy which extends from the illusory images of artists to ideal forms possessing optimal existence. In the *Laws* he writes more mythologically in commending the rule of the divine: "Wherever a state has a mortal, and no god, for ruler (ἀρχη), there the people have no rest from ills and toils; . . . we ought by every means to imitate (μιμεῖσθαι) the life of the age of Cronos, as tradition paints it, and order both our homes and our states in obedience to the immortal element within us, giving to reason's ordering the name of 'law.' "[65] Aristotle states more metaphysically his conviction that rule of the many by the few is the way of nature and not merely a social convention: "In every composite thing, where a plurality of parts, whether continuous or discrete, is combined to make a single common whole, there is always found a ruling and a subject factor (τὸ ἄρχον καὶ τὸ ἀρχόμενον), and this characteristic of living things is present in them as an outcome of the whole of nature, since even in things that do not partake of life there is a ruling principle (ἀρχή)."[66]

Aristotle presents this principle as part of his notorious justification of the institution of slavery. It shows how social relationships became generalized to the status of an eternal metaphysical principle for which God provides the prime exemplification. Clement appropriates this theme of the static hierarchy as the constitutive principle of social and transcendent order, modifying it only modestly to include Christ, angels, and other new gradations. By making immediate subordination to God an inherent part of the vision of God, Clement gives yet a higher experiential valuation to this theme than did his Greek forebears. The common identity of Christians as "slaves of God" (Rom. 6.22) is deemed a precondition of righteousness and the stuff of salvation. Pascal's postconversion submission to the authority of his spiritual director is a paradigmatic expression of this tendency to seek security by location in an authoritarian social hierarchy.

In summation, then, Clement provides a philosophical rationale for the spiritual life of chastity, poverty, and obedience by means of his employment of the philosophically generalized notions of suprasensual vision, unencumbered causality, and static hierarchy. Suprasensual vision informs the goal of the Christian spiritual life— the contemplation of God. Unencumbered causality is used to articulate the prerequisite for such contemplation as a passionless state of being and it is also used to describe the exercise of power in activities not devoted to pure contemplation. Static hierarchy helps describe the social prerequisites for the attainment of this goal, and insofar as the vision of God is constituted by an experience of rest, it also contributes substantially to the goal of the spiritual life by assuring rest to those who attain immediate subordination to God. In each case these ideas also contribute to a philosophical rationale for a spiritually disciplined life: Clement promises that his prescriptions make possible not only salvation, but also the optimum of well-being that can be attained by rational human beings. In the next chapter I shall investigate the extent to which this promise is fulfilled; I shall evaluate the extent to which Clement's rationale is adequate guidance for contending with Pascal's predicament. At times Pascal thought this traditional remedy was adequate; other aspects of his life and writings suggest otherwise.

CHAPTER 2

A Contemporary Evaluation

It is now possible to ask directly whether Clement's account of the spiritually disciplined life responds satisfactorily to Pascal's predicament. In doing so it is important to note that the rationale being considered, while culled most directly from Clement's writings, represents a much broader tradition. For instance, the three themes of suprasensual vision, unencumbered causality, and static hierarchy are evident in Augustine's writings: the first could have been introduced by citing the discussion of the vision of God in *De civitate Dei* (22.29); the second by citing Augustine's reflections on "God and the soul" in the very Platonic *Soliloquia* (1.2–6); and the third by referring to his remarks on church authority in anti-Donatist writings. Also, a theme like suprasensual vision is present in diverse contexts: in systematic treatises like Origen's *De Principiis* (1.1) and Aquinas's *Summa Theologiae* (1.q.12); in epic poems like Dante's *The Divine Comedy* (*Paradise* 30.34–63) and Milton's *Paradise Lost* (1.61–105); in texts of popular piety like Thomas à Kempis's *The Imitation of Christ* (1.1) and John Bunyan's *The Pilgrim's Progress* (1). All of the themes are especially evident in the hymnody of the Church. Recognition of the wide occurrence of the themes under scrutiny is important because it means that criticism of them can not aspire to refutation and eradication. Rather such criticism is offered as an admonition that these themes do not deserve unimpeachable standing and may well benefit from reformulation.

Pascal himself was mostly satisfied with traditional ways of describing and justifying Christian spiritual life: passages from *The Memorial* and *The Mystery of Jesus* quoted above showed his congeniality with themes initiated by Clement. It has also been noted that while Pascal did not permanently retire to Port-Royal and adopt an ascetic life after his 1654 conversion, he did renounce his intention of marrying, commence a program of charitable distribution of his wealth, and accept the authority of a spiritual director at Port-Royal. Indeed, if one considers early seventeenth-century adaptations of

47

traditional devotional teachings to the circumstances of the laity, Pascal's postconversion life comes remarkably close to fitting this ideal. Francis de Sales, who died the year prior to Pascal's birth, summarized these developments in his *Introduction to the Devout Life* and other writings; he claimed no philosophical or theological novelty, and one of his inherited traditions was the philosophical rationale for the spiritual life constructed by Clement and others. Clement wrote prior to the emergence of the monastery as a religious institution; Francis wrote after its decline from prominence. Thus in the sense that Pascal offers an example of a lay person seeking to adopt spiritual disciplines while still in commerce with the secular world, his spiritual life was more modern than medieval. He did, though, seek to address his modern predicament with some quite traditional remedies.

Pascal's testimony to the cogency of Clement's rationale is not itself binding. His example is instructive but not authoritative. Two sorts of questions can be raised in regard to Clement's rationale. For instance, one might ask whether the vision of God, as described by Clement, really should be the goal of the spiritual life. This is primarily a theological question, and as was noted in my introductory remarks, theology is not the immediate concern here. A second and more philosophical sort of question asks if a notion like suprasensual vision is adequate to the task of articulating a purportedly exemplary experience of God. Is the theme of suprasensual vision as formulated by Plato and Platonic theologians a reliable instance of philosophical generalization? Relevant to this question are empirical findings from scientific disciplines. Equally germane are conceptions of philosophy and philosophical method. Finally, it is appropriate to ask whether particular philosophical generalizations are defensible in light of the attitudes and actions they have historically fostered: this is an ethical criterion. By evaluating Clement's categoreal themes from these three vantage points—of empirical science, philosophical method, and ethical probity—I believe that some compelling conclusions can be drawn about how he sought to describe and justify various spiritually disciplined regimens of behavior.

Briefly put, I think that scientific, philosophical, and ethical considerations combine to make a strong case for the relative incoherence and inadequacy of the three categoreal themes identified in Clement's rationale. Certainly these themes, along with the conception of the spiritual life they help to portray, represent the serious reflections of a previous era and are even now capable of yielding insight. Yet I also believe that they bring presuppositions and bear connotations which are destructive of current attempts to understand the world rationally and to live peacefully in human community with one another. Hence in the first section of this chapter I offer criticisms of Clement's rationale. Subsequently, in light of these criticisms, I seek in the chapter's remaining two sections to redirect the rationale in a way that preserves some of its insights, and then to reformulate the predicament given exemplary expression in Pascal's life and writings.

First to be examined will be the categoreal theme of suprasensual vision evident in Plato's *Republic* and Clement's *Stromata*. Problematic here is the Platonic understanding of the relation between visualization and conceptualization in scientific knowledge. For Plato knowledge was certain and informative to the extent that it was free from reliance on the senses. Knowledge is a relation of an agent to objects in the intelligible world of ideal forms. Plato called the highest form of knowledge "dialectic (διαλεκτική)," a Greek word also used to designate logical theory (*Republic* 511). Mathematics—and he specifically had geometry in mind—counts as knowledge because it employs visual imagery in only an ancillary and illustrative way. Yet even scientific investigation of sensible objects fails to attain genuine knowledge, being at best a variety of correct belief. In this realm of opinion the sense of touch was most suspect to ancient Greek intellectuals; vision, though still flawed by sensuality, was less objectionable than the other faculties of sense. For Plato, then, conceptualization is fostered and improved to the extent that it transcends visualization and operates in an intelligble realm immune to the variability of the senses. This is the essence of Platonic idealism, and it is not difficult to understand how congenial such an epistemological model was for persons like Clement who sought to account for human knowledge of a transcendent God.

At first glance it may seem that some developments in twentieth-century natural science confirm the ancient Greek depreciation of visualization. Niels Bohr wrote about Max Planck's discovery of the quantum of action: "Only by a conscious resignation of our usual demands for visualization and causality was it possible to make Planck's discovery fruitful in explaining the properties of the elements on the basis of our knowledge of the building stones of atoms."[1] The adequacy of visual imagery and causal principles for the purposes of classical mechanics depended upon the relative smallness of the quantum of action in comparison to the size of the objects investigated. In a like manner, Einsteins's theory of relativity teaches that the sharp division of space and time effected by the human senses is tolerable only for the consideration of objects moving at velocities that are small when compared with the speed of light. Hence both quantum mechanics and the theory of relativity are predicated upon relinquishing the traditional demand for visualization. Bohr did not regard this new situation as an impediment to scientific progress; it merely implied that scientific theories must take on a new degree of abstract formulation. Werner Heisenberg's formulation of basic principles of quantum mechanics with the aid of matrix algebra effected just this new level of abstraction; Bohr interpreted Heisenberg's celebrated indeterminacy principle "as a direct expression of the absolute limitation of application of visualizable conceptions in the description of atomic phenomenon."[2]

These abstract modes of physical description might seem to suggest that conceptualization exceeds visualization in the newest frontiers of science, relegating visual imagery to an inferior and dispensable status. Bohr concluded otherwise in an addendum to his celebrated principle of complementarity. Both quantum mechanics and relativity theory introduced novel insights about the role of observation in physical theory: the latter specified the different ways in which observers moving relative to one another will describe physical objects, while the former posits an interaction between objects and measuring instruments which establishes a limit to the degree to which atomic objects can be said to be independent of the means of their observation. Bohr's famous principle of complementarity says that information obtained about an object under one set of experimental conditions is complementary to information obtained about the same object under different experimental conditions. Again, while these two sets of information cannot always be combined by ordinary concepts so as to form a single coherent "picture" of reality, they can always be integrated by more abstract methods into a coherent account, as, for instance, the wave and particle theories of light and matter are visually incompatible but are mathematically expressible in Heisenberg's quantal formalism.

Upon recognizing that atomic objects cannot be specified independently of the means and conditions for their observation, Bohr adds that these means and conditions are describable in natural languages pervaded by visual imagery and classical conceptions of causality. Even scientists working in the most arcane areas of physical research must be able to describe informally the experimental setup from which their observations come. This implies that even atomic phenomena which are not themselves visualizable are intrinsically related to visualizable descriptions via the conditions which make them possible. Heisenberg followed Bohr on this point, though he stressed somewhat more strongly the extent to which the images and concepts of classical physics are embedded in natural languages: "We know that any understanding must be based finally upon natural language because it is only there that we can be certain to touch reality, and hence we must be skeptical about any skepticism with regard to this natural language and its essential concepts. Therefore, we may use these concepts as they have been used at all times."[3]

Heisenberg's confidence in natural language concepts seems a bit excessive to students of twentieth-century philosophy. Natural language concepts like reality and truth have been proved to be notoriously ambiguous, and efforts to specify them precisely have led to unsuspected limitations. Alfred Tarski's formulation of a "semantic conception of truth" illustrates both of these points. Tarski began with Aristotle's conception of truth—the correspondence theory that avers a sentence is true if it designates an extant state of affairs. He then tried to characterize this notion precisely by using mathematical logic to define truth for languages with a rigorously specified structure.[4] However, a certain incompleteness was found to govern formal languages having such a precise notion of truth because they can not consistently include predications of truth for all sentences of this language. Self-referential paradoxes like 'This sentence is not true' introduce inconsistency. Hence an appeal to natural language concepts does not provide an easy solution to the problems of reflexivity troubling philosophically inclined quantum physicists. Tarski's work implies that formal definitions of truth are dependent upon richer but less precise ideas of truth conveyed in natural languages. As such it provides an interesting parallel to Bohr's point that abstract descriptions of physical space are dependent upon perceptual intuitions. Also, as I shall argue in detail later, semiotic self-reference provides a more adequate idiom than suprasensual vision for talking about paradoxicality—an aspect of human experience that Pascal showed to be central to the human spiritual predicament.

A brief summary of this first criticism is now appropriate. The Platonic theme of suprasensual vision was attractive to Clement and other religious thinkers because it seemed to provide an intellectually respectable way of articulating an individual's apprehension of the divine. Since the attainment of a type of knowledge transcending all ties to sense perception and colloquial language is no longer believed to be possible, or even particularly desirable, the descriptive and justificatory power of the notion of suprasensual vision is considerably lessened. When Plato's ideal of dialectical knowledge loses cogency, so too does a rationale for the spiritual life indebted to it.

A second way of challenging Clement's theme of suprasensual vision is to criticize the conception of philosophy from which it emerges. The criticism offered here is directed not only to Platonic idealism but to any philosophy which makes perception the model for knowledge and vision the model for perception. My views reflect the linguistic and hermeneutical character of much twentieth-century philosophy which is more concerned to support articulate truth claims with relative adequacy than to facilitate the apprehension of objects with absolute certainty. The clear visual perception of a stable object has an immediacy and irrefragability about it that makes it seem a promising starting point for more elaborate systems of knowledge. In a contrary manner, conversation as an exchange of questions and answers has an open-ended quality which makes the support of one verbal affirmation with another seem to be an endless and indecisive process. Ancient Greek philosophers and early modern thinkers like Descartes and Locke were devoted to the task of making knowledge systematic and secure. More recent philosophers have become less optimistic about their callings and more aware of the negative consequences of secular dogmatisms. Hence philosophers as diverse as Ludwig Wittgenstein, Martin Heidegger, and John Dewey have contributed to the liberation of epistemology from the paradigm of perception and the release of philosophy from the quest for certainty.

Particularly congenial to my philosophical temperament is Dewey's critique of what he calls the "spectator theory of knowledge."[5] It is especially relevant here because Dewey claims that the same quest for certainty which leads Plato to identify real knowledge with a mental vision of unchanging objects leads him to depreciate all forms of practical activity: such activity is ineluctably fraught with uncertainty. If Dewey is correct, then spiritual practices rooted in a Platonic conception of philosophy are recipes for the cessation of meaningful practical activity. They are practices which anticipate their own cessation in the experience of the vision of God. A philosophical rationale for spiritual practices that depreciates the practical seems hardly well suited to responding to the predicament of someone like Pascal. In his case, which I have offered as representative of many subsequent thinkers, the reality of incomplete knowledge and the necessity of action amidst conditions of risk are essential elements of the human spiritual predicament. Pascal's Wager shows that his own theological thinking had innovative and practical elements. Dewey frequently stressed this point; indeed, it is a pragmatist principle that human decision making, including the decision to trust and seek God, is an activity of a biological organism in a natural and social environment such that uncertainty, peril, and passion are never completely absent from the situation preceding and succeeding the decision. For Dewey this means that philosophy is ever in need of "reconstruction"; for the present project it means that the human spiritual predicament will continaully need to be addressed with new strategies as circumstances change.

Richard Rorty is a contemporary philosopher who has carried on Dewey's critique of spectator theories of knowledge.[6] Rorty has been especially vigorous in tracing the connection between metaphors of cognition as seeing and mirroring, and conceptions of philosophy as a foundational discipline—a discipline which, in deference to the natural and social sciences, admits that it has no privileged access to any empirical domain, but which allots to itself the task of insuring that various bits of knowledge are logically related to one another and securely rooted in the world that verifies them. In this foundationalist conception of philosophy Rorty sees a covert apology for philosophy's continued existence as a unique and, in some way, superior discipline. He argues further that this covert agenda vitiates the practical value of philosophy. One practical service that philosophers have historically rendered is to provide resources for the description and justification of the disciplined practices that figure in some remedies for the human spiritual predicament. With this book I aspire to do the same. In my view, following Rorty, one is more likely to render this service well—in a way that fosters rather than obstructs the adoption of the relevant practices—if one is not also seeking to exemplify and justify the privileged status of philosophers. Although Pascal did not give much significance to his own status as a philosopher—a trait that endeared him to Nietzsche—both Clement and Augustine accorded exaggerated honors to Plato and uncritical credence to elements of his epistemology.

The ethical deficiencies of a model of knowledge of God based upon the metaphor of suprasensual vision arise from its negative assessment of the body. Given Albinus' definition of spiritual praxis (which stresses the expression of an agent's spiritual character through the instrumentality of the body), the depreciation of the body is a direct implication of the depreciation of practical activity that Dewey detected in the Greek origins of the spectator theory of knowledge. Of course, Christians like Clement had Biblical injunctions which set limits on the degree to which corporeal existence could be devalued; for instance, married life retained honor if not the highest praise, and suicidal mortifications were condemned even though martyrdom was extolled. Yet knowing God as the soul's triumph over the body still has unfortunate ethical consequences; several are dramatically evident in a narrative instantiation of the theme of suprasensual vision—Athanasius' *Vita Antonii.*

Athanasius and Antony were Alexandrians who lived about a century later than Clement. Athanasius, while bishop of his native city, wrote Antony's biography with the pastoral intent of presenting him as a example to be imitated. He used as the central theme of his narrative the drama of temptation such as Christ experienced in the wilderness after his baptism by John. Though the narrative theme of temptation is Scriptural, the specific temptations themselves have a consistently Hellenistic content: "The beleaguered devil undertook one night to assume the form of a woman and to imitate her every gesture, solely in order that he might beguile Antony, but in thinking about the Christ and considering the excellence won through him, and the intellectual part of the soul, Antony extinguished the fire of his opponent's deception."[7] The female figure embodies sensual irrationality while the male figure of Christ is allied with the intellectual part of the soul; the former is an emblem of spiritual death and the latter of spiritual life. If one hesitates to conclude that this theological idiom becomes the vehicle for bias, then consider that in the next two visits the devil comes as a "black boy" and as "irrational beasts."[8]

Spiritual well-being is identified here and in many other Platonic sources with an intelligence unmarred by sensible contamination, and, in turn, intelligence is identified with that aspect of white male human beings which supposedly makes them superior to other sensate creatures. It may be argued that the link between the theme of suprasensual vision and these prejudicial views is more a historical than a logical one. I recognize that an idealism of a Platonic sort does not logically imply sexism and racism, but there is a misguided devaluation of embodied sensuality in such a philosophy, and I believe that even the historical link to virulent social attitudes supports the case for a critical rethinking of traditional Platonic ways of describing and justifying spiritual practices. Pascal certainly shared this negative view of human physicality, even to the extent, it is reported, of criticizing his sister Gilberte for hugging her children in public. Yet he also shared his spiritual life with his sisters Jaqueline and Gilberte as much as with anybody else; in this he signals that the spiritual predicament in its more contemporary forms is unlikely to be well addressed when sexes and races are needlessly alienated from one another. If themes like suprasensual vision even indirectly promote such alienation, then this is sufficient to warrant its re-evaluation.

Like suprasensual vision, the theme of unencumbered causality is a product of the Greek intellectual temperament epitomized by Plato and systematized by Aristotle. Plato sometimes spoke of his ideal forms as causes, thereby positing causes not physically mediated. This transcendent nature gave such causes immunity to change. Aristotle more consistently spoke of causal relations as crucial for knowing the world, writing at the beginning of the *Metaphysics* that "it is when we think that we understand its primary cause that we claim to know each particular thing."[9] He was the first to distinguish clearly between the four types of causes invoked by ancient philosophers. In terms of the traditional example of a sculpted statue the four causes are: the material cause or that out of which the statue is made, i.e., bronze; the efficient cause or that by which the statue is made, i.e., the hammer blows of the sculptor; the formal cause or that in accordance with which the statue is made, i.e., the essence of a human figure; and, the final cause or that for which the statue is made, i.e., the contemplation of beauty (*Metaphysics* 1013a).

Hellenistic Jews and Christians used three of these four types of causes in their philosophical descriptions of God. God was spoken of as an efficient cause in the sense of being the creator of the physical world and as a final cause in the sense of being that to which the spiritual aspirant sought to be assimilated. Also, God was sometimes described as a formal cause by early Christian philosophers, usually in order to stress divine immateriality and immutability. All three of these usages are present in Clement's essay on spiritual life. (Aristotle's own theology involved a different employment of the notion of causality: God, the Unmoved Mover, does not give the world its first physical impetus as an efficient cause, but rather as a final cause attracts the world into being by itself being the acme of existence—pure thought thinking itself.)

Several features of the Greek theme of unencumbered causality led to difficulties for descriptions of practical spiritual life. First, Plato's notion of a formal cause as something immune to change becomes obscure when the formal cause is embodied, specifically, when the soul is regarded as the form and source of motion for the human body. This obscurity is compounded by Plato when he speaks of the soul as including an intellectual part assigned to rule over spirited and appetitive parts. Aristotle mitigated these difficulties by denying the existence of forms not joined to matter, but he also in a sense ratified them by allowing the soul to be an once a formal, final, and efficient cause. Thus it is not surprising that the ideal of divine self-sufficiency was communicated to Clement and his generation by the mediation of Stoic thinkers like Chrysippus who eschewed formal causes altogether and who had a psychology that posited a unitary rational soul.

Empirical objections to the continued use of ancient conceptions of causality for the description of God's nature and human spiritual practices are several. First, only something like efficient causality survives in empirical scientific usage. Physically unmediated formal causes are entirely foreign to contemporary experimental sensibilities, and teleological ideas conveyed by Aristotle via final causes are no longer deemed necessary for adequate explanations in the physical and biological sciences, and where they are still used, in some psychological literature, they are more commonly expressed by talk about intentions and plans. Thus while Clement's recommendation that the Christian "gnostic" know God as First Cause may have counted as an injunction to pursue the sort of knowledge deemed most rigorous by ancient philosophers, this same recommendation can no longer claim such a status. The justificatory value of language of God as an unencumbered cause is thereby weakened.

Second, in the natural sciences the idea of causality has lost its aura of deterministic certainty because of the recognition of the probabilistic character of physical law, both in the sense that the laws of thermodynamics are statistical in nature, and also in the sense that all physical laws have an irreducible element of indeterminacy for reasons first enunciated by Heisenberg. Causes have lost precisely those properties which made them suggestive of classical conceptions of deity. This demotion from absolute standing does not imply that causality is an entirely antiquated notion: Bohr noted that even though it must give way to more generalized conceptions in order to account for very small and very fast entities, it is still an appropriate if informal notion for the realm of phenomenon described by classical physics. Changes in scientific conceptions of causality do imply, however, that religious certainty can not be gained by conflating theistic with causal knowledge.

Third, the existence of changeless causes of change, or unmoved movers, violates basic conservation principles. If operative in a concrete physical system subject to no external forces, such a cause violates the principle of the conservation of momentum. The momentum principle, as applicable in this context, is related to

Newton's third law of motion—a more familiar expression of the interconnectedness of physical forces frequently paraphrased as saying that for each action there is an equal and opposite reaction. Hence the stars of the highest heaven are not so unchanging as Aristotle believed, and so they do not provide an intermediate stage in a process of philosophical generalization which posits that the most potent causes are ones most immune to reciprocal influence from what they effect.

Actually, conservation principles have a greater generality than Newton's laws of motion; for this reason their violation is much more serious. The physicist Richard Feynman describes them as the laws which govern physical laws:

> When learning about the laws of physics you find that there are a large number of complicated and detailed laws, laws of gravitation, of electricity and magnetism, nuclear interactions, and so on, but across the variety of detailed laws there sweep great general principles which all the laws seem to follow. Examples of these are principles of conservation, certain qualities of symmetry, the general form of quantum mechanical principles, and. . .the fact that all laws are mathematical.[10]

In the next paragraph Feynman says what he means by a conservation law: "A conservation law means that there is a number which you can calculate at one moment, then as nature undergoes its multitude of changes, if you calculate this quantity again at a later time it will be the same as it was before; the number does not change.[11] It is noteworthy that this definition implicitly makes use of the idea of symmetry which he defines in a later chapter: "A thing is symmetrical if there is something that you can do to it so that after you have finished doing it looks the same as it did before."[12] (A circle has rotational symmetry in that no matter how you rotate it around its center it still looks the same.) The similarity between Feynman's definitions of conservation laws and symmetry is not accidental. A central theme of the book in which these quotations occur is that physical law is in some ways more adequately articulated by talking of physical symmetry than by talking of physical causality.

More will said about physical symmetry in a later chapter. Important to note at this juncture is that both the Greek words for 'cause' ($\alpha\check{\iota}\tau\iota o\nu$) and 'symmetry' ($\sigma\upsilon\mu\mu\epsilon\tau\varrho\acute{\iota}\alpha$) originally had applications to human beings and only subsequently became generalized so as to be applicable to impersonal natural forces. The generality of the idea of causality is important for Clement's rationale because he wants to recommend certain practices not simply on the basis of God's will—a Biblical and theological reason—but also for the philosophical reason that such practices are in accord with the laws of nature. Stoic philosophers were especially concerned that virtuous action be in accordance with nature and Clement's thinking shows evidence of their influence. A philosophical deficiency of the theme of unencumbered causality is the flawed nature of the generality achieved by it.

In another context I cited Niels Bohr as saying that even a scientifically tempered principle of causality does not apply to scales of the very small, the very large, and the very fast. In this sense causality does not have the same degree of generality as Feynman, for instance, attributes to symmetry as it figures in the formulation of physical laws. The principle of casuality employed by ancient authors was much less precise than the one to which Bohr alludes: it was applied variously to the causal agency of God, stars, and human beings. Today's natural and human sciences evince that it is far easier to predict the behavior of stars than of human beings. Human beings are very much more complex. A generalization, about causes or any-thing else, is cognitively vacuous if it indiscriminately ignores the relative complexity of the differing objects brought within its ambit.

A second and related reservation is philosophically just as basic. The idea of an unencumbered cause posits a severe discontinuity between the subject and object of causation. Regarding God's activity as an unencumbered cause, this discontinuity underscores the attribute of divine transcendence. When both creative power and self-sufficiency are ascribed to human beings via the process of assimilation to God, then a similar dualism develops between the subjects and objects of human action and knowledge. A Platonic conception of the soul is thereby confirmed over against a more unitary Stoic conception of human selfhood, and severe problems arise in accounting for embodied human practices. As in the case of the theme of suprasensual vision, philosophical notions used to describe and justify spiritual life become vehicles for a prejudice against practical activity, and as a result, Clement's philosophical case for spiritual fulfillment in the *Stromata* becomes disconnected from his practical prescriptions of the *Paedagogus*. For a practically minded thinker like Pascal this divorce is even more undesirable; it contradicts the intimate way he envisages habit working with grace and reason in the formation of faith.

The eschewal of a severe dualism between human subjects and physical objects has been a widespread feature of philosophical psychology in the twentieth century. Positivist philosophers and behaviorist psychologists have overcome this dualism by insisting upon the purely physical and material nature of the human mind. For behaviorists like B.F. Skinner this approach implies that such complex human behaviors as language use must be explained by the same stimulus-response paradigm as pigeon pecking behavior, and that psychology must heed the same observational strictures as physics; the philosopher Willard Van Orman Quine makes a similar case with a greater sensitivity to the danger of replacing rationalist with empiricist dogmas.[13] Still I think both men give an extreme response which replaces a undiscriminating spiritualistic generalization with an undiscriminating materialistic one. Noam Chomsky's critique of the inability of Skinner and Quine to account adequately for creativity in sentence production, inconsistency in linguistic intuitions, and complexity in language acquisition processes is telling for me.[14] He emphasizes properties of human behavior important to this discussion of spiritual discipline.

Phenomenological psychologists and philosophers have been critical of subject/object dualisms as well. William James was an early representative of this tradition, one who presented his critique by giving an emphatically negative answer to the question of whether consciousness exists. What James meant to deny was that consciousness is an entity composed of fundamentally different stuff from the content it purportedly encounters. He, of course, wished to affirm the integrity of vivid perceptual and intellectual experiences, but this integrity implied for him that subject/object differentiation is a "practical distinction" emergent from experience rather than an *a priori* ontological dualism.[15] For James, the classification of experience into subjective and objective elements—into thoughts and things—is a continuous and revisable activity; it is a function of particular human purposes and environment contexts. From this same context of practical activity consciousness of causal efficacy arises:

> But in this actual world of ours, as it is given, a part at least of the activity comes with definite direction; it comes with desire and sense of goal; it comes complicated with resistances which it overcomes or succumbs to, and with the efforts which the feeling of resistance so often provokes; and it is in complex experiences like these that the notions of distinct agents, and

passivity as opposed to activity arise. Here also the notion of causal efficacy comes to birth.[16]

Causal efficacy is just the sense that one's activity does overcome resistance and promote the realization of a desired end. It is embodied creativity. Hence James's integrated account of the subjective and objective elements of experience is one from which conceptions of practical activity and causal efficacy follow closely. It contrasts sharply with Platonic conceptions of selfhood, knowledge, and causation such as influenced Clement and other early Christian writers about the spiritual life. In addition, it dispenses with the arbitrary reconciliations to which Clement and Pascal must resort when trying to respect both Platonic and Biblical attitudes toward human embodiment.

The portrayal of God as both powerful and self-sufficient suggests the circumstances of an autocratic king who can deliver arbitrary fiats. Aristotle explicitly claimed that the authority of the learned should extend to the political sphere. "The wise man should give orders, not receive them; nor should he obey others, but the less wise should obey him."[17] The prominence of obedience to the abbot as the surrogate for Christ in the *Regula Benedicti* shows that this dimension of the theme of unencumbered causality found expression in Christian spiritual life. Equally unsurprising is that there would be alternative rules recalling the gospel portrayals of Jesus as one who adopted the role of the servant out of radical compassion instead of insisting upon the privileges of power because of his wisdom. The *Regula Primitiva* of St Francis of Assisi is perhaps the best example of this alternative. The ethical argument against using the theme of unencumbered causality in expositions of the spiritual life is that in glorifying power that is unilateral it promotes an authoritarian ethos. It is arrogant to want to act and influence others but remain immune to their response to one's actions; it is an attitude at odds with the professed humility of character that Clement and Pascal recommended for Christians. There is also a real danger that religious leaders will use this theme to justify their own powers and privileges.

In the twentieth century the Aristotelian maxim that the wise person should give orders, but not receive them, takes on a particularly ominous complexion. The experience of totalitarian states has shown that modern technologies can marshall immense forces of intimidation and coercion for controlling both professions of belief and beliefs themselves. Propaganda is born from the misguided conviction that the proper fruit of instruction is obedience. In the cases of Nazi Germany and Soviet Communism efforts toward making the "less wise obey" deliberately included efforts to corrupt and extirpate religious belief. This has led the Christian Church and other religious institutions to see the value of principles of human rights they resisted in times of their own social and political dominance. However, as evident in the recent resurgence of politically assertive religious fundamentalism, and especially in Islamic countries, the combination of religious dogmatism and state authoritarianism is still a reality of the present age. I do not believe that rationales for the spiritual life should give any support, direct or indirect, to such political developments. This conviction is an ethical reason for supplementing the notion of unencumbered causality with another categoreal theme.

A similar authoritarian impulse undergirds Clement's identification of safety, security, and endurance with social relationships in which persons are ordered by strict relations of dominance and subservience. This way of thinking I have summarized as the theme of static hierarchy. As noted previously, the Greek word 'hierarchy' (ἱεραρχία) was not used by Clement. It was of later Greek origin, gaining wide currency after it appeared in the titles of writings by the Pseudo-Dionysius about heavenly and ecclesiastical principles of order. It is an impersonal nominative form of a Greek word for 'high priest' (ἱεράρχης)—itself an inverted cognate of the more frequent ' ἀρχιερεύς'. Literally the word means governance by priests, or more generally, by that which is holy. This word is certainly apt for describing Clement's portrayal of the assembly of spiritual beings because he says all are subordinated to Christ as "High Priest" (ἀρχιερέα). The coincidence of worldly power and religious prominence has a long history in the ancient Near East, manifesting itself in Clement's day by the imperial cult of the Roman Emperor, a ruler at once a religious, civil, and military leader. Military organizations are prime examples of social relationships in which differentiation between individuals is accounted for by the persons one obeys and the persons one commands. Clement's portrayal of the heavenly assembly in hierarchical terms thus involved no special inventiveness.

The theme of static hierarchy had wide expression in ancient Greek philosophy and art. The Greek word ' ἀρχή' means not only governance but also beginning, and in philosophical contexts, first principle. In Aristotle's logical writings it describes the primary, basic, true premises of the various areas of knowledge; from them were deduced specific items of scientific knowledge (*Posterior Analytics* 74b). Aristotle's causes and Plato's forms figured in first principles of this sort. The axiomatic development of geometry which inspired both the Platonic and Aristotelian conceptions of scientific knowledge is hierarchical in the sense that premises dominate conclusions by the authority of the logical implication relation; it is a static hierarchy in that the presumably self-evident character of axioms and rules of inference were thought to assure a similar certainty for derived truths. Axiomatic structure is the logical analogue of Clement's vision of the heavenly hierarchy of spiritual beings.

Classical Greek temple architecture offers a physical analogue of Clement's heavenly hierarchy. I noted this in introducing the theme. A more detailed consideration of the Parthenon illustration suggests an empirical criticism of this theme. The temple of the goddess Athena achieves a classical exterior form by its elegant integration of the simple elements of outer and inner colonnades, a three-step foundation, and a modest entablature. A sense of awe and splendor is communicated by the vertical thrust of the columns, each of which consists of cylindrical marble sections piled on top of one another. The immense weight of each stone section insures that gravitational and frictional forces will keep the column upright and unmoved. The fluting on the Doric columns accentuate the upward thrust as do the diminishing diameters of their upper sections. The transverse slabs of the architrave and the triangular pediments were originally sculpted surfaces showing scenes from the myths of Athena and Greek legend; they provide religious beginnings or principles which inform the temple's cultural meaning.

Actually, the architrave represents one of the engineering limitations of the temple style. Originally the Greek temple was constructed of timber in a post-and-lintel fashion; later the construction material was changed to marble, probably under Egyptian influence. Timber has some flexibility in responding to structural stress and weather changes. Marble obviously lacks this flexibility. One consequence was the necessity of placing the columns quite close to one another so that the transverse slabs of the architrave would not buckle; this limited the architect's ability to modify the temple's basic form. Thus the endurance of the Greek classical style of temple architecture was due, in part, to its engineering limitations!

Modern architects and mechanical engineers have learned that large-scale structures depend for stability on their capacity to move within certain limits in order to compensate for changes in structural and environmental conditions. The steel cadre of a modern skyscraper is expected to sway, especially at its upper levels where winds are most vigorous. Some well-engineered modern buildings, especially in earthquake-prone Tokyo, have computer-controlled counterweights on their roofs that are made to sway in rhythms slightly variant to the building itself so as to counteract the reinforcing effects of repeated structural oscillations. In summation, stability and stasis are not coincident notions in physical engineering, and this fact militates against achieving durability by means of static, hierarchical structures. Dynamic processes of equilibration have replaced the static hierarchy as a structural ideal of engineers.

If the static hierarchies envisioned by Clement are not quite the emblems of stability that he thought them to be, then at least they seem to have the recommendation of simplicity. A soldier acts as his commander orders him and he recognizes that a reward for correct action may be elevation from a lower to a higher rank of authority. Clement's portrayal of the spiritual life has a similar simplicity about it: the Christian acts in accordance with Christ's commandments and by so doing ascends to a position of immediate subordination to Christ and spiritual repose. Yet this simplicity is purchased at the price of practicality because the world is complex. Embodied spiritual life must attend to this complexity; Pascal witnessed to this injunction in deed if not always in word. Complete avoidance of the world's complexity is at best temporary, and, at worst, deadly.

This point is can be clarified with the aid of the visual simile of a hierarchy as an inverted tree-like structure. Contemporary social scientists are apt to stress the branching span of a hierarchical structure rather than its vertically oriented trunk. For instance, in an article entitled "The Architecture of Complexity," the social scientist Herbert Simon defines a hierarchy as "a system that is composed of interrelated subsystems, each of the latter in turn being hierarchic in structure until we reach some lowest level of elementary subsystem."[18] One consequence of this different emphasis is that hierarchical systems are construed to be vehicles for complexity rather than emblems of simplicity. Simon understands endurance and continuity in evolutionary terms; both natural and social forms endure by evolving in ways that maintain some measure of integrity. In this context he writes:

> Complex systems will evolve from simple systems much more rapidly if there are stable intermediate forms than if there are not. The resulting complex forms in the former case will be hierarchic. We have only to turn the argument around to explain the observed predominance of hierarchies among the complex systems nature present to us.[19]

Simon believes his remarks apply to the evolution of social institutions and biological species alike. The Roman Catholic Church made the transition from the medieval to the modern and contemporary world not in the form of a Benedictine monastery—a community wherein the abbot exerts a direct line of authority over subordinates in the fashion of Clement's spiritual hierarchy. Quite to the contrary, the Benedictine monastery has survived to the extent that it has as a subsystem within a differentiated hierarchical structure of an increasingly pluralistic church. This pluralism is maintained within the borders of a single social institution by a dispersion of authority, in fact, if not in principle. For instance, the papal infallibility affirmed by the first Vatican Council is seldom explicitly invoked for contemporary teachings, and excommunicable beliefs and practices are fewer and less frequently cited now than prior to Vatican II. Simon says that any social organization must maintain an equilibrium between the inducements that motivate people to belong to social organizations and the deterrent of lost autonomy which participation of in such an organization involves.[20] Maintenance of such an equilibrium is a dynamic process which becomes more complex as more persons are members and as more of the members are allowed to make more decisions. Members continue to receive guidance from superiors, especially regarding organizational goals; their decision is informed, even constrained, but not rigidly dictated. Why should more persons be allowed this decision-making power? Quite simply, they are often more knowledgeable of the specific complex conditions which influence whether actions achieve their goals. In that sense it is efficacious for them to do so. It is also more compatible with the dignity of the organization member and so less a deterrent to continued identification with the organization. The difference between receiving the command of a Benedictine abbot and the guidance of a Salesian spiritual director well illustrates this transition toward a less authoritarian organization.

Here arises a philosophical criticism of the theme of static hierarchy as a theme descriptive of the life of spiritual practice. Making decisions in a complex world with imperfect knowledge is a process that sometimes leads to unsuccessful actions. Decisions lead to new decisions and new sets of alternative behaviors, so that one major constituent of the imperfect knowledge agents have is that they can realistically anticipate only some of the alternatives that any given decision will allow or foreclose. Stated more actively, decisions have consequences, sometimes unforeseeable. Uncertainty in deliberations of this sort arises from the necessity of assigning probabilities to the consequences of alternative behaviors and the difficulty of assigning values to imperfectly conceived consequences. Two social strategies are available for mitigating these difficulties. First, only allow those thought to be most knowledgeable the power to make decisions of serious import. Second, involve many persons in the decision making process so that errors can be anticipated before action is taken or corrected afterwards. Clement and Pascal clearly favor the first strategy and employ the notion of a static hierarchy to illustrates the structure of authority in the Christian Church. The second alternative is best modelled by the self-corrective process of reasoning which is most fully realized in some modern communities of scientific research. Representative democracies have sought to combine elements of each strategy: in recommending the United States Constitution Alexander Hamilton stressed the importance of government being administered by superior citizens and James Madison the importance of government reflecting society's competing interests; both appreciated the value of regular elections for correcting past mistakes.

The claim that wisdom earns its possessors a license to exercise authoritarian powers suffers from inconsistency as well as from ethical flaws mentioned earlier. It has also become increasingly clear in the twentieth century that the advance of scientific knowledge is attained more readily in social contexts that allow for an untrammelled communication of ideas and that legally insures this and other human rights. Charles Sanders Peirce's conception of scientific research as a communal venture of self-corrective reasoning in which uninhibited observation, experimentation, and conversation makes possible an increasingly close approximation of truths about reality is a signal development in the wedding of philosophy of science with democratic principles of American political philosophy. The benefits to American society of the refugee scientists who have sought a congenial context for doing their work provides an authentically pragmatic testimony to the value of such a philosophical combination. On the other hand, Nazi condemnation of the "Jewish science" of Einstein and others and the Soviet promotion of Lysenkoism as a Marxist alternative of evolutionary biology well demonstrated that coercion in the search for knowledge cannot prevail intellectually nor promote human flourishing except for very short times for very few persons. Hence to recommend that wise persons exercise authoritarian powers is to recommend relinquishing one of the preconditions for wisdom.

I will conclude this section of criticisms with one final point. Clement, and in his more conservative moments, Pascal, conceived of salvation as the attainment of a subordinate place within a differentiated whole. This sensibility was informed philosophically by Middle Platonic conceptions of cosmic restoration and Stoic feelings of personal resignation. Education as it applies to the spiritual life becomes instruction in finding one's place in a pre-established structure. John Dewey challenged this traditional view; he held that education in a democratic society enables the individual to adapt to extant social structures, but also to transform them in the direction of greater social viability.[21] Dewey's view is informed by his understanding of education as part of a broader process of dynamic development operative in individuals and societies. Well-being for individuals and societies is conceived less as a perfected condition than as a continuous activity which makes human experience more meaningful and human action more efficacious. Educating persons about the meaning and efficacy of spiritual disciplined practices should be a similarly dynamic process. In this spirit I turn next to the tasks of redirecting and reformulating the traditional material thusfar reviewed.

THE RATIONALE REDIRECTED

Criticisms of Clement's rationale have now been given. I have argued that the themes culled from Clement's *Stromata* revealed assumptions about the nature of the world that are unsupported by contemporary science, and presuppositions about the nature of philosophy that are uncongenial to contemporary sensibilities. Insofar as the themes have continued currency they largely endure in the form of outdated science doing service as stale metaphors. It is even more serious that while surviving in this way the themes are often employed in rationalizations for unjust practices, such as the religious condemnation of many expressions of human sexuality and the concentration of church power in very few offices. Respect for religious leaders and institutions extends this destructive influence into the broader secular society. Yet the continuing allure of these themes suggest that they touch upon something of value to many persons. In preparation for reformulating Pascal's predicament, I will summarize these criticisms, and at the same time, supplement them with an articulation of what I think are the valuable contributions of this prominent tradition of thinking about spiritual life.

Criticism of Clement's rationale—a summary term for the interrelated themes of suprasensual vision, unencumbered causality, and static hierarchy—came from three quarters: empirical science, philosophical methodology, and ethical reflection. Criticism from the first of these quarters argued that the classical conceptions invoked by Clement misrepresent how physical objects appear, endure, and evolve. Indeed, Platonic idealism posits that the most enduring things neither appear nor evolve at all, but are apprehended as immutable intelligible forms. Also, Aristotle's Unmoved Mover attains the status of eternal deity not by being the prime instantiation of physical principles underlying the world's causal nexus, but by being something which is singularly irrelevant to them. Finally, principles of hierarchical rulership commend an absolute chain of command as the means by which community members perpetuate habitual dispositions and actions, yet they are uninformative about how continuously revisable relations of mutual dependence help constitute such communities. Religion is intimately concerned with the human quest to resist death; however, supposedly eternal and absolute principles are not the best resources for explaining actual human flourishing.

In its various forms the fixation of Platonist theists like Clement upon endurance in an hostile environment—or even better yet, transcendence of it—militates against attentive explanations of the phenomena that constitute that environment. In the *Paedagogus* (2.8) Clement teaches that Christian men and women should shun embellishments like jewelry, ointment, and perfume. His philosophical borrowings confirm this abjuration but do not help to explain the allure, for example, of precious gems. Similarly, Clement banishes clapping, dancing, and raucous singing at Christian feasts, invoking Platonic confirmations of Biblical injunctions (*Paedagogus* 2.4). Yet his secular philosophy does little to explain the social function of celebratory occasions in which normal standards of behavior are relaxed. In many cases Clement's philosophical importations do not complement theology with a distinctive sort of explanation, but merely repeat a theological message in a different rhetorical idiom. Pascal was a much more accomplished social psychologist than Clement, but in moments of spiritual crisis he retreated to many of the same moral censures.

The general thrust of the philosophical criticisms of Clement's portrayal of the spiritual life was to challenge his presuppositions about human rationality. Specifically, I noted the absence of hermeneutical, phenomenological, and pragmatic elements which root

human rationality in history and biology, that is, which place
thinking in the temporal, sensual flux of life. Clement followed Plato
in identifying the most reliable sorts of knowledge with the
apprehension of unchanging objects by the "eye of the mind"; to this
I opposed the hermeneutical process of supporting articulate
affirmations with relevant warrants. Clement adopted an Aristotelian
metaphysical spirit which mingles together causal descriptions of
gods, stars, and human agents, making them all bearers of a radical
dichotomy between subjects and objects; to this I opposed a
phenomenological insistence upon describing things and relations as
experienced wholes in which distinctions are accorded a practical and
revisable status. Finally, Clement invoked the idea of a static
hierarchy for relating a plurality of elements, be they ideas or human
beings, into differentiated wholes; I argued that a more flexible
conception of hierarchical ordering conjoined with notions of dynamic
equilibration can better deal with complexity, and, specifically, can
facilitate the process of pragmatic decision making in a complex
environment.

Criticisms from the ethical point of view remarked that the three
categoreal themes had in common a tendency toward the unilateral
and coercive exercise of power. It is now regarded as an affront to
human dignity to treat people as objects of such power, and is also
regarded as an ineffective strategy for eliciting cooperation and
creativity from them. As Aristotle noted, a authoritarian ruler may
be capable of a crude efficiency in ending social conflict, but the tyrant
is not able to experience friendship (*Nicomachean Ethics*, 1161a).
Hence the exercise of coercive power is incompatible with something
that both Greek and Biblical traditions regarded as an almost
unquestioned value. When Jesus tells his disciples "You are my
friends if you do what I command" (John 15.14), he seems to contradict
this Aristotelian principle by making obedience a prerequisite of
friendship. Yet, of course, the commandment at issue here is that the
disciples "love one another," or, in other words, that they be friends
(John 15.12). With this paradoxical affirmation Jesus indirectly
accentuates the importance of friendship to the spiritual life and the
inappropriateness of ideas and practices which militate against it.
Clement's portrayal of salvation as the marshalling of angels and
saints in subordination to Christ is not an image of flourishing
friendship, and on this ground I think it is ethically suspect.

Criticisms of the components of Clement's rationale for his
favored spiritual practices have been lengthy and severe. Words of
appreciation for this heritage are perhaps long overdue. Certainly

the three themes reflect important psychological realities. Apprehensions of extraordinary light and heat, feelings of freedom and empowerment, and the association of structured ascent with repose—these are all commonly reported elements of religious or spiritual experiences. Of more philosophical interest are the recurring features of paradoxicality, creativity, and complexity. These ideas figured prominently in Pascal's reflections about his predicament; indeed, French commentators like Goldmann and Marin believe that his true genius lies in just his ability to manifest them so well in French prose. Also, reference to them has been repeatedly made in the course of articulating Clement's rationale for the spiritual life. In my view they are crucial ingredients for any philosophical account of spiritual practice. They help constitute that project by giving an outline of what meaningful spiritual practices should be: such practices should be creatively self-transformative responses to paradox and complexity as they are engendered by experiencing the world as a maximally inclusive whole. They are practices which creatively transform paradox and complexity from noxious to ennobling forms. This is not yet a definition of spiritual discipline, but it does indicate the basic direction in which such a revised conception should move. I believe that the most valuable service provided by Clement's rationale is that it boldly highlights these features of human existence. Progress in philosophically thinking about them requires further elucidation of these ideas as they pertain to spiritual discipline and as they contribute to a reformulation of the predicament to which such disciplined practices are intended to respond.

Spiritual discipline consists of those human practices and attendant teachings which promote a fullness of life experienced as a right relationship of one's truest self with the whole of reality. Practices adopted to express and promote this fullness of life are many and varied, as are their related conceptions of true selfhood and cosmic reality. As a Christian by faith Clement sought a right relationship with the Biblical God who is identifiable with the whole of reality, not in an immediate and pantheistic sense, but in the mediate capacity of being the creator of all that exists. Clement's God is also triune, at once incarnate in Jesus Christ and also extant in the incorporeal persons of the Father and the Holy Spirit. The paradox of simultaneous immanence and transcendence is strikingly proclaimed in the orthodox doctrine of the Incarnation. As a Christian by baptism Clement professed to partake of this paradox, affirming that his "sinful body" had been effectively destroyed by Christ's resurrection and delivered to a new life enlivened by Christ's godliness; but at the same time he acknowledged that his "mortal body" lives on and is still tempted by sin (Rom. 6.6,12).

Pascal too revelled in such subtleties, especially in thoughts about God as being both hidden and revealed. He favored the anthropological form of the paradox expressed in the Christian doctrine of original sin: at once the Christian is by nature good because of his or her created status on the sixth day of creation; yet also, by Adam's fall, there is a sense in which all subsequent humans are by nature sinful. When confronted with paradoxes like these Pascal characteristically sought reconciliation of the two opposing elements rather than eradication of either one of them. "A good portrait can only be made by reconciling all contradictory features"; solace for sin is found in the image of Christ: "In Christ all contradictions are reconciled."[22] Given these paradoxical renderings of the Christian God and believer, it is not surprising that Clement and Pascal understand the most intimate human encounter with God in a similarly paradoxical way, i.e., as an experience of radiant illumination that transcends merely visual sensation.

These paradoxical formulations are not only Christian, or even theistic, but have expression in many religious accounts of an maximally inclusive reality that is at once immanent and transcendent, and of any person that is spiritually transformed yet not spiritually perfected. In the Vedanta, the expression of Hinduism typified by the *Upaniṣads, brāhman* is understood as absolute reality; Sarvepalli Radhakrishnan says this includes both a "supra-cosmic transcendence and a cosmic universality. . . . In the former aspect (it) is in no way dependent upon the cosmic manifold; in the latter (it) functions as the principle of the cosmic manifold."[23] In Buddhism anthropological paradoxes abound: the enlightened but compassionate Buddha delays his final release to *nirvāna* in order to teach others still suffering. Mahāyāna Buddhism elevates this incident to paradigmatic status in its *bodhisattva* ideal of a person who transcends suffering by insight, but shares it by love. Daisetz Suzuki describes it this way: "In spite of self-sufficient blessings, the Bodhisattva would not seek his own ease, but he would mingle himself in the turmoil of worldly life and devote all his energy to the salvation of the masses of people."[24] For some Mahāyāna thinkers chief among these blessings is a spiritual fullness identified with a realization of emptiness—*śūnyatā*.

Paradoxical apprenhensions of oneself and the world often give rise to ambivalent feelings. Rudolf Otto nominated fear and fascination as prime expressions of this ambivalence. Merold Westphal in his recent reworking of Otto's phenomenology says that these feelings are what give some encounters with the whole of reality their religious quality.[25] Thus he says that while the Hindu *brāhman* and Buddhist *nirvāna* are not portrayed as personal deities, their existential engagement has a religious quality because they evoke fear and fascination nevertheless. Relevant here is the fact that spiritually disciplined practices often evoke ambivalent feelings. Ascetic practices, for instance, promise enhanced vitality when moderately pursued, but they threaten bodily harm when too harshly undertaken. The ambivalent feelings evoked by this simultaneous promise and threat is not something entirely eliminable by spiritual prudence, because ambivalent feelings such as these are also partially a response to the paradoxical realities outlined above which it is the character of the spiritual life to engage.

Spiritual life may take religious and theistic forms, as in Western monotheistic religions, or it may take religious but less directly theistic forms, as in Hinduism and Buddhism in the above mentioned variants. Also, spiritual discipline may occur in irreligious and atheistic forms such as have been advocated by some modern philosophers sometimes labelled existentialists. One thing all forms share is an experiential engagement with paradox. Of course, Pascal and Kierkegaard were Christian existentialists, Kierkegaard's portrayal of Christ as the "Absolute Paradox" in the *Philosophical Fragments* being a classic modern elaboration of the incarnational theme.[26] Martin Heidegger's project in *Being and Time* of questioning into the meaning of Being as a way of achieving a more authentic human existence is, to my mind, a variety of irreligious and atheistic spiritual discipline.[27] Heidegger calls questioning a sort of intellectual piety, and he claims that such inquiry both pursues Being (qua *Sein*) and yet is Being (qua *Dasein*), a formulation that resounds with paradox.

A certain inconsistency informs the action of any person who seeks to live in a spiritually disciplined way because such a quest presupposes conflict between a lamentable past and a desired, transformed way of being. One is always midway between these extremes: the experience of realizing a fullness of life does not entirely replace the life that preceded it. Nietzsche, another atheistic and irreligious philosopher, wrote a literary autobiography whose title suggests well the sense of spiritual paradox relevant here: *Ecce Home: How One Becomes What One Is*. Its first part echoes Pilate's words about Jesus (John 19.5) and the second suggests the author's didactic intent. The injunction to become what one is has an odd sound to it, because if one already is something then it seems redundant to bid one to become it. Yet what this phrasing accentuates is that a person has a certain nature only by realizing that self in decisions, choices, and actions. Fifty years ago Nietzsche was commonly portrayed as a precursor of existentialism who affirmed that people are better identified by their peculiar actions than by their essential nature; today he is more likely portrayed as a forerunner of the school of literary deconstruction who affirmed that authorial selves are more the creations than the creators of meaningful texts. There is some truth to each description. Nietzsche shall play a large role in this essay's third part because he associated spiritual self-mastery with imaginative acts that constitute and vanquish the self. The phenomenon of semiotic self-reference especially well reveals this capacity of language, and I shall soon recommend it as a way of describing the paradoxical intuitions which underlie many regimens of spiritual practice.

Creativity is a desideratum of all spiritual life that shuns a radical quietism. Generally, creativity is the ability to overcome opposition in apt and novel ways; as such it is closely related to James's pragmatic definition of causal efficacy. As a spiritual quality creativity is the ability to live vitally while being both in the world but not of it. It turns to good advantage the tension consequent upon this paradoxical standing.[28] For Clement creativity as the fruit of the spiritual life is understood primarily in ethical terms: the idea of assimilation to God is Greek, but the conception of God is the Hebraic one of a radically good ethical will. The Christian is a new creation by his or her loving intentions and by demonstrably upright actions. Faithful Christians are able to be spiritual teachers like Christ because of their creation in God's image and likeness, and because of their baptism into Christ's dying and rising again (*Paedagogus* 1.3,6).

This divinely empowered creative agency was understood by Clement in very personal terms; he stressed individual moderation as a way of resolving the lay person's struggle with the competing extremes of asceticism and profligacy. Clement spoke little about programs of social transformation. This is understandable given his idea of static hierarchy as the principle governing social relations. His concrete ethical teachings were also sexually prudish; this too is not surprising given his relative devaluation of things corporeal. For the most part Pascal shared the personal orientation of Clement's piety; however, his institution of a charitable bus service for the Paris poor suggests a socially progressive impulse. Declining health quickly frustrated Pascal's more ambitious social projects.

In the history of the Christian Church the baptismal profession which says that "if any one is in Christ, he is a new creation" (2 Cor. 5.17) has sometimes been connected with the eschatological vision of "a new heaven and a new earth" (Rev. 21.1). This has especially been the case when reform and tumult in the Church has coincided with the secular revolt of dominated classes. Millenarian movements characteristically feature this combination, as did the more extreme groups of the Protestant Reformation. Friedrich Engels spoke of Luther's one-time theological disciple, Thomas Münzer, as a sort of proto-Marxist because in his political actions at Mühlhausen and elsewhere he was willing to overthrow the established social structure so that a new egalitarian Christian society might be born.[29] In the social sphere it is more evident that creation implies concretely, and not only metaphorically, the destruction of something old so that something new may prevail. The post-Enlightenment metaphysics of both Hegel and Whitehead begin with this insight.

Whitehead made creativity the ultimate stuff of his organismic conception of reality; he defined it as the "production of novel togetherness."[30] In a dynamic, creative process there is an antecedent stage in which articulate apprehension is made of diverse and opposed realities. These may be contradictions in the intellectual sphere or conflicts in the social sphere. The consequent stage involves the production of something that brings novelty and unity to the environment it influences: this may involve a cultural work which realizes the overcoming of destructive oppositions in way that promotes human betterment. Usually religious personalities and institutions do not themselves effect significant intellectual breakthroughs or social transformations. It is true that medieval religious thinkers like the Franciscan William of Ockham pondered logical paradoxes under the rubric of "Insolubilia" and anticipated some of the insights that Bertrand Russell fostered with his reintroduction of these paradoxes as a central theme of philosophy in the twentieth century; and medieval monks like the Cistercians appreciated the conflict between the demands of the feudal economy and realization of an irenic contemplative life in a way that anticipated utopian protests against the social consequences of industrial capitalism. Historically, however, religious persons have more often served the prophetic role of acknowledging the relevant contradictions and conflicts, such that their concrete individual and communal actions point to an something extraordinary, often God, which offers hope and assurance that such oppositions are capable of being overcome. Liberation theologians have coined the term 'orthopraxis' to describe actions of self-mastery, compassion, and justice which embody this sort of spiritual creativity.

Creativity is characteristic of Eastern religions also, but there it takes a more aesthetic than ethical form. Writing about features of Japanese culture influenced by Zen Buddhist sensibilities, Daisetz Suzuki says: "The artist, at the moment when his creativeness is at its height, is transformed into an agent of his creator; this supreme moment in the life of the artist, when expressed in Zen terms, is the experience of *satori*."[31] Here the experience of creativity and enlightenment are intimately connected. The artistic enlightenment is especially realized in poetry and painting, but also in the less craftlike activities of swordplay and tea ceremonies. Chang Chung-yuan gives a similar centrality to creativity in Chinese religious thought; he writes:

> When we are struck by the utter tranquility of landscapes by Mi-Fei and Ni Tsan, or moved by the simplicity and purity of poems by T'ao Ch'ien, we come close to experiencing aesthetically what the Taoist hopes to experience spiritually. There is something inherent in these works that leads us to the inexpressible ultimate that man shares with the universe. There is in them a dynamic process that interfuses with a higher grade of reality. They draw us to a spontaneous and even unintentional unity which, as the Taoist sees it, refers back to *Tao* itself, the primordial source of creativity.[32]

I believe that Taoist and Buddhist traditions provide a helpful perspective on creativity as an attribute of the spiritual life because they provide correctives for traditional Western emphases. First, Taoism especially presupposes a positive valuation of the natural world, including human corporeality. Nature is appreciated in its "suchness" (Chinese *chen-ju*). Creativity in the arts and life is thus a cooperation with nature more than a domination of it. In the *Tao Te Ching* of Lao Tzu the image of an uncarved block is invoked to say that a pristine but unpretentious simplicity is the quality that most surely promotes human well-being. (*Tao Te Ching*, 15) This usage contrasts sharply with Aristotle's illustration of the four causes by appeal to a stone sculpture; even more it contrasts with the ideal of the unencumbered cause. Second, Eastern thought in Taoist and Zen Buddhist forms places constraints on the role of conscious rational thought, and does so not for the sake of obedience to authority, or even for a deferential quietism, but on behalf of a natural human spontaneity. Spontaneous action (Chinese *tzu jan*) serves as a dynamic correlate of "suchness." It especially characterizes the action of the creative artist. This is why Asian art places less value on principles of perspective and symmetry than does Western art in its classical expressions. Indeed, the breaking of symmetry is here an expression of aesthetic creativity.[33] In the next part I shall suggest that notions of symmetry making and breaking are helpful for describing the role of creativity in a spiritually disciplined life.

That the spiritual life is a response to the world's complexity is evident in the injunction, almost ubiquitous in the literature of this genre, to pursue a simple life. At its best *sancta simplicitas* is not attained by pure self-denial, but rather presupposes creative self-transformation. As a character trait it connotes the ability to bring together into unity numerous complex facets of existence, yet it brings them into a new arrangement of order and thereby produces an appearance of simplicity. Clement consistently recommends simplicity in the second book of the *Paedagogus* where he gives practical advice about things like food and dress. In its first chapter he encourages readers to live as "simple and artless children" and he aphorizes in its final chapter that "simplicity provides for sanctity."[34] Pascal admired and envied "simple people believing without argument."[35] His railing against *divertissement* betrays a yearning for a more simple life; in this context he speculates "that the sole cause of man's unhappiness is that he does not know how to stay quietly in his room."[36]

Simplicity has always been a part a distinctively American spiritual sensibility. Emerson's advice to "Converse with a mind that is grandly simple" suggests a secular ethos of prayer.[37] Having left behind the aged and intricate social behaviors of their European homeland for a stark wilderness society, many early American immigrants extolled simplicity, thereby seeking to make necessity a virtue. Subsequent generations came to idealize the simple life of their historic past and the austere promise of the wilderness further westward. Henry David Thoreau's experiment in living at Walden Pond best typifies this American spiritual quest. Early in his record of this experiment he observes:

> Our life is frittered away by detail. An honest man has hardly need to count more than his ten fingers, or in extreme cases he may add his ten toes, and lump the rest. Simplicity, simplicity, simplicity! I say, let your affairs be as two or three, and not a hundred or a thousand; instead of a million count half a dozen, and keep your accounts on your thumb nail. . . .

Simplify, simplify. Instead of three meals a day, if it be
necessary eat but one; instead of a hundred dishes, five; and
reduce other things in proportion.[38]

Christians like Clement associated simplicity with obedience to
authority and moderation of the passions. For a secularist like
Thoreau it is part of a strategy of self-reliance. Yet both would agree
with Pascal that a simple life allows what is really important to
receive its due regard. Both affirmed that implicit in the call to
simplify is the desire to endure and flourish. The drive for simplicity
is so strong among spiritual seekers because their conception of
human flourishing is extraordinary, both in the sense of being
uncommon and being ambitious. Hence the spiritual impetus for
simplification arises from the conviction that attaining a novel order
of simplicity is productive of spiritual well-being in a complex and
not entirely hospitable world. On this conviction traditional Christian
and American wisdom agree.

To explain the practical value of spiritual simplicity requires some
reflection first about the nature of complexity. Thoreau associates
complexity with multifariousness. Something is complex because it
is the aggregation of numerous parts. A complementary way of
understanding complexity is in terms of the absence of deterministic
order, or stated more, positively, in terms of order amidst randomness.
Something is complex if it is neither simple or chaotic. A rose is
complex because its carbon atoms are not arranged in the symmetrically simple way characteristic of diamonds. Also, a rose is complex
because its molecular motion does not have the chaotic randomness
that typifies hydrogen gas. The hydrogen gas has less order than
roses—and diamonds—and so less information can be gleaned from
it. The world as an arena of action is complex to the extent that an
agent has a number of alternative paths of action and limited
information about the probability of the consequences of any given
action producing a desirable outcome. The simple life is a quest for
order and meaning amidst the potentially chaotic complexity of life.
Spiritual simplicity consists of the insight that a host of apparently
distinctive alternatives are effectively identical from the vantage
point of the spiritually undesirable consequences they yield. The
alternatives before one are not as numerous (i.e. complex) as they
seem: choices between many elaborate ways of eating and dressing
really do not matter if what you value is a spiritual fullness of life.
Yet this is a wise simplicity because the reduction in the number of
alternatives is predicated upon a judgment of equivalence, e.g., an
apprehension of order and information.

A second judgment of equivalence may take the form of reckoning alternative options as equivalent in their capacity to promote spiritual well-being. Mohandas Gandhi said, "Religions are different roads converging to the same point of view. What does it matter that we take different roads, so long as we reach the same goal?"[39] The syncretism of Hinduism or the undogmatic nature of many Buddhists (like Shunryu Suzuki quoted above) are examples of this point of view. In either form such judgments are intuitive as well as calculative. This is not to say that they are arbitrary. They have a practical orientation in the sense of being the result of an implicit process of means-ends reasoning which concludes that such simplification does, in fact, promote spiritual well-being. As was the case for Clement's notion of static hierarchy, simplicity is both a goal and precondition of the spiritual life. It is both an attribute of spiritual well-being and of the practices designed to promote that end. The simple life offers the promise of new and higher manners of equilibration between self, society, and the natural world. It is a promise of equilibrium with the world through continual self-regulation, not the least of which is the continual refinement of the mix of aesthetic intuition and calculative reasoning in decisions about adopting specific regimens of spiritual discipline.

A human being grows—like the human species has evolved—in the direction of greater complexity; these are truths of embryology and evolutionary biology. It is a truth supportive of the ethical imperative that all human life be respected and nurtured so that it may attain its optimal fulfillment. John Dewey regarded this evolution toward complexity as a fact necessitating that education be something more than naturalistic apprenticeship:

> As a society becomes more complex it is found necessary to provide a special social environment which shall especially look after nurturing the capacities of the immature. Three of the more important functions of this special environment are: simplifying and ordering the factors of the disposition it is wished to develop; purifying and idealizing the existing social customs; creating a wider and better balanced environment than that by which the young would be likely, if left to themselves, to be influenced.[40]

By this definition regimens of spiritual discipline certainly count as educative practices: their stress on simplification and idealization are functions of the sort Dewey identifies. Yet when the peace and repose cultivated by spiritual aspirants are identified with static conceptions of order, then spiritual regimens do not provide the diversity of experience of which Dewey speaks in his third criterion. They become shelters for the timid. Yet if that repose is more dynamically conceived and if the drive for simplification is regarded as a species of self-regulation rather than self-abnegation, then spiritual disciplines can claim to be educative strategies for flourishing in diversely complex environments. Biological notions of equilibration will be suggested in the next part as means for describing how spiritual regimens may simplify one's life while at the same time counting as an informed and sophisticated attempt to deal with the complex realities that oppose human well-being. A philosophical consequence of embracing this conception of spiritual discipline is that intellectual reflection upon such practices should not yield absolute claims nor even compulsory methodologies. Histories and contexts differ; they require flexible responses both practically and theoretically.

THE PREDICAMENT REFORMULATED

Pascal's predicament was multiform. It included a sense of estrangement from the natural world whose impersonal vastness reminded him of his personal mortality; he felt this despite his extraordinary intelligence which contributed in several ways to scientific knowledge in the seventeenth century. It involved a perceived lack of meaningful community life, even though Pascal had close family members who sincerely loved him and friendships with the some of the most talented persons of his era. Finally, it embraced a discontentment with himself as a feckless sinner; he felt this in spite of his great literary talent for reflecting upon his personal situation with insight, wit, and eloquence. What to do given these circumstances was Pascal's predicament. It was a spiritual conundrum because the consequences he anticipated were so momentous. What was at issue was his right relation to the whole of reality—in his mind, to God as the beginning and end of all things.

As an intellectual Pascal rejected a life devoted to the unreflective pursuit of wealth and power; he also rejected *divertissements* which keep the mind active in matters of inconsequence. Pascal seriously confronted the issues of human ignorance, sin, and death, bringing much creativity to his reflection on these topics: the celebrated Wager argument is the product and emblem of his formidable innovative energies.

Yet at many crucial points Pascal reverted to the tenets of Augustinian theology and Platonic philosophy, opting for traditional certainties instead of novel solutions. He sought in Jansenism a system of thought he might inhabit with security, its foundations provided by faith, its superstructure fortified by deductive logic, and its integument sealed with polemical wit. His replacement of a philosophical foundationalism with a theological simulacrum illustrates how his remedy lacks the novelty of his diagnosis. The criticisms advanced here of Clement's rationale for the Christian spiritual life argue that this sort of house cannot stand; it can provide no enduring shelter for contemporary persons who share in Pascal's predicament. Hence, the predicament arises anew, and with a special urgency for the passage of time.

Philosophical reflection can be helpful to persons embarked on a venture of spiritually disciplined living by reformulating traditional beliefs in light of new evidence. Both the words of criticism and appreciation directed toward Clement's rationale for the spiritual life motivate a reformulation of Pascal's predicament. The model of practical reasoning that emerged with Pascal's Wager argument remains valuable, but it needs to be inserted in a more temporal context of biological and historical flux such as was assumed by American pragmatist philosophers. The Platonic urge to transcend this flux was still strong in Pascal and shaped his conception of his spiritual predicament. I believe a more relevant challenge is to find the rhythms within this flux that are most supportive of a spiritual fullness of life. One way of looking at the dynamic regularities of lived experience is in terms of habitual behaviors. This is the idiom my reformulation will adopt. Successful egress from Pascal's spiritual predicament should be sought, according to this revised conception, by creatively fostering good habitual behaviors while self-critically resisting bad ones. Regimens of behavior effecting a vital engagement of the whole of reality give this project a practical and spiritual complexion. Full recognition of the paradoxicality and complexity which pervade the context in which it is undertaken frees it of excessive moralism. These, at least, are the rudiments of the proposal I shall offer for reformulating Pascal's predicament; clarifications and implications of it comprise the rest of this chapter.

The English word 'habit' derives from the Latin root 'habere' meaning 'to have or to possess'. Habits were once construed quite literally as characteristic possessions, for instance, as one's clothing; even now one speaks of a nun's or a monk's habit to specify their distinctive religious dress. More usual today is to identify habits with behaviors and dispositions. In this context habits will be understood prospectively as dispositions to act repeatedly in certain identifiable ways, and retrospectively, as histories of having so acted. Habits are something people have—dispositions and histories—and people have them in the form of repetitious actions for which dispositions and histories are respectively preludes and postludes.

Repetitious acts are crucial constituents of human forms of order. Repeated mental acts of adding 1 to 0 and its successors are crucial for generating the series of natural numbers, and the mental act of demonstrating that a property occurring in some first element of a series will have a repeated occurrence in the successor of some arbitrarily chosen element of that same series if it occurs in the arbitrarily chosen member itself—this mental act proves that the property occurs in every member of the series and is crucial for establishing mathematical truths. Repetition in these ways gives rise to abstract forms of order. Habits give rise to practical forms of order in human existence when repetition is conceived concretely as occurring in the temporal flow of experience. David Hume believed that habit or custom is what explains human beliefs about causes and effects. Dismissing any metaphysical meaning for the idea of causal force or power, Hume contended that one feels a connection between the occurrence of one event and a second which follows it only because one has previously experienced them together and now anticipates a repetition of their conjunction. While not agreeing on all points with Hume's account of causality, I do share his assessment of the philosophical importance of habit in accounting for regularity in human experience.

In colloquial speech habits are most frequently understood as unhealthy and addictive behaviors—destructive patterns which people are unable to alter easily. Drug-taking and overeating are physiological habits of this sort. Extravagant, promiscuous, and violent behaviors are social variants. Speech about good habits continues, but almost always attributes a jejune quality to such behavior. One tells children to develop good habits of personal hygiene, such as brushing their teeth after every meal, or one lectures students to develop good study habits. Presupposed by such language is the belief that rational adults know what is good for them and do not need the aid of unreflective contrivances like habits. Irony often accompanies attributions of good habitual behavior to adults. In *Adam Bede* George Eliot describes Arthur Dimmesdale by saying: "Deeds of kindness were as easy to him as a bad habit: they were the common issue of his weaknesses and good qualities, of his egoism and his sympathy."[41]

In *Washington Square* Henry James writes of his female protagonist: "She was excellently, imperturbably good; affectionate, docile, obedient, and much addicted to speaking the truth."[42] These few illustrations from life and literature are sufficient, I think, to show that talk of habits is inextricably part of a more inclusive language of moral praise and censure.

Habitual behaviors are also prominent topics in religious psychologies. Augustine's confessional account of the inveterate misdirection of desire toward material objects instead of toward a spiritual God is a Platonic account of the pathology of bad habits. "For my will was perverse and lust had grown from it, and when I gave into lust habit (consuetudo) was born, and when I did not resist the habit it became a necessity."[43] Pascal's description of hunting and gambling as *divertissements* is a psychologically perceptive elaboration of this Augustinian tradition. In a non-Western context, the Four Noble Truths of classical Buddhism attribute the origin of suffering to craving and to the patterns of manic behavior it engenders. Buddhists recommend an Eightfold Path including meditative discipline as a means to overcome this craving and achieve release from the cycle of death and rebirth. For good and ill, and in ways superficial and sublime, habits are intimately associated with human needs and desires: they manifest in human behavior both the process of continual sustenance by social and physical environments, and the capacity for physiological and psychological addictions.

Habits figured prominently in ancient philosophy. The Latin 'habitus' was a translation of Aristotle's 'ἕξις'; it was understood by him to be an acquired power to act in a certain way. It figured centrally in Aristotelian ethical theory because the virtues of courage, justice, and temperance were regarded as habitual dispositions toward specific types of action. The conception of virtues as habits was crucial for making Aristotle's moral theory an ethics of character rather than of rules or consequences. This conception had, of course, great influence on Christian thinkers like Thomas Aquinas who gave the classic formulation of faith, hope, and love as distinctively Christian theological virtues. Pascal also drew upon this tradition, though it vied irresolutely for dominance in his thinking about ethical behavior with Augustine's Platonism.

At the conclusion of the Wager section of the *Pensées* Pascal says that if one does not opt for faith after comprehending his argument then it is passion and not reason which is the restraining force. He recommends the example of persons who, while not having faith, nevertheless adopt religious behaviors as a means of taming their passions. Of such persons Pascal wrote:

> Learn from those who were once bound like you and who now wager all they have. These are people who know the road you wish to follow, who have been cured of the affliction of which you wish to be cured: follow the way by which they began. They have behaved just as if they did believe, taking holy water, having masses said, and so on; that will make you believe quite naturally, and will make you more docile (vous fera croire et vous abêtira).[44]

Literally, this last passage means that habitual religious practises "will make you believe and become like a beast." Elsewhere, when he speaks of habit Pascal uses the image of an automaton:

> Proofs only convince the mind; habit (la coutume) provides the strongest proofs and those that are most believed. It inclines the automaton, which leads the mind unconsciously along with it. Who ever proved that it will dawn tomorrow, and that we shall die? And what is more widely believed? It is then habit that convinces us and makes so many Christians.[45]

Pascal's mention of beasts and automatons in the course of his advocacy of habitual religious behavior shows that he retained considerable allegiance to the view that people are quintessentially human only insofar as they are consciously rational. Reason, grace, and habit coexist uneasily in Pascal's psychology: what unites them in his thinking is that they all can act to tame passion and promote faith. Fixation of religious belief is accomplished by the three interrelated process of ratiocination, inspiration, and habituation. The first process is undoubtedly given novel formulation by Pascal with his adoption of probabilistic and practical techniques of reasoning; the second is just as surely informed by traditional Augustinian theology; while the third, I contend, contains some insufficiently appreciated novel elements that emerge when Pascal's understanding of habit is interpreted under the rubric of paradoxical practice instead of the more traditional rubric of obedient avowal.[46]

Nietzsche criticized Pascal on the grounds that he decried a multitude of secular bad habits, like gambling and carousing, only to urge the equally execrable religious habits of taking holy water and having masses. Both sorts of behaviors were decadent in Nietzsche's judgment because they sought to destroy passions instead of satisfying or sublimating them. Nietzsche was not prompted to this criticism by any categorical disparagement of habits. It was Jean-Jacques Rousseau who advocated the banishment of habit for the sake of preserving passionate spontaneity and reflective rationality.[47] Instead Nietzsche favored a more nuanced view:

> I love brief habits and consider them an inestimable means for getting to know *many* things and states, down to the bottom of their sweetness and bitterness. . . . Enduring habits I hate. I feel as if a tyrant had come near me and as if the air I breathe had thickened when events take such a turn that it appears that they will inevitably give rise to enduring habits.[48]

I think Nietzsche's views on this subject are very insightful, and I shall seek to develop them. Yet his reading of Pascal seems seriously amiss; in fact, I think that Pascal anticipates Nietzsche's own position quite remarkably!

That Pascal did not unreservedly advocate pious religious practices is evident in the tenth of his *Provincial Letters* where he argues against the Jesuits' practice of general confession. Pascal there argued that allowing inveterate sinners to confess generally, for example, without acknowledging the habitual nature of their sinning, was only to encourage indirectly the persistence of such sinful behavior; this, wrote Pascal, "is in my view one of their (the Jesuits') most pernicious principles, and most likely to maintain the wicked in their bad habits (mauvaises habitudes)."[49] Confession and absolution become incorporated into a pattern of habitual, sinful behavior. Pascal urged genuine contrition and change of heart. For him, habitual religious practices were aids in a complex process of arriving at a genuinely faithful Christian life; they were not a sheer capitulation to arbitrary church authority. In the broad context of the history of Christian theology Pascal's Jansenism was conservative—a self-conscious return to Augustinian doctrines of grace and election—but in the proximate context of seventeenth-century Roman Catholic France it was radical in its challenge to the theological and ecclesiastical dominance of the Jesuits.

Nietzsche probably did not read the *Provincial Letters*, but a second piece of relevant evidence was surely familiar to him. In one of numerous references to his French predecessor Nietzsche criticized

Pascal for arguing that Christianity is true because it is necessary. Nietzsche says that Christian faith and life seem necessary or "second nature" to Pascal only because he regards them as the product of habit as well as reason. Nietzsche concludes that even if Pascal is right in saying that Christianity is something to which one must be habituated, this fact does not make Christian conversion any less an error; it only shows that it is a variety of what Nietzsche calls "nöthige Irrthümer" (necessary errors).[50] He seems at this point to be alluding to Pascal's definition of habit in the *Pensées*:

> Habit is a second nature that destroys the first. But what is nature? Why is habit not natural? I am very much afraid that nature itself is only a first habit, just as habit is a second nature.[51]

By so closely associating habit with nature Pascal also associates with habit the contradictory duality of human nature as great and wretched. Aspects of human nature like calculative reasoning can be emblems of both greatness and wretchedness; I contend that for Pascal religious habits have this same dual capacity. Going to mass can tame passions and promote faith; going to confession can routinize absolution and make sinful behavior more egregious. As the apostle Paul realized, sacramental actions may redound to one's salvation or damnation depending upon whether they are undertaken with contrite discernment or arrogant insensitivity (I Cor. 11.17–32). This is the paradox of religious practices, and though Pascal most especially associated it with sacramental actions it extends in his thinking to other practices like prayer (*Pensées* 930). More generally, he wrote: "It is superstitious to put one's hope in formalities, but arrogant to refuse to submit to them."[52] The marks of faith are paradoxically similar to the symptoms of sin.

I believe that habitual religious practices have a similar sort of duality for Pascal as Nietzsche posits when he distinguishes between brief habits that suggest self-mastery, and so enhanced vitality, and enduring habits which signal a deadening sameness. This claim is supported by Pascal's own habitual practices which were more of the brief than the enduring sort. He sought retirement at the Abbey at Port-Royal for short stays, but he never completely renounced the world for monastic life. Part of Nietzsche's great love and sympathy for Pascal was rooted in an apprehension of similarity between them; in regard to their assessments of disciplined habitual regimens of behavior I think that their views and behaviors were more similar than Nietzsche realized.

Of course, Nietzsche took this line of thought further than did Pascal. Although he rejected all Christian and specifically religious practices, he did recommend disciplines like solitude, fasting, and sexual abstinence as irreligious forms of spiritual self-mastery. These he enjoined only in a qualified way. He urged adopting spiritually disciplined practices with a self-conscious conviction that the elevation of these practices to inveterate habits will surely bring about noxious consequences; perforce, all spiritual practices must be provisional and revisable. Furthermore, ascetic practices should not be pursued exclusively; their celebratory counterparts must also be affirmed. Fasting without feasting becomes a denial of life in Nietzsche's view. So much does Nietzsche emphasize the revisable and contrastive character of warranted regimens of spiritual practice that he might be said to enjoin the spiritual practice of paradox—the practice of some disciplined regimen followed by the practice of its opposite, each undertaken for the sake of realizing one's truest self in the context of the world most expansively conceived. This characterization is supported by Nietzsche's distinction between brief habit and enduring habits. It is also motivated by the theme of creative self-overcoming which pervades *Thus Spoke Zarathustra* and his later philosophical writings. Briefly stated, then, Pascal appreciates the paradox of religious practice and anticipates Nietzsche's advance to the spiritual practice of paradox.

In light of these observations it is evident that Pascal's spiritual predicament, as conceived in terms of habits, may not be simply stated as the task of avoiding the bad ones and embracing the good ones. Certainly there is a measure of serious moral intent in this strategy of which Pascal would have approved, but it is a formulation lacking sensitivity to the contradictions which Pascal thought pervade even the most pious of human practices. Besides the exegetical arguments just rehearsed, there are two types of practical considerations, one traditional and one rather modern, which make the situation more complicated than is acknowledged by the bald prescription to adopt religiously requisite good habits and no bad habits. The first type arises upon examination of the individual careers of cynics and romantics, and the second from the way in which economic and political forces have come to influence habitual behaviors.

A cynic for present purposes is a person who believes that good habits tend to become bad ones. Diogenes of Sinope was probably the first philosophical thinker to be labelled a cynic, and as was mentioned earlier, he is said to have earned that title because he emulated dogs (κυνικοί) and other animals which defecate in public

(Diogenes Laertius, *Vitae Philosophorum* 6.70–73). Diogenes was a contemporary of Aristotle and in his own manner a student of Socrates. He believed that rationality is a natural human quality and the essence of virtue. Unlike most other students of Socrates he combined these beliefs with an ascetic and antinomian cast of mind, concluding that social conventions which did not directly promote one's physiological or intellectual well-being could be ignored. Indeed, it seems he felt they should be flouted because they almost always acquire pretensions they do not deserve. They masquerade as rational moral norms when they originated with, at best, the warrant of practical convenience. Cynics tended to shun duties of family, property, state, and cult; they adopted ascetic regimens requiring only the simplest forms of food, shelter, and companionship. They strove for an ideal of autonomy which they believed made them godlike. Their particular interpretation of this ideal in terms of "shamelessness" (ἀναίδεια) was not widely emulated, but their influence in other respects upon Stoic philosophers, and indirectly upon Christian thinkers like Clement, was considerable.

Cynics contend that good habits can become bad. A corollary to this teaching is that the more rigidly one keeps to a regimen and the more strenuous are one's efforts to justify it, the more likely it is that the behavior will acquire inimical features. Even brushing your teeth too regularly and too vigorously can have the negative consequence of wearing away tooth enamel, and a too adamant insistence upon the virtues of tooth brushing can prevent one from adopting new strategies of oral hygiene such as flossing or mechanical plague removal. More seriously, Sigmund Freud's classing of much religious behavior as a variety of obsessive neurosis, while to my mind an expression of Freud's excessive reductionism regarding religion, is still insightful in pointing out that a religious regimen, like a daily office of prayer, when applied too scrupulously can become a instrument for attenuating life instead of fulfilling it.[53] Jansenism is often portrayed by Roman Catholic scholars as a species of excessive scrupulosity, and while Pascal accused the Jesuits of moral laxity, he was also cynical—in the sense defined above—about the Jesuits' understanding and practice of general confession, believing that they had transformed a good habit into a bad one.

A romantic is defined here as someone who believes that bad habits can become good ones. The word 'romantic' dates back to descriptions of the popular form of Latin spoken in the city of Rome. This *Romanus* Latin was the progenitor of the vernacular romance languages of Italian, French, and Spanish. It was regarded as inelegant and vulgar, but it became the medium of popular storytelling. A romantic in this context is someone who accords aesthetic value to stories and poems expressed in these popular idioms rather than in traditional Latin forms. In French 'roman' today means 'a novel', and dates back to late medieval tales of adventure written in the French vernacular; similarly, 'romance' in Spanish today is a poetic ballad that has roots in late medieval verse forms.

A more contemporary type of literary romantic is epitomized by the French poet Arthur Rimbaud. Writing as a sixteen-year-old poetic prodigy, Rimbaud explains to his teacher how he is making himself a poet:

> Now, I am degrading myself as much as possible. Why? I want to be a poet, and I am working to make myself a *seer (voyant)*: you will not understand this, and I don't know how to explain it to you. It is a question of reaching the unknown by the derangement of *all the senses*. The sufferings are enormous, but one has to be strong, one has to be born a poet and I know I am a poet.[54]

According to the best estimates of his biographers, Rimbaud actually employed many vices to attain such a state of derangement: alcohol and drugs, blasphemy and obscenity, vagabondage and sexual experimentation.[55] In extreme or superficial forms this theory of the *voyant* degenerates into a rationalization for self-indulgence. Still it is analogous to some traditional religious practices. Fasting and feasting, which are essential parts of the archaic seasonal calendar of ritual, certainly involve a sort of derangement of customary physiological patterns. Ritual intoxicants were sometimes part of the mortification and jubilation periods of ritual activity—*soma* use in Hindu ritual is the most celebrated archaic example. More dramatically, the rites of passage to adulthood in many Native American Indian societies involve so-called "vision quest" experiences which include austerities designed to promote religious insights.

Pascal was romantic in the sense that he believed gambling, and most specifically, the gaming mentality it produces, can become a means for rationally promoting belief in God. Although he never went to the Rimbaldienne extreme of encouraging dice-playing so that faith might flourish, he clearly felt that familiarity with this bad habit could be put to good use. Good habits become bad, and here the bad are made good: habits suffer from a radical axiological instability in Pascal's view. Even habits serving as instruments of morality were accorded a fundamental ambivalence. He notes in the *Pensées* that what counts as just varies from place to place; no essential nature informs these disparate manifestations, at least, none that fallen human reason can perceive. Thus even the most acclaimed conceptions of human justice gain sway only by force of habit—a force itself often consisting of little more than the administered will of a tyrannical ruler. Should these pretentious norms be publicly unmasked and flouted? No, says Pascal; so long as they are believed to be just they can serve justice: "Men must often be deceived for their own good."[56]

Although I stop short of advocating deception or derangement, I do believe that one can not roundly condemn romantics and cynics without significantly impoverishing spiritual life in deference to conventional standards of morality. Their persons and practices embody a paradoxical creativity which spiritual aspirants seeking to contend with a predicament like Pascal's can not afford to ignore. Nietzsche's criticism of traditional ascetic ideals presupposes their subservience to conventional morality, and as will be evident later, when this presupposition is granted his criticisms are trenchant. Hence persons undertaking a variety of spiritually disciplined life would be well served by being both a little romantic and little cynical about this project, at least to the extent of not mistaking their endeavor as one of simply substituting bad habits for good ones, and replacing old tyrants by new masters.

A second more modern complication also undermines a rigid distinction between good and bad habits. Since psychologically and physiologically addictive habits are not easily changed, their promotion in others is an indirect way of exerting power over them. In contemporary times, when authoritarian models of government have come into at least nominal disfavor and most methods of interpersonal coercion are legally eschewed, the inculcation of bad habits in others has become a way of exerting power over them while apparently respecting their autonomy. Traditional forms of sophistry condemned by Aristotle and other philosophers were said to appeal to irrational emotions such as fear, envy, and greed. A newer and more vicious form of sophistry—one associated with the development of totalitarian governments and advanced capitalism—tries not only to appeal to these irrational dispositions but also to engender them. Addiction epitomizes human folly and misery in the twentieth-century. Political propaganda and provocative marketing are manifestations of the new sophistry which promotes it.

Governments in recent times have promoted drug trafficking and drug use as a way of weakening the social and economic vitality of adversary populations. During the Vietnam war the Communist and American sides accused each other of promoting the Asian heroin trade for political purposes. On a more individual scale, taking advantage of individual vulnerabilities to bad habits is a common theme of political espionage; the Soviet spy Kim Philby was a master at the genteel art of fostering bad habits in persons who had access to information he desired or power he wished to control. Governments more passively implement these same strategies toward their own populations by tolerating levels of drug use and violence in poor and minority populations that they would not tolerate in their primary constituencies. Malcolm X forcefully aimed this charge at the U.S. government. Increasingly governments are finding that such policies do not really promote social stability, nor even the long-term economic well-being of privileged classes that dominate the government. The disease and criminality spawned by alcohol and drug abuse tend to move beyond minority communities into the larger population.

More popular now is governmental inculcation of bad habits for the purpose of regressive taxation. So-called sin taxes are levied on alcohol and tobacco products, even in countries like the United States that do not have broad-based consumption taxes. Members of Congress sanctimoniously say that they levy taxes on these items so as to discourage their use, yet at the same time they vote subsidies for the grain and tobacco farmers who provide the raw material for such products. Also, more and more states are promoting lotteries as a way of raising revenues because of political hostility to more direct forms of taxation. Advertising agencies are hired to run clever campaigns designed to convince people that government lotteries are innocent fun that have the added benefit of helping public education, care for the elderly, or some other commendable program. Unfortunately many people are enticed into habitual and destructive forms of gambling by these public-spirited games of chance. So governmental and corporate services are now being instituted to address the gambling problem!

Many varieties of unhealthy and habitual behaviors are encouraged in order to sell products and services. Corporate advertising is the most prominent medium for this new sophistry, though, of course, the appeal originates in strategies of individual sellers addressing individual buyers. Restriction on the advertising of alcohol and tobacco products indicates a public judgment that it is neither salutary nor moral to encourage bad habits for profit. Still the libertarian conviction that people should be free to pursue bad habits which do not directly harm others gives a certain legitimacy to those who foster these pursuits by selling relevant products. Besides, another type of corporation—an insurance company—will very likely sell you their products so as to protect you against the harmful consequences of purchasing and consuming other products. Health insurance will cover the costs of treatment for liver damage, lung cancer, and venereal disease. If insurers balk at covering certain medical costs, like those related to AIDS, on the grounds that they are the result of self-inflicted injuries, then lobbyists and lawyers are available to work to make such coverage a legal right. Complexities abound!

At each stage of a predicament aggravated by addictive habits there are many alternatives from which to choose because there are always people willing to sell products or services which they claim will extricate people from that predicament. Yet what promises to relieve the problem may just as well compound it. Lawsuits make enemies at least as readily as they reconcile them. Stimulants promote dieting but lead to a new form of dependency. For these reasons an ethos of personal liberty and economic opportunity makes the ability to obtain and assess relevant information a prerequisite for exercising these privileges wisely. Yet education itself is a social process and can not be exempted from complicity with the political and economic forces that shape a consumerist ethos. Educators who fashion themselves as providers of information services may themselves inculcate the bad habit of slavishness before technical expertise. Even philosophy may be presented more as a consoling potion—as "adversity's sweet milk," in Shakespeare's phrase (*Romeo and Juliet*, 3.3.55)—than as a critical remedy. Paradoxes proliferate!

The examples of cynics and romantics teach that good habits may become bad, and bad ones good. The lesson to be learned from the plight of the contemporary citizen and consumer is that human behavior occurs in a competitive and conflictive social context. This implies that estimates of the value of behavioral regimens become relative to the array of interests active there. I am convinced that not all of these interests are benign. As my criticisms of Clement's rationale suggested, I believe spiritual disciplines should provide practical means for resisting the inculcation of bad habits by governments and corporations (and professions and churches!), and in general, for opposing the exercise of coercive power. Spiritual regimens should be enlisted for this task both for the sake of one's own spiritual well-being, but also on ethical grounds; solidarity with persons oppressed in this or any other way is a moral obligation as well as a social prerequisite for attaining the fullest measure of spiritual well-being. Summarily stated, in a social context where governments, corporations, professions, and religious institutions use sophisticated techniques of persuasion to promote habitual behaviors and thereby control putatively free populations, spiritual discipline must be understood as an intellectually critical form of political resistance. Such resistance is most effective when the enduring habits inculcated by dominant social institutions are undercut by multiple and adaptable regimens of spiritual discipline—by, in short, the practice of paradox.

The insertion of a discussion of spiritual discipline as habitual behavior into the temporal context of embodied, social experience has suggested that simple dichotomies must be eschewed. A daily office of prayer can become an obsessive ritual and instruction in yoga may amount to little more than consumption of an imported product slickly merchandised. Histories and contexts count; paradoxicality and complexity can not be willfully absented from spiritual life. Two broad criteria retain general validity: no spiritual practice should bring physiological and psychological harm to oneself or others, nor should it directly or indirectly foster the coercive and harmful use of power. The two criteria are related. Judging spiritual discipline to be both an antidote to addictive behaviors and a means of political resistance is not inconsistent when the inculcation of bad habits of consumption by powerful institutions is acknowledged to be a method of coercive social control. Given the precariousness of human life in its physical and social environment, there is constantly the need to respond flexibly to new circumstances; being the object of a coercive use of power inhibits one's ability to respond in this requisite way. On the other hand, a very destructive psychological trait is the need habitually to control other people's destinies in order to feel personally satisfied with one's own life.

Together these criteria of personal health and social justice specify the broadest prerequisites for the fullness of life that spiritually disciplined behavior has traditionally sought to promote. To be free from addictive needs and behaviors requires constant vigilance and considerable creativity. This is especially so when one recognizes with the cynic that good habits can become bad. To cultivate compassion and excellence requires persistence and creativity, especially if one seeks to convince persons who suffer from their own and other's actions that they are not without allies nor their plight without remedy.

How concrete examples of spiritually disciplined behavior can be understood to be a creative response to elements of paradoxicality and complexity in human experience is the subject of the next part of this essay. Arguments for discriminating between traditional spiritual disciplines will be offered but will not be the crux of what is to follow. Rather an imaginative rethinking of the nature of spiritual discipline through novel description of concrete practices is the primary purpose of this next stage of the project. The third and final part will return to a more argumentative mode of discourse, parrying some of Nietzsche's harsh criticisms. Nietzsche will then be shown to offer constructive resources for understanding how spiritual practices can be restorative of fundamental rhythms of life from which many persons in recent years have become estranged. In doing this, I hope that the meaning of the idea of spiritual discipline itself might be enriched.

II

Categoreal Themes and their Practical Applications

CHAPTER 3

Semiotic Self-Reference

The next three chapters will provide a speculative interlude in this book's case for philosophically rethinking the meaning of spiritual discipline. Thus far I have argued that several philosophical notions which have traditionally informed Western conceptions of spiritual discipline are no longer adequate. The first consequence drawn from this conclusion was the reformulation of the predicament which spiritually disciplined practices seek to remedy. This has been done by substituting for the traditional goal of denying the body so that the soul might flourish the alternative task of discovering habitual practices which give life meaningful structure but which do not become themselves instruments of deadening conformity. In Nietzsche's pithy phrasing, the task is one of cultivating brief habits which do not endure tyrannically.

In this part of the essay a second consequence will be confronted. The philosophical borrowings criticized above were acknowledged to be valuable insofar as they showed that spiritually disciplined regimens of behavior aspire to be creative responses to the large-scale features of paradoxicality and complexity in human life. If one judges this aspiration deserving, but the old vehicles for achieving it flawed, then a need for alternative means is evident. The categoreal themes outlined in the following chapters will offer these alternatives. When the argumentative case resumes in the essay's third part with an actual redefinition of spiritual discipline, these themes will be constitutive elements of that new conception. Hence the following somewhat speculative reflections about self-reference, symmetry, and equilibration will be an interlude, but not an interruption of the book's main line of thought.

Semiotic self-reference is the first alternative notion I shall consider. The criteria for being a satisfactory alternative are several. Rational coherence, empirical applicability, and imaginative appeal are foremost among them. The contents of this chapter on semiotic self-reference, and of the two succeeding chapters, are structured so as to address each of these three points. Two preliminary criteria can be addressed immediately. First, an initial plausibility is required

95

of each proffered theme. It should be possible to state clearly how a given categoreal theme is helpful for describing the relevant feature of religious experience, or, more generally, of the spiritual dimension of existence. Second, the alternative should have historical relevance to some of the philosophical and religious traditions from which have emerged the spiritual practices that it purports to better describe and justify. Philosophical speculation is necessarily abstract and potentially arbitrary; to relate speculative notions to historical antecedents is one way to make these characteristics less objectionable. Such historical relevance was certainly present in case of the themes of suprasensual vision, unencumbered causality, and static hierarchy; they were all shown to have fairly direct origins in Greek philosophy and more indirect relations to the religious sensibilities of the Hellenistic Mediterranean world.

By semiotic self-reference I mean the process whereby signs refer to themselves; or, if one prefers a more behavioral account, it is the phenomenon of persons making reference to the very signs they use as they speak or write.[1] It has been known intuitively since antiquity that some language which refers to itself is paradoxical. Diogenes Laertius attributed to Eubulides of Miletus, a contemporary of Aristotle, the insight that whenever he says of himself that he is lying, it is problematic whether he is speaking truly or falsely in saying this (*Vitae Philosophorum* 2.108). If he speaks truly, then he is lying— saying something false; yet if he speaks falsely, and is not lying, then he speaks truly. Since the medieval era some logicians explicitly attributed this paradox to the presence of linguistic self-reference; in his summary of extant solutions for the Liar paradox Paul of Venice explicitly mentions one dealing with the capacity of language for "super se reflexionem" (*Logica magna* 2.15).[2] It was Bertrand Russell who coined the term 'self-reference' in the sense used here and who began the modern tradition of investigating the close tie between paradoxicality and linguistic self-reference.[3] This philosophical tradition establishes a general relation between the two notions, yet it does not indicate how linguistic self-reference is pertinent to paradox and contradiction as these notions figure in the religious career of someone like Blaise Pascal. I believe this relevance is established by something common to them both which I shall call 'a simultaneity of perspectives'.

The peculiarity of instances of the Liar paradox like 'I am lying' disappears if this bit of language is excluded from the domain of things to which it refers. Qualifying phrases such as 'when I talk about my age' or 'if I promise complete loyalty' turn the Liar sentence into unexceptional assertions. It is only when one tries to maintain that 'I am lying' is both objectively descriptive of a linguistic phenomenon—so in that sense outside of it—and also integrallly a part of that same phenomenon—so in that sense inside of it—only then does this expression acquire a peculiar status. The simultaneity of perspectives which counts this sentence both inside and outside of language is crucial here. It is analogous to the potentially paradoxical religious experience of being both in the world but not of it, of being an immanent agent of something transcendent. From this analogy comes the initial plausibility of semiotic self-reference as a categoreal theme for describing religious practices.

Martin Luther described the Christian's status as being *justus simul peccator*, i.e., justified while still a sinner. Not all religions express this reality via legal metaphors; for instance, Chinese religious sensibilities experience a simultaneity of perspectives more as a realization of natural duality than as an juridical condition. Still spiritually disciplined practices in both contexts are most often ordinary actions which are presumed to introduce the practitioner to an extraordinary quality of existence. Older Christian idioms spoke of spiritual practices as embodied actions seeking to transcend embodied existence, for instance, by promoting a "suprasensual vision" of God. The theme of semiotic self-reference is intended to explore this religious realization of a simultaneity of perspectives without invoking meanings that disparage human corporeality.

Semiotic self-reference received attention in the Western philosophical tradition prior to the medieval period. It is implicitly operative in Aristotle's definition of truth and in the Stoic trichotomy of sign, meaning, and referent; it is most fully explicit in the Porphyrian distinction between names of first and second imposition—a precursor of what is now known as the use/mention distinction. To my knowledge Augustine of Hippo was the first author to appeal to this sort of philosophical material in the course of a theological treatise. Each of these facts serves to establish the historical relevance of this theme to the religious tradition receiving primary attention here. Indeed, Augustine, like Pascal, will prove to be not only a proponent of many traditional notions criticized here, but also a resource for effecting needed changes in thinking about spiritual discipline.

Aristotle provides his famous definition of truth in Book Gamma of the *Metaphysics*: "To say that what is is not, or that what is not is, is false; but to say that what is is, and what is not is not, is true."[4] Clearly Aristotle is saying that truth and falsity, rather than inhering in things themselves, are properties of thoughts about such things and these thoughts are given expression in declarative sentences and other linguistic instruments for making statements. Alfred Tarski cites Aristotle's formula as the prime antecedent for his own semantic conception of truth. In Tarski's account metalinguistic predications of truth figure prominently: " 'snow is white' is true if, and only if, snow is white" is his favorite example. He regards such formulations as explicated instances of Aristotle's definition, and he demonstrates in the course of his articles on this topic how crucial such examples are for understanding the type of self-referential language operative in the Liar paradox.[5]

Aristotle did not explore the semantic provinces of logical theory as systematically as did the Stoic school of logicians. It was these intellectual descendants of Chrysippus, Aristotle's junior by a century, who first clearly distinguished between a physical sign ($\sigma\eta\mu\alpha\hat{\iota}\nu o\nu$), the meaning signified ($\sigma\eta\mu\alpha\iota\nu\acute{o}\mu\epsilon\nu o\nu$) by that sign, and the physical referent ($\tau\upsilon\gamma\chi\acute{\alpha}\nu o\nu$) to which that sign refers through the agency of its meaning.[6] By clearly acknowledging that signs and referents are physical objects, and thereby distinguishable from abstract meanings, the Stoic logicians made possible the identification of signs which are the referents of other signs or of themselves. Porphyry, a third-century Neoplatonist, explicitly identified this class of signs in his commentary on Aristotle's *Categories*; two centuries later Boethius gave Latin terminology for essentially the same distinction: "The first imposition of a name (prima positio nominis) is made in accordance with the signification of the word, and the second is made in accordance with its form; the first imposition is made so that names might be imposed for things, and the second so that names themselves might be designated by other names (ut aliis nomibus ipsa nomina designarentur)."[7] In the medieval logical tradition names of second imposition were especially associated with words frequently used by grammarians, words such as 'nomen', 'verbum', and more broadly, words like 'modus' and 'tempus'. From Porphyry onward the distinction between names of first and second imposition was used to distinguish between inquiries having ontological as opposed to logical or linguistic interests.

This brief account of the development of awareness of the phenomenon of semiotic self-reference is sufficient, I think, to show that this development parallels the progress of philosophical logic as a species of self-reflective inquiry. Historically, interest in the Liar paradox coincides with periods of great advance in logical theory—classical Greece, the late Middle Ages, and the early twentieth century. Through textbook summaries of logical theory Augustine became acquainted with the Aristotelian and Stoic conceptions requisite for clearly conceiving of semiotic self-reference.[8] He did so under the rubric of *signa quae significant se ipsa* (signs which signify themselves) in *De magistro* (4.10) and more casually in other texts.[9] He represents, therefore, the combination of interests characteristic of the philosophy of religion; he brought a self-reflective philosophical temperament to the project of describing religious experiences and justifying religious practices.

Augustine was familiar with the how the Liar paradox was used by Academic philosophers of late antiquity to strengthen their case for philosophical skepticism. He cites a version of it in his early text *Contra Academicos* (3.17.37). There he provides a fairly unsophisticated defense of logical truth against the skeptical arguments summarized, for instance, in Cicero's *Academica*—a text with which Augustine was very familiar. Two important changes occur when Augustine takes up this argument again in *De magistro*. In acknowledging the difficulty of ascertaining and communicating reliable knowledge he appeals generally to self-referring signs rather than to the Liar paradox in particular. Also, in affirming how these difficulties can be overcome he no longer defends a strictly Neoplatonist epistemology, but instead, argues on behalf of a specifically Christian adaptation in which Jesus Christ as the *intus magister* (inner teacher) is the ultimate guarantor of true knowledge. In short, Augustine enlists his philosophical insight into the phenomenon of semiotic self-reference in the service of Christian apologetics.

Pairs of signs that were both self-referential and mutually referential especially impressed Augustine. For instance, the Latin word 'nomen' refers to signs which are nouns; it refers to itself and nouns like 'verbum'. In turn, 'verbum' means 'word' and refers to itself; it also refers to 'nomen'. He notes that 'nomen' then refers to 'verbum' which, in turn, refers back to 'nomen', such that in this particular path of reference one never reaches a thing which is not a sign. Since Augustine inherited as part of his North African intellectual makeup a strongly extensional bias in semantics—he was inclined to think that the meanings of signs gained clarity and utility by referring to physical objects—the case of self-referential and mutually referential signs seemed highly problematic to him. He offers the following analogy: "For discussing words with words is as entangled as interlocking and rubbing the fingers with fingers, in which case it may scarcely be distinguished, except by the one himself,

which fingers itch and which give aid to the itching."[10] The sense
of sight is insufficient to distinguish between the itching and
scratching fingers; appeal must be made to a second sensory source—
the sense of touch—in order to settle the issue. What is needed is two
different but simultaneous perspectives. Augustine concluded that
signs as a sensory medium of inference and communication can not
be a self-sufficient instrument for acquiring and sharing knowledge
reliably. The arguments of Academic skeptics, including their
interpretation of the significance of the Liar paradox, were useful to
Augustine in making this point. Yet he was neither philosophically
nor theologically inclined toward skepticism as a final position. For
instance, he recognized that one could interpret the ability of signs
to refer to all things, including themselves, as an asset contributing
to their efficacy as instruments for learning. Furthermore, as a good
Platonist he believed that eternal and intellectual principles must
supplement signs and provide a transcendent perspective. He is so
much a Platonist that he even says that such transcendent items of
knowledge are apprehended by recollection, only accenting a
specifically Christian point when he identifies the soul's recollections
with the activity of Christ as an inner spiritual teacher.[11]

For present purposes what is important in Augustine's religious
epistemology is, first, his claim that a purely human perspective on
how human knowledge is gained and communicated must be
conjoined with the divine perspective introduced by the activity of
Christ, the second person of the Trinity; and, second, the fact that
the example of self-referential signs is used by him in making this
point. This use of semiotic self-reference for describing a simultaneity
of perspectives as a potentially paradoxical characteristic of the
Christian's intellectual life serves, I think, as something of an
historical precedent for the project undertaken in the subsequent
pages of this book. Establishing the historical relevance of a categoreal theme will not always involve citing an historical precedent
of this sort, but it is one way of preemptively defending speculative
constructs against accusations of arbitrariness.

SIGNS AND THINGS

Crucial to any philosophical theory of semiotic self-reference is an
account of how signs signify things. Essential to almost every such
account is the already mentioned Stoic trichotomy consisting of the
physical sign, the meaning signified, and the individual objects to
which significant reference is made. The utility of this division is

evident in illustrations. For instance, smoke, being a natural sign consisting of a mixture of gases and suspended carbon particles, usually denotes fire as its origin, and connotes danger or warmth. Another example is the word 'red', an audible or inscribed conventional sign, which denotes all objects of a certain color and connotes a property that seems intrinsic to human blood, but not to woven cloth. The Stoics were among the first philosophers to differentiate between classes of signs such as the natural and conventional types just illustrated. Efforts at theorizing about signs, things, and their classification has not so much discovered confirmable scientific facts as they have yielded general philosophical strategies for making sense of the world. I contend that understanding the nature and varieties of semiotic self-reference can help reveal some strategies for attaining a fully meaningful life which practitioners of spiritual discipline employ. Review of some rudiments of semiology will prove helpful for this task.

Individual things and sets of individual things are what signs signify. When a sign makes reference to a set of things it is said to denote them. In the special instance when a sign makes reference to a single thing it is said to designate that thing. Singular signs (names to logicians) designate; general signs (predicates to the same) denote. Referents may be concrete or abstract; for instance, the signs 'Aristotle' and 'the tallest building in New York City' each designate concrete things, while '7' and 'honesty' each designate abstract objects. The general signs 'man' and 'house' denote concrete things, while 'prime number' and 'virtue' denote sets whose individual members are abstract. Hence signs may be classified not only in terms of the nature of the vehicle of signification, as between natural and conventional signs, but also in terms of the nature of their referents. An implication that follows from the attention philosophers have given to such distinctions is that people—philosophers and arguably others too—organize the things in their world by means of the signs they choose to signify them.

Important philosophical differences can be specified according to how signs are related to what they denote. Aristotle believed that the metaphysical structure of the world was accurately mirrored in the structure of the Greek language: to know language is to know the world. Quite oppositely, Cratylus, a follower of Heraclitus and an influence on Plato, believed that language shares in the world's state of flux, such that this lack of fixity implies limitations on the human ability to attain and communicate sensible knowledge. As the sensible media for expressing conceptual thought and for representing the natural world, signs implicitly pose the question of what is most real—enduring substances or transient flux, signs themselves or an independent reality with which they are correlated.

In the modern period, Bertrand Russell believed that ordinary language distorts the reality to which it refers, and so is in need of logical reformulation if it is to be a reliable aid of inquiry. Russell's work in seeking to bring about this reformulation has been very influential, especially in English-speaking countries, and it has also served to make the theory of reference a central rubric of twentieth-century analytic philosophy. Not all philosophers, though, have followed Russell's example; in a quite contrary manner, Martin Heidegger held that logical, scientific language is oriented toward the manipulation and control of the natural world, and is therefore antithetical to the world's urge to reveal itself in language.[12] For him, to know the world is to experience language as poetry. Though himself an atheist like Russell, Heidegger's philosophy is indebted to his early theological training and has proved helpful to many modern religious thinkers. The emphasis on semiotic self-reference in this essay implies that Russell's relevance to the philosophy of religion is likewise not confined to his professions of atheism, but can be gleaned indirectly from his other philosophical accomplishments.

Arthur Danto, a contemporary American philosopher, has advocated a conception of philosophy that allows attention to the issues and emphases favored by both scientific and aesthetic philosophical temperaments. He has written that the space between language and the world is the locus of philosophical investigation. Since an inscribed or spoken sentence has physical reality, as a visual or acoustic phenomenon, it is a part of the world and may be studied scientifically by the linguist. Yet a sentence may also be a vehicle for a proposition which says something true of the world. As such, says Danto, the sentence attains a singular status, becoming distant from the world by reason of its being a vehicle for a truth claim about it. Hence self-referential language like the Liar paradox, which in a certain way has been shown to be both inside and outside the world to which it refers, embodies in concentrated form the singular status of language generally. Like art objects, sentences expressing propositions exist in a different way from more ordinary objects. Danto argues that human beings as the users of sentences are themselves both part of the world, so an object of scientific study, and yet also at a distance from it because they entertain and assert propositions. According to Danto philosophers are persons who persistently reflect upon themselves in their dual capacity for being inside and outside of the world in this sense. This conception of philosophy's way of reflecting about signs is helpful for mediating the conflict of views between philosophers like Russell and Heidegger; more specifically, it is also helpful for addressing the phenomenon of the simultaneity of perspectives which I have identified as crucial to the spiritual predicament of Pascal and like-minded persons.[13]

Western philosophers have traditionally been more theoretical than their Asian counterparts. As Danto's description of philosophy attests, they understand themselves in terms of how they represent the world more than in terms of how they engage it in sagacious action. The writings of Hindu yogis and Taoist sages may also be understood as reflecting upon the space between language and the world, yet their characteristic concern is not primarily cognitive. They are concerned lest this space become a barrier to enlightenment. Hindu yogis use language (e.g., as mantras) to transcend language and the multifarious world it posits, while the Taoist sage seeks to remove language as a barrier to identification with the world's rhythmic flux. Chuang Tzu wrote, "If the Way is made clear, it is not the Way. If discriminations are put into words, they do not suffice."[14] I find this Eastern perspective on language and the world another helpful qualification to traditional philosophical approaches. It is especially germane if philosophy is to productively reflect upon spiritually disciplined human practices.

What exists and how extant things are related to one another were perhaps first signified by cosmographic structures and images. Mesopotamian ziggurats, Ptolemaic armillary spheres, and less directly, Christian churches embody such conceptions; Pueblo sand paintings, Indian mandalas, and again, somewhat less directly, Chinese landscape scenes delineate them. They are expressions of the characteristically religious desire to establish a relation to the whole of reality. They are also self-referring signs: if they denote the entire world then they denote themselves as part of that world.[15]

Cosmographic representations, or cosmograms, are relevant to spiritual practices in two ways. Most directly, the act of creating cosmographic artifacts is itself often given a spiritual significance. Archaic religions like those of the Pueblo Indians sometimes understand the making of cosmograms as part of the annual ritual act of recreating the orderly world. A less archaic spiritual meaning is evident in interpretations of the creative process offered by artists in the tradition of Chinese Taoist and Buddhist landscape painters.[16] Japanese culture is especially pervaded by an aesthetic sensibility that understands artistic creation less an individual act of expression than as a manifestation of impersonal force of natural creativity. The activity of creating an object which symbolically embodies the entire world, including its creator, is a sort of self-creation in which the features of paradoxicality and creativity are strikingly coincident.

Cosmograms also provide the context in which spiritual practices are undertaken. Cosmographic architecture provides the most literal instance of this phenomenon. The significance of this contextualization is revealed when one examines what difference such a setting makes to spiritual agents. Why is prayer in a church (or a temple or a mosque) especially apt and moving? For Western monotheists it is not simply because God is there to hear one's prayers; God is confessed to be omnipresent. Nor is it because in church one finds like-minded persons engaged in similar activities. This may be an explanation credible to outside observers, but it is hardly a self-description that practitioners of such prayer would give. Rather, I think, that it is especially powerful to pray in church because the church, as a physical edifice and human institution, models an ordering of the world in which prayer is a meaningful, and indeed, an obligatory act. It symbolically models the world which prayer pragmatically presupposes. The cosmogram serves the function of positing what is most real.

Critics like Russell might charge that this cosmological symbolism falsifies the world; those schooled by Heidegger might say prayer seeks to magically control things and events. Surely religious or spiritual cosmograms falsify the world in the sense that they require its practical simplification. Models are not models if they are as complex as what they represent. Surely spiritual practices are techniques of control to the extent that they are goal-oriented activities. Practical activity is inconceivable without the positing and pursuit of desired ends. Placing prayer and other spiritual practices in cosmographic contexts enables them to be interpreted as strategies for arriving at spiritual meaning. They are strategic actions undertaken with a consciousness of inhabiting but transcending a not entirely hospitable world, of confronting but not succumbing to a complexity pregnant with chaos.

Western Christians are mostly ignorant of the cosmological significance of church architecture, being capable of identifying only in the vaguest of ways how the church building represents a sacred dimension of space. The tradition of having the church face east, the direction of the rising son and the Holy Land, has given way to practical considerations. The altar or communion table is commonly sensed to be a place where God is especially manifest, yet the traditional meanings attached to its placement are mostly forgotten. Gothic cathedrals placed the altar against a wall in a sanctuary separated from the nave by a chancel screen: this emphasized God's presence in the Mass as a sacrifice administered by clergy. Churches of Reformation heritage, and especially Calvinist communities, placed both the communion table and baptismal font much more in the midst of the congregation and under the elevated survey of the pulpit: this arrangement stressed God's presence in the Word as read and preached. Not only the symbolism of God's presence but the prominence and function of the clergy is quite different in Reformed worship. Nevertheless, Riverside Church in New York City, home to a liberal Protestant congregation, was constructed in a Gothic revival style that has the major altar against a northern wall, and St. John's Abbey Church in Minnesota, serving one of the world's largest Benedictine communities, features an entirely centralized altar in a church designed by the Bauhaus architect, Marcel Breuer.

Mandalas are especially instructive for illustrating how cosmograms contribute to spiritually disciplined practices; the efforts of some psychologists may also have made them more closely associated in the minds of many Westerners with this process than is indigenous religious architecture. 'Mandala' is the Sanskrit word for 'circle'. This same term is used in the study of religion to signify a ritual drawing which integrates a circle with a square, a vision of the self with a vision of the world. Mandalas in the form of complex geometrical designs were first systematically used in Hindu rituals as devices for representing the entire cosmos; for instance, they were used in the construction of Vedic altars. They were first described in Hindu Tantric texts and later became topics for speculation in Vedantic wisdom literature. There mandalas are said to portray the process of disintegration and reintegration which consciousness undergoes as it devolves from an original unity through the agency of *māyā* or illusory appearance, and then subsequently returns to wholeness through the realization that inner and outer reality are one—*ātman* is *brāhman*. In its creation the mandala is a pictorial representation of this process. As an object of meditation it serves to promote the concentration necessary for restoration of spiritual wholeness. Yogic practice uses mandalas to establish body/cosmos identifications in an experiential way.

Mandalic images became most pictorially elaborate and most ritually specific in Buddhist religious communities, especially in Tantric Buddhism as practiced in Tibet. Drawing upon the rich Buddhist pantheon of deities, disintegration and reintegration were frequently pictured as malevolent and benevolent deities descending into or emerging from consciousness. In this context, meditation upon a mandala is thought to effect a realization of the cosmos depicted, an animation of the deities and forces symbolized, and, finally, an identification of the self with the central deity. In summary, the mandala's meaning consists of a series of identifications between self, world, and deity. Here the self/world identification is mediated by images of deities.

The creation of a mandala involves a pictorial clearing of a sacred space. The addition of a square within the circle shows symbolically that this space is inhabited by nontransients. Hence the mandala evokes meanings inherited from the earliest phases of cultural life associated with the transition to organized agriculture and the domestication of animals. A circle within the square is included as a symbol of the self. Sometimes the square is conceived to be a courtyard, inside of which is a human habitation and outside of which are graveyards. The square is often cut by transverse lines which then mark out a set of four triangular spaces corresponding to the four compass directions. Lotus flowers as images of unfolding harmonious creation and crystalline gems as images of radiant endurance are frequent ornamentations. Sometimes the interpretations are psychological as well as cosmological, the transverse lines, for instance, marking out dimensions of consciousness as well as compass directions. In this Buddhist context the original unitary consciousness is understood in quasipsychological terms; for instance, the *ālayavijñāna* or "store-consciousness" of the Vijñānavādins is a sort of universal congeries of psychic contents.[17]

The psychologist C.G. Jung understood mandalas as "archetypes of wholeness," archetypes themselves being formal aspects of instincts. Jung believed that a drive for wholeness is a universal human characteristic such that a frustration of this drive is unhealthy in a similar way as is the repression of sexual urges. He further held that the creation of personal mandalas and meditation upon them counts as an attempt at self-healing, and he supplemented Freud's psychoanalytic interviewing with this essentially pictorial technique. By reason of Jung's influence practices involving mandalas in Western countries straddle the line separating psychotherapeutic and religious practices.[18]

For Jung, the central image was always a reference to the self and the outlying images were psychic contents in various stages of integration with the self conceived as a total personality consisting of personal consciousness, the personal unconscious, and then the collective unconscious. Jung's views on the collective unconscious remain very controversial; however, this idea is crucial to Jung's way of maintaining specificity for a microcosm/macrocosm key capable of interpreting mandalas in ways similar to the religiously conceived dynamics in Hinduism and Buddhism. A mandala pictures the self and its world; it is a sort of psychic and cosmic inventory.

Pictures, like words, are vehicles for reference; they are signs referring to things (and sometimes to things which are signs). The rational coherence of semiotic self-reference as a categoreal theme for describing spiritual practices has been provided by a systematic account of the relevant principles of semiology. As noted previously, cosmograms in their various forms seek to signify all of reality, such that if they succeed, they end up signifying themselves—because signs are things also. The empirical applicability of semiotic self-reference to spiritual practices has been achieved by describing the relationships between cosmograms and practices like prayer and meditation. The final criteria of imaginative appeal is best met, I think, by explicating cosmograms as cosmic and psychic inventories.

If one were asked to visualize a room which one was not presently occupying and then to answer questions regarding the contexts of that room, I think that the peculiar appeal of mandalic images would become evident. As one went about listing a dozen objects in the room, and then a half-dozen more; as one listed groups of objects on pieces of furniture or on walls, one would become aware of how such listing involves processes of selection and organization. Individual objects are identified by inclusion in the list, by their grouping into sets of objects, and their relation to other individuals and sets. Pictorial representation would further specify these relationships and promote insightful interpretation.

If different persons perform this sort of inventory exercise, a comparison of their listing and grouping reveals much about their personalities and preoccupations. If inventories by the same persons are performed for different rooms from different times in their lives, interesting processes of memory and history come into play. Memories of childhood domiciles are shaped by the quality of life that they nurtured. Then, finally, if activities are subsequently undertaken in a room so inventoried, they are shaped by it in its capacity as both a real and idealized environment. Indeed, the coexistence of the two contextual representations influences how these activities are experienced, remembered, and recounted to others. How parents treat their children, lovingly or abusively, is influenced by their memories of their own childhood—by the child's world they inhabited.

These thought experiments are suggestive of the ways in which cosmographic signs inform religious practices. Cosmograms are self-referential signs and so they also intuitively portray the relevance of semiotic self-reference to spiritually disciplined practices. Another sort of self-reference is suggested by contemplating activities undertaken in the cosmographic contexts, and that is how the human self may be denominated as yet another item in a cosmogram and as an element of the reality it posits. How semiotic self-reference is constitutive of selves as well as worlds, and is thereby potentially directly descriptive of embodied human practices, is the topic of the next section of this chapter.

WORDS AND SELVES

Thus far signs have been described in terms of the things to which they refer. This correlation of physical signs with referents invokes two elements of the Stoic trichotomy, leaving the third unused. This way of theorizing about signs is called extensional: it holds that signs are identical in meaning when the sets of objects to which they refer—their extensions—have exactly the same members. That the meaning of signs can be completely described by these resources seems attractive to certain philosophical temperaments, classical expressions of which are the termist logic of the nominalist William of Ockham and the theory of names of the archempiricist John Stuart Mill. Despite the fact of Ockham's vocation as a Franciscan brother, this philosophical temperament has not been very congenial to philosophical theologians nor does it offer much promise to philosophers of religion concerned with spiritual discipline.

Objections to concepts, properties, and possible worlds—all intensional notions—are both ontological and epistemological: they seem to require the existence of abstract objects and to deprive meanings of optimal clarity. It is the extensionalist's ideal that singular signs designate one and only one thing, and that general signs denote a set for which it can be determined whether any given individual is a member of it. Yet most signs, and especially words of natural languages, suffer from vagueness and ambiguity, from an underdetermination or an overdetermination of meaning. Religious thinkers are apt to apprehend mystery and the touch of the transcendent in the vagueness and ambiguity which accompanies speculative generalities; hence for the philosopher of religion it is essential to have the intellectual means for grappling with meanings of this sort.

In his influential essay, "On Sense and Reference," Gottlob Frege reemphasized the necessity of supplementing reference with sense, extensions with intensions.[19] He said that in many cases a referent can only be fixed by a prior determination of the sense of a sign; an intensional dimension of meaning is needed at least for signifying how referents are fixed. In his preferred example, the phrases 'Morning Star' and 'Evening Star' both designate the planet Venus; they share the same extension. Yet they have different "senses" because they differently specify how this heavenly body appears and, presumably, how it was named. Frege's strategy involves a compromise of sorts: abstract and potentially unclear intensional notions are employed to clarify ambiguities of reference that arise in a very complex systems of signs like natural languages. Philosophical investigation of a topic like spiritual discipline requires this same strategic compromise: the meaning of the word 'spiritual' itself signifies a property not strictly reducible to specifiable instantiations. It requires other strategies as well.

Insights about the ways signs are vague and ambiguous are insights about the space between language and the world, and so they are preeminently philosophical. For instance, singular signs like proper names are especially likely to be ambiguous unless a context of usage is specified. Such linguistic information about the context of usage is pragmatic because it concerns the relationship between language as a representation of the world and language as an agent's action within the world. Human actions in specific contexts provide information which gives definite meaning to crucial signs. Again this is especially the case for proper names. Consider the different referents of the proper name in the following two sentences: 'Ask John to meet me in the conference room' and 'I'm sorry I can not, because John has a cold and was not able to come to work today.' In the first sentence the speaker presupposes that John will arrive in the conference room clothed, with personal accessories like a watch and wallet, and perhaps even with items relevant to his job. In the second John is referred to more exclusively as a biological organism; it is not assumed that his wallet and pen are beset with a viral malady. No serious ambiguity is apt to arise because implicit information about context, intention, and action enables the interlocutors to handle the diverse meanings appropriately. Spiritually disciplined actions give like specification to conceptions of spiritual selfhood, and sometimes they do so through the mediation of self-referential signs.

If the human self is conceived to be a composite whole, then one of its parts can signify this whole. This is called synecdochic signification and it is a variety of semiotic self-reference because the physical sign, as part, is a member of the whole set it denotes. Common literal examples are phrases like 'hired hand' and 'private eye'. Poetic variations occur, for instance, when Homer describes Helen as "Helen of the white arms" and "Helen with the light robes" (*Iliad* 3.121, 228). Important religious examples of this sort of signification are relics understood as the venerated physical remains of a saint, usually ashes, or pieces of bone or hair. The notion of a relic has just the sort of ambiguity discussed above because it sometimes is interpreted to include objects that came into touch with a holy person during his or her lifetime. Splinters from the cross of Christ or the shroud of Turin, traditionally claimed as the burial cloth of Jesus, are the most popular Christian instances of this expanded notion of a relic.

A medieval Christian knew that a splinter of wood qualified as relic even though it was not part of Jesus' physical remains. The splinter was recognized to be sacred: the pious Christian knew the story of the passion and the context of action whereby the cross came to have physical contact with Jesus. The pious practice most closely associated with relics was pilgrimage. Such travel to the tomb of a saint or to a church reliquary often involved considerable hardship; ideally this hardship was endured in a spirit of humble obedience to church tradition, and ultimately, to God. In many cases the pilgrimage was experienced as an analogue to Christ's passion and as a way of conforming to the practice and selfhood of Christ. The inverse operation of the pilgrimage was the translation of relics to new sites. Peter Brown, in his book *The Cult of the Saints*, notes how important this practice was for the spread and integration of the Christian Church in the early Roman world.[20] Thus both spiritual conceptions of self and society were promoted by practices associated with the veneration of relics.

Other practices related to relics arose because these objects were understood to be sources of spiritual power, effective for bringing about cures, for warding off evil, and for assuring both heavenly and worldly blessings. Prayers offered in the presence of relics petitioned the venerated saint to intercede with God. Sacramental acts sought to share in this power; the celebration of Holy Eucharist at a saint's tomb, or on an altar embedded with relics, was a common early Christian practice. Indeed, the Second Council of Nicaea in 787 prescribed that the enclosure of relics in the altar was a prerequisite for the formal consecration of a Christian church. This prescription anticipates a scene in which the religious practices of administering and partaking of the sacraments occur in the context of the church as cosmogram and the altar as reliquary—two self-referring signs respectively providing conceptions of world and self which make the related religious practices meaningful.

The veneration of relics is not a universal religious phenomenon. Of the major world religions only Buddhism has been like Christianity in showing official approval and popular support for this practice. Emperor Asoka's distribution of relics of Buddha (supposedly 84,000 of them!) throughout his empire figured prominently in the spread of Buddhism in India in the third century before the Christian era.[21] Reasons for this uneven pattern include the highly paradoxical nature of relics as symbols and the abuses which their veneration invited. The remains of a dead person are regarded as impure in most cultures, not venerable; they normally signify death and impermanence, not the power of transcendent spiritual life. This taint of impurity probably accounts for the relatively small role that relics played in classical Hinduism. The potential for idolatry cautioned Jewish and Islamic monotheists from encouraging the veneration of relics.

By the late Middle Ages abuses were evident in the practices associated with Christian relics. Geoffrey Chaucer satirized the venality of Pardoners and others who trafficked in relics; John Calvin trenchantly condemned the superstitious mentality of those who venerated them. Their works stand at the beginning of modern Christian and humanist traditions which deprecate relics and their veneration. Yet I do not think that even widespread concurrence with these criticisms diminishes the importance of the phenomenon underlying the veneration of relics, though it does impugn some official theological rationales for it. Even the secular activities of travelling to museums to see "first-hand" a Pablo Picasso painting or Hank Aaron's bat are partially motivated by a desire to be transformed in some way by the power of these objects and to be conformed to the human character of the persons with whom they had significant physical contact. Though shunned by sophisticated psychological portraitists, synecdochic significations of personal identity thrive in the popular imagination. They figure as favorite clues in detective stories: a "tuft of tawny hair" is a central clue of guilt in Poe's "Murders in the Rue Morgue," and "fiery red hair" serves as a clue of misdirection in Conan Doyle's "The Red-Headed League." Relics of the second order continue to provide symbolic signatures for mythic heroes: the Jedi Knights in the *Star Wars* trilogy have swords as distinctive as Arthur's Excalibur.

Suspicions about traditional vehicles of extraordinary meaning like relics has helped make words the preeminent signs of contemporary intellectuals. Words used as predicates sometimes create a similar type of ambiguity as was displayed by relics. When one says "the desk is brown" one is designating some specific desk as a physically singular entity, but when one says "the desk is cluttered" one is referring to some specific desk along with the things on or in the desk; the predicate 'cluttered' tells how these various constitutive elements are arranged. Thus these two predicates suggest the potential ambiguity of the designating phrase 'the desk': it may signify a bare physical object or that object along with a collection of associated objects. The increase in syntactic complexity of this last example makes possible problems of multiple meaning as subtle as found in the Liar paradox. 'I am a liar' is one of its variants. In this case the ambiguity in the scope of the predicate—does it extend to all assertions the speaker makes or all except this assertion itself?—infects the self designated by the name 'I'. Is that self a liar or a truth-teller? The supplementation of extensional by intensional semantic notions expands the varieties of semiotic self-reference.

This example is also especially noteworthy because the individual name which is its grammatical subject directly designates a human subject, a self. The contemporary American philosopher Robert Nozick has recently formulated a conception of selfhood which relies heavily on the notion of semiotic self-reference. In *Philosophical Explanations* he writes with provocative brevity: "To be an I, a self, is to have the capacity for reflexive self-reference."[22] As I understand it, what is involved in this claim is something more complex than just using language to name oneself, as, for instance, a chimpanzee who has learned gestural sign language might do by signing "Feed me." It is also more complex than using language to refer to itself as language, as, for instance, a computer might do via the contrivance of "Gödel numbering" in a formal language.[23] "Something X which could refer to X, but not reflexively, is not an I, not a self."[24] Reflexive self-reference is using language to refer to the self as a user of language, or, put somewhat differently, using language to refer to language via the self which uses that language. The utterance of the Liar sentence 'I am lying' achieves this end, as does the non-paradoxical utterance 'I am speaking English.' The use of the first person pronoun is not essential in either case, but some indexical device which relates speaker and utterance in a common context is required.

Nozick offers his conception of selfhood as an alternative to views which assume the self's independent existence, as do, for instance, traditional notions of the soul, or which infer its precarious unity, as does Hume's understanding of the self as a bundle of perceptions. Reflexive self-reference for him involves a dynamic yet integral process of "self-synthesis." An implication of Nozick's view is that to be a self is to use language in a way that is sufficiently complex to generate ambiguity and paradox, yet sufficiently structured so as to avoid radical skepticism. Many religious thinkers come to this conclusion via a different route. They insist that one cannot speak of God, or the ultimate principle of reality, without broaching ambiguity and paradox; yet they insist at the same time that one cannot be fully human without seeking to understand and address what is ultimate in life, through prayers of praise and confession or through some other spiritually disciplined practice. The practice of prayer gives excellent evidence of the paradoxical character of embodied spiritual existence and of the utility of using semiotic self-reference to describe spiritual practices.

Prayer is typically conversation with God. The success of conversation requires that participants heed certain pragmatic rules. For instance, they must forsake idiosyncratic word meanings, and forego dishonest or deceptive discourse. Practically acknowledging the context of interest and action in which a conversation occurs is part of this prerequisite. At least in Western monotheistic traditions, prayer is conversation which occurs in the context of a drama of salvation. Sincere conversation with God presupposes a turning toward God, or repentance, and on God's part, a predisposition to mercy. Understood in this way prayer constitutes a decisive moment in a spiritual biography and is as much a devotional act as an act of verbal discourse.

Prayer may be divided into two general forms: praise of God or confession of fault. Prayers of gratitude and prayers of petition both presuppose that God has something of which human beings are needful, and they thereby serve the broader themes of praise. The opening prayer of the Koran prayed by pious Muslims many times a day strongly stresses the theme of praise:
    In the Name of God, the Merciful, the Compassionate
       Praise belongs to God, the Lord of All-Being,
       the All-Merciful, the All-Compassionate,
       the Master of the Day of Doom.

> Thee only we serve; to Thee alone we pray for succor.
>   Guide us in the straight path,
> the path of those whom Thou hast blessed,
> not of those against whom Thou art wrathful,
>   nor of those who are astray.[25]

So great is the emphasis on praise of God that human faults are only mentioned indirectly in the reference to "those who are astray." Still even this reference occurs in the third person and in the context of a petition for guidance.

No writings illustrate confessional prayer better than those of Augustine of Hippo. Yet his confessions are too complex to be merely typical. For instance, he alludes to the basic duality of praise and confession when he begins the *Confessiones* with the following prayer: "Grant me, Lord, to know and understand whether a man is first to pray to you for help or to praise you, and whether he must know you before he can call you to his aid."[26] Should the person who prays to God first acknowledge human need, or divine greatness? Conflict is crucial to drama and Augustine clearly appreciates that it is central to the act of prayer. Notice that in asking this question about petition and praise Augustine is himself requesting something from God— "Da mihi, Domine . . ." His way of speaking in questioning answers implicitly the questions he asks. Prayer is not only a conversation with God but it is a devotional act before God and amidst the church. Insofar as prayer concerns how one should act in God's presence it is self-referring: it speaks about itself and not always with complete clarity and consistency. Augustine was a master at using rhetorical practice to exemplify how fallible human beings encounter a transcendent God.

The nature of prayer as a religious speech act is succinctly revealed in the New Testament pericope about the Pharisee and the tax collector recorded in Luke 18:9–14:

> He (Jesus) also told this parable to some who trusted in themselves that they were righteous and despised others: "Two men went up into the temple to pray, one a Pharisee and the other a tax collector. The Pharisee stood and prayed thus with himself, 'God, I thank thee that I am not like other men, extortioners, unjust, adulterers, or even like this tax collector. I fast twice a week, I give tithes of all that I get.' But the tax collector, standing far off, would not even lift up his eyes to heaven, but beat his breast, saying, 'God, be

merciful to me a sinner!' I tell you, this man went down to his house justified rather than the other; for every one who exalts himself will be humbled, but he who humbles himself will be exalted".

Both prayers have a self-denying or apophatic character. The Pharisee's prayer is an act of self-praise, commending his own justice and piety. Yet if humility and charity are regarded as integral to these virtues, then the Pharisee's prayer is an impious action because of his quick praise of himself and his peremptory condemnation of the tax collector. What the Pharisee affirms in words he denies by deed. The tax collector's confession of sin is simple, direct, and genuinely humble. The most profound confession is one which acknowledges that sin is an enduring condition, not only marring past acts but also making present actions less than perfect. Hence when the speech act of prayerful confession is obediently performed it admits that even confessions are tainted by some disobedience; it implies that if a confession of sin is well done, then it is not done well enough. Both the prayer of the Pharisee and the tax collector have an apophatic character arising from the capacity of prayer to refer to itself as a certain type of action. However, the self-denial of the tax collector is conscious and contrite, and so compatible with God's mercy, while the self-denial of the Pharisee is inadvertent and unmotivated, and so not incompatible with God's condemnation. Crudely stated, the former counts as a spiritual credit and the latter as a spiritual debit.

Prayer as a spiritual discipline, for instance, as formalized in a daily office of prayer, involves a commitment to make God a constant actor in the drama of one's spiritual life. It is also an acknowledgment that the language of prayer should not aspire to the eloquence that might please or persuade an audience, but must always be bound up with paradoxical limitations especially well revealed in speech in the presence of transcendent divinity. Prayer is that type of human speech which constitutes human selfhood in its spiritual dimensions—in its capacity for relating itself to the totality of things. Bertrand Russell said that the possibility of paradox arises when one tries to speak of totalities of which one is oneself a member. It just such inclusive totalities that Ludwig Wittgenstein said one must pass over in silence. Prayer refuses to be silent before the greatest totality it recognizes as God. Augustine prays: "Can anyone say enough when he speaks of you?" and assuming a negative response, he continues, "Yet woe betide those who are silent about you!"[27]

Confessional prayer is an exemplary spiritual practice because it gives uncommonly articulate expression to the paradox of spiritual life. It points to an encompassing transcendent reality with which it seeks to establish a right relationship and thereby find spiritual peace, yet the very action which accomplishes this signification reveals its agent to be particular, fallible, and distinct from what it signifies. The claim made here is that semiotic self-reference is peculiarly helpful for describing such practices: self-referring cosmographical signs reveal the world posited, self-referring relics reveal the self presupposed, and self-referring confessional prayer reveals the problematical status of spiritual practices designed to reconcile self and world.

Although very few attestations of the utility of this descriptive theme have and can be made now, I do contend that its relevance is not restricted to theistic prayers of confession. The opening pages of the *Kena Upaniṣad*, for instance, contain a speculative dialogue where similar material occurs. It begins with a pupil asking the master what empowers mind, speech, and life. The master responds by saying that this power is something transcendent: "There the eye goes not, speech goes not, nor the mind; we know not, we understand not how one can teach this."[28] This is an instance of apophatic self-reference; it is like predicating ineffability of God, saying that no statements about God are ultimately true, yet then recognizing that the very predication of ineffability is one such statement.[29] The master proceeds to specify, indirectly, the transcendent power as *brāhman*: "That which is not expressed through speech but that by which speech is expressed; that, verily, know thou, is *brāhman*, not what people here adore."[30] The fully paradoxical character of this divine wisdom is then explicitly acknowledged: "To whomsoever it is not known, to him it is known; to whomsoever it is known, he does not know."[31] The teaching ends with a recommendation of "austerities, self-control and work" as aids for securing knowledge of *brāhman*.[33] Practice and knowledge are closely connected, and the practice by which a pupil gains knowledge from a master exemplifies this truth.

PRESENCES AND ABSENCES

Signs are used to refer to things in the world; they do so by pointing selectively to certain objects, thereby making them the precise foci of human attention. From the phenomenological point of view, one which takes intentional acts of consciousness to be the essential dynamic of signification, they also contribute to the constitution of objects and the world in which they reside. This object-constituting and world-making capacity is what qualifies phenomenological intentions as something more than just another intensional semantic notion. By investigating the interplay of the full and the empty, and the whole and the part, especially as they are manifest in language, Edmund Husserl made a case for the distinctiveness of intentionality as a font of meaning, and in so doing, he inaugurated phenomenology as a movement in twentieth-century philosophy.[33]

According to Husserl, intentional acts of consciousness may be filled or empty, being filled if the object intended is perceptually present, and empty if it is absent. The whole of which empty and filled intentions are parts is the recognition of identity. The empty intention of an apple is the consciousness of that apple as we remember or anticipate it in its absence. Its filled intention is the consciousness of holding it in one's hand, seeing it, and biting into it. The same object is intended in both cases; indeed, the identity of the apple is constituted by the distinctive ways in which it can be present and absent. Identity is the constancy within presence and absence. One way in which signs help to constitute the objects to which they refer is by promoting this process of identification.

All intended objects have an accompanying sensible content; there is no pure thought. Perceptual intentions partake of the sensible content of the actual object intended; the interplay of presence and absence in this case is constituted by the arising and passing of partial intentions in the experience of a perceptual whole. Signs effect the presentation of what is absent; this definition dates back to the Stoics. It was adopted by Augustine who found it suggestive of divine revelation because an immaterial God always remains partially absent, even when sensed to be present. (*De doctrina Christiana* 2.1) In general, the sensible character of the sign is not identical nor even similar to the sensible content of the intended object. The object signified may be currently absent though once conjoined to the sign, as in the case of smoke signifying fire or footprints signifying animals. In a different manner the object signified may be more radically absent, absent for some principled reason, as in linguistic signs whose general character is to be arbitrarily related to what they signify. Thus there is a dynamic of presence and absence within perception, but also there is a doubling of this dynamic in the special case of perception via signs, because signs, even when perceptually present, are presenting something which is absent. By promoting a diversity of ways of being present and absent signs help to identify objects.

The phenomenological approach to semiotic reference differs appreciably from the extensional and intensional semantics previously noted. They are not compatible on all points. I myself resist Husserl's more idealistic claims, preferring to understand the natural world instead of the transcendental ego as the most concrete reality; accordingly, I regard meaningful identification via signs as only a partial constituent of the objects of consciousness. Still I believe that naturalistic and phenomenological perspectives can complement one another in describing how signs refer. The contemporary American philosopher Robert Sokolowski has described the relationship between them in a very helpful way:

> If phenomenological discourse is to brighten natural language, it must be continuous with it; but if phenomenological discourse speaks of objects as phenomena, there must be a break between it and mundane language which speaks about objects in the world. . . . Since natural language actualizes objects for us, phenomenological language has to take natural language into itself in order to secure its own objects, i.e., the objects as phenomena. Transcendentalese has to quote the vernacular.[34]

Quotation, of course, is a device by which language users refer to language; usually speakers and writers cite the language of someone other than themselves.[35] Quotation thus counts as an indirect or global form of linguistic self-reference. The phenomenological quotation of natural language is, for Sokolowski, just another instance of the method of "bracketing existence"—of suspending belief in the existence of an object as a natural entity so as to engage it as a phenomenological object. In this context semiotic self-reference is not a special variety of sign, but instead, it is how all signs are construed when approached from the phenomenological point of view, i.e., when interpreted as quotations of natural language simulacra.

Phenomenological inquiry into the way things are involves a quest for a consciousness of fulfillment. In Husserl's view the identity of an object is most fully experienced when there is a lived transition from an empty to a filled intending of the object: the more diverse and novel is this transition, the more fully is the object engaged. Signs promote this fulfillment in a specific way. Signs present to the human mind a reality which is something more than what the sign itself is. Signs allow one to think about an object in its absence. This thinking includes developing strategies for re-engaging the object as a filled intention in novel ways, thereby making the object more distinctive and meaningful. The fulfillment of consciousness in this sense requires a fullness of meaning; the prescription to pursue truth and fulfillment are one and the same. When the re-engagement of the object involves relating it to the parts or moments of other objects, then this articulation is called a fact by Husserl. A fact is registered when it is experienced perceptually and it is reported when it is experienced in the absence of the perceptual ingredients. Reflection upon facts brings about a shift of focus which is synonymous with the framing of judgments. Descriptive human judgments—supposed facts as supposed—are full if they provide genuine knowledge of the world. The world both confirms judgments and is constituted as a *Lebenswelt* by ways of living with facts.

In this essay spiritually disciplined practices have been identified as regimens of action which relate the practitioner to the world as a whole in ways that are believed to promote a fullness of human life. They cultivate a certain way of living with facts, especially as the relevant parts or moments are subsumed within the most extensive of wholes. Husserl's phenomenology of signs helps to give more definite meanings to key elements of the conception of a spiritually disciplined life emerging here. Husserl provides a semantics that explains meaning not only in terms of individual objects and ideas, but also in terms of a self's intentions and encompassing world, both of which figure prominently in the meaning of spiritual discipline. The fullness which is the goal of spiritual life is given a greater definiteness by its parallel to Husserl's notion of a filled intention: it comes to include a directing of consciousness towards reality as a whole which has a sense of an experienced presence as its fulfillment. Theists describe this experience of maximum fulfillment as an encounter with God.

Since Paul Ricoeur's adaptation of phenomenological methodology for the study of religion in his *The Symbolism of Evil*, there have been increasing attempts to describe religious experiences via a phenomenology of signs.[36] It seems a plausible strategy; a philosophical method placing great stress on the interplay of presence and absence seems suited for describing religious symbolism, something said to convey a commanding presence by many and an equally impressive absence by others. Also, even many religious persons report that alternating experiences of God's presence and absence are an ineluctable feature of religious life. Consideration of fasting regimens and icon veneration will illustrate the descriptive value of a phenomenological account of semiotic self-reference.

Fasting is a spiritual practice of great antiquity. Fasting, and its counterpart, feasting, are practices which together constitute a very visceral realization of a sacred presence and absence. Religious fasting is commonly a preparatory act in which people abstain from food so as gain some esoteric communication. In the Western philosophical tradition fasting was a practice attributed to the mystical and philosophical followers of Pythagoras. Of Apollonius of Tyana, a Neopythagorean, Philostratus wrote that his extraordinarily clear and prescient dreams, were in large part due to his eating habits (*Vita Apollonii* 2.37). In the Bible Moses, Elijah, and Jesus are said to have fasted for forty days before they received important communications from God. In the Biblical context fasting is not only preparatory, but penitential. Food is an organic material subject to decay and contagion, and so ridding the body of food readily signifies spiritual purification. The fasting of Jews on Yom Kippur and Christians during Lent are communal expressions of this purificatory meaning of fasting.

By engendering the experience of the absence of food fasting is thought to promote the experience of the presence of God. Feasting, in a quite different way, presupposes food to be the organic material that sustains life; feasting consists of consuming food with joy as a gift from God. In the Islamic religious year the month of Ramadān, during which dawn to dusk fasts are maintained by pious Muslims, concludes with the celebration of 'Īd al-Fitr—a feast of fast breaking. In a similar manner the yearly period of pilgrimage, or *hajj*, includes penitential fasting and concludes with a feast—the 'Īd al-Adha. Fasting and feasting are empirically correlative practices. Philosophically they are inseparable as well. They are both practices in which the human body is a vehicle of signification as well as the agent which perceives the sign's meaning. Abstention from food gives rise to intense bodily sensations and unusual states of consciousness; so too does the consumption of food and drink, especially of intoxicants. That hunger pangs may be interpreted as the pain of a sinner or the exaltation of the saint is very important. That God's presence may be bodily symbolized by the abstention or consumption of nourishment is equally significant. The paradoxical consciousness wrought by pious fasting in anticipation of pious feasting serves to bracket the naturalistic experience and give it a phenomenological character. The literal existence or nonexistence of food in one's stomach is not the crucial issue. What is phenomenologically encountered in either case is some form of ultimate reality which is thought to be a font of spiritual fullness. The visceral character of this encounter contributes to a vivid apprehension of intentions being "filled" in the phenomenological sense, whether the fullness be also biological, as with feasting, or paradoxically spiritual, as with fasting. Fasting and feasting are in a sense paradigmatic spiritual disciplines according to the description offered here: they most literally involve a process of intentional emptying and filling-of creative self-transformation through an embodied realization of paradoxical self-conceptions.

In the three sections of this chapter dealing with semiotic self-reference, meditation, prayer, and fasting have been treated as characteristic types of spiritual discipline. In each section, signs, either pictorial, verbal, or bodily, have been used to intensify self-consciousness in a manner designed to promote consciousness of God or sacred totality. Spiritual discipline has been implicitly identified with practical modes of cultivating self-awareness via semiotic self-reference. Given the discussion of the interplay of presence and absence in perception and signification it may be concluded that this emphasis on self-presence is one-sided. Spiritual discipline also involves practical modes for cultivating self-absence. Christians may seek the righteousness of faith—the right relation of the soul to God, but Buddhists seek the cure for suffering—the vanquishment of the phenomenological self. Yet it is wrong to see Christian and Buddhist spiritual practices as simply polar opposites. Self-presence and self-absence are correlative terms and give rise respectively to processes one might call self-referencing and self-vanquishing—a representation of the self to the self and then the overcoming of that representation in deference to a totality which embraces but transcends it. A philosophical conception of spiritual discipline must give full acknowledgment to both dimensions.

Celebratory disciplines are specific types of action. Celebrative techniques include feasting, dancing, ritual eroticism, spectacles, singing, dreaming/hallucinating, and all communal rituals. To the extent that selfhood is associated with the characteristic possessions and actions of a biological self, each of these celebrative techniques involve a cultivation of self-presence. Yet insofar as communal activities involve deference of personal consciousness to a consciousness of group actions, they are techniques of self-absence. In a contrary manner, ascetic disciplines are specific types of inaction. Ascetic techniques are fasting, sitting (*zazen*), chastity, poverty, silence, vigils, and solitude. By denying the self food, motion, possessions and such, these activities promote self-absence. Yet by directing consciousness away from ordinary activities of eating, speaking and socializing, they also promote an intensified self-consciousness or self-presence.

Naturalistic and phenomenological perspectives differently interpret the interplay of presence and absence in spiritually disciplined practices. I think that it is as a spiritual dialectic of self-presence and self-absence—as a process of self-referencing and self-vanquishing in the context of some apprehension of a maximally inclusive reality—that spiritual discipline obtains a distinctive identity. Religious doctrines tend to immobilize this interplay by giving substantive and propositional content to these correlative moments; religious fervor tends to accent the ascetic and celebrative elements unequally. Spiritual practices, when undertaken in the plurality of its celebrative and ascetic forms, works to reactivate the process by which the self is identified in its relation to the natural world, and then is overcome in deference to the inclusive totality that contains but transcends it. In this sense spiritual practice is the experiential counterpart of religious doctrines both as their practical fruition and as their practical antagonist.

This twofold movement of spiritual discipline was operative in Pascal's solution to his exemplary predicament. It was noted earlier that Pascal believed that spiritually disciplined practices could help a person break the hold of diverting habits by concentrating the mind on what really matters. They helped to vanquish the gaming mentality and absent the practitioner from the social milieu in which it flourished. Yet, also, if the practices were acts of prayer or ritual, they could help to incline the personality toward a faith that may not yet have been acquired. It could help introduce one to the company of persons who experience God's presence as revealed in Jesus Christ. Under the influence of Jacques Derrida it has become common to portray Christian theology as an epitome of a "metaphysics of presence" in which God is accorded a manner of presence more total than any other thing perceived or signified.[37] Religious life then becomes the project of cultivating divine presence. Yet this characterization of Christian theology only acknowledges one part of the self-presence/self-absence dynamic discussed here. The feaster fasts and the faster feasts because no degree of consumption or abstention is adequate to embody symbolically the paradoxical apprehension of complex wholeness to which both the faster and feaster defer.

Icons reveal the interplay of presence and absence with special clarity. At the same time they raise issues that challenge the appropriateness of the idiom of semiotic self-reference to the task of resolving Pascal's predicament. Like mandalic images icons are frequently objects of meditation, and like relics they are often prayerfully venerated; icons are thus important aids for important spiritual practices. In Eastern Orthodox Christianity icons of Christ are paradigmatic. The challenge of iconoclastic emperors led theologians like John of Damascus to acknowledge that while God is present in the iconic image insofar as it is a vehicle for communion with the transcendent, God is also absent because the icon is a material object; this latter point protected its venerators from accusations of idolatry.[38] The icon is both different from and similar to what it represents; it does not simply represent the embodied selfhood of the saint, its proximate referent, nor does it adequately capture the transcendent reality of God, its ultimate referent. It is both material and spiritual; in the former capacity God is absent, while in the latter God is present. This duality mirrors the two natures of the Incarnate Christ.

Technical implications of this understanding were that the margins and frames for icons were handled to stress materiality, while realistic mediums of representation, like oil-based paints, were shunned as incompatible with the icon's spiritual subject matter.[39] Artistic conventions changed from realism to abstractionism to accentuate the picture's materiality and the spirituality of its ultimate referent.[40] In a sense, one could say that the icon's most proximate referent was to itself as a visual medium. This self-reference has the effect Sokolowski describes: it brackets the icon's existence as a natural object so as to make possible its phenomeno-logical engagement. Given the Athanasian formula that God became human so that human beings might become God, the meditation on icons in Eastern Orthodox spirituality may be construed as a means for both encountering the sacred and for being conformed to it. Such meditation promotes an identification of self and sacred totality not unlike the microcosm/macrocosm dynamic operative in mandalic and relic symbolism.

Icons are not unique in their receptivity to dual description as material and more than material objects. If one hands a volume of a Shakespeare play to a printer and a critic, and then asks for a description of the book, one should expect different sorts of answers. The printer will most likely respond by speaking of the book's paper quality and binding strength, while the critic will perhaps summarize its plot and categorize it as a comedy, tragedy, or historical drama. Of course, a full description of the volume would need to integrate both types of responses. Increasingly this sort of descriptive duality is an issue in modern forms of art. Martha Graham's dances have no narrative structure; Jackson Pollock's painting no naturalistic object; and John Ashberry's poems no realistic voice. Hence they resist description in terms of what they are about; they invite phenomenological and formalistic accounts. Yet people almost instinctively bring naturalistic expectations to art works, and while they may not be eradicable, they can be resisted. Each of the artists just mentioned employ artistic strategies that encourage the bracketing of naively existential questions in order that a more vivid encounter might be had of movements, images and words as self-subsistent phenomena.

Unlike icons, works of modern art rarely have associated with them a doctrine indicating what, though materially absent, is being spiritually presented. In modern art the question may be raised as to whether there is a spiritual dimension to the art work's meaning, but it is seldom expressly answered. Many persons for whom religion has ceased to be meaningful as dogma and confession still are attracted to its stories, rituals, and art. For them these religious varieties of signification take on the tentatively questioning character of modern art. Religion, in a sense, then becomes a province in the art world. Not a bad change many critics of religion may say, but, in turn, a more traditional adherent of Biblical traditions might counter by noting that just as forces in contemporary culture tend to remake religion as art, so to do these same forces tend to remake art as mere entertainment. Crassly commercial considerations can transform artistic presentations into the sort of diversion which Pascal said people use to avoid inquiring honestly into life's profounder meaning. The salvific doctrines and fervent devotion which accompany religious practices of discipline and worship have traditionally prevented them from devolving to the status of diverting entertainments. Thus conceptions of spiritual discipline which shun schemes of salvation, prefer aesthetic descriptions, and encourage critical reflection become particularly vulnerable to the charge of a lack of spiritual seriousness. A major aim of the next chapter will be to counter suspicions that philosophically rethinking spiritual discipline in terms of semiotic self-reference and like notions is not itself a manifestation of *divertissement spirituelle*.

CHAPTER 4

Physical Symmetry

Something which is balanced and well-proportioned, and which has parts comprising an integral whole, is commonly called symmetrical. In Greek 'symmetry' ($\sigma\upsilon\mu\mu\epsilon\tau\rho\iota\alpha$) literally means 'with measure' or 'in accordance with a rule'; its Latin translation is 'commensurable'. In a development similar to how semiotic self-reference has become an important idea for explaining linguistic paradoxes, symmetry has emerged in the twentieth century as an important idea for explaining physical reality and human creativity.[1] In fact, it has regained something of the prominence it had in ancient Greek thought. I shall review the meanings of symmetry in order to give an initial plausibility to its use as a categoreal theme for describing spiritually disciplined practices. In preparation for arguing that symmetry, in both its structural and functional expressions, is a preferable way of describing what Clement and other traditional thinkers described in terms of unencumbered causes, I shall also indicate some historical precedents for employing symmetry in philosophical reflections about spiritual life.

A distinctive feature of the rational strain of ancient Greek culture was an abhorrence of everything indefinite. The geometrical method canonized in Euclid's *Elementa* sought to minimize the number of undefined concepts and underived axioms in formal proofs; its relative success in doing so set a standard of logical rigor which philosophers have long emulated. The Pythagorean identification of number as the cosmic *Urstoff* improved upon the Ionian alternatives of water and air in the sense that it postulated as fundamental something readily specifiable in form and magnitude. The discovery of incommensurable magnitudes, such as the length of the diagonal of an isosceles triangle with sides of unit length, was deeply disturbing to Greek mathematicians, especially the Pythagoreans. Equally problematic for Pythagoreans were the paradoxes of Zeno of Elea which argued that motion is impossible if one assumes the infinite divisibility of space and time. Pythagoreans believed that to be is to be something with form and measure; incommensurability and infinity as a consequence took on the connotation of nonbeing.

Parmenidean Eleatics agreed, but more radically added plurality to the list of illusory qualities and accepted the consequence that all reality must be one and unchanging.

Plato was a disciple of both Pythagoras and Parmenides, and he speculated in the *Timaeus* (53–56) that physical reality was originally constituted by the combinations of the five regular, i.e., highly symmetrical, polyhedra. This was a memorable, if implausible, compromise. Still, it vividly captures how symmetrical form was taken by an influential tradition of Greek rationalism to be the quintessential property of physically created reality. In more subtle variations this rational tradition persists. Willard Van Orman Quine's semantic formula that "To be is to be the value of a variable (in the language of first-order logic)" shows how some philosophers believe that traditional standards of logical rigor are requisite, if not to determine what there is, then certainly to converse productively about it.[2] Among contemporary physicists intuitions about symmetry have provided crucial guidance for theorizing about the number and classification of elementary particles; however, even the most attractively symmetrical account of the basic units of matter is today subjected to experimental verification in a way not at all Platonic.

Greek religion was far from consistently rational; and Biblical religion is even much less so. Thus if symmetry is to be helpful for philosophically informed descriptions of spiritual practices it must account for apprehensions of the mysterious dynamism of the world as well as for its enduring structure. As Nietzsche has forcefully reminded philosophers, the Greeks have bequeathed to Western culture not only the spirit of Apollo, but of Dionysus as well. In this regard the truism of rationalist ontology, that what is is symmetrical, should be compared with a second truism, this one from romanticist psychology, that says that human creativity in its profoundest expressions involves a willingness to depart from traditional forms and rules. Symmetry making needs supplementation by symmetry breaking.

Perhaps the most ancient use of the word 'symmetry' was to describe the ideal of physical perfection embodied in classical art. Two magnitudes were deemed commensurable if there was a third which could be divided into them both without remainder; a statue or building was symmetrical if it was a whole composed of commensurable parts. One perceptible part was regarded as a modular unit whose elaboration was the aesthetic key of a given art work; for instance, the finger was sometimes accorded this significance for human statuary. An explicit definition of symmetry in modular terms is contained in the *De Architectura* (111.1) of the Roman Vitruvius. The ideal, however, was articulated much earlier in the fifth-century BCE "Canon of Polykleitos"; this treatise has not survived, but Roman copies of statues attributed to Polykleitos have endured, and one, in particular, the Doryphoros, was thought especially to embody the principles of the Canon.[3] Through the influence of this exemplar the Canon came to include the aesthetic imperative of counterbalancing elements in the human figure; for instance, the alternation of tensed with relaxed musculature was enjoined, this being especially appropriate as a chiastic pattern of tension among the shoulders and hips. Here is suggested the breaking of a rigid bilateral symmetry; so there is evidence from the most ancient sources that due proportion and the breaking of symmetry are capable of being complementary aesthetic phenomenon.

More vivid illustrations of symmetry breaking as a mark of creativity are provided by the musical arts. Music, of course, takes place in time instead of space. So instead of having the duplication of a temple column at some fixed distance, for example, one has the repetition of a melody at some regular temporal interval; in technical terminology, there is translation in time instead of space. A major part of the appreciation of music consists of the listener's ability to identify musical structures, often intuitively, in a way that allows him or her to anticipate the music's temporal unfolding. Enjoyment comes both from correctly anticipating the composer's intentions, but also from being surprised by novel variations and departures from established musical structures.[4]

Musical structures are fashioned within a given musical composition, but they are also more globally established by conventional musical forms. For instance, Joseph Haydn is generally credited with crystallizing the string quartet as a musical form: in contrast to the rare quartets of his Italian precursors he published a large body of music for this genre, often in related sets of six; in contrast to Baroque string trios and violin concertos he gave the violins, viola, and cello independent and nearly equal voices; and in contrast to his own symphonic works which shared the sonata form, he maintained a spirit of conversational intimacy while adhering to strict structural requirements. Although Haydn wrote the first masterpieces for the string quartet genre, the title of its greatest master is usually reserved for Ludwig van Beethoven.[5] In part this accolade is an acknowledgment of historical circumstance, because unlike Haydn and more than Mozart, Beethoven had a corpus of great classical string quartets from which to learn and for which he provided stunning formal and emotional variations. Even in his first Opus 18 quartets Beethoven's modulation to third-related keys (instead of to the classical fifth or dominant key) is more frequent and pronounced than in Haydn's last works for this medium. The sheer length of the Razumovsky quartets—often attained while shunning traditional repetitions, thereby increasing the wealth of musical material—was said to have stunned initial listeners into incomprehension, but they are now credited with having elevated the string quartet from private entertainment to serious art. Beethoven was able to achieve a higher level of formal complexity than his predecessors because the modular elements he elaborated were themselves more complex; he was thereby able to elicit more subtle anticipatory expectations from the listener and to confirm or surprise them more variously.

The slow movements of Beethoven's final quartets are often cited as model communications of emotional depth and sensual intensity by purely musical (i.e., nonvocal) means. The classical ideal of symmetry in Greek statuary likewise combined abstract principles of form with a vivid sensual immediacy; it helped establish a conception of beauty which Stoics like Chrysippus bluntly identified with symmetry itself. Platonist philosophers applauded the generalizing impulse of their Stoic counterparts, but balked at any formulation involving reason and sense wherein the former did not dominate the latter. Beauty in its sensual manifestations should be subject to absolute beauty as the correlate of eternal goodness and truth; this is the concluding lesson of the dialogue recounted in the *Symposium* (211–12).

Through Stoic influence of this sort symmetry subsequently became a central idea in classical conceptions of virtue. Panaetius of Rhodes, the founder of Roman Stoicism, affirmed the traditional Stoic belief that virtue is identifiable with knowledge and informed action, yet he understood knowledge less scientifically and informed action less rigorously than did his Greek forebears. Knowledge was characteristically self-knowledge for him, and ethical action was decorum, or actions in harmony with the larger wholes of personal character, societal duties, and natural regularities. Symmetry thus came to characterize not only beauty of body but also beauty of soul and action. The eclectic thinker Galen in *De temperamentis* understood symmetry to connote that state of mind equally removed from opposite extremes; John Chrysostom used this same meaning in his homiletic exegesis of Christian Scripture.

Augustine of Hippo imported this sensibility into the Western Christian tradition. He did not explicitly use the word 'symmetry' in *De ordine*, his philosophical dialogue about the order of the universe; I suspect he was influenced in this respect by Plotinus' rejection of symmetry as the distinguishing mark of beauty (*Enneades* 1.6.1). Even so, through one of the student interlocutors, he does affirm that whatever is opposed to order is nothing, *nihil,* literally nonexistent. These remarks anticipate his later embrace of the Neoplatonic idea of evil as nonbeing. In his own voice he explains the appearance of disorder by an implicit appeal to the classical Greek notion of symmetry:

> If one were examining the details in an inlaid pavement, and if his searching eye could grasp no more than the outline of one little cube, he might censure the artificer for lacking skill of arrangement and order. On this account he might think the uniformity of the little stones disarranged, just because the drawn lines harmonizing into one integral form of beauty could not be seen and examined all at once.[6]

Augustine is saying here that people who observe disorder in the world see one modular unit of reality, but they do not apprehend the rules which combine a plurality of these units into an ordered, integral whole. In a second geometrical illustration Augustine describes orderly forms as ruled by a "law of equality" (aequalitatis iure).[7] (See also *De vera religione,* 31.57.) A law of symmetry would be a more modern description of this governing principle.

Augustine gives his conception of order an ethical and practical meaning when he says order is "that which will lead us to God, if we hold to it during life."[8] The practical question thus becomes how one apprehends this order so that one might live well. There follows affirmations of the immovability of the wise person's soul as a mark of being in right relation to God; this builds upon previous indirect affirmations of order that say "Nothing can be done without a cause."[9] Hence elements of the theme of the unencumbered cause are present here, as is advice that most persons should simply follow the dictates of authoritative teachers. Yet also there is this: for the intellectually gifted, Augustine says, reason is the best guide, especially as human rationality is realized in the quest for increasingly inclusive unity in the study of the liberal arts. In a very Pythagorean way he writes near of the end of *De ordine:*

> For to the soul that diligently considers the nature and the power of numbers, it will appear manifestly unfitting and

most deplorable that it should write a rhythmic line and play the harp by virtue of this knowledge, and that its life and very self—which is the soul—should nevertheless follow a crooked path and, under the domination of lust, be out of tune by the clangor of shameful vices.[10]

The same principles of order that rule mathematics, poetry and music, rule moral life!

Although Augustine never renounced this view, it does not reflect his mature thinking. What is lacking is a full appreciation of the problem of evil experienced psychologically as a power perverting the will to sinful actions. In *De libero arbitrio* of two years later, Augustine began formulating how human beings are responsible through abuse of God-given freedom for their captivity by sin. In later writings he charts out the three great stages of the spiritual life: the human condition in Paradise of *posse non peccare* where people are able not to sin; the fallen human condition of *non posse non peccare* where they are not able not to sin; and finally, the redeemed perfection of *non posse peccare* where Christians are not able to sin at all. The crucial point here is that redemption is not mere restoration, a return to Paradise. It is not symmetry repaired, but a broken symmetry that is creative of a new and yet greater spiritual well-being. Thus in Augustine the idea that the symmetry immanent in the whole of reality is emblematic of the spiritual fullness one realizes by being in right relation to God comes to be complemented by a related affirmation: the symmetry of an original wholeness, upon being broken by sin as the personal appropriation of evil, can lead to an unprecedented creative transformation. The goal of the spiritual life is to embark on a quest for this experientially unprecedented quality of spiritual fullness.

After the early Christian era the use of symmetry in descriptions of the spiritual life becomes less frequent. There are some significant exceptions; one is Jonathan Edwards's invocation of symmetry in his *Treatise Concerning Religious Affections* as the tenth sign of "affections that are truly holy and gracious."[11] There Edwards writes that, to be genuine, religious affections should be constant in time and space: they should be manifest upon occasions of good and bad fortune, and in contexts both social and solitary. These are injunctions in which the notion of symmetry is fairly meaningful in the sense that it bears resemblance to the way this word is used in describing physical reality; at other times Edwards exhorts symmetry when he means little more than consistency of character. In the pages that follow I shall revive this tradition of talking about spiritual dispositions and practices in terms of the notion of symmetry; I shall seek to do so in precise and informative ways. In a way similar to how semiotic self-reference proved instructive for revealing the dynamic of meaning operative in many spiritually disciplined practices, physical symmetry, I believe, will be helpful in revealing the distinctive integrity and value to which such practices aspire.

SELVES AND REFLECTIONS

The most familiar variety of symmetry, and the variety treated as exemplary by classical writers, is the bilateral kind, the symmetry of left and right; it is the kind and degree of symmetry characteristic of higher animal life. It was noted previously, in a quotation wherein Richard Feynman paraphrased the mathematician Hermann Weyl, that things are symmetrical to the extent that there is something you can do to them, such that after you have done it, they look the same as they did before. Mirrors effect such transformations. The bilateral symmetry of an image of a human body can be vividly grasped by looking into a mirror placed perpendicular to a line vertically bisecting that body—the doubled halves seems to create a whole body.[12] Of course, several important qualifications apply to the bilateral symmetry of human beings. Many internal organs are not symmetrically situated in the human body, the heart being to the left, the liver to the right, for example; and almost all people have a distinct handedness when they become adults. More important from the phenomenological point of view is that subtle departures from symmetry give human beings their unique identity. Birth marks and scars are almost always distinctive and asymmetrical; mirror images of human faces constructed by doubling one of its lateral halves are oddly amiss, suggesting a sibling similarity, but falling short of complete identity with the individual's natural countenance.

Upright posture gives animals of the primate order a second type of symmetry—the reflective symmetry which makes the experience of one primate viewing another similar to seeing his or her own frontal mirror reflection. Hence to recognize a kindred intelligent being, another self, is to envisage bilateral symmetry; quite literally, it means coming face to face with another bilaterally symmetrical organism. An enduring insight of Hegel's *Phenomenology of Spirit* is that people know themselves to be, at least, partially, what others see them as being.[13] Self-knowledge is gained from existential encounters with others. Spiritual self-knowledge is acquired by engaging the whole of reality as an existential counterpart, a famous illustration of this maxim being Rudolf Otto's phenomenology of the holy as the Wholly Other. Considerations of symmetry as a human trait give these phenomenological truths increased specificity.

Especially since the advent of religions of love like Christianity and Buddhism, a second relationship of self and other has become important for understanding spiritual life. "You shall love your neighbor as yourself," says Jesus (Mk. 12.31). Christians are enjoined to compassionately encounter other persons as if these persons were themselves transformed by placement in another body and human history. Loving actions of this sort presuppose recognition of another person as like oneself, and so deserving of care comparable to the instinct for self-preservation; yet they also presuppose the differences of circumstance which motivate particular practical activity on their behalf. "Truly, I say to you, as you did it to one of the least of these my brethren, you did it to me" (Mt. 25.40). Here Jesus is portrayed as explicitly identifying with the hungry, the sick, and the imprisoned in a way that commends compassionate service to them. Also, insofar as Jesus is an exemplar for his disciples, he is shown to encourage them to make a similar identification—to see themselves as Jesus sees himself and as Jesus wants to see them as his disciples.

The aim of this section is to explore the implications of bilateral symmetry for the spiritual life, and especially for the relationship between masters and disciples. Spiritual masters are a nearly ubiquitous fact of spiritual life; "Behind every saint stands another saint," Friedrich von Hügel wrote.[14] This relationship is especially relevant to spiritual practices because practical activities generally are not easily learned by self-instruction or text study alone. So central are spiritual models to religious life that introductions to the diversity of religious traditions can be organized around the basic types of exemplary religious personalities. Denise and John Carmody do this in their text *Shamans, Prophets, and Sages: A Concise Introduction to World Religions.*[15] They acknowledge that in pursuing this pedagogical strategy they should not allow the utility of their abstract typology to obscure the historical individuality of the human religious data. In a similar manner Robert Neville uses the models of soldiers, sages, and saints as vehicles for philosophically studying spiritual development. He shares the concern that this typological strategy may be unduly abstract, and he provides a second caveat. He cautions that the models he discusses are ideally sources of spiritual guidance, yet, in fact, they are sometimes used as guises for spiritual fakery. He urges upon his readers a strong but not immobilizing dose of skepticism.[16]

I likewise urge that historical sensitivity and skeptical reserve be brought to the understanding of the master-disciple relationship. One way to do this is describe spiritual discipline with ideas predisposed both toward the creation of orderly regimens of behavior and toward their creative transformation. I believe that the notion of unencumbered cause does not have this dual predisposition, but that the ideas of symmetry making and symmetry breaking do. The relation of symmetry breaking to processes of physical creation will be discussed in subsequent sections, but an intuitive illustration will be helpful at this point. In the late medieval period there circulated the story of Buridan's ass (though it probably did so without the aid of its putative author Jean Buridan, a fourteenth-century Parisian philosopher). The story goes that an ass became situated midway between two heaps of hay exactly equal as regards their quantity and quality. Since the ass had no grounds for preferring one heap over the other, it remained still, deliberating, and eventually starved to death. Aristotle alluded to an earlier version and G.W. Leibnitz was among those who attributed the story to Buridan (*New Essays in Human Understanding* 2.1.15.). Philosophical tradition generally linked the story to Buridan's defense of free will: a free act of will breaks the hold that equal attractions have on a person and prevents such circumstances from being a serious predicament for human beings.

There are two reasons why the predicament of Buridan's ass is chimerical, and each is instructive for the use of symmetry in describing aspects of spiritual life. First, no two heaps of hay are exactly equal; no situation is perfectly symmetrical. Symmetry as a mathematical notion is abstract and as an aesthetic one it is ideal; as applied to human behavior it can claim considerably less precision. Hence symmetry as a property of spiritual practices should not pretend to justify unyielding prescriptions or proscriptions. Second, formal constructs consciously entertained or biologically encoded serve the interests of nourishment, growth, and reproduction, not vice versa. It is more generally true that people philosophize in order to eat than that they eat in order to philosophize. An actual ass's indecision would readily be overcome by instinct, and a human being's act of free will has the same effect of extricating himself or herself from an unavailing situation. For spiritual discipline this implies that the goal-oriented nature of the spiritual life is philosophically rooted in the embodied intentionality of the agent and not in absolute ordinations authoritatively interpreted by religious specialists. It is assumed here that spiritual discipline is philosophically warranted because it purportedly promotes fullness of life for its practitioners and their community, not because it heeds God's will or natural law. Of course, dogmatic theological assertions may be made to this effect; they simply do not receive philosophical support from the alternative categoreal themes now being suggested.

Traditional Christian theology places great emphasis on the office of religious instruction. Christological reflection has often taken the form of elaborating the meaning of Jesus's special claim to the title of 'Rabbi' or 'Teacher'. Clement's *Paedagogus* and Augustine's *De magistro* well substantiate this fact. The Damascine theology of icons makes it explicit that divine revelation is typically incarnational: what is spiritual is characteristically mediated by a material medium, and the divine is mediated by the human. For the Christian who undertakes some specific form of spiritual practice, this implies that such practices are always inculcated by an authoritative teacher. Historically, this sort of authoritative teacher has taken a variety of forms—the apostolic witness, the anchorite of the Egyptian desert, the abbot of the Benedictine monastery, the Jesuit spiritual director, the Orthodox staretz, the Methodist itinerant preacher, and so on. In each case the teacher provides a sort of symmetrical self—an agent of the sacred who speaks and returns one's gaze. One need not embrace Hegel's conception of *Geist* as the transcendental subject of world history to affirm that spiritual life becomes practical when it becomes social.

Christian conceptions of spiritual mastery urge the disciple to model his or her behavior on the example of Christ: "Be imitators of me, as I am of Christ," writes Paul to the Corinthians (I Cor. 11.1). Thomas à Kempis provided an influential medieval interpretation of the *imitatio Christi* theme in his text of that same name:

> Let all the study of our heart be from now on to have our meditation fixed wholly on the life of Christ, for His holy teachings are of more virtue and strength than the words of all the angels and saints; and he who through grace has the inner eye of his soul opened to the true beholding of the Gospel of Christ will find in them hidden manna.[17]

Instructive here is the apparent equation of the Christ's life with his teachings. Note also the movement from meditation on Christ's life to a penetrating spiritual vision with "the inner eye of the soul." It is Christ's obedience to God and his suffering at the hands of a sinful world which gives Christ his salvific potency. Thomas has Jesus say the following:

> Our Lord Jesus says to His servant: As I offered Myself to God the Father for your sins, hanging all naked with My arms spread wide upon the cross, so that nothing remained in Me, but all went in sacrifice to please My Father and to appease His wrath against mankind, so in the Mass you daily ought to offer yourself freely to God as much as you can, as a pure and holy oblation.[18]

This sacramental partaking of Christ's brokenness is a prelude to yet a greater vision and a less mediate communication of grace:

> When what is perfect shall come, all use of the sacraments will cease, for they who are blessed in the heavenly glory have no need of this sacramental medicine. They take joy without end in the presence of God, beholding His glory face to face, and transformed from brightness to brightness by the Godhead.[19]

Thomas says that imitating Christ means sharing his cross and that such suffering is requisite for a "face to face" vision of God, the goal of the spiritual life. Writing as an Augustinian Canon Regular, Thomas assumes that following Christ includes fulfilling the proximate demand of obedience to one's monastic superior. So single-minded should the disciple be in the pursuit of spiritual fulfillment and so strict should the master be in enforcing the discipline which makes this fulfillment possible, that Thomas portrays human friendship as a suspect comfort: "Learn to forsake some necessary and well-beloved friend for the love of God."[20]

Even brief quotations from *The Imitation of Christ* reveal traditional Christian themes discussed and criticized in previous chapters: Thomas à Kempis is representative of the spiritual ethos that seeks "by despising the world to draw daily nearer and near to the kingdom of heaven."[21] Presently I am interested to note the unqualified character of his call to conformity to Christ's model and obedience to spiritual authority. I want to contrast with this the handling of a similar theme by Ignatius Loyola in his *Spiritual Exercises*. Ignatius cited *The Imitation of Christ* as one of his primary sources and similarities between the religious sensibilities of the two men are considerable. For instance, they both looked to the images of Christ's passion for indispensable spiritual guidance and understood Christian humility to include self-abasement and self-contempt. Nietzsche regarded these aspects of *The Imitation of Christ* as so decadent that he claimed he could not touch the book, much less read it, without feeling tainted; I suspect he would have the same reaction to the *Spiritual Exercises*. Yet because the latter work was written more for lay Christians than for monks—for persons who had not yet decided whether a life of poverty, chastity, and obedience was their true vocation—it prescribes a very different relationship between the spiritual master and disciple. For present purposes this difference is crucial.

The *Spiritual Exercises* outlines a method for the examination of conscience in which the theme of *imitatio Christi* is given an innovative and practical turn.[22] Ignatius begins with a description of his practical intent: "For just as strolling, walking, and running are bodily exercises, so spiritual exercises are methods of preparing and disposing the soul to free itself of all inordinate attachments, and after accomplishing this, of seeking and discovering the Divine Will regarding the disposition of one's life, thus insuring the salvation of his soul."[23] This passage is contained in a prefatory section giving advice to "the master of the Exercises." A master-disciple relationship is presumed throughout the text, and at the very outset, even though Ignatius is generally quite willing to enjoin obedience to the "hierarchical Church," he stipulates that the master's role is not a dictatorial one. Christian life demands a decision regarding one's true vocation but "the one who gives the Exercises should not lean to either one side or the other, but standing in the middle like the balance of a scale, he should allow the Creator to work directly with the creature, and the Creature with its Creator and God."[24] By even-handed guidance the spiritual master's task is to aid the disciple in choosing a proper vocation of service of the church, and thereby, he promotes that disciple's salvation.

Ignatius' portrait of a spiritual master differs significantly from traditional images of the monastic abbot. According to *Regula Benedicti* the abbot is "esteemed to supply the place of Christ in the monastery" and is due in every instance such total obedience as "if God Himself had given the command."[25] Since the monks have already decided upon their vocation, the abbot's task is govern and instruct by word and example. So much is the abbot the agent of decision that "at the dreadful day of judgement he is accountable for the obedience of his disciples as for his own teachings."[26] In sum, for

Benedict the person of the abbot becomes at once merged with the person of Christ and with the persons under his care; ideally they are intended to share the single salvific destiny earned by Christ.

Ignatius intends something quite different. He presents the spiritual master as another human self who facilitates the enrichment of Christian life by administering a method for the examination of conscience. The content of the exercises amplifies the manner of their administration because the exercises consist largely of imaginative encounters with Christ as a divine figure demanding response.[27] For instance, in the exercises for the second week the disciple is asked to imagine a human king appointed by God, hear his words to subjects, and respond with humility. The student is then led to engage Christ as King in the same three forms of visual imagery, verbal engagement, and active response. This pattern of visual, verbal, and attitudinal engagement is repeated several more times in this cycle of contemplations: imaginatively engaged are the three persons of the Trinity, the Virgin Mary, the Christ child at the nativity scene. The exercises frequently adopt the form of imaginative face-to-face encounters. Finally, an encounter with Christ and Lucifer is made part of the imaginative regimen. This latter exercise clearly delineates the choice between good and evil which Christian must constantly make in their lives, and it anticipates the choice of vocation which the exercises progressively approach. At the conclusion of this material for the second week of activity Ignatius provides the following exemplary reflection which he assigns to the disciple seeking discernment.

> I must have as my aim the end for which I am created, which is the praise of God our Lord and the salvation of my soul. At the same time I must remain indifferent and free from any inordinate attachments so that I am not more inclined or disposed to take the thing proposed than to reject it, nor to relinquish it rather than to accept it. I must rather be like the equalized scales of balance, ready to follow the course which I feel is more for the glory and praise of God our Lord and the salvation of my soul.[28]

Again the image of balanced scales occurs; significantly, in this usage it describes the disciple instead of the master, and it includes the tipping of the scales to one side or the other. This tipping represents the act of discernment and decision which is taken to be the disciple's own, though, made, of course, with the master's aid.

Practically this guidance includes choosing only from options approved by Christian church authorities; more subtly it means being conformed to the spiritual model of the master as someone empowered with the ability for decisive action regarding spiritual life.

The Ignatian portrait of the spiritual master is of a person, essentially similar to the disciple, but especially possessed of a balance and tranquility which trusts in God. In respect to his physical embodiment, his psychological qualities, and his theological integrity, the spiritual master possesses properties which are connoted by the several classical meanings of symmetry. The disciple learns from the master so as to appropriate this symmetry, but also the disciple breaks this symmetry, always potentially and sometimes actually, in deciding for a specific variety of disciplined life.

The categoreal theme of symmetry making and breaking is well suited to describing the Ignatian practice of spiritual direction. Its adoption, for instance, in preference to the theme of unencumbered causality, also undermines the more authoritarian conception of the master-disciple relationship evident in the *Regula Benedicti* and other traditional spiritual writings. I think that spiritual discipleship in which the tyro imitates a master but only fully attains spiritual mastery by a critical and personal appropriation of traditional teaching is a promising way to achieve the creative self-transformation which is a chief desideratum of the spiritual life. In discussing the pursuit of spiritual development in a contemporary context, Neville says something similar: "The disciple imitates the master in order to attain his or her own discipline, not in order to be a disciple of the master."[29] He further says that a modicum of skepticism and a resistance to authoritarianism means that paths of spiritual discipline today will be catholic, flexible, and syncretistic. I find this likewise to be a consequence of the process of personal appropriation I have recommended. Neville adds that this characteristically contemporary approach has its unique dangers.

> Any given individual's path of discipline is likely to be syncretistic. This is very dangerous, of course, because syncretism in discipline lends itself to the tendency never to face an absolute showdown. When a given trial of discipline becomes demanding, the temptation is to be "catholic" and to try some other path. But the crucial events in a path of discipline are indeed the showdowns. One may practice thinking of oneself as capable of autonomous decisions, but the discipline is not firm until a momentous situation is faced and grasped with confidence.[30]

In Pascal's terminology, paths of spiritual discipline are apt to devolve into diversions, not in the sense of losing their distinctive orientation, but by becoming so spiritually shallow as to become a specifically spiritual form of diversion. A dilettante is rarely seriously challenged by any of his or her many delectations. Superficiality of spiritual practice may arise from two quite opposites tendencies. A first tendency is to so uncritically follow a master that one does not deeply reflect upon the significance of what one is doing. The effort to rethink spiritual discipline from a philosophical point of view, invoking new categoreal themes in its redescription, and construing it as a species of political resistance—this effort militates against an uncritically timid form of superficiality. A second type of superficiality consists of the tendency to refrain from engaging any single spiritual path so seriously that one wagers on the way of life it presumes to be most valuable. In Neville's phrase, one avoids "showdowns." The deeper understanding of symmetry making and symmetry breaking attempted in the next two sections will allow, I think, for an antidote to this more subtle variation of the danger of diversion.

WORLDS AND COMPLETIONS

Thus far two perceptually intuitive identifications of symmetry have been given; one stressed commensurability and the other transformability. In the first case an object was said to be symmetrical to the extent that its parts were commensurable with that object taken as a whole: well-formed arms bear this relation to the entire human frame. In the second something was deemed symmetrical insofar as the effect of certain transformations retained that thing's original appearance: rotation of a sphere around any of its axes retains its spherical appearance. The close connection between the two descriptions becomes clearer as the definition of symmetry becomes more abstract, i.e., as it is defined in terms of arbitrary elements and rule-governed operations upon them.

The systematic generation of two-dimensional symmetrical patterns makes a first step in this direction. The basic elements in this process are called 'cells'; a cell may be any recognizable and repeatable visual image. Operations on cells combine them into "core patterns." There are a strictly limited number of ways in which cells can be combined into two-dimensional core patterns: (1) by the operation of translation, in which a cell moves vertically, horizontally, or diagonally a specified distance; (2) by the operation of rotation, in which a cell turns around a central point a specified number of degrees; and (3) by the operation of reflection, in which a cell is given a mirror image relative to a specified axis. Operations can be executed jointly, for instance, effecting a translation and reflection at once, and operations may be applied to core patterns as well as to original cells. In these ways more complicated patterns may be created; however, these three operations are sufficient to generate all two-dimensional symmetrical patterns.[31]

Given this account of two-dimensional symmetrical patterns it is evident how the features of commensurability and transformability are closely related to one another. Commensurability occurs because of the existence of pattern cells and core patterns; they assure that pattern parts will be related by integral ratios to the pattern whole. Transformability occurs because of the rule-governed nature of the operations performed upon basic cells and core patterns. By abstractly characterizing these operations as well as the elements upon which they act symmetry becomes identifiable as a type of mathematical structure called a group. A group in this sense consists of a system of elements and an operation applicable to two elements such that (1) every application of an operation to elements yields a single element that is also a member of the group; (2) every operation is associative in the sense that the grouping of a sequence of operations does not change the resulting element; (3) there is an element, the identity element, such that when the operation is applied to this element it remains the same element; and (4) finally, for every element there is some other element such that if the operation is applied to them both the identity element is the result.[32]

Mathematical group theory provides a formal account of symmetry. Since its initial formulation by the French mathematician Évariste Galois in the mid-nineteenth century, group theory has increasingly proved to be a powerful tool for the description of physical reality.[33] For instance, many structural traits of molecules and crystals are governed by considerations of symmetry. Of special relevance to molecules is point symmetry in which symmetry operations leave one point in space fixed. Included in the operations requisite here are rotation around an axis and reflection through a plane—variants of the two-dimensional operations already discussed. (A third operation, inversion through a point, is also crucial.) Linus Pauling succinctly indicated the role group theory plays in the description of molecular structure when he wrote: "There are no restrictions on the point symmetry elements that individual molecules can have, except that, for any molecule, the symmetry elements taken together must form a *group* in the mathematical sense"; then he provided his own paraphrase: "In essence this requires that the collection of symmetry operations be internally consistent."[34] Hence group theoretic symmetry considerations provide a principle of order that systematically specifies ideal molecular configurations. So, for instance, when individual molecules combine to form larger crystalline structures, group theory provides the descriptive chemist investigating these structures with a classification scheme that systematically denominates thirty-two distinct kinds of crystal symmetry.

Michael Polanyi, both a chemist and a philosopher, says that the theory of crystal symmetries "is not merely a scientific idealization but the formalization of an aesthetic ideal."[35] Part of what he means by this is that no principle of order is purely empirical, i.e., entirely consequent to specific observations of some circumscribed domain of physical data; rather such principles, including the theory of crystal symmetries, depends upon some antecedent distinction between order and randomness. To the extent that this distinction is more a product of perceptual intuition than methodological application it has an aesthetic character. It arises partially from the human propensity for pattern recognition and appreciation.

The physical theorizing of early Greek cosmologists sought principles of order by generalizing observable patterns of physical processes. For example, the ancient Greeks observed that changes in the weather are characterized by processes of condensation (raining and freezing) and rarefaction (melting and evaporation); one philosopher, Anaximenes, made such processes central to his account of nature, i.e., all natural change was explained as the condensation and rarefaction of air, the basic stuff of which the universe was thought to be made. Air was said to be what remained the same amidst physical transformations. Anaximenes employed a technique of generalization—he identified one pattern in nature and expanded this one pattern to account for all natural phenomena. Of course, we know now that his generalization was not well motivated by the empirical evidence, nor capable of genuinely explaining all that it tried to explain. Still his example is instructive because it shows that the impulse to speculate philosophically about the large-scale structure of the world is related to the aesthetic satisfaction which comes from completed patterns. Indeed, symmetry is a rubric which reveals the interconnection of Greek aesthetic and intellectual ideals; symmetrical commensurability is the key to the sense of proper proportion manifest in Greek art, and symmetrical transformability is the notion which underlies the Greek quest for the primary stuff which remains the same amidst the changes of the physical world. Monumental religious architecture often combines regular form and cosmographic significance; this is true of Greek temples like the Parthenon, and even more so for Egyptian pyramids like those at Giza.

Philosophical generalization was an historical precursor of physical law. Contemporary physical scientists likewise seek the regular patterns immanent in physical phenomena, and they seek to represent these regularities in systems of mathematical equations. There is a technical sense in which equations can be symmetrical, the degree of symmetricality being a measure of the extent to which they are completely solved. A more intuitive way of understanding the symmetrical character of physical law is to realize that a methodically executed scientific experiment will not yield different results if it is repeated in a different location or at a different time.[36] Translations in space and time are symmetrical operations—changing the translated entities in certain respects, while retaining essential observable physical features. This fact explains why the results of a scientist's experiment can be repeated and confirmed by scientists working in different laboratories, even in very different cultural settings. The concept of symmetry helps to explain how physical law attains its generality.

A more profound symmetrical operation from the point of view physical law is the change effected by uniform velocity in a straight line. Under this change the laws of physics remain constant—a truth first systematically stated by Isaac Newton and known as the principle of relativity. Einstein's celebrated general theory of relativity confirmed the constancy of physical law amidst changes in a physical system introduced by nonuniform motion, such as the acceleration of objects falling freely in a gravitational field. For a variety of reasons, some related to theoretical developments in quantum physics from which Einstein dissented, symmetry is increasingly supplementing causality in articulations of the character of physical law. Hence, instead of saying that when a given set of conditions satisfies the antecedent of a conditional law, this set of conditions will cause an event to occur as specified in the consequent of that same law, one might alternatively say that the set of initial conditions gives rise to an event because that event is an integral element of a second set of conditions whose symmetricality with the first is expressed by a physical law.

The Stoics were the first philosophers to connect symmetry, physical law, and human well-being. The goal of the good life for

materialists like Chrysippus was to "live in accordance with nature."
Diogenes Laertius summarizes Stoic views as saying:

> Living virtuously is equivalent to living in accordance with
> experience of the actual course of nature, as Chrysippus says
> in the first book of his *De finibus*; for our individual natures
> are parts of the nature of the whole universe. And this is why
> the end may be defined as life in accordance with nature, or,
> in other words, in accordance with our own human nature
> as well as that of the universe, a life in which we refrain from
> every action forbidden by the law common to all things, that
> is to say, the right reason which pervades all things, and is
> identical with this Zeus, lord and ruler of all that is.[37]

One establishes a relation of commensurability with the law-governed
and god-permeated natural world of which one is a part—this is
happiness ($\epsilon\upsilon\delta\alpha\iota\mu o\nu\iota\alpha$). One makes the intellectual part of the self
a point that remains fixed in the midst of the transformative swirl
of natural phenomena that can provoke intense and fluctuating
passions—this is passionlessness ($\alpha\pi\alpha\theta\epsilon\iota\alpha$). In attaining these states
one achieves virtue; and according to the Stoics, this means also that
one becomes morally beautiful, attaining a state of being that is
symmetrical (Diogenes Laertius, *Vitae Philosophorum*, 7.100–01).

   In later Hellenistic tradition these Stoic ideas became subsumed
within a framework of Platonic idealism. One version of this mixture
of philosophical ideas influenced Christians like Clement in ways
already described: the unitary psychology of the Stoics gave way to
the Platonic tripartite soul in which the rational part rules, and Stoic
materialism yielded to the Platonic division of of the world into visible
and intelligile realms. The commensurability of self and world came
to be expressed in terms of the assimilation to God of an inner divine
principle, and the self was capable of a passionless fixity amidst the
transformations of the world because of its ontological difference from
all things material. Some Christian spiritual disciplines incorporated
these Platonistic versions of the Stoic ideal of symmetry. Hesychast
prayer in Eastern Christianity did so with special vividness. This
technique of prayer is described in the practical teachings of
Nicephoros the Hesychast and Gregory of Sinai, fourteenth-century
monks centered at Mount Athos. Prominent elements of the
Hesychast spiritual discipline are the following: (1) adoption by a
spiritual guide and teacher, not necessarily a priest; (2) maintenance
of a stable bodily posture during prayer with attention concentrated

on the physical location of one's heart; (3) regulation of the rhythm of breathing during prayer; (4) recitation of the Jesus Prayer as a means for ridding the mind of all mundane and discursive thoughts; and (5) search for the divine light within oneself as evidence of God's presence and a source of divinization. These prayer practices, of course, were frequently adopted with a monastic and liturgical context that included other types of spiritual discipline, especially celibacy and fasting.

The Hesychast model of prayer was defended by Gregory of Palamas in a way that has striking continuity with Clement's rationale for the sprital life. Gregory, like Clement, held that the human experience of God is typically an experience of divine radiant light. He quite explicitly says that this light "is not a sensible light," thereby very strongly exemplifying the theme I have called suprasensual vision.[38] Also, to defend against any charge that he identifies God with something sensibly apprehensible, Gregory distinguishes between God's essence, which is unknowable to human beings, and God's energies which human beings can apprehend, characteristically as radiant light. In this way Gregory adds a rank to the hierarchy of divine things. Finally, the experience of God as divine light causes the beholder to become a vessel and vehicle of divine grace. The purpose of Hesychast prayer is to attain an inner stillness or quietness (ἡσυχία) that, with God's grace, promotes this salvific process.

Gregory of Palamas defended the bodily aspects of Hesychast prayer by saying that they promoted the psychophysical integration characteristic of Biblical accounts of human nature. Still, the ontological dualism which accompanies the theme of suprasensual vision and the disparagement of the body which comes with ideas of passionless agency are part of the Hesychast tradition. Hence if I am to employ the notion of symmetry for the description and justification of spiritual practices such as Hesychast prayer and remain consistent, I must do so without resorting to these Platonic notions. Yet it is just these notions that have traditionally provided a philosophical rationale for spiritually disciplined practices: the ontological rift between the spiritual and material realms motivates disciplined regimens for overcoming the soul's estrangement from its spiritual source. On the other hand, a thoroughgoing Stoic naturalism threatens to ignore the spiritual dimension of existence altogether.

My solution to this problem is to recast ontological and dogmatic points in phenomenological and pragmatic ways. What is needed for a philosophical rationale for spiritual practices is not so much a distinction between a spiritual self and material reality, but a distinction between a relatively enduring agent of action experienced inwardly and an arena of transformation externally encountered. Also needed is a conviction that the external world to which the self seeks commensurate relations is such that it should not be naively understood or impulsively desired; this external world need not be radically depreciated.

A classical presentation of these distinctions is given in the opening pages of Hegel's *Phenomenology of Spirit*; there he says: "In sense-certainty, pure being at once splits up into what we have called the two 'Thises', one 'This' as 'I', and the other 'This' as object."[39] This basic phenomenological differentiation of consciousness and the objects which it engages allows for spiritual practices to be understood as disciplines of maintaining a singular concentration of consciousness amidst the flux of physical reality. This intentionally self-disciplined behavior, in turn, allows its practitioner to choose between alternative habitual regimens, and specifically, to avoid automatic responses to physical and social stimuli. In the same context Hegel notes that sense-certainty as a form of consciousness is one in which external objects are experienced as immediately given, and in that sense, fundamentally true; however, this truth is revealed to be contradictory in the sense that the generality of linguistic instruments like 'This' and 'Now' are ill-suited for the task of designating what is uniquely particular. Sense-certainty cannot, therefore, be both immediately and meaningfully true. For Hegel, only an intensification of the subject's self-consciousness offers access to more adequate truths. One need not subscribe to Hegel's dialectics of historical consciousness to agree that engaging in reflective deliberation and disciplined forbearance when confronted with sensual stimuli, both pleasurable and painful, are prerequisites for the most effective interactions of the human organism with its environment.

In summation, symmetry is descriptive of practices like Hesychast prayer in two ways. First, such practices seek to realize the ideal of symmetry in which an element of fixity exists amidst a multiplicity of changing elements. The pious concentration of spiritual devotion, as evident in the regular recitation of the Jesus Prayer, is maintained amidst the multifarious deliverances of the senses. Here is symmetry understood in terms of transformability. Second, such practices seek to achieve the ideal of symmetry in which a part is commensurable to the whole in which it participates. The gracious apprehension of the spiritual self, experienced as an inner, heart-felt source of radiant light, is correlated with the intelligible order discoverable within the flux of sensual manifestations. Here symmetry is understood in terms of commensurability. Hesychast prayer, then, is a religious instance of the ideal of symmetry also manifest in the aesthetic ideal of Greek statuary and the metaphysical ideal of the Pre-Socratic *Urstoff.* It exemplifies how a regimen of spiritual discipline provides a definite structure to the human experience of the world at large.

Hesychast prayer has frequently be compared to the yogic disciplines of ancient India. From the vantage point of the issues being examined here, this comparison is fortuitous. The *Yoga-Sūtras,* an ancient collection of aphorisms about yoga attributed to Pantañjali, commences by saying that "Yoga is the suppression of the modifications of the mind." It is the confusion of these modifications— the sensing, thinking, feeling, and willing which comprise human mental life—with one's true self *(puruṣa)* that is the source of human sufferings. This true inner self is pure, eternal, blissful, and free; it does not change with the fluctuating impressions of the mind and body. To believe otherwise is to become subject to affliction *(kleśa).* The greatest affliction is this ignorance itself *(avidyā);* of it Heinrich Zimmer has written: "As a consequence of this impairment we are bound to the prejudices and habits of naive consciousness."[41] Among these bad habits are the attachments and antipathies born of nature and shaped by society. Yogic practice is designed to break the bondage of these habitual sufferings. It does so by promoting the realization that there is a true self that remains stable and tranquil amidst the mental activities rooted in a changing natural world.

Unlike the later Hindu school of philosophy called Vedanta, yogic thinkers like Pantañjali affirmed the reality of nature *(prakṛti);* yogic practices seek to establish a proper relation between self and nature. Concentration *(samādhi)* is the state of being that establishes this proper relation and it is likewise the means by which ignorance, as the identification of self and mental modifications, is dispelled. The bodily postures *(āsanas)* and breathing techniques *(prāṇāyāmas)* most familiar to Westerners through the dissemination of Hathayoga are means for attaining this state of concentration. Mircea Eliade has commented that the precise relation between self and nature is one of the most complicated aspects of yoga philosophy.[42] One simile, used by Pantañjali and favored by Eliade, expresses this relation in a way particularly appropriate for present purposes. When concentration is directed toward the subtlest type of natural object, it takes on some qualities of that object, as does a crystalline gem when its surface appears tinged by the color of an object placed near it and reflected by it.[43]

Frequently Indian thinkers speak of the true self and the teaching which reveals the true self as a crystalline jewel. It is entirely appropriate that this symmetrical object is used to represent a self that is thought to be fixed amidst a flux of naturalistic transformations and that is thereby thought commensurate with the subtlest and most real aspect of natural reality. Yet in a quite different way, Pantañjali thought that achieving a state of yogic concentration caused changes in the nexus of action (*karma*) which requires rebirth as the consequence of persistent afflictions: yogic practices fosters removal of afflictions, prevention of rebirth, and thereby, attainment of lasting liberation (*mokṣa*). The elaboration of a Stoic conception of spiritual well-being in terms of symmetry in order to describe the practices of Hesychast prayer and yogic concentration does not entail a commitment to a notion of salvific causality of this sort. From a philosophical point of view I think that this freedom from salvific presuppositions is advantageous.

The spiritually disciplined practices described here with a generalized notion of symmetry are promising candidates for rational legitimation because they are understandable in continuity with descriptions of physical reality and in isolation from supernatural schemes of salvation. For instance, practices described in terms of symmetry making and symmetry breaking receive, in my view, a *prima facie* rational recommendation greater than practices such as daily casting one's horoscope do from the astrological idiom for accounting for regularities in human experience. One is very unlikely to adopt a practice that cannot be coherently described, much less rationally justified; for instance, people are generally reluctant to heed the advice to undertake a journey if their advisor cannot coherently describe their goal and route. Yet one is also more likely to heed directions taken from a map that in previous instances has proved reliable for oneself and others than one is to follow a map that has not provided comparable utility. To elaborate the analogy: the adoption of a regimen of spiritually disciplined practices represents a journey into rationally uncharted territory, but by favoring those practices describable via the scientific and philosophical meanings of symmetry one at least undertakes this journey with standards of measurement and direction drawn from a reliable conceptual map. Terminologies and principles drawn from supernatural schemes of salvation cannot make a parallel claim.

The conception of spiritual apprenticeship and practice articulated by means of notions of symmetry also has a presumptive defense against charges of fostering superficially diverting spiritual pastimes.

No supernatural shortcut to spiritual well-being is offered; this discourages the dilettante. Likewise the profundity of the terms used to describe and recommend spiritually disciplined practices requires diligence to understand and employ reflectively. They militate against spiritual frivolity. A second extreme should be avoided. No description or justification of a spiritually disciplined practice, no matter how informed or elegant, can rid its adoption of risk. Spiritual life is a risky venture. As Pascal said, it is a high stakes wager.

The bilateral symmetry of the human body, in which parts are commensurate with the whole, is an ideal; the translation symmetry of crystal lattices, in which possible transformations have group-theoretical properties, is an abstraction. As such, these conceptions of symmetry are well-suited for describing the enduring structure of the created world; yet these same aspirations to permanence makes them less appropriate for describing the dynamic processes of natural change. The Stoic equation of natural and moral beauty with symmetry has frequently been criticized by philosophers on the grounds that the ideal and abstract character of symmetry makes this equation vague and uninformative. The present effort to retrieve symmetry as a feature of spiritual discipline seems vulnerable to the same criticism. This is so because a prominent feature of the spiritual life is a vivid experience of sudden transformation and gradual growth: this type of life involves a temporal quest for a personal sense of peace sustainable in different times, places, and circumstances. The traditional criticism of symmetry would be seriously damning of the present project if recent science had yielded only abstract and static conceptions of symmetry; however, recent research has also provided an account of symmetry breaking far more informative than was suggested by the example of Buridan's ass.

Contemporary physicists appeal to the physical process of symmetry breaking in order to explain the relative simplicity of physical laws that hold in the complex world of human experience. Isaac Newton thought that laws of nature can be simple because the initial conditions to which they apply are so complex. The description of the positions and momenta of a system of particles at a specific instant is undoubtedly a complex task, and beyond certain limits, it is now known to be theoretically impossible. Newton's observation allows for the simplicity of natural laws but does not realistically explain it. The simplicity of physical law, or more precisely its symmetry—the fact that physical laws hold constant amidst multiform transformations of time and space—is explained in contemporary cosmology by making reference to an antecedent symmetry extant at the moment of the universe's creation. This is the "perfect symmetry" of the title of Heinz Pagels's second book, where he wrote:

> The universe begins in a very hot state of utmost simplicity and symmetry and as it expands and cools its perfect symmetry is broken, giving rise to the complexity we see today. Our universe today is the frozen, asymmetric remnant of its earliest hot state, much as complex crystals of water are frozen out of a uniform gas of water vapor.[44]

The contemporary world is the product of a history of broken symmetries. For instance, the four fundamental forces that govern the interaction of physical matter—the electromagnetic, strong, weak, and gravitational forces—are distinct yet related. They are capable of description within a uniform theoretical framework because they are manifestations of a single force that prevails in conditions of high temperature such as existed at the beginning of the universe. They are distinct because the universe has cooled and the uniformity of the initial conditions has been altered—an original symmetry has been broken. The great diversity of elementary particles which physicists are now discovering shows that matter underwent a similar process of differentiation.

The idea of a broken symmetry is based on the simple fact that some symmetrical states of open physical systems are less stable than related asymmetrical states. Pagels uses the illustration of the "Heisenberg ferromagnet" to make this point. A magnet may be thought to consist of a multitude of small constituent magnets. Suppose one shields the large magnet from the earth's magnetic field. Then the north poles of the constituent magnets will be arbitrarily oriented, and the large magnet itself will have no north-south polarity: in that sense it is symmetrical. Now suppose further that the orientations of the some constituent magnets become subject to a local and temporary magnetic field such that this group of physically proximate constituent magnets becomes oriented in the same direction. This new orientation, in turn, will generate a small magnetic field that will attract other constituent magnets to this same orientation. Eventually the common orientation will become sufficiently widespread so that the large magnet will acquire a

definite north and south pole; it will become asymmetrical. Furthermore, it will be stable in this asymmetrical state; a group of locally
opposite orientations produced by random fluctuations will be drawn
back into relative conformity by the magnetic field of the large
magnet.

To say that the creation is the product of a history of broken
symmetries is simply to acknowledge that the world as an physical
system empowered by the initial "Big Bang" has at crucial junctures
achieved a relative equilibrium in asymmetrical states. This is
fortunate for human beings: perfect symmetries and absolute
equilibria are incompatible with meaning and life. Scientists like
Pagels and his mentor, Richard Feynman, appreciate the peculiar
aspects of what scientists have learned: that there exists anything
at all seems due, recounts Pagels, to the asymmetry between the
amount of matter and antimatter that resulted from the primordial
process of cosmic cooling; but that one can know anything at all, notes
Feynman, is due to the remarkable but imperfect symmetries which
govern the interactions of material reality.[45] For both men the world
of broken symmetry seems puzzling but purposeless, best met by a
playful curiosity and a modest skepticism.

Broken symmetry has prompted some scientists to bolder claims,
and this is well illustrated by the variety of broken symmetry that
has been discovered to characterize living organisms. Protein
molecules, essential to all living organisms, have a spiral structure
that can be compared to the threads of screws. Screws may be
threaded to the right or to the left, though, in fact, most screws are
threaded to the right for the convenience of right-handed persons. All
types of protein molecules have, in fact, a definite handedness, or
chirality, which they inherit from the amino acids which compose
them. Only leftward spiralling amino acids are constituents of protein
molecules. Louis Pasteur, who in the 1850s was the first person to
investigate the chirality of protein molecules, believed this
asymmetry of left and right was "the only well-marked line of
demarcation that can at present be drawn between the chemistry of
dead and living matter."[46] Scientists now are much less inclined to
see this chemical property of proteins as an intrinsic property of living
things, yet they do recognize it to be a peculiarly pregnant fact. Some
suggest that it shows the uniformity of the ancestry of life on earth;
others say that both chiral forms of protein molecules were originally
formed, but that this symmetrical situation proved unstable due to
random irradiations or the lack of parity in nuclear forces.

Theories about the meaning and origin of the chirality of protein molecules are now speculative. Equally speculative are interpretations of the fact that human beings are the only mammals born with a literal preference for using one hand rather than another. This asymmetry reflects the left-brain/right-brain differences which are characteristic of the highly developed central nervous system of *homo sapiens*. The psychologist Julian Jaynes has speculated that phenomena so basic as archaic theism and modern consciousness are best explained in terms of the broken symmetry in the evolution of the higher primates which endowed human beings with an asymmetrically "bicameral mind."[47] I am not here interested in arguing on behalf of the grand generalizations of Pasteur or Jaynes, or in celebrating the playful skepticism of Feynman or Pagels, but I share with them a conviction that the breaking of symmetry in the evolution of complex physical systems is something unusually rife with significance for understanding the creation of novelty and complexity. I shall even extend this significance to a sort of creativity one might label spiritual. As before, the transition from symmetry in physical theory to symmetry as a descriptive theme for spiritual life is effected with the help of relevant phenomenological insights.

Symmetrical objects attract a human observer's attention more readily than do thoroughly asymmetrical objects; yet generally symmetrical objects with a minor asymmetrical element retain an observer's attention more consistently than do completely symmetrical forms. Psychological experiments with newborn children attest that there is some instinctive component to these phenomenological truths. Religious imagery puts them to work in symbolically representing the power of salvific personalities: the outspread arms of Christ on the cross emphasizes the bilateral symmetry of the human form, while his crossed feet and sagging head break that symmetry; also the Buddha meditating in the lotus position has his arms and legs symmetrically arranged, but his hands and feet are crossed. The ancient Asian yin-yang sign now used on the Korean flag and the Aryan swastika appropriated by the Nazis are perhaps the most striking abstract emblems of broken symmetry. Philosophers often elevate phenomenological insights to the height of metaphysical principles: Hegel did this for the phenomenology of broken symmetries when he claimed that the most enduring and embracing knowledge—Absolute Knowledge—attains this status by containing and overcoming contradictions and conflict.[48] He here departs radically from the Platonic ideal in which the highest objects of knowledge exists transcendentally in a realm beyond imperfection.

For Plato, rational subjects gain knowledge more by rising above the conflicts of historical existence than by living through them. By insisting that symmetry, when conceived as a descriptive theme for the spiritual life, include elements of symmetry achieved and symmetry broken, I follow Hegel more than either his Platonic or Stoic predecessors. I acknowledge that negation as intellectual and social process is as much an instigation as an obstacle to human creativity.

Hegel's phenomenological insights have been called upon in previous sections of this chapter. First, I appealed to the idea emergent from his master-slave dialectic that people come to know themselves by knowing how others sharing their world see them: I added that recognizing an intelligent being like oneself means facing a bilaterally symmetrical organism. In this chapter's first section I used these points to describe the fact that persons seeking to know themselves as spiritual beings—as true selves related to the world as a maximally inclusive whole—almost always enlist the aid of a spiritual master. The chapter's second section began with the truism that the spiritual master is more a practical exemplar than a doctrinal pedagogue: he or she models practices that promote a concentration of consciousness and a discernment of what is really valuable and what is not. This spiritual goal I described as the cultivation of an aspect of one's inner experience—be it the true self or the felt truth that there is no self— which is constant amidst the multiform transformations of the objects of consciousness and which is commensurate with true reality. Such inner constancy is like a point of symmetry in the structure of one's experience of the world. Hegel's account of the dialectic of sense-certainty posited the phenomenological differentiation of consciousness and its objects presupposed by this spiritual self-conception. Now a third aspect of symmetry can be employed for the description of spiritually disciplined practices: it avers that imitation of a spiritual master leads to contestation, and, potentially, to preeminence. To truly learn from a master involves the personal appropriation of that master's expertise in a way that spontaneously departs from slavish repetition and becomes an aspirant overcoming. To truly learn from a master involves the creation of a new form of excellence. Stated in the idiom I am recommending: if learning is not confined to mastering some preexistent corpus of truths—and the experiential, practical learning characteristic of the spiritual development surely is not—then it is an unstable and unpredictable process such that traditional inculcated forms of thinking and behaving are liable to be spontaneously broken.

The account of apprenticeship, practice, and creativity given here in terms of notions of symmetry can be illustrated by examples drawn from diverse quarters. Perhaps the most literal exemplification is provided by the case of masters and students playing complex board games like the game of chess. Chess is a game of strategy in which the goal is to secure the resignation from play of your opponent, or else, force the cessation of your opponent's ability to continue play— a outcome known as checkmate. Chess originated in ancient India sometime in the early centuries of the Christian era, travelling eventually to Western Europe by way of Persia and the Arab world. This fact is attested to by the earliest recorded names for the game and its pieces; they are Sanskrit terms which coincide with ancient Indian military terms. For instance, the word 'chess' itself comes from the Arabic 'shatranj' and the Persian 'chatrang', which both, in turn, are derived from the Sanskrit word for army 'chaturanga'.[49] Chess is played on a square board subdivided into sixty-four squares arranged in eight rows and eight columns. This board ('ashtāpada' is the Sanskrit term) was used in both ancient and modern times in games other than chess, most notably today, in checkers, and it seems to be of even greater antiquity than the chess pieces. It possibly was a very archaic cosmographic artifact used in divination rites. In brief, chess began as a ritual game of war.[50]

Chess players face one another across a board arrayed with pieces. In learning to play the teacher instructs the novice to make legally permissible and strategically recommended moves. Though the rules of chess may be learned abstractly, there is a more basic sense in which the novice learns to play by imitating the actions of the teacher, by seeking to be a mirror image of the master. Symmetry also figures in the commencement of play in a more literal way because the pieces on a chess board at the start of a game form a bilaterally symmetrical formation relative to an axis of symmetry drawn between the 4th and 5th rows. The first move by white breaks the symmetry of the initial situation; white is said to have the "initiative" because white has control of more space and greater mobility for the white pieces. Players in a chess game cannot forego moving a piece when it is their turn to play. This promotes dynamic play; it assures that a symmetrical array of pieces, if regained, will be repeatedly broken.

Black's task is to "equalize" by gaining comparable control and mobility for the black pieces. This can be done, temporarily, by mimicking white moves and restoring a symmetrical array of pieces. However, to persist in this strategy makes Black's play passive and unimaginative—and almost certain to lose. Furthermore, since each sides' eight pawns can move only forward, the rules of the game virtually require that symmetry eventually be broken. Black's best strategy is to achieve strategic goals by a more radical departure from symmetrical play than is achieved by white's advantage of playing the first move. Knowing how to depart from the initial position of symmetry while also maximizing the development of your pieces and their control of space is crucial to good chess play; it requires intense concentration in order to calculate combinations that might win a piece and to intuit more subtle positional advantages. The primary pedagogical benefit of chess playing has proved to be its ability to promote concentration on abstract activities.

The example of a student's innovative chess play presents concretely the general situation in which a student departs from the example and instruction of a teacher. The most conformist learning situation occurs when a student literally repeats authoritative teaching. Like a melody repeated in a musical composition, the student's reiteration of taught truths may be represented as mere translations in time of the teacher's original assertions. In that sense the assertions of master and tyro are quite literally symmetrical and any deviation by the student in expression and meaning breaks that achieved symmetry. A more realistic instance of this phenomenon occurs in interlocutory instruction where the master quizzes a disciple in a practice designed to elicit correct responses. Some logicians say that logically structured questions contain two parts: a subject element which presents alternative assertions and a request element that specifies the manner of choice the respondent is to make.[51] Hence answers conform to the structure of their paired questions to the extent that they count as an appropriate choice from the proffered alternatives. Examples are legion of religious personalities deliberately confounding their more orthodox questioners by responding in ways that challenge the structure of thought inherent in the questions addressed to them. The replies of Jesus to questions from the Pharisees often have this character. Asked by them "Is it lawful to pay taxes to Caesar, or not?" Jesus responds with his famous saying "Render to Caesar the things that are Caesar's, and to God the things that are God's" (Mk. 12.13–17). The Pharisees' question presents two alternative assertions regarding paying taxes to the Romans, and requests that the Jesus choose at least one of them. Declaring taxpaying to Caesar unlawful seems bound to offend the Romans, but declaring this activity lawful seems equally likely to offend many Jews. The question harbors an apparent dilemma. The response of Jesus is not an affirmation of the legality of paying Roman taxes.

He answers a different question which concerns the more fundamental issue of the nature of God's sovereignty for one's life. He speaks of Caesar only indirectly. Jesus frequently spoke in parables about the kingdom of heaven and the sort of life one should lead to prepare for its coming: this showed a consistent resistance to his audience's expectation of legalistic pronouncements about what is right and wrong behavior.

The Zen Buddhist conception of enlightenment is often urged upon inquirers by a master's singularly erratic response during a conversational interchange. Known popularly by the Japanese word 'koan', historical accounts of this master-disciple interchange so emphasize idiosyncratic appropriation that the master is portrayed as the one who departs from symmetrical convention. The disciple is implicitly urged by the example of this behavior to make a like departure, but, of course, in a distinctively individual way! For instance, the Chinese master Huang Po is more than once portrayed responding to inquiries about the "Transmission of Mind" by giving a sharp slap to his interlocutor's face.[52] The image of the symmetrical repose of master and student facing one another in mediative postures being broken by a single outstretched slapping arm is a visual epitome of the moment in a spiritually disciplined tutelage that I am seeking to describe. Huang Po's occasional response of silence to his disciples' queries is a comparable, though less dramatic, interruption of this type of edifying discourse.

Expert chess playing highlights several features it shares with spiritually disciplined practices like Hesychast prayer, yogic austerities, and koan-like wordplay; these are the master-student model of learning, the practical cultivation of intense concentration, and the personal appropriation of knowledge via novel forms of excellence. Chess playing especially well illustrates how the language of symmetry breaking is helpful for describing advancement in a disciplined practice as a creative overcoming of one's teacher. Important dissimilarities exist also. Success at chess is more easily measurable than is expertise at performing spiritually disciplined practices like prayer and meditation; this is especially the case if one divorces these practices from particular doctrines of religious salvation as a philosophical treatment is likely to do. Related to this first dissimilarity is a second which notes that in contemporary Western culture, chess, while certainly a highly disciplined creative practice, is rarely a spiritual undertaking. It may be for some individuals, but issues of professional status and commercial success dominate the chess world at the grandmaster level; little concern is given there to the significance of chess for the player's sense of deepest selfhood and cosmic wholeness. The current world champion, Garry Kasparov, has been widely quoted as saying that his victory over the most powerful chess playing computers has vindicated human integrity against technological challenges. Yet these remarks are more commercial hucksterism than existential conflict; even Kasparov admits that eventually a computer will be able to defeat all human players. Perhaps only when computers can defeat even the best human chess players will the game's playful and aesthetic elements return to prominence!

In contemporary Western culture chess retains spiritual significance mostly through its incorporation into works of art. Vladimir Nabokov's novel *The Defense* attests to this fact; in this story a chess master's strategy of developing a completely reliable response to an aggressive opponent is shown to evolve into a way of dealing with all of the unpredictable and menacing aspects of life itself. In *The Master of Go* Yasunari Kawabata similarly attributes a spiritual significance to the ancient Chinese board game of Wei-Ki, known as Go in Japan. The book is a novelistic account of a 1938 Go championship match in which a old master is defeated by a young, brash challenger who has been influenced by Western commercial and competitive values. Kawabata well describes of the old Master's reaction to a decisively devastating move by his opponent.

> The Master had put the match together as a work of art. It was as if the work, likened to a painting, were smeared black at the moment of highest tension. That play of black upon white, white upon black, has the intent and takes the forms of creative art, It has in it a flow of the spirit and a harmony as of music. Everything is lost when suddenly a false note is struck, or one party in a duet suddenly launches forth on an eccentric flight of his own. A masterpiece of a game can be ruined by insensitivity to the feelings of an adversary. That Black 121 having been a source of wonder and surprise and doubt and suspicion for us all, its effect in cutting the flow and harmony of the game cannot be denied.[53]

The price of creativity was the breaking of symmetry! The crassness of the young master's personality and behavior prevented the old master from anticipating the play of his opponent or even of acknowledging retrospectively its own distinctive beauty.

Kawabata's old Go master laments the professionalization and commercialization of a practice he understands primarily in spiritual and aesthetic terms. Winning and losing are of paramount interest to general audiences who know little of the subtleties of games like Go and chess, and commercial promoters of game matches accentuate this aspect of competitive practices in order to attract wide audiences. Today chess promoters seek to imitate the successful example of professional athletic competitions: games are shorter and purses larger; competition is fiercer and marketing crasser. Chess becomes thereby more a diverting entertainment and less a spiritual art.

The fate of games like Go and chess in the contemporary world has implications for a new conception of spiritually disciplined practices. If spiritually disciplined practices include elements of contestation and if they aspire to new forms of excellence; furthermore, if these aspects of such practices are no longer understood in salvific ways, as, for instance, overcoming the devil or ascending toward God, then it is as an aesthetic phenomenon that these aspects of spiritually disciplined practices are manifested. I think that the instincts of artists like Nabokov and Kawabata are correct in this respect. In addition, I think that it is by means of cultivating the impulse for aesthetic excellence in such practices can maintain their spiritual character in radically pluralistic and secular contexts. Regimens of prayerful devotion or yogic austerity can bring a quality of excellence to the lives of practitioners in a same way as regimens of playing music do to the lives of musicians.

In the most creative spiritual disciplines I detect the spirit of aesthetic contestation—the agon of the ancient Greek festivals of Olympic athletics and Athenian drama; and because of this I think that describing such practices in terms of symmetry, a concept with artistic origins, is quite appropriate. Also, the way in which the notion of symmetry has been developed in the mathematical and natural sciences enables talk of symmetry to convey the accent on personal fullness and cosmic wholeness which marks the spiritual dimension of human existence. In the last chapter it was noted how the categoreal theme of semiotic self-reference promoted understanding spiritually disciplined practices as meaningful activities; in the present chapter symmetry has shown the meaning generated by such practices has a pronouncedly aesthetic and axiological character. In the next chapter—the final one in the speculative part of the present rethinking of spiritual discipline—the categoreal theme of biological equilibration will show how the meanings and values made possible by spiritually disciplined practices promote human vitality in its physiological, intellectual, and social expressions.

CHAPTER 5

Biological Equilibration

In this book's third chapter the notion of semiotic self-reference was first used to describe how certain spiritually disciplined practices are meaningful, and specifically, how they signify the paradoxical meaning born of the practitioner's belief that he or she at once participates in the natural world yet also transcends it. In the last chapter the notion of physical symmetry was used to describe how certain spiritually disciplined practices are valuable, and specifically, how they are bearers of an aesthetic integrity arising from the practitioners's belief that he or she is a creative agent who is both the product and instrument of a greater totality. In a small way a transition from description to justification has begun: presumably a rationally justified practice will be one bearing some measure of meaning and value. This step is only preliminary, though, because the relevant meanings and values remain unspecified. For some philosophers this preliminary assignation is sufficient. As the next chapter will document, Nietzsche argued that ascetic ideals deserve a minimal approval because they give meaning to suffering; any meaning at all deserves some approval, he claimed, because the deepest suffering is meaningless suffering. Likewise any ascription of value is warranted so long as it is a self-generated revaluation. The greatest calamity for Nietzsche is to accept values prescribed by others. I think that more needs to be said than this, and so the movement from description to justification will continue in subsequent pages.

In the present chapter I will argue that the notion of biological equilibration is helpful for describing how spiritually disciplined practices are vital in the sense they promote individual health and communal flourishing. Insofar as they do that, they are, I believe, rationally justifiable means for contending with the predicament that Pascal embodied. The rational justification of a belief or practice may be required to meet stronger or weaker standards. One might argue, as, for instance, John Locke did, that a nonintuitive belief (like belief in the existence of God) is rationally justified only to the extent that there is relevant evidence for holding that belief. (See his *Essay*

Concerning Human Understanding, 4.15–16.) Alternatively, one might say along with William James in "The Will to Believe" that one is rationally permitted to hold a belief whenever one lacks grounds for judging it irrational: if the available evidence does not demonstrably impugn a belief's rationality, then James allows, volitional factors may tip the balance in favor of adopting it. Pascal partially anticipates James's point of view by allowing assessments of the desirability of a belief's truth to figure in the decision as to whether to adopt that belief. One wagers on God's existence, in part, because faith in a God that really exists will presumably be amply— perhaps infinitely—rewarded. As will be indicated in the next chapter, Nietzsche's development of the will to power as the will to truth gives great importance to conative factors in belief formation, and in that sense he extends the tradition of Pascal and James. From another point of view, he inaugurates an entirely different project than either Locke or James because he does not share their commitment to an ethics of belief; he acknowledges no moral obligation to favor beliefs which are rationally commended over those which are not.

At least thus far I have assumed James's weaker interpretation of belief justification. (Of course, I am really interested in the justification of practices, but the two issues become integrated by focusing on the rational justification of the belief that certain spiritually disciplined practices warrant adoption.) Spiritual discipline has been recommended on the basis of the negative judgment that a vulgar hedonism is not likely to bring about the well-being of oneself and others. Indiscriminate gratification of desires often breeds anxious and habitual craving, and brutish competition for desiderata often leads to destructive social conflicts. To allow the rationality of denying oneself something pleasurable is a first step toward establishing that spiritually disciplined practices are rationally permitted. In the last two chapters I have moved yet farther in this direction, contending that spiritually disciplined practices are not themselves diversions: they are not devices for avoiding the profoundest human issues. In the present chapter I shall similarly argue that some practices professing to promote vitality in its most singularly human sense—its spiritual sense—are not themselves decadent: they are not inclined to extinguish instinctive desires.

In several ways this book will increasingly deal with the person and thought of Friedrich Nietzsche. His critique of ascetic ideals in *On the Genealogy of Morals* forces any thorough philosophical treatment of spiritual discipline to contend with matters of justification as well as description. The accusation of decadence just cited is Nietzsche's; it compels a commentator on spiritual discipline to question whether such practices may become actively harmful. Nietzsche's importance for this book, however, is not only as a critic of asceticism. His own conception of a spiritual self-mastery, which I shall soon illustrate with his remarks on solitude, emphasizes just the elements of meaning, value, and vitality that have emerged in these three speculative chapters. Although Nietzsche's work on spiritual discipline did not begin the modern philosophical treatment of this topic—this honor belongs more credibly to Kierkegaard's account of life's stages or to Schopenhauer's interpretation of asceticism—Nietzsche did, in my view, establish the basic outline for any viable contemporary conception. Soon arguments will be offered in support this judgment.

So greatly was Nietzsche devoted to defending the value of embodied human vitality against the calumnies of priests and theologians that he said philosophers themselves must become physicians and physiologists (*Beyond Good and Evil*, 212). From the other direction, so highly did the physiologist Walter Cannon appraise the value of processes of biological equilibration for human well-being and self-understanding that he spoke of them as "the wisdom of the body."[1] As befits a student of William James, Cannon was a philosophically minded medical researcher.[2] I share his estimate of the philosophical suggestiveness of biological equilibration, believing myself that it is as crucial for explaining vital complexity as semiotic self-reference is for explaining paradoxical meaning and physical symmetry is for explaining creative agency.

Briefly stated, processes of biological equilibration are the means by which the human body maintains an internal stability essential to its endurance in a variable environment rife with both nurture and threat. They consist of automatic and internal processes of adaptation which make possible the conscious adaptive behaviors of individual organisms. It is because it serves these regulatory functions that biological equilibration is essential to human embodied vitality, for as J.B.S. Haldane has remarked, "Life is adaptive. We might almost say that it is adaptation."[3] Processes of biological equilibration have themselves proved to be very complex: this fact is evident in Cannon's work early in the century which emphasized the stabilizing mechanisms of the circulatory and digestive systems, and it is even more manifest in recent work which has extended this same approach to the neurological and immunological systems. Also, biological processes for maintaining stability include self-regulation informed by the return of exerted bodily output as sensed environmental input, i.e., by feedback mechanisms. Self-correcting processes of biological equilibration make possible the complex behaviors of human beings and other highly evolved animals.

A simple illustration of this variety of physiological self-regulation is the maintenance of constant body temperature by the fluid matrix of the body. The production of heat by the human body is a continuous process; every activity in which organs engage produces heat. The maintenance of a constant body temperature is achieved by increasing or decreasing the speed of heat production, or alternatively, increasing or decreasing the speed of the inverse continuous process of heat loss. Most people know how heat loss is promoted under conditions of extraordinary muscular exertion. In the first instance, blood vessels near the surface of the skin dilate so as to accommodate a greater volume of blood flow; more blood warmed by the heat generating organs in the interior of the body is thus allowed to pass near the skin's surface where it radiates more heat into the cooler ambient air. If air temperature is greater than body temperature, then heat loss will be achieved by evaporation instead of radiation. Bodily water warmed by both internal organs and circulated blood passes through to the exterior of the skin as perspiration; as it changes into water vapor it draws heat from surrounding body tissue, thereby cooling it. In the opposite circumstance, when body temperature falls, metabolic activity increases so as to generate more heat internally. If at any time the body overcompensates by too rapidly promoting heat production or loss, then it senses this and decreases the speed of the relevant process. Thus this process of temperature regulation is an example of negative feedback.

The Scottish physicist Clerk Maxwell first explained negative feedback in an 1868 paper on the "governors" of steam engines—devices invented by James Watt for maintaining the constant velocity of steam engines under conditions of variable load. The self-regulating processes described by Cannon are a considerably more complex form of self-regulation because they involve the integration of numerous physiological systems and because they maintain stability in many respects and relative to many types of environmental change. Both the physiological and purely mechanical varieties of negative feedback were cited by Norbert Wiener as instrumental in his formulation of the basic principles of the science he called "cybernetics." Indeed, Wiener acknowledged the influence of Cannon's person and work on the writing of his 1948 book, *Cybernetics: or Control and Communication in the Animal and Machine.*[4] I mention this fact for several reasons. It shows the status of the notion of biological equilibration as one of the few biological ideas, clearly joined in this regard by Darwin's and Wallace's idea of evolution by natural selection, which has shaped other areas of scientific research. Also, it accents its relevance to human sciences like biology, economics, and computer science which contend with the explanation of complex phenomenon and which struggle with the formulation of a coherent notion of complexity. Finally, it indicates that the utility of the computer as a research tool and as a conceptual model for the human sciences is due in part to the genesis of cybernetic principles in physiology. This relevance of biological equilibration to the ways that organisms thrive in complex environments, and to the ways that such behavior is scientifically represented, makes it useful here. If spiritual fullness as a goal of life is something enhanced by disciplined bodily practices that enliven rather than endanger physical health, then the notion which summarizes the physiological processes presupposed by healthy persons, i.e., biological equilibration, is an intuitively plausible resource for describing spiritually disciplined practices.

Biological equilibration, I will admit, is not a very familiar or felicitous phrase. Claude Bernard did occasionally use the French word 'equilibre' in his physiological account of the *milieu intérieur*—a notion Cannon credits as the most direct anticipation of his own work. Early in his classic book, *The Wisdom of the Body*, Cannon explains his own choice of words:

> The constant conditions which are maintained in the body might be called *equilibria*. That word, however, has come to have fairly exact meaning as applied to relatively simple physico-chemical states, in closed systems, where known forces are balanced. The coordinated physiological process which maintain most of the steady states in the organism are so complex and so peculiar to living beings—involving, as they may, the brain and nerves, the heart, lungs, kidneys, and spleen, all working cooperatively—that I have suggested a special designation for these states, *homeostasis*. The word does not imply something set and immobile, a stagnation. It means a condition—a condition which may vary, but which is relatively constant.[5]

Cannon's neologism fails to capture fully the dynamic quality of the physiological processes it is intended to denote; still it has prevailed among biologists and the physiological meaning of biological equilibration goes by the name of 'homeostasis'.

The word 'equilibrium' identifies a specific state of a dynamic system of forces or processes. It and its cognates have long been associated in Western scientific parlance with Robert Boyle's employment of it in research which provided the theoretical basis of modern chemistry.[6] Already Boyle was generalizing a notion that had received its first precise interpretation in Archimedes' treatise on planar statics ('Ἐπιπέδων ἰσορροπιῶν). Chemical equilibrium is a state of balance in which two opposing and reversible chemical reactions proceed at equal rates so that there is no net change in the system. Human beings attain chemical equilibrium only at death. Biological equilibrium is a state of human organisms conceived of as an open system far from equilibrium with its physical environment. What is in equilibrium are forces internal to the human body. As noted above, a constant temperature is maintained when there are organs that produce heat in roughly equal measures as there are organs that dissipate it. To achieve this desired result a continual interchange of materials with the environment is required; this need for things like air and food is what qualifies human organisms as open systems. Preserving life and internal systems of biological equilibration in this way amounts to the same thing as resisting death and chemical equilibrium with the external world. In other words, to preserve its high degree of order relative to its environment living things must appropriate order from that environment. Indeed, Erwin Schrödinger cites this importation of order, or "negative entropy," as the hallmark of living things.[7]

Equilibration models of explanation have also been extended to processes that are interpersonal rather than intrapersonal. A commodity's price is in equilibrium when the number of persons who want to sell it at a certain price matches the number who want to buy it at that same price. So long as this match lasts the price will not change. Equilibrium in economics refers to a state of a market system—an active community of buyers and sellers. In principle a market system seems not to require constant augmentation of the available quantity of buyers and sellers or of the relevant commodity in order to maintain price stability. In fact, though, particular markets are always part of larger markets which influence them and are shaped by augmentative forces of population growth, discovery, and invention. Social systems are analogous to market systems in that equilibrium notions are definable relative to processes of observable individual behavior. As evidenced in Simon's work previously cited, the joining or leaving a particular organization is an example of a process that can be understood in these terms.

A figure cited by Cannon as a precursor, and a person who anticipated many of the meanings of equilibration mentioned above, is the ancient Greek physician, Hippocrates. While an actual historical personage—a contemporary of Plato—Hippocrates did not write all, if any, of the medical writings attributed to him in antiquity.[8] Still, books in the *Corpus Hippocraticum* posit a loosely defined force the medieval scholars called the *vis medicatrix naturae*— a self-corrective power that tends to restore health after physical trauma or enervation. This notion is less an express principle than it is an implication drawn from two outstanding features of the Hippocratic writings. They are, first, an effective rejection of religious and other superstitious explanations of the causes of diseases—this trait is especially evident in the treatise on epilepsy; and second, a characteristic pattern of treatment that emphasized "regimen" ($\delta\iota\alpha\iota\tau\alpha$) over more active measures.[9] Programs of diet, rest, exercise, and mild purgation predominate in the Hippocratic treatise on acute diseases. Such treatments would hold little promise if the body was not deemed to have powers of self-regulative healing.

In a second polemical treatise from the Hippocratic collection philosophical theorizing about the body and disease is rejected.[10] This is somewhat inconsistent with the physiological doctrine of "humours" ($\chi\upsilon\mu\iota$) presented in another text, *Natura Hominis*, because this doctrine has a significant philosophical ancestry. Part of the latter text reads:

> The body of man has in itself blood, phlegm, yellow bile and black bile; these make up the nature of his body, and through these he feels pain and enjoys health. Now he enjoys the most perfect health when these elements are duly proportioned ($\mu\epsilon\tau\varrho\iota\omega\varsigma$) to one another in respect of compounding power and bulk, and when they are perfectly mingled.[11]

Prior to this formulation of the doctrine of humours Alcmaeon of Croton, a younger contemporary of Pythagoras, had enunciated the principle that health was an "equilibrium of forces ($\iota\sigma\upsilon\nu\upsilon\mu\iota\alpha\nu\ \tau\hat{\omega}\nu\ \delta\upsilon\nu\acute{\alpha}\mu\epsilon\omega\nu$) and disease the domination ($\mu\upsilon\nu\alpha\varrho\chi\iota\alpha$) of one bodily force by another.[12] He understood these forces less as dynamic fluids than as opposed qualities of the wet and dry, and the hot and cold. In this he shows the influence of Greek cosmological speculation that had water, air, fire and earth as the basic constituents of nature; he may also have been influenced by the cosmological speculations of Anaximander of Miletus who was said by Aristotle to have invoked the notion of an equilibrium of opposite forces to explain the stability of the earth in space (*On the Heavens* 295b), and who, like Alcmaeon, used political metaphors to explain the interaction of opposed forces.

Plato, too, in the *Timaeus* used the notion of equilibrium to explain both cosmological and anthropological ideas. He insisted there that the change from primitive chaos to ordered cosmos was a movement from disequilibrium to equilibrium ($\iota\sigma o\varrho\varrho o\pi\hat{\epsilon}\iota\nu$) (*Timaeus* 52e). He later affirmed the humoural theory of health and disease, even extending it to claim that an optimum of human well-being require an equilibrium ($\iota\sigma o\varrho\varrho\acute{o}\pi\omega$) between soul and body (*Timaeus* 88b). Unfortunately, from my point of view, Plato did not consistently develop this insight. In the *Republic*, to which the *Timaeus* is an addendum, he used very different language in describing the virtue of self-discipline ($\sigma\omega\phi\varrho o\sigma\acute{\upsilon}\nu\eta$), saying that this virtue consisted of the proper ordering of the parts of the soul. Of course, he said that the rational part of the soul should rule the spirited and appetitive parts (*Republic* 431). In describing this relationship Plato explicitly appealed to political analogues, but instead of stressing equality as did Alcmaeon, he consistently employed language of rulership, domination, and control. Since the spirited and appetitive parts of the soul were especially associated with the heart and lower abdomen by Plato, later commentators—Neoplatonists, Gnostics, and some Christians—interpreted self-discipline as domination of the body by the soul. This tradition of interpretation culminated in the anthropological and cosmological conceptions of static hierarchy implicitly expressed by writers like Clement and literally present in the writings of the Pseudo-Dionysus.

The young Augustine provides an exemplary and influential instance of a Christian Platonism which construes spiritual discipline as a subjugation of bodily senses for the sake of a spiritual ascent to God. In the *Soliloquia* he writes:

> There is only one thing that I can command you—I know no more. These things of sense must be forsaken entirely, and as long as we bear this body, we must have care lest our wings be entangled by their sticky lime, as we need whole and faultless wings to fly from this darkness to light. For that light does not even deign to show itself to those who have been shut up within the prison of the body, unless they are strong enough, after breaking and destroying their prison, to take wing into their own lofty realm.[13]

As Augustine matured as a Christian theologian, he became a more Biblical and historical thinker, and his conception of the body changed.[14] The body became less an intrinsic locus of lust and nonbeing, and more an arena of change and death. His valuation remained primarily negative, though the Christian professions of Christ's incarnation and resurrection prevented this devaluation of the body from ever being categorical. In his commentary on the Psalms he contrasts the eternity of God with the mutability of the human body:

> Consider this, brothers: what your body has, it does not have of itself, because it is not fixed in itself. It is changed by each period of life; it is changed by changes of place and time; it is changed by diseases and carnal failings. It is not, therefore, fixed in itself. . .(yet) You (O God) change things, and they are changed; however, you remain yourself the same.[15]

In a late sermon he even more succinctly made this same point: "Take away death and the body is good."[16]

The shift from sensuality to temporality as the distinctive feature of embodied human existence is a distinct improvement in Augustine's theology. For instance, it approximates the observation of the biologist C.H. Waddington that one of the things that makes living things so complex is that scientific accounts of them must make reference to multiple frames of temporal reference: the seconds and minutes of physiological process, the years and decades of embryological development, the several generations of hereditary influence, and finally, the many generations of species evolution.[17] Still, Augustine's understanding of the relationship between the experience of temporality and the experience of spiritual fullness posits that such fullness is achieved by transcending the temporal rather than by finding stability and peace within the flux of its rhythms. He took one step in the right direction, but he did not go far enough in my judgment. Hence this latter form of stable well-being—this "wisdom of the body," operative within time rather than outside it, will be the chief concern of the remainder of this chapter.

BODIES AND MOVEMENTS

Rather than think metaphorically of spiritual agents as souls imprisoned in bodies one should think naturalistically of them as organisms living in environments: this was the main thrust of this chapter's introduction. To think this way makes it much easier to argue that at least some spiritually disciplined practices enhance human vitality in tangible ways. The environments in which most people live are generally capable of sustaining human life with food, water and other resources, but they vary. The maintenance of an internal equilibrium in the presence of changing environmental conditions is achieved by the coordinated activity of numerous physiological processes: this phenomenon has been called homeostasis. It is a necessary condition of living beings. Claude Bernard wrote, "It is the fixity of the *milieu intérieur* which is the condition of free and independent life, and all the vital mechanisms, however varied they may be, have only one object, that of preserving constant the conditions of life in the internal environment."[18] Activities of bodily movement and intellectual reflection are quickly robbed of their efficacy in the absence of a stable inner environment. Even the relatively sedentary and intellectual act of reading a book becomes difficult when hungry or feverish!

Most physiological processes of self-regulation are governed by the autonomic nervous system, and so, are not under conscious mental control. The degree to which a homeostatic process is automatic correlates roughly with the organism's sensitivity to disruption of the aspect of internal stability that process preserves. The circulation of blood throughout the body is not something to which a healthy person has to attend consciously. This is fortunate because a sharp drop of blood pressure within moments leads to a life- threatening state of shock. During the First World War, Walter Cannon inaugurated the modern practice of treating wound victims with intravenous colloidal solutions as a means of quickly raising their blood pressure. Eating and drinking, however, are deliberate activities. Accordingly, most healthy persons can survive for days without water and for weeks without food. Cannon made important discoveries about the digestive system as well, demonstrating that the wavelike movements of the stomach wall cease when a person experiences strong feelings of rage or fear.

Food digestion and blood circulation are directly relevant to two varieties of spiritual discipline. Regimens of fasting presuppose a considerable capacity for consciously desisting from food consumption, while some rigorous forms of meditation require an extraordinary ability to bring within conscious control physiological activities normally left to the governance of the autonomic nervous system. One rationale for these spiritually disciplined practices is that they diminish bodily activity so that spiritual activity might flourish. A second rationale, which I prefer, is that both activities make the body less vulnerable to physical and emotional disturbance. If performed intermittently—alternating periods of quietude and abstinence with periods of more robust activity—they prepare one for effective responses to conditions of want, harm, or danger. They are, in that sense, adaptive.

The body's ability to maintain the physical stability of the head, i.e., to keep one's balance, is mostly outside of conscious control. Physical orientation in space is maintained by the cooperative efforts of the eyes and the vestibular system of the inner ear. People can swirl around to make themselves dizzy and they can remain still to suppress sensations of movement, but they cannot suppress the working of their vestibular system itself. Practices developing one's sense of balance cannot be spiritually recommended for their diminution of a bodily sensation because this homeostatic process is not a sense organ; rather it functions to quell disorienting sensations that impede the primary organs of perception. In my view, this fact is instructive, directing efforts to justify spiritually disciplined practices to the relevant criteria of individual vitality and social comity.

Very often practitioners of regimens of bodily movement that develop one's sense of balance—soldiers and athletes and dancers—attribute spiritual significance to what they do. Athletic competitions and dance performances are communal celebratory activities. Like most aspects of human culture their most archaic meaning is religious. The masculine physical contests recounted in Homer's *Odyssey* (Book 7) and the frenzied dancing portrayed in Euripides' *Bacchae* (lines 55-170) are believed to have played roles in cultic rites before they were transformed into episodes of literary epic and drama. Athletics and dance, one might argue, still retain elements of this ancestry of wondrous spectacle. There is another sense, though, in which practices designed to enhance a person's capacity for physical balance are inchoately spiritual, and it stems from the accent on wholeness and deeper selfhood which was stipulated previously as the characteristic feature of the spiritual dimension of human existence.

The vestibular system consists of the semicircular canals and the otolith organs, the utriculus and the sacculus. They are filled with fluid and contain hair cells that transduce the physical displacement of fluids into electrical nerve signals. The semicircular canals are responsible for sensing angular acceleration and the otolith organs for sensing linear acceleration. What causes the displacement of fluid upon movement is the earth's gravitational force. Hence unlike the respiratory system which is oriented toward the vaporous part of the external environment, or the immunological system which is keyed to toxic materials which invade the body, the vestibular system is correlated with no particular aspect of the environment; rather it is sensitive to the environment in its most global sense—to the earth's center of gravity which is the theoretical point of origin of its gravitational force.

Upon sensing acceleration of the body, the eyes and vestibular organs communicate this message to nerve centers in the spine, and when possible, muscles are activated to compensate for the insurgent force and maintain bodily stability. As noted previously, feedback in a homeostatic process is present when sensory neurons detect the output of a physiological process so as to trigger afferent neurons which accordingly augment or diminish the relevant process. The vestibular system is a very sophisticated system for detecting changes in the position of the head. It thereby contributes to the sensory phase of the feedback process governing the human sense of balance. It is the upright and stable position of the head that the vestibular system has evolved to promote, yet because it responds primarily to the earth's gravitational force, it achieves this end by promoting a stable center of gravity in the human body. This fact is confirmed by the observation that most people's sense of balance works quite well when standing on their heads, even though this position makes them vulnerable to hostile attack and so is not something which itself is favored by natural selection.

The human system of balance seeks to maintain a stable relation between the earth's center of gravity—an emblem of the world in its totality—and the human center of gravity, likewise an emblem of one's deeper self. There is some subjective confirmation of this description in the reports of dancers, athletes, and soldiers. For instance, the dancer Isadora Duncan professed that dance movement emanates from a central inner source; she rhetorically asked the novice dancer: "Do you not feel an inner self awakening deep within you—that it is by its strength that your head is lifted, that your arms are raised, that you are walking slowly toward the light?"[19] She was also insistent that the dancer's movement must be "one with the great movement that runs through the universe; and therefore the fountain-head of the art of dance will be the study of the movement of Nature."[20] It was especially the undulatory movement of ocean waves to which Duncan directed her student's attention. Self-descriptions invoking similar themes come from athletes; for instance, marathon runners often report quasimystical experiences in which they feel some intimate connection between an inner source of strength and the natural environment through which they move.

In addition to such anecdotal evidence, there is phenomenological support for the attribution of an inchoately spiritual dimension to graceful embodied movement. Maurice Merleau-Ponty frequently stressed that people are not only biological organisms having environments, but are also existential beings having worlds. What was distinctive in his variety of phenomenology was the way in which he intimately associated the body with this existential experience of "being-in-the-world": "To be a body is to be tied to a certain world."[21] As the center of this world, the body gives it both permanence and perspective:

> The body therefore is not one more among external objects, with the peculiarity of always being there. If it is permanent, the permanence is absolute and is the ground for the relative permanence of disappearing objects.... Not only is the permanence of my body not a particular case of the permanence of external objects in the world, but the second cannot be understood except through the first: not only is the perspective of my body not a particular case of that of objects, but furthermore the presentation of objects in perspective cannot be understood except through the resistance of my body to all variations of perspective.[22]

Merleau-Ponty denied that the body is just another object in the world in a second way. He claimed that it is capable of attaining not only a balance of corporeal parts, but an equilibrium of meanings as well: "Whether a system of motor or perceptual powers, our body is not an object for an 'I think', it is a grouping of lived-through meanings which moves towards its equilibrium."[23] A vivid illustration of the body as a grouping of meanings moving toward equilibrium is found in the experience of visually examining one's own hand or foot. The extremity examined is the body as most objectified, while the eyes which do the examining are the body most strictly in its role as a perceiving subject. Yet both eyes and hands are intuitively experienced to be part of the same body. The way in which dancers sense their feet when engaged in a sequence of dance steps is a much more subtle instance of this same phenomenon: here the body as perceived and perceiving attains experiential unity by their common integration with the musical rhythm propelling the dance.

To develop a sense of bodily unity amidst an experience of intense body self-consciousness constitutes the sort of phenomenological equilibration Merleau-Ponty describes. Like other activities of perception it presupposes processes of physiological homeostasis, but it is not identifiable with any one of them, not even with the vestibular balance system. I think that this phenomenological variety of equilibration is a characteristic feature of disciplined practices. Be it meditation or dance, or chess playing or praying, any practice that requires tutelage by a master for competency and self-appropriation for proficiency requires a balance of supervision of self and sensitivity to a broader flow of experience.[24]

Phenomenological equilibrium can be absent from a disciplined physical practice in one of two ways. On the one hand, mental self-scrutiny may interfere with bodily performance. If a person is too deliberate in executing prescribed physical motions, for instance, when ice skating or riding a bicycle, then he or she risks sacrificing a requisite fluidity of motion. In many cases the bodily adjustments needed to maintain one's balance on skates or on a bicycle are just too subtle to be consciously accomplished. Something similar applies to the performance of music. The plodding playing of neophyte pianists announces their lack of subliminal control of finger movements. Since musical composition and performance have become distinguishable activities, an excessive emphasis on the abstractly intellectual component of music is sometimes expressed more vividly than by plodding playing. Composers can compose music having an abstractly beautiful form which musicians cannot actually perform on the scored instruments! Less dramatically, composers may give their music rhythmic and harmonic structures so subtle that performers have difficulty learning them because they cannot rely on their customary intuitions about musical form. Arnold Schoenberg's serial string quartets sufficiently depart from the tradition sonata form so as to present this sort of challenge. Asian approaches to sport and art, especially those influenced by Chinese Taoism and Japanese Zen Buddhism, actively resist such extreme intellectualism. In *Zen in the Art of Archery*, the German philosopher Eugen Herrigel describes the Zen notion of an "artless art" that paradoxically commends relinquishing conscious control as a means for assuring expert results in practices like archery.[25]

The activities of dance, sport, and combat are prone to an opposite sort of extreme. They can be undertaken with a passionate abandon that gives vivid expression to sexual and aggressive human feelings. Some religious traditions revere this primal energy as much as more studied creative efforts. An apotheosis of this duality is the Hindu god Śiva who is mythologically portrayed as both dancing the world into being and dancing it to its destruction. Christian writers have generally censured dancing in its more unrestrained forms. They have allied even its secular expressions with pagan worship and with pagan opposition to Christianity: the New Testament story of Salome's dance which won the death of John the Baptist gave scriptural warrant for this point of view (Mk.6.14-29). Clement of Alexandria certainly shared this low regard for dancing (*Paedagogus* 3.4). He like most Christian theologians understood dancing as permissible only in it restrained forms, and preferably as an expression of Christian worship. The perpetual dance of angels before the throne of God provided him with a paragon of balletic propriety and praise.

While assigning no moral opprobrium to passionate dancing, I believe it is helpful to distinguish between disciplined and undisciplined forms of dance. Religious dance sometimes has an ecstatic character: rhythmic bodily movement brings about a loss of customary self-consciousness that is experienced as an intimacy with the sacred. Clearly this experience is different from the phenomenological equilibration I have offered as the distinguishing feature of disciplined practices. The dance practices of American Shakers well illustrate this distinction. Like the Quakers from whom they descended, the United Society of Believers in Christ's Second Appearing received their colloquial name from the excited movements and gestures which their members claimed as religious manifestations. During the formative days of the American Shaker community in the mid-eighteenth century, these communal "laboring" experiences were not formalized as part of an organized worship service. They were assigned the common meanings of casting off doubt and mortifying the flesh, but they actually consisted of an uncoordinated assembly of agitated persons: trembling, shouting, stamping, dancing, and so forth. When in 1786 the first Shaker meeting-house was erected in New Lebanon, New York, the community became more structured and its worship more formal. Ecstatic laboring experiences began to be referred to as the "quick," "back," and "promiscuous" style of dancing. New liturgical dance forms were instituted such as the "square order shuffle." Specific steps and rhythms were requisite for this dance, and it could not be performed without some measure of conscious concentration. Song lyrics sung while dancing the square order shuffle reveal the simple yet structured nature of the dance: "One, two, three, steps, foot straight at the turn/ One, two, three, steps, equal length, solid pats/ Strike the shuffle, little back, make the solid sound/ Keep the body right erect with every joint unbound."[26]

This last lyric alludes to just those features of disciplined bodily practices that I have highlighted. An upright torso with flexed knees and elbows is an optimal posture for maintaining physical equilibrium. Also suggested by the lyric is a perceptual consciousness of the body as an object having a desired property ("Keep the body erect"), yet at the same time it enjoins melding this body image into a deeper consciousness of rhythmic experience ("with every joint unbound"). The relevant rhythm is musical, yet because song and dance are here part of religious worship, a wider rhythm of the interaction between self, world, and God is also suggested. For this reason the practice is not only disciplined, but spiritual.

Combat training offers examples of practices that are disciplined, but not spiritual. Learning how to break the neck of an adversary requires an accurate application of force in order to inflict lethal damage, yet it also requires a fluid quickness so that the opponent's defenses might be overcome. This is true whether the deadly act is a single, elegant karate chop, or a more cumbersome aggravated headlock. A talent for phenomenological equilibration seems as necessary here as in an expert dancer. Yet so long as the purpose of the combat training is the bodily harm of an adversary, soldiers must be concerned with the very particular physical beings of the engaged combatants. Thoughts of deeper selves and cosmic wholes are dangerous distractions. Furthermore, when soldiers are engaged in potentially fatal combat they usually undergo the physiological responses that Cannon identified in studies of fight or flight behavior. Nonessential processes abate in favor of ones absolutely needed for physical survival. I suspect too that spiritual intentionality diminishes in this context. Hence in my view, even apart from ethical considerations, there is no spiritual dimension to the act of killing. I would make a similar argument regarding certain sex acts. Spiritually disciplined practices, as described here, are incompatible with primarily instinctual biological behaviors.

Traditional Asian martial arts are commonly accorded spiritual significance, and thus they potentially challenge the implication I have drawn from making phenomenological equilibration a crucial characteristic of spiritually disciplined practices. I admit that the sense of duty which motivates soldiers to engage in combat may be spiritual, as may be the meaning they assign to past conflicts in which they participated, and certainly military training practices may be spiritually disciplined. Thus I concur with an ascription of a spiritual character to martial arts, but only to the extent that such practices are absented of actual lethal intent. For two reasons this qualification is not an arbitrary abstraction of Asian martial arts from their historical contexts. First, many martial arts have antecedents in practices that have an independent basis in religion and medicine. This is the case, for instance, for the Chinese defensive martial art of T'ai-Chi Ch'üan, many of whose underlying principles are articulated in Lao-tzu's *Tao Te Ching* and in the *Nei Ching*, an ancient medical text. Second, many martial arts have been transformed into sports in which the intent to inflict lethal damage on an opponent is replaced by the goal of attaining a noninjurious competitive advantage. The Japanese sport of judo in which colored belts are differential emblems of attainment well illustrates this course of evolution.

T'ai-Chi Ch'üan is a Chinese martial art that clearly exemplifies a spiritually disciplined practice. As a defensive form of martial art, it never stressed lethal aggressiveness. Also, it clearly incorporates the Taoist sensibility regarding natural phenomena into a physical discipline that emphasized the body in motion, and specifically, the body in simple, balanced, and healthful motion. The reputed origin of T'ai-Chi Ch'uan is instructive. One legend has it that during the reign of the Emperor Yu (circa 2200 BCE) a great flood devastated China, leaving stagnant bodies of water in its wake. These waters gave rise to infestation and disease. Observing the harm done by the stagnant water, the Emperor decreed that great ritual dances be undertaken as a way of providing a social antidote of vital motion to the natural stagnation afflicting his land. According to this account the initial meaning of T'ai-Chi Ch'üan was religious and medicinal, not martial.

T'ai-Chi Ch'üan is an ancient Chinese system of medicinal exercises that consists of physical movements which are slow, flowing, and very much integrated with mental dispositions which are themselves calm and concentrated. It is a particular instance of Kung-fu—a regimen of bodily movement devoted neither to communal ritual nor public entertainment, but to the well-being of the practitioner. For Taoists and Confucianists alike, the well-being of an individual is synonymous with his or her participation in the world's natural movement. To conceive of oneself apart from this movement is to entertain an unhealthy sense of self. Yin and yang are the Chinese terms for aspects of this cosmic movement: yang specifying the more active phase and yin the more tranquil phase. Movement in this context is often symbolized by the fluid alternation of crest and trough in an ocean wave. T'ai-Chi Ch'üan consists of regimens of movement that promote the experience of being "one body with the world."[27]

This emphasis on realization of vital selfhood as enfolded in a pattern of cosmic movement gives this practice an indubitably spiritual character.

T'ai-Chi Ch'üan promotes a dynamic mental and physical presence of slowness, lightness, calmness, clarity, and balance. By stressing the quality of balance, or *Heng*, T'ai-Chi Ch'üan is clearly related to the physiological activity of maintaining one's balance; however, Chinese medicine also stresses the maintenance of balance in regard both to the yin-yang movement and the basic substances of the world, and so the balance sought is more than physiological. It is interesting to note that ancient Chinese medicine includes a notion of health as the realization of balanced forces and substances that is not unlike the theory of humours in ancient Western medicine. Yet more than in the Platonic traditions of spirituality, the medicinal emphasis on balance remained crucial for the major Taoist, Confucian, and Buddhist conceptions of spiritual well-being.

An emphasis on balance is evident in the basic stance adopted by practitioners of T'ai-Chi Ch'üan. The individual stands upright with feet parallel and apart, separated by approximately one foot. The knees are slightly bent; the back is kept straight but not arched; the buttocks are tucked under. No joint is locked, nor any muscle tensed. Arms hang down at the sides of the body, straight but not stiff. Eyes look forward at the horizon. This stance presents a vivid contrast with the military posture of standing at attention used in Western armies. Here the individual stands upright with heels together and feet facing forward. The shoulders are pulled back, the back is arched, and the arms and hands are extended down along the thighs. Eyes face forward and the chin is pulled in. The body's muscles are kept very taut. Standing at attention is not a posture that the body naturally adopts. It is deliberately imposed upon the body in a twofold sense. First, the body is conformed to the soldier's own conscious will. Second, the soldier is obedient to the superior officer who commands adoption of this posture. It suggests the imposition of static relations of hierarchical dominance as a strategy for obtaining stability and order amidst a dangerously complex world. The T'ai-Chi Ch'üan stance is suggestive of an alternative strategy. It seeks to make one immune to threatening changes, both internal and external. Conceiving the threat to be internal stresses the medicinal value of the art, while conceiving it as an external threatening adversary emphasizes its value as a martial art. In this latter capacity T'ai-Chi Ch'üan is an art of gaining advantage by yielding gracefully—of using opponents' aggressive movements against them. It is a fluid dialectic that engages reality by transforming it into its opposite; this is part of its spiritual meaning. Whether one construes the opposites in the Chinese metaphysical language of yin and yang, or in the Western semiological categories of the full and the empty, it remains true that this aspect of T'ai-Chi Ch'üan exerts a transformative yet irenic power. "Do that which consists in taking no action, and order will prevail."[28] This maxim from the *Tao Te Ching* is embodied in an individual's movement, but lays claim to cosmic correspondences as well. It suggests that generalized notions of equilibration have relevance to the vitality of community life. An insalubrious community life was earlier shown to have aggravated Pascal's predicament, and so this thesis will be explored in the next section.

EVOLUTIONS AND INTERPRETATIONS

Biology differs from chemistry and physics because of the relative complexity of its object of study. Consequently, one of its distinctive tasks is to explain the emergence of complexity in specific living forms. As noted previously, C.H. Waddington has remarked that the complexity of life is manifest in the multiple dimensions of time which must be invoked in its description and explanation. Answers to simple questions, such as why the human heart beats as it does, include specification of the relevant time scale. For instance, a physiological response speaks of the fibrous composition of the heart muscle, the neurological causation of its rhythmic contractions, and the fluid dynamics of the circulation of blood. In a different manner, an evolutionary answer mentions how differences in heart shapes are inherited and contribute differentially to the adaptation and survival of mammals.

Just as a body organ can be studied in different time frames, so too can the phenomenon of physiological homeostasis. For instance, the development and demise of specific processes of biological self-regulation can be charted throughout an organism's lifetime. Also, the notion of homeostasis is itself capable of being further generalized for use in an evolutionary context. Several projects of this sort have been undertaken by contemporary biologists. In each case the evolutionary context shows that the stability maintained through self-regulation is not directly a property of individual organisms, but instead, belongs to some community of organisms. Notions of biological equilibration thereby take on a social character. By reflecting upon biological equilibration in this wider evolutionary perspective I hope to gain a vantage point from which to survey philosophically the social character of spiritually disciplined practices, and especially, I hope to assess their potential for promoting the stable social preconditions of genuine human vitality. This, at least, is the agenda of the current section.

One very expansive generalization of the notion of homeostasis occurs as part of J.E. Lovelock's provocative "Gaia hypothesis." Simply stated this hypothesis claims that Gaia is "a complex entity involving the Earth's biosphere, atmosphere, oceans, and soil: the totality constituting a feedback or cybernetic system which seeks an optimal physical and chemical environment for life on this planet." The passage continues, "The maintenance of relatively constant conditions by active control may be conveniently described by the term 'homeostasis.' "[29] In the technical writings of Lovelock and his colleagues, detailed evidence is presented to show how the earth maintains the moderate temperatures, chemical compositions, and other conditions requisite for the flourishing of earthly life. Most evolutionary biologists remain unconvinced. Strict Darwinians argue that there is no mechanism of natural selection that allows organisms to restrain reproduction for the sake of a global community: virtuous genes that somehow favor distantly related living things or promote long-term environmental viability will lose out to selfish genes seeking proximate advantages. Lovelock has rejoinders to such criticisms, but he has not dissuaded critics from finding a veiled ethical import to his Gaia hypothesis. To many critics his writings do not so much advance the scientific hypothesis that the earth is a living organism as they do the ethical imperative that it should be treated as if it were alive. This commingling of scientific speculation and moral conviction has made the Gaia hypothesis attractive to ecological activists. The popularity of the Gaia hypothesis among a portion of the politically active public attests to the imaginative appeal of the notion of a self-correcting balance of forces in descriptions of human and cosmic vitality.

A second controversial proposal has differently imported the notion of homeostatic equilibrium into the context of evolutionary biology. From their studies of the earth's fossil records the paleontologists Niles Eldredge and Stephen Jay Gould have concluded that "The history of life is more adequately represented by a picture of 'punctuated equilibria' than by the notion of phyletic gradualism."[30] By this latter notion they mean the view that new species arise— and thereby evolution occurs—from slow and constant changes in large populations. Their own theory holds that "The history of evolution is not one of stately unfolding, but a story of homeostatic equilibria, disturbed only 'rarely' (rather often in the fullness of time) by rapid and episodic events of speciation."[31] In other words, the equilibria which natural selection maintains between species and their local environments are periodically "punctuated" by the emergence of new species, and it is these speciation events that are the primary source of evolutionary change.

Gould especially has sometimes written of "punctuated equilibria" as a refutation of Darwinism and a new theory of evolution.[32] Few informed commentators accept such sweeping characterizations. Instead they regard the theory as a more or less warranted minor modification in the Neo-Darwinian synthesis achieved early in the twentieth century. This synthesis of Darwin's theory of natural selection with Mendelian genetics may be summarized with the following maxim: "Genes mutate; organisms are selected; species evolve." Evolution requires a population of mortal organisms that is not perfectly adapted to their environment, but which is sufficiently fertile so as to generate an overproduction of individuals. The theory of natural selection explains how such organisms become adapted to survive in particular environments by the fact that random genetic variations allow some organisms to survive and reproduce more readily than others. The synthesis of the theory of natural selection with Mendelian genetics has yielded the discipline of population genetics with its mathematically rigorous formulation of evolution as the differential inheritance of gene frequencies in living populations. Eldredge and Gould depart most from this synthesis when they infer from the fossil record a sharp distinction between brief periods of dynamic speciation and long periods of relative stasis.[33]

Two mechanisms of equilibration are basic principles of evolutionary biology. The first is a statistical axiom of population genetics called the Hardy-Weinberg equilibrium principle. Informally construed, it says that processes of sexual reproduction do not by themselves change the frequencies of genes in a randomly mating population; this implies that evolution can not occur by means of sexual reproduction alone. Hence there can exist populations of randomly mating organisms which undergo no significant evolutionary change. So crucial are such stable populations in evolutionary genetics that they have a special name; they are called "demes." Stated another way, the equilibrium principle says that regardless of the initial relative frequencies of genes (more specifically, of diploid genotypes) in Mendelian demes, these frequencies will come to fit the

Hardy-Weinberg distribution in the next and subsequent generations. The temporal context here spans only two or three generations, and so the Hardy-Weinberg principle identifies a hereditary mechanism of biological equilibration.

To say that no significant evolutionary change occurs in demes does not imply that natural selection is inoperative. Indeed, even in an unchanging environment a stabilizing variety of natural selection often takes place that eliminates the most extreme genetic variations introduced by mutation and migration. In other words, the organisms which this second evolutionary variety of equilibration allows to survive and reproduce are not only the fittest, but also the most typical individuals in the population. Evolution occurs in the sense that natural selection takes place in an environment that is never absolutely unchanged, but it is not the dramatic sort of evolution manifest in the origin of species.[34]

Darwinians have so successfully used the ideas of chance variation, natural selection, and equilibration in their explanations of the emergence of biological complexity that social scientists and philosopher have been enticed to follow their example: this same process has become an important resource for explaining aspects of cultural evolution. Recent decades have brought the emergence of theories of the "the development of the noosphere" from the Jesuit paleontologist Teilhard de Chardin, of the "ecology of mind" from the radical anthropologist Gregory Bateson, and of "memic evolution" from the reductionist biologist Richard Dawkins.[35] Philosophers had much earlier engaged in generalizing the Darwinian conception of natural selection, Herbert Spencer and Charles Sanders Peirce being among the first to cast philosophical cosmology and epistemology in evolutionary terms influenced by Darwin. Both philosophers introduced what are now regarded as unscientific elements into Darwin's account of evolution. Spencer's "Lamarckism," or his belief that acquired traits could be passed on to offspring, gave his philosophy a sanguine view of the role of education in human cultural evolution, while Peirce's "agapism" posited a purposeful course of development in the history of life. Such evolutionary optimism is not scientifically warranted because biological evolution is not intrinsically directed toward complexity as, for instance, in an opposite way, closed physical systems move toward conditions of maximum entropy and minimum structure in accordance with the second law of thermodynamics. Environments exert a selective pressure for suitably adapted forms, whether they are more or less complex than their predecessors. The evolution of asexual species from sexual ones well attests to the movement from heterogeneity to homogeneity in the history of life. Yet since more complex forms allow for more numerous and more differentiated strategies of adaption, they may be regarded as having an indirect favoring by natural selection.

In the twentieth century philosophers like Karl Popper and Stephen Toulmin have been foremost advocates of an evolutionary epistemology. This variety of the theory of knowledge uses the Darwinian idea of a selective system to explain the development of adequate scientific theories about the world. In his Herbert Spencer Lecture at Oxford University in 1961 Popper said:

> The growth of our knowledge is the result of a process closely resembling what Darwin called "natural selection"; that is, *the natural selection of hypotheses:* our knowledge consists, at every moment, of those hypotheses which have shown their comparative fitness by surviving so far in their struggle for existence.[36]

In the language of his earlier writings, fit hypotheses are those which have been "corroborated," i.e., they are falsifiable conjectures that have consistently passed logical and empirical tests of their adequacy; unfit hypotheses are those that have been refuted or have been shown to be unfalsifiable.[37] Popper says his account of the natural selection of hypotheses is "not meant metaphorically, though of course it makes use of metaphors."[38] Toulmin is equally emphatic in denying the metaphorical status of the claim that scientific thought develops by variation and selection; his major work *Human Understanding* supplements Popper's more logical approach with a portrayal of the social processes by which scientists formulate, evaluate, and perpetuate theoretical accounts of nature.[39]

There are at least two ways in which a selective system applies differently to scientific hypotheses than it does to gene-bearing organisms. First, selection is not entirely natural in the former case because unfit hypotheses do not meet as definitive a fate as do dead organisms and extinct species. Aristarchos' heliocentric theory of the solar system was rejected by Ptolemy, but revived by Copernicus. Astrology has been debunked by scientists but survives in popular culture because it serves other purposes than scientific explanation. Popper admits that most theoretical problems in science are only distantly related to human physical survival. He rejects a vulgar Darwinism that says ideas are valuable only to the extent that they give direct biological advantages and he even implies that the evolutionary model is relevant to the growth of unfalsifiable humanistic attempts to understand the world.[40]

A second qualification Popper does not acknowledge. It says that in the epistemological context variations are not randomly generated; instead, they are intentionally formulated in order to solve a specific problem.[41] Hypotheses which seem to their author only distantly related to prominent competitors may not be publicly offered for discussion and criticism. In this way logically possible but improbable ideational variants are deemed unfit prior to their entrance into a competitive environment. Hence a sort of stabilizing process of selection occurs before as well as after hypotheses are fully and publicly formulated. Peirce wrote about the "sympathy" of ideas for one another and the "continuity" of mental processes as speculative reasons why ideas do not emerge by random variation alone.[42] The social psychology of conformity also plays a role.

If the variation of hypotheses are not random and their selection is not natural, then what remains of the project of evolutionary epistemology? Is it merely an elaborate analogy? In my mind and for my present purposes, it is at least that, and as with most good analogies it is just as insightful for how it fails as for how it succeeds. The intentional disinclination to formulate possible but unpromising hypotheses in public is partially due to the fact the differential selection of ideas presupposes a cooperative social environment as well as supportive natural environment. An evolutionary epistemology, of either the Peircian or Popperian variety, stipulates that intellectual problem solving is always a social process and thereby always requires a relatively stable social environment. Hence a problem presupposed in all other intellectual problems is how to maintain stable social institutions of disciplined scholarship under changing circumstances. Confirmation of this necessity is provided by the way intellectual extremists—both crackpots and geniuses—are resisted, and even persecuted, by scientific and other scholarly institutions. Thomas Kuhn has written how "normal science" proceeds by workers conforming to the intellectual guidance of a shared "paradigm" and Toulmin describes how participation in institutionally situated "disciplines" encourages work that preserves the social status of one's discipline and oneself within that discipline.[43]

Religious creeds and theological speculations are not offered by believers, nor are they countenanced by doubters, as empirically falsifiable theories whose truth awards their adherents some direct sort of biological advantage. Hence if the history of religious thought is described via a selective system in which variant conjectures are articulated, criticized, and perpetuated on the basis of their ability to withstand criticism, the criteria of selection cannot be empirical or biological. They must be theological and social: proposals survive and flourish to the extent that they solve theological problems, and promote social stability and cooperation among the groups that subscribe actively or passively to them. The relevant disputants may be conservative priesthoods of state religions or radical prophets of discontented minorities, but among them, the theological proposals which successfully overcome competitors will be those that foster cooperative social solidarity in addition to solving strictly theological problems.

Understanding religious intellectual life with the assistance of the idea of a selective system becomes more plausible to the extent that one attributes a role to social and political factors in shaping the course of religious controversies. It not essential here to specify what it means to solve a theological problem beyond observing that theologians cannot so readily appeal to publicly observable tests of their contentions as can scientists. Thus the social criterion of selection takes on relatively greater prominence in accounting for the evolution of theology and other humanistic disciplines. It is not surprising that as biologists have come to speak about religion from a evolutionary perspective they do so assuming the Durkheimian maxim that "religion is something eminently social."[44]

Attention to the social and political factors at work in the evolution of religious belief systems is also increasingly evident among historical theologians and historians of religion. The history of Christian doctrine from the Jerusalem Council to the Council of Nicea offers an apt illustration. Prior to the Enlightenment, Christian historians commonly attributed developments in this period to struggles between orthodox church leaders inspired by the Holy Spirit and heretical schismatics doing the work of Satan. In the nineteenth century historical scholarship revealed the plurality of views even within the orthodox ranks; this prompted historical accounts of the gradual development of Christian beliefs toward full doctrinal explicitness such as was given to the doctrine of the Trinity at Nicea. Though historically mediated, the processes active in the development of Christian doctrine as described by figures like F.C. Baur and John Henry Newman were still subject to transcendent guiding forces.[45] Prompted by the discoveries of further historical research and by the challenge of secular social theory, historical theologians in the present century have become even more attentive to social and political matters.[46] Walter Bauer's *Orthodoxy and Heresy in Earliest*

Christianity is an instructive representative of the movement of academic scholarship. In this book Bauer argued that theological positions which Christian tradition has deemed orthodox were not always and everywhere established prior to the emergence of opposing views later named heretical. Hence orthodox views, said Bauer, sometimes gained dominance via a process of controversy, even sometimes surviving competition from heretical views for reasons not strictly theological. For instance, Bauer argues that Ignatius, the first-century bishop of Antioch, unabashedly used his centralized ecclesiastical powers in order to overcome heretical opponents.[47]

The trends toward employing evolutionary motifs in sociology and sociological motifs in historical theology combine in the recent work of Gerd Theissen, a German historian of early Christianity. In the 1970s Theissen began interpreting the faith of early Christians in light of the sociology of both the Jewish Christianity of the Palestinian community founded by Jesus and the Hellenistic Christianity of the Gentile mission undertaken by Paul.[48] Regarding this latter context, he is especially noted for his thesis that the Church there adopted the social form of *Liebespatriarchalismus* (love patriarchalism): this means that it embraced traditional forms of social differentiation, including those based on gender and class, but it did so in a way theologically qualified by the Christian love ethos. Women, for instance, became excluded from positions of church leadership, but were granted an eschatological equality with men "in Christ Jesus" (Gal. 3:28). Both features, says Theissen, promoted stability of the Church as a growing social institution. By recognizing differences in social roles the Church gained a continuity with its ambient society and an efficiency in its administration which aided in the integration of large numbers of new members. The "itinerant radicalism" of Jesus and his immediate followers were generally unwilling to make such practical accommodations. By appealing to the Christian love ethos, church leaders assuaged social tensions inherited from the similarly diverse population of the Roman empire. Elitist Gnostic groups did not seek so diverse a membership; they thereby avoided certain social tensions but insured at the same time their marginality as a form of religious social life. Love patriarchalism weds a compensatory belief system with a centrally organized but flexible social system, thereby instantiating forms of social equilibration emphasized by the American sociologist Talcott Parsons.[49] Theissen believes that this combination of elements was crucial for the growth and endurance of Christianity, not in the least because it was a social form that served the interests of the Emperor Constantine, a Christian convert and the convener of the Council of Nicea.[50]

Although I do not concur with all aspects of Theissen's work, I think that his sociological and evolutionary perspective is helpful for understanding the social meaning of spiritually disciplined practices. The only social feature so far mentioned in this discussion of spiritual discipline is the requirement of a spiritual master. The master-disciple relationship was portrayed as having just the salient features of Theissen's love patriarchalism: the master exerts authority over the disciple based on age, office, and practical skill, but this authority is recognized by both as itself subservient to an ethos of love and enlightenment. In a sense love patriarchalism is a sociological generalization of the more intimate master-disciple relationship. Also, just as many spiritually disciplined practices can claim to be life affirming by their promotion of the physiological processes of equilibration required for human individual health, so too can some claim to affirm social well-being by promoting sociological processes of equilibration: ascetic practices temper aggressive and sexual drives that undermine social solidarity and celebratory rituals require social cooperation for their performance and thereby foster such cooperation more generally.

While arguing for the relevance of physiological processes of biological equilibration to spiritually discipline practices, I mentioned a correlative notion of phenomenological equilibration. Indebted to Merleau-Ponty this notion specified the experience of attending to a part of one's own body in a way that objectifies it, but does so only in conjunction with the experience of the body's unity as both the agent and the object of perception. Disciplined embodied practices like dancing or T'ai Chi Ch'üan deserve their status as disciplined, I claimed, because they involve a discriminating awareness and control of bodily movements at the same time that they exhibit sensitivity to a wholeness of bodily form which encompasses its parts and is in turn encompassed by a natural environment. In concluding this section I will sketch a related notion of phenomenological equilibration which is suggested by the way some spiritually disciplined practices promote a dynamic sort of social stability. It is most evident in spiritual practices having a character more intellectual than embodied, and is especially evident in the interpretive study of religious texts.

Almost all religious traditions with a corpus of sacred scriptures regard the study of these writings as a commendable if not obligatory practice, yet nowhere has such study been more central to a community's religious life than in rabbinic Judaism. The example of rabbinic Judaism is especially appropriate because of how it combines textual piety and historical stability. Enduring as a dominant social form from its formation in the first century after the destruction of the Jerusalem Temple until the nineteenth century and its dissolution by secular forces, rabbinic Judaism showed remarkable stability as a social modality of Jewish life. It was able to adapt, survive, and flourish in an often hostile environment of pagan, Christian, and Islamic culture. At the center of social life was the rabbi—a figure whose diligent study and extensive knowledge of Torah enabled him to be, like Moses, a personal paragon of Jewish life and a juridical administrator of Jewish law. Given the particular circumstances of individual Jewish communities, the effort to embody and administer the Torah involved interpretation. The central myth of rabbinic Judaism was that God handed down a dual revelation at Sinai, a written part recorded in the Hebrew Bible, and an oral part, some of which was later recorded in mishnaic and talmudic texts, and some of which remains to be explained by rabbis as they and their communities face new circumstances in which Torah must be applied. So highly valued was the interpretive study of Torah, or Midrash, that God and the angels in heaven were said to do it. The rabbis had not only Moses, but God, too, as an exemplar!

The way rabbis transmitted religious and cultural traditions with a social sensitivity to the changing circumstances of their community is a major factor contributing to the stability of rabbinic Judaism. The witness of Torah and the labors of Moses reveal above all else that it is God's will that the Jewish people endure and flourish. Practices which manifestly obstruct this will are suspect; so, for instance, celibacy never became a Jewish religious ideal. Interpretation of Torah in its various forms thus becomes responsible to the contemporaneous community of interpretation as well as to the text itself, previous respected commentators, and the individual's own convictions.[51] This is especially the case for halakhic Midrash— exegesis concerning Jewish religious and civil law. Literary theorists have recently shown great interest in other varieties of Midrash, and especially in mystical kabbalistic exegesis. They have been attracted by the imaginative resourcefulness of these Jewish kabbalistic exegetes.[52] I am emphasizing here something different which is the combination of a commitment to the figurative fecundity of sacred text with a social responsibility to a community of interpretation. It is the acceptance of this dual responsibility which constitutes one dimension of the disciplined character of scripture study as a variety of spiritual practice.

Toward the end of his life, after he had encountered Husserl's *Logical Investigations*, Wilhelm Dilthey articulated a hermeneutical framework for the human sciences. Crucial to this hermeneutical project was what Dilthey called a "community of life unities" (die Gemeinsamkeit der Lebenseinheiten)."[53] This community is characterized by a double dynamic of wholes and parts, one of which is directly relevant here. Dilthey says that a shared language provides a community with an intersubjective medium in which both mutual identification and individuation occurs. Shared language allows for the communication of beliefs, values, feelings, and hopes which enable people to identify with one another's lives, yet it also empowers the conversational disputes that sets individual interlocutors apart from their community. The experience of the community is the presupposition of understanding, including the individual's understanding of himself or herself.

The phenomenon of reflective interpretation begins with an objectification of that which a person seeks to understand, whether it be a text or a text's interpretation. The text is made an object of consciousness. The same experience individuates the interpreter by making that person a conscious bearer of a possibly novel textual interpretation. Yet at the same time, because the interpretation is carried out in the medium of shared language, it implicitly identifies the interpreter with the text and competing interpretations. Something counts as an interpretation of some specific text, and as an alternative to other actual interpretations, only because it is offered with a consciousness of its participation with them in a single linguistic community. The workings of this interpretive consciousness is a species of phenomenological equilibration. By means of the medium of language the phenomenological equilibration that Merleau-Ponty detected in body consciousness is elevated to a social sphere by interpretive action undertaken within the context and for the sake of a social body. Continual self-regulation seeks to adopt the best balance between individual creativity and communal cooperation in interpretation. Adverting to the previous discussion of rabbinic Judaism, kabbalistic Midrash so greatly favored individual creativity that it was resisted by the orthodox rabbinate responsible for Jewish juridical life. On the other hand, halakhic Midrash proved insufficiently attentive to creative aspirations in post-Enlightenment European Judaism and so many individual Jews forsook the juridical Jewish community for secular society. Clearly the social viability of a religious community requires a balancing of the innovative energy that sustains creative individuals and the communal forces that preserve traditions and mobilize social action. By referring to the example of Torah study by Jewish rabbis I have sought to identify a social experience of phenomenological equilibration that promotes this balance and reveals the disciplined character of scriptural study as a spiritual practice.

The second dynamic of wholes and parts that Dilthey counts as part of his community of life unities is the relation between individual experiences in a person's life and the recollected and projected whole of that person's life history. Here is a diachronic life unity mediated by the experience of history; it complements the linguistically mediated synchronic unity just described and makes possible historical understanding as a communal venture, and specifically, it makes the human sciences possible. It also explains how the life of someone like Pascal can be exemplary of a widely shared human predicament. It is to this process of individual life development that I turn in the last section of this chapter on biological equilibration.

STAGES AND ILLUSIONS

It was noted earlier that the quest for spiritual wellbeing is often born from encounters in which the complexity of the natural and social worlds is experienced as a chaotic impingement upon one's peace of mind, and, perhaps, one's health. From such experiences comes the injunction for simplicity in action and intention. Accordingly, spiritual discipline frequently takes the form of abstaining from certain behaviors. Yet, also, it often involves thinking about customary behavior in a disciplined way, i.e., with the aid of unifying religious symbols, narratives, and maxims. In this second approach, complexity is not absolutely reduced, but rather complex phenomena are rendered more intelligible and so less effectively chaotic.

Simplicity of conception and application has long been regarded as an attractive attribute of scientific theories. For example, the Copernican account of the solar system was originally less accurate in tracing planetary orbits than was its Ptolemaic rival, yet its theoretical parsimony won it advocates who later demonstrated its empirical superiority. Simplicity is at least as much an asset for reflective accounts of the spiritual life. Kierkegaard even wrote a guide to the Christian life as an exposition of the maxim that "Purity of heart is to will one thing."[54] The spiritual quest for simplicity can be more concretely illustrated. In periods of rapid social change—the late classical period of Clement, the early modern era of Pascal, or contemporary North America—the demands of diverse and changing social relationships are extraordinarily stressful. Some persons seek to relieve such stress by restricting the number and variety of their social contacts; others seek to regularize the contacts they do have. Each of these responses has sometimes taken spiritually disciplined forms. To reduce social contacts anchorites adopt a rigorously solitary life. Missionaries respond in an opposite manner: they uniformly address others in the distinctive ways their religious convictions require, sometimes with loving service, sometimes with coercive instruction, and usually with an admixture of both. In the first case spiritual discipline takes on a more practical and privative character, while in the second, it is more didactic and dynamic. This dichotomy, however, should not be too sharply drawn. I have favored the phrase 'spiritual discipline' just because it is inclusive of both spiritual instruction about behavior and behavior undertaken in accordance with such instruction.

Following Plato's lead, Clement described an ideal of stability of self and society with the aid of the idea of a static hierarchy, and he predicated his spiritual prescriptions on this philosophical basis. I have argued that physical vitality and social comity are better described by notions of biological equilibration, specifically with the notion of self-regulation by negative feedback manifest in processes of physiological homeostasis and the notion of evolution toward complexity manifest in processes of natural selection. A practical consequence of this alternative way of looking at one's spiritual predicament is that disruptive environmental forces may be dealt with by efforts to have compensation for them and not simply control over them. This strategy acknowledges that efficacy at dealing with the threats of a complex world is gained only by becoming more complex oneself. Specifying the meaning of this vague but pregnant statement is a major aim of the section which follows.

A second reason for turning to notions of biological equilibration is to parry Nietzsche's criticism of "ascetic ideals," a phrase I take to be inclusive of ascetic practices and their rationalizations. Nietzsche criticized—indeed, calumniated—Clement's and Pascal's understanding of spiritual discipline because he thought it decadent. It negates bodily life and frustrates individual creativity, said Nietzsche. It perverts social relationships, too, because these ideals are sustained by feelings of resentment. Construing life in terms of "the instinct for growth, for continuance, for accumulation of forces, of *power*," Nietzsche decried traditional spiritual disciplines for thwarting the vital process by which "One Becomes What One Is."[55] Conscious of this Nietszchean critique I have described spiritually disciplined practices with the aid of notions of biological equilibration because they are descriptive of the preconditions of individual and social well-being. I have yet to counter the Nietzschean point that ascetic ideals are inimical to the invigorating processes of life itself. Thus it remains to be shown here that the categoreal theme of biological equilibration is helpful for understanding how individuals grow, and specifically, for understanding how they grow more complex and more vital.

The growth of individual organisms constitutes the subject matter of developmental biology and psychology. The time span relevant to this variety of biological investigation is the organism's individual lifetime. Already mentioned have been notions of biological equilibration relevant to the other temporal frameworks of biological science—the momentary contexts of physiologists and the multigenerational contexts of geneticists and evolutionists. A developmental conception of biological equilibration will thus be part of a series of notions which effect a progressive generalization of physiological homeostasis. Different methods of generalization have been mentioned less directly. Introspective psychologists like William James or Sigmund Freud theorized about human personality in terms of stabilizing interactions of psychological forces, in this way extending a medical paradigm of equilibration to less tangible mental phenomenon. Social scientists like Alfred Marshall and Vilfredo Pareto pioneered mathematical representations of systems of interpersonal economic and social forces, in effect, applying physical models of equilibration to human behavior[56]. Talcott Parsons, as noted before, has sought to combine these perspectives by rooting a formalistic theory of social systems in a psychologically articulated theory of action. I am undertaking a yet more bold generalization in which notions of biological equilibration are given philosophical breadth so as to be useful for describing spiritually disciplined practices, and in this section, for showing how such practices promote spiritual growth.

Growth for the developmental biologist is just an organism's irreversible increase of mass, usually by means of cell division and protein synthesis. The full development of an organism from embryo to adult involves a multiform process of differentiation: in time, whereby cells become specified as certain types of tissues; in space, whereby like cell tissues become localized in certain parts of the body; and in shape, whereby cells, organs, and bodies adopt a nested group of configurations. The actual course of an embryo's growth and differentiation is determined by a combination of genetic instructions and environmental interactions. Differentiation constitutes one way in which growth brings increased complexity. A second emerges from the fact that biological development is a self-regulating process that occurs in stages. This is true in several respects. Growth and differentiation occur at varying rates at various time's in an organism's development, ceasing in some important respects at the achievement of adulthood. More importantly, the passage from embryo to adult is characterized by repeated transitions from relative stability to relative flux, and then to a more complex form of approximate stability. The passage from the blastula to the gastrula stage which follows quickly upon the fertilization of an egg cell is an archetypical example of such a sequence of stable forms. The organism's adult form has a singular status: its physiological integrity is identifiable with the results of the proper functioning of homeostatic processes of physiological equilibration. The realization of stability of this sort relies on others; for instance, it relies upon the fact that protein molecules, under proper conditions, are thermodynamically more stable than the collection of their component elements, thereby allowing for the spontaneous assembly of protein macromolecules. Even more fundamentally, equilibrium at the cellular and organismic levels of complexity requires a constant importation of energy from the environment—an adaptive equilibrium.

Self-regulation of development is effected by the genetically determined synthesis of proteins. Enzymes—proteins whose structure enables them to be catalysts of chemical reactions—play an especially important regulatory role. They can speed up or slow down chemical reactions. In response to environmental changes the concentration of enzymes in a cell can be increased manyfold. Also, negative feedback mechanisms operate in this context to maintain constant rates of reactions. In these ways, enzymes, and their respective genetic determinants, work to insure the pace and integrity of an organism's development toward adulthood. Much recent research in embryology is concerned with the processes by which genes keep a maturing organism within certain developmental pathways despite the presence of genetic and environmental abnormalities.[57] Illustrations of developmental constraints imposed by more general physical forces and geometrical forms are plentiful in D'Arcy Thompson's classic text, *On Growth and Form*.[58] For instance, an organism's heat loss is proportional to its surface area (the square of its linear dimension) while its heat gain is proportional to its bulk (the cube of its linear dimension). Hence as its size diminishes the ratio of heat loss to heat gain increases: to maintain a stable temperature the smaller organism must have a higher metabolism and a shorter life span.

Relative to their size, mice eat more than elephants, but pachyderms live longer! This fact vividly shows that an organism's development is constrained by the need to maintain a high degree of internal and external equilibrium.

The relationship between development and equilibration can be stated even more directly by equating biological development with the emergence of stages of progressively more complex processes of biological equilibration. Such a conception of biological development has influenced the thought of the Swiss psychologist Jean Piaget; indeed, Piaget frequently acknowledged his debt to embryologists like Waddington. He stressed the aspects of development noted above, positing, for instance, that "Life is essentially auto-regulation."[59] An emphasis on stages is also notable in Piaget: central to his developmental psychology are sequential stages of intelligence in which the sensory-motor operations of a child are said to give rise to concrete, semilogical interactions with objects, and then to fully abstract, logical operations.[60] Principles of equilibration are invoked by Piaget to explain how psychological structures are constructed by operational interaction with the environment; they allow him to resist wholesale appeals to biological innateness such as Noam Chomsky has made in regard to linguistic structure.

Piaget's developmental psychology assumes a biological description of human beings as organisms acting to maintain their structural integrity. Internal organization and external adaptation promote this end. Successful adaptation involves the creation of more complex structures which allow for an increase of productive interchanges between the organism and environment. It consists of assimilation and accommodation. When an organism assimilates aspects of its environment, it transforms them so that they become a part of its internal structure and functional activity, i.e., consumed food is transformed into the organism's unique bodily substance and process. Accommodation, in a complementary manner, is the process by which organisms change themselves so as to more adequately interact with salient features of their environment: mammals living at high altitudes utilize atmospheric oxygen more efficiently than do sea-level residents. Adaptation, in brief, is an equilibrium between assimilation and accommodation; it is the equilibrium of the organism changed by the environment with the environment changed by the organism.

Piaget conceives of human knowledge in these same terms:

> Human knowledge is essentially active. To know is to assimilate reality into systems of transformation. Knowing

an object does not mean copying it—it means acting upon it. It means constructing systems of transformations that can be carried out on or with this object. Knowledge is a system of transformations that becomes progressively more adequate.[61]

Intelligence is an adaptive activity of highly complex organisms. Logical form is the principle of internal organization to which environmental data is assimilated, and experience is the organism's accommodation of logical form to the particularities of its environment. Cognitive judgment integrates logical form and experience, and thereby integrates an organism and its environment into a single meaningful reality. By elaborating more complex logical forms through intelligent action human beings gain access to enriched experiences and a more adequate knowledge of the world. Intelligence includes the capacity for effectively responding to novelty. It enables one to compensate for environmental disturbances so that they not endanger health and equanimity, and to appreciate rare and wondrous occurrences so that they might accrue in satisfying patterns of meaning.

Piaget believes that intelligence is the type of biological adaptation which contends with the most variable and inclusive environments. I would further say that when the world is attended to in a maximally inclusive way, as the totality of all that is, and when the self that endures is likewise optimally construed, as one truest self, then intelligence becomes a process of adaptation that can be said to have spiritual dimensions. There are precedents for extending a Piagetian model of developmental psychology in a spiritual direction. Lawrence Kohlberg does so when he posits a seventh, religious stage to his six stage account of moral development.[62] James Fowler also does so by positing six stages of faith development that parallel Kohlberg's moral stages and Piaget's cognitive stages.[63] Kohlberg's psychological portrayal of moral life has a markedly Kantian character, the highest stage of moral thinking being identified with the formulation and application of universal principles. His understanding of religion is also Kantian in the sense that he sees moral development as necessary, though not sufficient, for religious development. Kohlberg has been criticized for his Kantianism; for instance, Carol Gilligan has argued that his rule-oriented account of morality is very rationalistic and so more germane to men than women.[64] I am sympathetic to this criticism, having sought to understand spiritual life in terms of habitual embodied practices rather than with the traditional category of supramental contemplation. Still, I find Kohlberg's remarks about religion congenial because, like my own, they seek to be mindful of Kant's critique of philosophical theology. Also, he finds in Kantian philosophy, with the aid of John Rawls, an important conception of intellectual equilibration which I think is of considerable relevance to rethinking the meaning of spiritually disciplined practices.

The relevance of biological and psychological strategies of adaptation to the predicament of the spiritual life can be indicated by reflecting on the several meanings of illusion. According to Piaget illusions frustrate the assimilatory mechanism of intelligence by fracturing the world into appearance and reality, into perceptual truth and cognitive truth. Illusions effect this split in two quite different ways. One is evident in the child's inability to grasp principles of quantitative conservation. A beaker of water is entirely emptied into two other beakers in a child's presence: questioning reveals that the child does not realize that the quantity of water in the second and third beakers is equal to the quantity originally contained in the first. Piaget contends that this illusion of nonconservation is characteristic of a certain stage of intellectual development in which logical operations are only partially grasped. Once such operations are fully grasped the child no longer perceives a divided whole as unequal to an undivided whole. Piaget understands intelligence as a more complex and inclusive relation of equilibrium between organisms and environments than is obtainable by perception alone. Specifically, intellectual operations are reversible; one can undo a group theoretical transformation by an inverse operation, but perceptual acts like scanning an optical illusion cannot be reversed—one cannot return to a point of not having seen what one did, in fact, see. Piaget's reliance on the reversibility of group theoretical transformations to explain the highest stages of intellectual equilibration is problematic. It betrays a formalistic bias in accounting for intelligence because other scientists have been able to confirm its empirical importance.[65] A richer notion of equilibration seems desirable.

A second kind of illusion—the optico-geometrical kind—is less amenable to intellectual correction. Knowing that the central shafts of two arrows are equal does not prevent them from appearing unequal when one has its arrowhead splayed outward and the other inward (the Müller-Lyer illusion). Intellectually mature adults still see two circles of equal diameter as unequal when one has a concentric circle just inside of it while the other has a concentric circle just outside of it (the Delboeuf illusion). In the nineteenth century

Hermann von Helmholtz established this basic principle for the scientific investigation of optical illusions: they cannot be perceptually negated by conscious intellectual knowledge, though their illusory appearance is diminished by repeated perceptual examination. He also correctly surmised that the illusions do not arise because of movements of the eye nor do they originate in the retina (points which Piaget was not so clear about in his treatment of this sort of illusion). Helmholtz explained optical illusions as errors in unconscious inferences by which the nature of the three-dimensional world is inferred from a two-dimensional retinal image. Though he appears to be wrong about the role of depth perception in optical illusions, contemporary scientists say that the illusions arise because of the way the visual system spontaneously interprets retinal images.[66] Hence correctly understanding an experience of optical illusion involves two sorts of adaptation. First, one must recognize that what has appeared to be the case is not really so; this may be realized by using a ruler to measure relevant distances. Then, second, one must ascertain that the original perception was not simply erroneous, due, for example, to haste or fatigue, but was attributable to healthy processes of perception led astray by unusual sensory input. Of course, what is described here is just a very specific instance of equilibration between assimilative and accommodative strategies of intellectual adaptation, and it provides the broader context in which Piaget's notion of equilibration as transformational reversibility should be located.

The scientific explanations of illusion given by Helmholtz and Piaget were much indebted to Kant. Kant entirely transformed the traditional Platonic understanding of the relationship between cognitive illusion and theological knowledge. First, he regarded as illusory the reification of entities that could not possibly be experienced sensibly; among such entities he included a transcendent God and a substantial soul. This stands in marked contrast to the Platonic attribution of an illusory quality to representations of sense data. Second, Kant thought that transcendental illusions, e.g., that there exists a transcendent God and an immortal soul, are not mistakes due to intellectual immaturity or inexactness, but are inevitable outcomes of reason's interpretation of the deliverances of the understanding and sensation. Illusion for Plato was a consequence of ontology: images are less real than the objects they depict, and these objects themselves, are less real than their ideal forms. For Kant its source is epistemological: illusion results from the misapplication of the rules of understanding in logical and optico-geometrical cases, and from the correct, but potentially deceptive, application of the rules of reason in transcendental illusions. Kant's criticism of traditional arguments for the existence of God were presented in a section of his *Critique of Pure Reason* entitled "Transcendental Dialectic," and dialectic was defined in this context as a "logic of illusion."[67]

Helmholtz, and to a lesser extent, Piaget, helped establish the integrity of perceptual knowledge by systematically explaining how human perception functions. In doing this they and kindred researchers provided a needed corrective to prejudices inherited from Parmenides and Plato which treated sense-based perceptual knowledge as inherently illusory. Jews like Philo and Christians like Clement generally followed Plato on the nature and meaning of illusion. They understood the spiritual life to be a journey from illusion to truth: life dedicated to the pursuit of meretricious pleasures is forsaken for a life devoted to contemplation of God as the epitome of transcendent reality. Several Platonic similes inform this account of spiritual well-being. Spiritual progress was pictured as enlightenment on the model of Plato's famous account of ascent, from a dimly lit cave where shadows cast by a fire are thought real, into a world of sunlight so brilliant that its source cannot be directly viewed (*Republic* 514–17). Even more influential was Plato's description of a contemplative ascent toward absolute beauty recorded in the *Symposium* (210–11). There Socrates speaks of beholding physical beauty in a particular person, and then of moving on to contemplate the ideal of embodied beauty, as, for instance, portrayed in Greek statuary. He next talks of the beauty of an individual's virtuous soul and passes on to the social forms of virtue. Finally, he reaches the intellectual beauty of the sciences that is higher than moral beauty, and yet a step below absolute beauty. With God substituted for absolute beauty this pattern of ascent was directly imported into Christian renderings of spiritual progress: Augustine's famous vision at Ostia recorded in his *Confessiones* (9.10) is one such example; more elaborate is Bonaventure's description of the soul's stages of illumination in his *Intinerarium Mentis ad Deum*.

The terminology for the three stages of the spiritual life was fixed by the Pseudo-Dionysius as purgation ($\kappa\acute{\alpha}\theta\alpha\varrho\sigma\iota\varsigma$), illumination ($\phi\omega\tau\iota\sigma\mu\acute{o}\varsigma$), and perfection ($\tau\epsilon\lambda\epsilon\acute{\iota}\omega\sigma\iota\varsigma$). The last stage was typically understood in terms of mystical communion with God.[68] The second was informed by the Platonic theme of suprasensual vision. The first stage was dedicated to the removal of all hindrances to acceptance of God's graced illumination; it is the sphere of embodied spiritual discipline. In a similar scheme Evagrius Pontus had called this first stage of spiritual life "practical" ($\pi\varrho\alpha\varkappa\tau\iota\varkappa\acute{\eta}$) because it consisted of human actions preparatory to divine illumination. Evagrius understood this preparation, like Clement, in terms of the Stoic notion of passionlessness. Practical spiritual life according to this conception should be dedicated to breaking the power that the passions exert over the human will and that prevent a person from attending fully to things divine, and preeminently, to God.[69]

There is some analogy between this classical problematic of the spiritual life and the predicament I outlined at the end of this book's first part. There I postulated that today one is faced with the task of avoiding enduring habitual behaviors that diminish human vitality and of adopting briefer ones that can inform human behavior with structure and meaning. The philosophical presuppositions, however, are very different—Platonistic in the traditional account, more pragmatic and phenomenological in my own. The Kantian critique of theology and biological notions of development require a different sort of model of spiritual development than the one early Christian writers culled from Plato. One such alternative has been prefigured by three phenomenological notions of equilibration introduced in this chapter. Although I do not claim for them a strictly temporal sequential status, I do think that they constitute idealized stages in the maturation of a spiritual agent engaged in spiritually disciplined practices. In analogy with biological development, then, I propose that spiritual development is the emergence of stages of progressively more complex processes of phenomenological equilibration. Definitive of the very notion of a developmental stage is a distinctive variety of dynamic equilibrium: the first stage in a career of spiritual discipline involves the bodily variety of phenomenological equilibration intimated in Merleau-Ponty's work. It consists of the experiential unity of the body's dual aspects as the subject and object of perception which it attains by their mutual integration into a rhythmic flow of practical behavior. This phenomenological process was exemplified by the sensibility cultivated in the Chinese discipline of T'ai Chi Ch'üan, but it is also capable of cultivation by many embodied regimens of prayer and meditation. It is not directly identifiable with the physiological equilibration of a homeostatic mechanism, for instance, as manifest in functioning of the vestibular balance system— but it is the assimilation of that physiological process into a system of intentional spiritual meanings. Physiological balance becomes transformed into the Chinese spiritual virtue of *Heng*.

Stages of biological equilibration are pregnant with higher stages of development: this preformative role is played by the organism's genetic endowment. In the eminently social and interactive account of psychological equilibration given by Piaget, stages of development are likewise enabled to reach their optimal functioning by contact with others who have attained a higher level of intellectual development. Analogous processes promote spiritual development as it is being portrayed here. Adepts at embodied spiritual practices learn them from masters; hence that very embodied variety of phenomenological equilibration is pregnant with the next higher stage which is the social dimension of phenomenological equilibration. Here Dilthey was crucial. Dilthey stressed that language provides an intersubjective medium in which mutual identification occurs so as to foster a sense of community, yet it also allows for conversation and disputation which enables the individuation of community members, i.e., their self-identification. Just as Dilthey allowed the interpretation of texts to be supplemented by the interpretation of other cultural works, so too did he see natural languages supplemented by nonverbal systems of communication. Hence both the verbal interchange of master and disciple, and their less direct communication through shared practices of spiritual discipline, promote identification with a shared spiritual community and the individuation of a distinctive spiritual self within that community. Maintaining a vital balance between the sense of belonging to a community and yet being still a distinctive individual is a social process of phenomenological equilibration. I suggest that it is important in the spiritual life that the initiate extend his or her sense of community beyond the personality of the master, but yet not so far as to become coextensive with the ambient community understood in its mundane economic and political manifestations.

A spiritual community, like its individual members, resists the direct and indirect forces of secular society which seek to conform it to its ways and interests. In our time, I have suggested, this means resisting the habitual behaviors which governments, corporations and other powerful institutions seek to instill as a way of exerting control over persons politically protected from their direct control. Thus the question arises as to whether the particular spiritually disciplined practices of some spiritual community actually constitute resistance to life-denying social forces or whether they are simply a differentiated manifestation of the same social structure they purportedly resist. Is a church just a business in pious disguise? Is a guru just a huckster peddling Eastern spiritual wares? Finally, to restate Nietzsche's query of Pascal, is a regimen of spiritual discipline just another bad habit? In my opinion a vital spiritual life requires that one ask these questions and that one seek to answer them by engaging in a third process of phenomenological equilibration—a distinctively intellectual one I shall call, following Rawls and Kohlberg, reflective equilibration.

In *A Theory of Justice* John Rawls says that reflective equilibrium is "a notion characteristic of the study of principles which govern actions shaped by self-examination."[70] The equilibrium holds in a system composed of principles regulating human behavior and of judgments made about actual behavior in particular circumstances. Ideally such judgments follow from the more general principles and when they do the system is in equilibrium. Rawls invokes this notion instead of the more usual logical criteria of consistency because the proper fit of principle and judgment is obtained not only be modifying the theoretical principle but also by modifying the practical judgment. He goes on to say that it is relevant to moral reasoning, and to human sciences such as linguistics which include mentalistic conceptions like grammaticality, but it does not have a place in physics or biology. One cannot change observational judgments to make physical theories work, but one can redescribe human behavior so as to accommodate them to moral maxims. Abortion is murder to an orthodox Roman Catholic and a medical procedure to a many a secular humanist. There is no reliable method for obtaining consent as to which moral description is preferable.

Thus reflective equilibration, though it contains an assimilative strategy of modifying principles and an accommodative strategy of modifying descriptive judgments, is a phenomenological rather than a biological process. Equilibrium holds not between an organism and its environment, but between principles and judgments as two varieties of intellectual structures internal to the organism. Of course, to the extent that one regards living with moral integrity and spiritual well-being as part of what it means to be a vital human being, reflective equilibration is adaptive in promoting favorable interactions between and agent and that agent's social environment. This can be said of all three notions of equilibration mentioned here and of spiritual development generally.

The specific principles at issue in spiritual development are ones which specify the nature and purpose of spiritually disciplined practices. For instance, I have claimed that habitual behaviors having an addictive character should be resisted by the inculcation of other habitual behaviors that have the character of spiritually disciplined practices. A judgment following from this principle is the following: impulsively eating foods high in fat, sugar, and salt should be resisted by a regimen of spiritual fasting as well as by a regimen of healthy diet. Practical experience and intellectual reflection will cause continual interpretation of both principle and judgment; it may also cause substantial modification of one or both of them. What is crucial is that the principle enjoining resistance not be made absolute in a way that leads to vilification of other persons and practices. Equally crucial is that particular descriptions of the addictive habits and spiritual regimens mentioned in the judgments not be reified in a way attributes to them an entirely objective, verifiable content.

This third and final aspect of phenomenological equilibration includes reflection upon its embodied and social antecedents; it is thereby dependent upon them and, yet, in another way, is emergent from them. If one's intention in undertaking a regimen of disciplined practice is to attain a vital relationship between the whole of reality and one's truest self—that is, if one's intention is genuinely spiritual— then a socially educative process of equilibration is requisite for that discipline to be thoroughly learned and an intellectually critical process is needed for it to be maintained with integrity. This is the case because of the unique promise and danger of life in community. Such a context makes possible the highest levels of individual development—biologically, psychologically, and spiritually; it provides the nurture which aids growth, the cooperation which allows differentiation, and the power which effects correction. Yet this same power may be used for more selfish ends, and may result in development— one's own or another's—to cease prematurely in the acquisition of a limited retinue of behaviors that serve parochial interests. A life of monotonous labor and mindless consumption counts as such a stunted development. It is just this sort of life, and the bad habits that constitute it, that spiritually disciplined practices are intended to overcome, and it is the difficulty of doing so that requires their rethinking.

III

Rethinking the Nature of Spiritual Discipline

CHAPTER 6

Nietzsche's Negation

THE PERILS OF ASCETIC IDEALS

The presentation of a set of categoreal themes for describing and justifying various forms of spiritual discipline is now complete. These new categories are offered as alternatives for ideas indebted to ancient philosophy that had been found wanting on scientific, philosophical, and ethical grounds. In the final part of the book a radically contrary point of view must be directly addressed. Friedrich Nietzsche's criticism of religious asceticism, besides being one of the few modern philosophical treatments of this topic, is also singularly sweeping. It includes within its scope all disciplined practices motivated by salvific considerations, whether correlated with traditional or contemporary categories of thought. Nietzsche reviled the Schopenhauerian rationale for asceticism just as strongly as he did the older Neoplatonic case. His views on this subject qualify as radical because of this comprehensiveness, but also for the unique perspective from which he approached the interpretation of all religious phenomena. It is an approach that challenges the feasibility and worth of most constructive ventures in the philosophy of religion, including, on some points, the one undertaken here.

Religion was a frequent topic in Nietzsche's philosophical writings. Mostly his remarks were disparaging. Also, they were not offered as part of a propaedeutic "critique" intended to insure the force of necessity in scientific and moral law, as was, for instance, the case for Kant. Nor did he criticize religion for the sake of philosophy's integrity—as Ludwig Feurbach did in his efforts to formulate a "philosophy of the future." Rather Nietzsche criticized philosophy and religion alike insofar as they were the vehicles for expressing certain moral notions. It is significant that Nietzsche's major discussion of asceticism occurs in a book entitled *On the Genealogy of Morals*. A "genealogy" is Nietzsche's preferred strategy for unmasking illusions. In a Nietzschean genealogy illusions are traced less to a human desire for comprehensiveness or consolation than to an unannounced intent to gain and exercise power.

Natural science was no more sacrosanct for Nietzsche than were religion and philosophy, and he did not criticize asceticism for the sake of some new scientific world view. This contributes to the uniqueness, and, I think, the cogency of his views on this subject. Marx implied that religious practices were narcotic and Freud described them as obsessive; in doing so both presupposed positivistic conceptions of scientific truth. Their case against religion seems less trenchant now, not only because their positivism has proved unrealistic, but also because their central theoretical claims have not been empirically verified by even moderate standards of contemporary social science. Nietzsche's critique of religion has not suffered this fate because he never privileged scientific discourse nor faulted religion for falling short of its standards; indeed, science, philosophy, religion, and art are all regarded by him as expressions of the same human "will to power." Thus Nietzsche's challenge to religious asceticism is not undertaken on behalf of truth objectively conceived; instead, it is undertaken on behalf of life epitomized by the will to power of individual human agents. Life, for Nietzsche, is human vitality conceived as the possession, exercise, and increase of power. Such life is a self-evident good, and others things are good to the extent they are so deemed by persons "filled with life and passion."[1] Here is the crux of the matter for Nietzsche, and here also is an issue of morality.

In the final lines of *On the Genealogy of Morals* Nietzsche writes that religious asceticism is a negation of the full realization of human life: "We can no longer conceal from ourselves *what* is expressed by all that willing which has taken its direction from the ascetic ideal: this hatred of the human, and even more of the animal, and more still of the material, this horror of the senses, of reason itself, this fear of happiness and beauty, this longing to get away from all appearance, change, becoming, death, wishing, from longing itself—all this means—let us dare to grasp it—*a will to nothingness*, an aversion to life, a rebellion against the most fundamental presupposition of life."[2] Religious asceticism is bad because it opposes life. It is a species of a passive nihilism that cultivates a diminished vitality in oneself and in one's adversaries. It is a mentality and activity that Nietzsche describes as decadent in the sense that it seeks neither to actuate nor sublimate powerful passions, but rather it seeks to extirpate them. Insofar as Nietzsche finds religious asceticism to be a negation of life, he negates this negation. One of the of the aims of the chapters just completed was to rid spiritually disciplined practices of life-denying associations, and thereby preemptively evade Nietzsche's negation. Still, the negation deserves further, direct response.

To social historians and historical theologians Nietzsche's identification of asceticism with a "will to nothingness" may seem tendentious. Margaret Miles, for instance, has more than once introduced discussions of asceticism by quoting Serapion of Thmuis saying "We beg you (God), make us truly alive," and since Serapion was a monastic companion of Anthony and an ecclesiastical protégé of Athanasius, he can be said to stand at the beginnings of Christian ascetic tradition.[3] What informs Nietzsche's thinking here is the philosophy of Arthur Schopenhauer. In *The World as Will and Representation* the latter philosopher writes:

That knowledge of the whole, of the inner nature of the thing-in-itself. . .becomes the *quieter* of all and every willing. The will now turns away from life; it shudders at the pleasures in which it recognizes the affirmation of life. Man attains to a state of voluntary renunciation, resignation, true composure, and complete will-lessness.[4]

Shortly thereafter he continues: "Thus it may be that the inner nature of holiness, of self-renunciation, of mortification of one's own will, of asceticism, is here for the first time expressed in abstract terms and free from everything mythical, as the *denial of the will-to-live*, which appears after the complete knowledge of its own inner being has become for it the quieter of all willing."[5] Nietzsche refers several times to Schopenhauer in the opening chapters of "What is the Meaning of Ascetic Ideals." In the body of the essay he very much wished to refute Schopenhauer's recommendation of asceticism as well as the more traditional theological rationales for it.[6] As is evident from comparison of the passages just quoted, the negation Nietzsche himself negated, was Schopenhauer's denial of the "will-to-live."

By speaking of knowledge of "the whole" and one's "own inner being" Schopenhauer is clearly alluding to the spiritual dimension of human existence as it was defined in this book's first chapter. By scorning all "mythical" vehicles for expressing the meaning of asceticism Schopenhauer thought that he was expressing the abstract essence of pessimistic religions like Hinduism, Buddhism, and Christianity. He thought the sustained abstractness of his formulation was a virtue. I think otherwise, and while Nietzsche's technique of genealogy is an attempt to overcome Schopenhauer's abstract idealism, I shall argue shortly that Nietzsche's treatment itself is flawed by its abstraction of the phenomenon of asceticism from its historical and behavioral contexts. A noxious abstractionism is an ever present danger when one speaks philosophically about asceticism and spiritual discipline. I have consciously sought to avoid it, though I doubt that I have been entirely successful in doing so. Still, one should resist this tendency as much as possible.

Whatever its origin, Nietzsche's philosophical censure of religious asceticism seems to contest the claim that spiritually disciplined regimens of behavior can be recommended as means for realizing an optimum of human well-being. It apparently strikes at the central thesis of this book that disciplined spiritual practices can promote a fullness of life. Certainly Nietzsche believed that advocates and practitioners of traditional forms of asceticism were hostile to persons he described as "strong, full natures in whom there is an excess of power."[7] Yet, no single passage—not even the crucial one quoted above—can adequately represent Nietzsche's views on this subject. As in all of the major themes of Nietzsche's philosophy, there is complexity and ambivalence to his treatment of asceticism. Indeed, there may even be inconsistency. This would not have daunted Nietzsche, for whom vitality was more important than veridicality, yet neither should it excuse his readers from attempting to understand precisely his views on an important issue like asceticism.

In Nietzsche's account ascetic ideals have different meanings for artists, philosophers, and priests. For artists, he says they mean many things; so many, in fact, that they mean nothing at all. Even the many things they mean are derivative from philosophy and religion. The meaning of ascetic ideals for philosophers is similarly indebted to religious exemplars, yet this philosophical meaning acquires definite import by serving a single purpose: it has enabled philosophers to survive!

> The peculiar, withdrawn attitude of the philosopher, world-denying, hostile to life, suspicious of the senses, freed from sensuality, which has been maintained down to the most modern times and has become virtually the *philosopher's pose par excellence*—it is above all the result of the emergency conditions under which philosophy arose and survived at all; for the longest time philosophy would not have been *possible at all* on earth without ascetic wraps and cloaks, without an ascetic self-misunderstanding. To put it vividly: the *ascetic priest* provided until the most modern times the repulsive and gloomy caterpillar form in which alone the philosopher could live and creep about.[8]

Nietzsche implies here that philosophers no longer need "ascetic wraps"; hence he associates the true meaning of ascetic ideals with the figure of the ascetic priest. Such priests advance ascetic ideals, says Nietzsche, as part of a religious revaluation of values that seeks to supplant a "noble morality" with a "slave morality." They do this in the context of self-appointed mission to preserve "degenerating life."[9] They can only protect the weak by harming the strong. The way in which they achieve this end is what Nietzsche found most insidious. The priest's ascetic "will to nothingness" replaces the noble values of courage, robustness, and conquest with the Christian values of humility, meekness, and love. It undermines noble personalities by instilling in them guilt and bad conscience. In brief, it effects a mobilization of hatred that becomes self-hatred in the strong personalities who adopt the values of the weak. Nietzsche used the French word 'ressentiment' to describe this psychological state of mind which sustains ascetic ideals, and he credited the priests with several imaginative strategies for relieving the suffering of ill-constituted persons like themselves. Practical regimens of ascetic behavior are among these strategies.

In "The Meaning of Ascetic Ideals" Nietzsche identifies five ways in which ascetic ideals console the weak in their suffering. The first involves cultivating "a feeling of physiological inhibition" through deprivations of things such as food, sex, property, and conflict. The second consists of "mechanical activity," especially the observance of a regular cycle of prayer and worship, and a third comprises the "petty pleasures" of almsgiving, nursing, counselling, and like charitable ministries.[10] The final two ways are less strictly discrete actions; instead, they concern the priest's role as an agent of morality, promoting the "formation of a herd" (i.e., establishing a religious community) and orchestrating "orgies of feeling," characteristically, paroxysms of enthusiasm and guilt.[11] The immediate purpose of these five strategies is to make bearable the painful existence of the majority of unexceptional human beings. One way in which the priest, in Nietzsche's view, forms a herd with him as its leader is by convincing its members that they are the ultimate cause of their own suffering. They suffer for their sins, both original and personal, and so they must repent by amending their lives in the above specified ways. In essence, the priest provides a cause and apparent remedy for human suffering; he provides a meaning for suffering. In the sense that a meaningless suffering is more bearable than suffering without meaning, the priest manipulates ascetic ideals so as actually to relieve suffering and sustain life. This is the meaning of ascetic ideals and the answer to the question regarding asceticism that concerned Nietzsche. Again one can see the radical nature of his approach to this issue: he is concerned neither with philosophy's identity nor the status of moral or natural law, but with the possibility of meaning which is a presupposition of them both.

The effort of weak natures to secure their own survival is something that Nietzsche, in principle, respected. Even a will to nothingness is better than no will at all. Meaningful suffering is better than no meaning at all. By harnessing the will to power of the great masses of humanity the ascetic priest becomes, says Nietzsche, "one of the greatest *conserving* and yes-saying forces of life."[12] In this appreciation one senses ambivalence: Nietzsche saw the ascetic priest, or in alternate ascriptions, Jews and Christians, as clever, shrewd, and perversely effective, yet he unreservedly decried the motivations and consequences of their propagation of ascetic ideals. He condemned the vindictiveness which sustain these ideals and the passivity they engender. He identified Paul and traditional Christianity with these vices, and while he exculpated Jesus from feelings of hatred or envy, he still denounced the Nazarene for the sterility of his particular form of spiritual self-mastery. Stated differently, Nietzsche respected the revaluation of values, but he condemned the transformation of vital values into decadent mores. He celebrated the capacity of spiritually disciplined practices to generate meaning and value without depreciating embodied vitality. The new descriptive resources offered in the last few chapters were intended to enhance just this aspect of traditional spiritual disciplines.

The subtleties of Nietzsche's position become more pronounced when the topic of religious asceticism is placed in relevant larger contexts. His unappreciative interpretation of Christianity is one such context. Nietzsche's critique of Christianity is most systematically presented in his last topical writing, *The Anti-Christ*. (This text was subtitled in some manuscripts *Attempt at a Critique of Christianity*, so the word 'critique' is appropriate here, but must be read in a non-Kantian fashion.)[13] There he clearly identifies Christianity with what he had called "bad" in the *Genealogy*: that which is vulgar, weak, diseased, and cowardly. He is equally clear that Christianity "has waged *a war to the death* against the *higher* type of man."[14] Furthermore, according to Nietzsche, Christianity is allied with other expressions of decadence in nineteenth-century European culture, especially Kantian philosophy, evolutionary optimism, democracy, and socialism. As was suggested above, Nietzsche partially exempts Jesus from his scorn. "In reality there has been only one Christian, and he died on the Cross."[15] This one Christian, he says, is not to be identified with religious feelings, like pity for the sick, or with theological beliefs, like justification by faith, but with practices. In *The Anti-Christ*, he writes:

> It is not a belief that distinguishes the Christian: the Christian acts, he is distinguished by a *different* mode of acting. Neither by words nor in his heart does he resist the man who does him evil.... The life of the redeemer was nothing else than *this* practice... his death too was nothing else.[16]

Nietzsche understood this practical orientation as of one of the virtues of early Christianity which later became lost.

Clearly Nietzsche admired the self-mastery inherent in the consistent refusal of Jesus to resist evil. Since he believed that noble characters are "rounded men replete with energy and therefore *necessarily* active," he approved of Jesus' self-identification with a characteristic type of action. For this same reason he was contemptuous of Luther's emphasis on "faith alone."[17] Still Nietzsche faulted Jesus because, while he was a "great symbolist" through his performance of significant actions, he was not a great creator; he failed to fashion and articulate an unequivocal message. "The history of Christianity—and that from the very death on the Cross—is the history of progressively cruder misunderstanding of an *original* symbolism."[18] Paul begins this tradition of misinterpretation, and for Nietzsche he is the first Christian in the negative sense of being the first to shape Jesus' message into a religion of resentment and decadence. Paul made Christianity the opposite of what Jesus practiced. Jesus extended loving forgiveness to the enemies who crucified him, but Paul built a system of theology upon his vindictive hatred for the Roman rulers who killed Jesus.

A second wider context for Nietzsche's critique of asceticism is his account of religion itself. His interpretation of the meaning of ascetic ideals as a "will to nothingness" is closely related to his account of the genesis of religion in priestly cunning. Both spring, according to Nietzsche, from a more archaic origin in an experience of a superabundance or fullness of power. In *The Will to Power*, a compilation of late unpublished manuscripts, Nietzsche writes that "the origin of religion lies in extreme feelings of power"; subsequently he claims that ideals are "the penalty man pays for the tremendous expenditure he has to make in all actual and pressing tasks."[19] That religion and ideality take on a pernicious character is due to physiological weakness: sick and cowardly persons cannot believe that such power is rightfully their own and so they attribute it to gods and other ideal projections. Nietzsche sees disastrous consequences following from this attribution. Locating power in the "other" involves a disparagement of the self. Positing a supernatural or ideal realm implies a contempt for what is natural and real. Priests exploit such persons alienated from feelings of power: they cultivate in them a hatred of life and then marshal this vituperative energy for their own aggrandizement.

The alliance of religious idealism with morality further mobilizes feelings of hate. Physiological weakness takes on a social dimension in morality: weak individuals, prompted by priests, join together in a "herd" and cultivate moral feelings and ideals. They do this in order to preserve themselves and oppose independent and strong personalities. Pagan moral ideals of courage and fortitude may plausibly be counted as instruments of self-mastery, but Nietzsche believed that Jewish and Christian religious ideals express a slavish moral impulse. Ideals of humility and pity demand nothing to which the weak are not already predisposed, their true intent being to instill a guilty conscience in the strong. They are vengeful ideals. To insure that their intended targets do not believe that they can escape punishment for doing evil, priests promulgate religious dogmas of a just and omnipotent god. The ways in which the weak come to deploy notions of evil, guilt, and revenge in their struggle against stronger opponents constitutes what Nietzsche called the genealogy of morals. How moral notions are used to attain dominance in social conflicts he called the "politics of virtue."[20] The gist of Nietzsche's case against ascetic ideals, especially as propagated and practiced in priestly religious forms, is that such ideals serve decadent interests. They are life denying and spirit corrupting; they honor the extirpation of instinctive drives more than their actualization or sublimation.

By placing Nietzsche's account of asceticism in the context of his similarly hostile treatment of Christianity and religion in general, it becomes evident that it belongs to an older and broader tradition of social criticism. Nietzsche's critique of religion is a later species of the variety of social criticism that identifies religion as an otherworldly system of beliefs and practices serving very worldly interests. Marx's critique of religion was an extension of the views of Enlightenment deists who attacked the Christian Church's alliance with persons of wealth and privilege; it was an atheistic and humorless updating of what had been said by church satirists like

Voltaire. Nietzsche also extends an earlier pagan tradition of deriding Christianity for its alliance with vulgar and ignorant peoples: Origen's literary nemesis, Celsus, for instance, accused Christian missionaries of shamelessly exploiting their followers' lack of education. Nietzsche is unlike his pagan predecessors only in identifying religious partisans of decadence with psychological types rather than with specific social classes. He should not be dismissed as a snob or bigot of the usual sort. For instance, for all his criticism of Judaism, he resolutely scorned contemporary German Anti-Semites. Nietzsche was more admiring of Goethe's haughty distaste for Biblical religion. Reflection upon Nietzsche's relation to these earlier critics of religion suggests two different ways of blunting his criticism.

First, Nietzsche can be made the object of a radical ideological critique. His disrespect for the interests and institutions of the poor and outcast can be read as promoting the case for their greedy oppressors who in some ways are just as decadent. Likewise, even though his portrayals of women avoided many stereotypes of German middle-class society, his alternative characterizations are sexist in their own way.[21] On this view, Nietzsche was right to criticize traditional Christianity, but he did so for the wrong reasons. Of course, the invocation of Nietzsche's writing by Nazi propagandists gives some plausibility to this line of attack; the wide adoption of this negative assessment of Nietzsche in the early postwar years caused a concurrent decline in the estimation of his philosophy. A dramatic change in intellectual climate has occurred in the last ten years. Indeed, in his recent book on Heidegger's Nazi associations, Jacques Derrida seems to suggest that Nietzsche was instrumental less in fueling Heidegger's romance with Nazism than in quelling it![22]

My own assessment of Nietzsche on these political points favors a middle ground between righteous denunciation and easy exculpation. I shall not attempt to identify my position more precisely because Nietzsche's hyperbolic rhetoric make his political comment-ary extraordinarily difficult to evaluate and to do so in this context would stray too far from the topic of philosophy and spiritual discipline. A second line of criticism I find more pertinent. Nietzsche can be plausibly accused of exhibiting some of the same psychological traits he vehemently condemned. Specifically, there is a tone to his writings, especially in later years, which is arguably hateful and vengeful, suggesting, therefore, that his own recipe for overcoming these impediments to a fully vital life was not personally successful. Also, his interpretations of theologians and other religious figures were seldom generous, even though generosity is a virtue he says can only be contained in a strong and noble personality. Nietzsche suffered himself, it seems, from foibles he rightly criticizes in religious personalities. His irreligiousness did not maintain Goethe's aristocratic reserve. Heidegger reproached Nietzsche for his "spirit of vengeance spiritualized to the highest degree."[23] This observation is offered not only as part of an *argumentum ad hominem* charging inconsistency; it also supports the view that Nietzsche did not effectively make the transit from a theoretical and highly personal conception of fullness of life to the practical and social vision of well-being to which most practitioners of spiritual discipline have aspired. I believe that Nietzsche's own proclivity for contempt led him to a one-sided representation of religious forms of spiritual practice and to a too categorical rejection of religion. In turn, this rejection of religion prevented him from extending his insights regarding individual forms of spiritual discipline, like solitude, to practical regimens for nurturing social forms of fullness of life. Since Nietzsche's critique of asceticism directly challenges major themes of this book he warrants a response. In the remainder of this chapter I shall seek to rebut his claim that spiritually disciplined practices promote decadence—not vitality—unless they are shorn of all religious and social elements.

Nietzsche's account of the origin of religion is not entirely idiosyncratic. Gerardus van der Leeuw's formulated a phenomenology of religion continuous with Nietzsche's thinking because he too identified religion with the experience of "extraordinary Power: whatever is successful, strong, plenteous." Of course, he developed this basic insight in ways quite different from Nietzsche. For instance, contrary to Nietzsche he argued that sacred power and the fullness of life it makes possible are only fully realized in community. Indeed, he states this point yet more strongly than I have: "Solitude excites dread in us all: for we possess power and life only in community."[25] Nietzsche, of course, held the quite opposite view; he associated solitude with the filling of Zarathustran figures with an extraordinary power that becomes subsequently depleted during the interaction between these energetic figures and their larger community. I think that Nietzsche underestimates the extent to which human beings are social beings, partly because of his own isolated personal circumstances, but also because of the prophetic idiom (albeit as an atheist prophet of eternal recurrence) in which he chose to communicate his thoughts about religion. The actual experience of most people lies somewhere between the dread of solitude posited by Van Der Leeuw and Nietzsche's unrestrained celebration of it. Solitariness as a habitual disposition cannot be permanently classified as good or bad in abstraction from a person's concrete circumstances. These circumstances change and thus so do people's experience of solitude. This judgment is a consequence of the reformulation of the human spiritual predicament necessitated by a rejection of the classical philosophical assumptions articulated by Clement and an acknowledgment of the complexity of a more modern situation anticipated by Pascal. The decision to engage in any variety of spiritual discipline retains a strategic character, being sometimes apt and sometimes inept at promoting genuine fullness of life. At issue here is whether solitude and other forms of spiritual discipline are compatible with ties to traditional religious communities. Nietzsche gave an emphatically negative response to this query while I shall offer a more positive and complex answer to it.

Nietzsche's disparagement of religious community is evident in his description of it as a "herd." In fact, he uses this term for any community which is an agent for promulgating slavish moral values; in *The Gay Science* he defines morality as "herd instinct in the individual."[26] Yet it is an infelicitous description of communities dedicated to the pursuit of spiritual disciplined practices because they are rarely familial. Indeed, both monastic communities and associations of lay persons receiving spiritual direction are deliberately founded institutions whose members quite consciously decline full participation in prevailing social institutions. Nietzsche at least implicitly acknowledges the founded character of ascetic communities by his assignation of an organizing role to the ascetic priest, but he consistently ignores the possibility of a spiritually disciplined community being socially dissident.

In this context, Joachim Wach's distinction between " 'natural' and 'founded' religious groups" is quite helpful.[27] For Wach a natural group is preeminently one rooted in biological ties of blood and marriage. Such family or clan groups usually further integrate their lives by joint efforts in securing food, shelter, and protection, so that Wach allows under the rubric of natural groups persons who engage in these fundamental activities but are not directly related by blood or marriage. Religion is, of course, another important bond by which natural groups are sustained. "Founded" religious communities are not coextensive with natural groups, either being small cults within natural groups or expansive religions that have adherents from a wide variety of racial, ethnic, and political backgrounds. They are "integrated exclusively by religious impulses."[28] The great world like Judaism, Christianity, and Buddhism are founded religious groups in this sense. So are monastic communities. Nietzsche believes that ascetic practices undertaken in the social and intellectual context of religious groups can do nothing except promote the interests of mediocrity and decadence. I deny that generalization, and believe this denial is made more cogent when one recognizes that communities of spiritually disciplined practice are rarely the naturalistic, instinctual, and kin-protective "herds" that Nietzsche says they are.

To further advance an argument against Nietzsche's disparagements of religious communities closer attention must be given to how such communities are integrated by religious impulses. Notice should especially be given to the role that concrete religious practices play in effecting this integration. One of the most ancient varieties of religious practices are the ritual activities which comprise the calendar of events that mark the seasonal transitions of archaic agricultural communities. Generally, in such contexts, each year is regarded as a lease on life that expires in the winter or fallow season and then requires renewal in new year's ceremonies. An important element of this aspect of ancient religious life was the interregnum period following the close of the old year and the commencement of the new. During this period activities of jubilation are typical—feasts, contests, sexual play, and so forth. In one sense these are sympathetic attempts to invigorate nature and bring on the new year, while in a more sociological and psychological perspective they present an opportunity for social rules to be temporarily relaxed and energies periodically restored. I shall place great emphasis on this element in the genealogy of religious practices, insisting that celebrative practices be conjoined with ascetic practices in any account of spiritual discipline. In *On the Genealogy of Morals* Nietzsche consistently isolates ascetic practices from their celebrative counterparts: he discusses fasting as a religious practice of self-denial, but not feasting as an activity communicating profound religious self-affirmation. Solitude is recognized as religious, but not communal dancing and singing. At best, he acknowledges these celebrative practices as belonging to non-Christian religions like the cult of Dionysus; yet then when he adopts the cause of "Dionysus versus the Crucified" he brings ambiguity to his claim to be strictly atheistic and irreligious. One way of countering Nietzsche's critique of religious practices is to reclaim the vitality revealed by genealogical accounts of their origins in celebrative rites.

Experiences of interregnal celebration are treated by anthropologists under the heading of liminality ('limen' in Latin means 'threshold'). Also included here are the in-between times that punctuate the lifetime sequence of rites of passages. In the passage of a person from youth to adulthood there is often a period where the initiate is assigned the status of neither the young nor the old: in some cultures a young male is allowed to have sexual intercourse without adopting formal marriage or kinship ties. The French ethnographer Arnold van Gennep made original contributions to the understanding of this ritual phenomenon; more recently, Victor Turner's reflections upon the Ndembu tribe of south central Africa have been especially insightful at generalizing liminality as a characteristic of ritual life.[29] He vigorously develops the theme that communal rituals serve to release individual tensions and strengthen social ties in times of transition or crisis. In making this case he correlates distinctive social arrangements with liminal and nonliminal periods, calling them respectively *communitas* and *societas*. The latter phrase designates society as it is customarily structured in accordance with economic necessities, kinship responsibilities, and political hierarchies. Religious beliefs and practices serve to support this natural and social order. In times of liminality conventional strictures are relaxed: an "antistructure" prevails in which improvident feasting may occur, excessive sociability is encouraged, and superiors become subject to inferiors in playful encounters.

Archaic experiences of *communitas* can provide inspiration for egalitarian and compassionate religious ethics such as the Christian doctrine of love. Nietzsche does not acknowledge this point; rather he understands the ideal of Christian love—*agape*—as a priestly stratagem for infecting the strong with guilt and with the many other psychological infirmities that make the weak what they are. For him Christian love, understood as pity, is an emotional complement of ascetic practices and a legitimation of waning vitality. I believe that this reading too is one-sided, ignoring as it does exalted potential of love as the concomitant of celebrative practices. Equality and love need not signal a passive resignation to the priestly schemes for mediocrity, but may be an anticipation of a new community creatively organized around overcoming tyrannical habitual patterns of social behavior. Even granting that compassion promotes the acceptance of another's burdens and faults, the effect upon a community may be the opposite of what Nietzsche predicts. Adopting Nietzsche's physiological language, I hold that slight exposure to an individual's malady may inoculate other community members so as to hinder rather than foster the spread of the contagion. Turner reads the Ndembu Isoma ritual in this fashion: he understands this ritual response to the perceived infertility of a women as a corporate acceptance of responsibility for the misfortune and as an augmentation of social ties in a time of stress. These remedies combine to lessen the women's individual sense of failure and society's corporate sense of misfortune. Prayers undertaken with love on behalf of the sick in Christian liturgical celebrations has a similarly vivifying effect on both the individual and the worshipping community. The example of communities responding to crises in this fashion is another rebuttal of Nietzsche's condemnation of communal religious practices.

Nietzsche's claim that religion is the product of a priestly exploitation of alienated feelings of power overlooks experiences of *communitas* in which ritual practices constitute collective and regularized experiences of a superfluity of feelings of power. Furthermore, he fails to appreciate that the priests and other religious specialists who integrate these religious impulses in systems of practice and belief are agents for social revitalization serving communities that include both weak and strong personalities. Certainly priests may sometimes be actors in a drama in which the weak seek to undermine the strong with ascetic ideals, but for there even to be such a precisely articulated pattern of conflict there must be an underlying measure of social cohesion. Religious leaders in many cultures are agents for achieving this cohesion by means of their expertise regarding the cycle of celebrative and ascetic practices that help to mark out a communities regular progression through periods of structure and anti-structure. Even the spirituality of strong personalities presupposes a social context shaped by the more traditional and communal expressions of spirituality. Nietzsche partially recognizes this point when he says that philosophers have had to adopt an ascetic stance in order to survive. He seems to imply that this social reality has changed with the advent of his own philosophy, but he gives no evidence to support this.

My final point in rebuttal to Nietzsche's critique of ascetic ideals and practices claims that he does not provide a fair portrayal of the relationship between religion and decadence. Moral decadence for Nietzsche has a twofold nature. It is either a slow ebbing of physiological vitality that militates against the satisfaction of basic instincts, or it is a deliberate strategy by which a pattern of activity, either privative or consumptive, serves to extirpate instinctive drives instead of satisfying them or sublimating them. The relation of asceticism to the first variety of decadence is straightforward: asceticism becomes equivalent to an ethics of self-denial in manifold forms. Celibacy, fasting, and related austerities constitute denial in a physiological sense; solitude, poverty, and meditation limit stimulating social interactions; almsgiving, humility, and good works restrict psychological satisfactions to indirect, altruistic forms. The second variety of decadence relates to asceticism in a more complex way, and presupposes distinctions between types of ascetic behavior.

Max Weber persuasively distinguished between a "world-rejecting asceticism" and an "inner-worldly asceticism."[30] The former is typified by the anchorite who through physical isolation experiences only a low level of physical sustenance and social intercourse. Monastic communities make a similar physical retreat from society and most often require vows of their members which likewise restrict physical and social activities. Still the cenobite is a less pure example because by being in a community he or she repeats there in miniature certain social patterns of relationship, sometimes even extending to sophisticated forms of economic cooperation. This was certainly the case for many Benedictine monasteries in the late Middle Ages. "Inner-worldly asceticism" describes a person's or group's disciplined behavior insofar as it occurs within the context of a larger society's institutions and social processes. Even in a secular context such behavior often maintains a quite consciously salvific purpose. Prohibitions regarding sensuality in sexual and recreational behavior, regarding ostentation in diet and dress, and regarding nonconformity in intellectual matters figure prominently here as in the other form of asceticism. Included sometimes within the scope of this project is a transformation of society in accordance with a communal vision of salvation. Weber identified the "Protestant ethic" as the paradigmatic example of this form of asceticism; it stressed, he claimed, productive labor as the unifying ideal for the Protestant variety of inner-worldly ascetic practices. He specifically associated the emergence of Reformed Protestant communities in Northern Europe with the development of capitalist modes of production, going so far as to make the controversial characterization that representatives of Reformed theology, if not Calvin's own theology, interpreted good works, including ones productive of economic success, as a sign of an inner grace.[31]

Often overlooked in favor of his more controversial claims was Weber's emphasis on the internal contradictions besetting the Protestant ethic. Wealth was condemned because it was thought to breed sloth, sensuality, and thereby, reveal faithlessness. Yet the very ethic articulated in contradistinction to the behavior of the rich—an ethic stressing frugality, diligence, learning, and innovation—tended to create wealth for the pious entrepreneur. Hence labor designed to be an antidote to the sloth of the wealthy itself promotes the acquisition of wealth, and, thereby, the adoption of the ways of the wealthy. Decadence in a moral sense follows from this development. Since wealthy persons whose success is indebted to an inner-worldly ascetic ethos rarely give away all income not needed for a modest but healthy style of living, their level of consumption rises and they approach the lifestyles of similarly wealthy persons. Yet they cannot revel in the satiation of their needs and desires lest they feel sinful. Hence they develop a pattern of consumption which, while sating one form of desire, suppresses another. Excessive eating and drinking suppress sexual appetite. Nietzsche frequently denounced the alcoholism and vulgar hedonism of the German bourgeoisie, not because such excess was actuated by economic exploitation of others, but because it was symptomatic of a morally decadent hatred of one's own embodied self.[32] In contemporary culture a zealous commitment to sports and recreational activities frequently leads to enervation and injuries that inhibit further expression of aggressive drives. The resultant behavior highlighted by these examples is a self-destructive *via media* determined by guilt. It is also the recipe for a pattern of consumption that is habitual and unhealthy. Spiritually disciplined practices of the ascetic sort can be useful in breaking these habits. Again, Nietzsche recognized this point, but it did not lead him to mollify his attack on religious asceticism.[33]

Weber artfully described the contradictory dynamic of an ethic which eschews the enjoyment of wealth but promotes its production. He also quoted John Wesley and others as evidence of that Protestant leaders were themselves aware of this tension.[34] Nietzsche, more than Weber, is more responsible for the above-cited description of how religious guilt dictates an ambivalent program of consumption. That Weber so stressed the relation of religion and economics via production rather than consumption is explicable by previous traditions of scholarship, including Marxism, and by the then immature states of marketing and advertising functions relative to manufacturing. Nietzsche's precocious sensitivity to matters of economic consumption is related to his understanding of human well-being in terms of feelings of power, including physiological vitality. Also, his own chronic ill-health surely contributed to his penchant for perceiving philosophical issues in vividly embodied ways.

Nietzsche does not credit religion for empowering creative labor by providing a rationale for an inner-worldly asceticism. Although his motivations for failing to do so are inaccessible to interpreters, his argument at this point fits a familiar pattern. Nietzsche's views are consistently one-sided to the discredit of religion. First, ascetic practices are abstracted from their celebrative counterparts. Then, ascetic priests are portrayed as agents for mobilizing a herd morality that wars against exceptional individuals, but they are not credited with effecting the social cohesion presupposed by such a drama. Finally, he explains how ascetic ideals motivate decadent consumption but is silent about its role in promoting innovative industry and practical antidotes to decadence. Balanced expositions are not characteristic of Nietzsche. Yet there is a shrewdness too about his omissions that makes them more than a rhetorical ploy. Perhaps the most generous interpretation one can offer—once having declined to attribute his irreligiousness to the madness and meanness presaged in *The Anti-Christ*—is that Nietzsche is engaged here in that form of nihilism which destroys in order that a new creation might follow. Nietzsche foresaw a new creation in the persona of *Übermensch* and the ideology of eternal recurrence. Still, understanding the role of the critique of religion in Nietzsche's larger philosophical project does not exempt in from charges of bias and inaccuracy.

Despite its flaws Nietzsche's portrayal of irreligious spirituality forces a new understanding of the relationship between spiritually disciplined practices, religious institutions, and society at large. Intimations of this new relationship have been given above in suggestions for rebutting Nietzsche's attacks on ascetic ideals, priestly cunning, and decadent forms of religious community. Summarily stated these concrete rejoinders advocated the cultivation of forms of community whose spiritually disciplined practices (1) promote experiences of celebration that makes a ethic of love less vulnerable to corrosion by calculating pity and institutional authority; and (2) foster regular experiences of austerity that allow for the differentiation of manic activity from productive labor and for the severance of productive labor from unhealthy and habitual overconsumption. A source for philosophically rethinking spiritual discipline along these lines is Nietzsche's own portrayal of the spiritual discipline of solitude. In the next section I shall draw on this resource in preparation for formulating a new way of understanding spiritual discipline as a practical strategy for resolving Pascal's predicament and for promoting fullness of life.

THE LESSONS OF SOLITUDE

A striking feature of Nietzsche's critique of religion is its practical orientation. Religion is most palatable to Nietzsche when it is construed as a type of practice; conversely, a collection of practices, like traditional asceticism, is most offensive to him when it is motivated by religious valuations. Nietzsche may be read as a philosopher who recommended spiritually disciplined practices rather than critically considered beliefs as the best resources for dealing with the human predicament he confronted. I shall make a case for this reading shortly. In this practical orientation Nietzsche is similar to Pascal, though Nietzsche places his practical recipes for human well-being securely within the natural realm and outside the purview of religion. Still Nietzsche culminates a modern philosophical tradition begun by Pascal which judges regimens of disciplined behavior to be the most effective weapons for combatting the diversions and decadence of modern European culture. Heidegger, for instance, continued Nietzsche's philosophical project by attending to embodied temporal existence and eschewing abstract metaphysics; yet he differed too in seeking a spiritual remedy that stressed receptivity to language more than verbal and nonverbal action. For Nietzsche, practices of disciplined self-mastery are prerequisites for poetical creativity and poetic creation is philosophically pregnant action.

This last affirmation leads back to the question of the meaning of ascetic ideals for artists and philosophers. In a typically dramatic fashion Nietzsche said that these ideals have no meaning for artists: "They do not stand nearly independently enough in the world and *against* the world for their changing valuations to deserve attention *in themselves!* They have at all times been valets of some morality, philosophy, or religion."[35] Although this pronouncement was part of a diatribe against Richard Wagner and so occurs in a quite specific context, it does indicate that for Nietzsche the case of the philosopher was more directly illustrative of the nonreligious meaning of ascetic ideals. Nietzsche says that for philosophers this meaning is "something like a sense and instinct for the most favorable preconditions of higher spirituality."[36] Here is mentioned a realization of ascetic ideals that is spiritual but not religious. It offers a precedent for reconceiving spiritual discipline in a way that is not tied to theistic soteriologies; it promises thereby to be more widely applicable to the variety of creative practices occurring in the contemporary context of cultural and religious pluralism. At least these are presumptive reasons for surveying Nietzsche's constructive views on spiritual discipline.

Asceticism serves as the precondition of the higher spirituality of the philosopher in both a genealogical and a physiological sense. Ascetic ideals are a genealogical precondition for philosophers because the ascetic priest was the best historically available precedent for how one can sever ties with customary society in order to pursue an extraordinary vocation. Nietzsche detests the mission of the ascetic priest, but he admires the boldness with which it is undertaken. Once philosophers acquire the courage for undertaking their own task, then this backward look to the ascetic priest will no longer be necessary. A new variety of self-discipline is needed to foster this type of courage, because courage for Nietzsche is not a mere attitude or habitual disposition: it is an instinctive preference for what is vital, fecund, and sublime. This courage is the physiological precondition for the philosopher's higher spirituality.

The philosopher embraces ascetic ideals—even poverty, humility, and chastity—because they establish "an optimum of favorable conditions under which it [i.e., '*la bête philosophe*'] can expend all its strength and achieve its maximal feeling of power."[37] Nietzsche uses the simile of the athlete who refrains from sexual activity on the eve of a contest. There is nothing in this action that is moral—nothing that implies a hatred of the senses or the body; rather there is just an exercise of self-mastery that is an expression of to the will to excel, achieve, and dominate. Nietzsche also uses the metaphor of entering a desert "where the strong, independent spirits withdraw and become lonely."[38] From the example of Zarathustra it is evident that the endurance of solitude is a leading theme of Nietzsche's narrative imagination, and from his autobiographical and aphoristic writings it is evident that Nietzsche included solitude as one of the ingredients of his own higher spirituality. In the essay on ascetic ideals he suggest the personal relevance of solitude as a spiritual discipline when he says that a desert may be "even a room in a full, utterly commonplace hotel, where one is certain to go unrecognized and can talk to anyone with impunity."[39] These were precisely the living conditions in which Nietzsche wrote many of his most important works of philosophy. His own life, then, demonstrated the vital connection between solitude and creativity; at least on this point he showed a remarkable self-consistency.

"There is nothing in me of the founder of a religion—religions are affairs of the rabble; I find it necessary to wash my hands after I have come into contact with religious people."[40] Nietzsche wrote these lines in the conclusion of *Ecce Homo*, his literary autobiography. There is hyperbole here, but also irony: Nietzsche did not want his life's work understood in religious terms, yet he did want it accorded an order of significance more like the legacy of a Jesus or a Buddha than of an academic philosopher. To contend, as I shall, that Nietzsche's understanding of solitude, of *Einsamkeit*, bears some significant similarity to traditional forms of spiritual discipline is not an indirect way of arguing for a religious dimension in Nietzsche's thought. However, I do intend to deal with the peculiarly prodigious character of his life and work, and I do so guided by the conviction that Nietzsche's personal greatness, and his estimate of greatness in others, cannot simply be equated with the irreverent passion suggested by the motto *"Dionysus versus the Crucified"*—the final words of *Ecce Homo*. More relevant is an elucidation of why Nietzsche recommended a spiritualization of the human will to power as a mark of the most fecund form of self-mastery.

To my mind, the willingness and the capacity to endure solitude best exemplifies Nietzsche's version of a disciplined spiritual practice. An examination of this theme sheds light on Nietzsche's philosophy, both illuminating strictly intellectual points, such as his understanding of sublimation which traditional critics like Walter Kaufmann have deemed crucial, and clarifying the relationship between the drama of Nietzsche's life and the central dynamic of his philosophy, a topic which has interested more recent commentators like Alexander Nehamas. Furthermore, I believe that investigating Nietzsche's portrayal of solitude in tandem with his critique of the ascetic ideal suggests a new way of thinking about spiritual discipline.

The theme of solitude figures prominently in two distinct genres of the Nietzschean corpus: in aphoristic reflections, often autobiographical, and in his masterpiece, *Thus Spoke Zarathustra*. In *Ecce Homo* Nietzsche explains why he is so wise by claiming for himself "the energy to choose absolute solitude and leave the life to which I had become accustomed."[41] Shortly thereafter, in the same text, he explains that solitude is not only a way to wisdom, but a necessity of life itself: "I need solitude—which is to say recovery, return to myself, the breath of a free, light, playful air."[42] At the time of writing *Ecce Homo*, in 1888, Nietzsche was approaching a descent into madness from which he would never emerge. In a sense, solitude was about to be forced upon him in an irrevocable way.

Yet in even his earliest writings very similar points are made. In "Schopenhauer as Educator," one of the *Untimely Meditations* written in 1874, Nietzsche identified solitude as one of the dangers that threatened Schopenhauer and kindred spirits:

Where there have been powerful societies, governments, religions, public opinions, in short wherever there has been tyranny, there the solitary (einsamen) philosopher has been hated; for philosophy offers an asylum to a man into which no tyranny can force its way, the inward cave, the labyrinth of the heart: and that annoys the tyrants. There the solitaries conceal themselves: but there too lurks their greatest danger.[43]

Note solitude's role in combatting "tyranny" (Tyrannie). In *The Gay Science* Nietzsche compares an enduring habit to a tyrant. Clearly he thinks brief habits, like regular experiences of solitude, are means for overcoming oppressive, enduring habits. That solitude must not be sustained too long is implied in the Schopenhauer essay when Nietzsche says that if solitude is unmitigated by friendship and creative expression, then the solitary person implodes like a bright, superdense star: Heinrich von Kleist, the dramatic poet and suicide, is the offered illustration. In a contrary manner, those who can endure and overcome this solitude are richly gifted: "Yet there will always be demi-gods who can endure to live, and live victoriously, under such terrible conditions; and if you want to hear their lonely (einsamen) song, listen to the music of Beethoven!"; Beethoven, Schopenhauer, Goethe, Wagner—these are the masters of a "productive uniqueness (productive Einzigheit)," the true educators.[44] They are the company in which Nietzsche placed himself; they are his teachers, his tradition. It was not entirely inaccurate when Nietzsche claimed in *Ecce Homo* that his essay on Schopenhauer would more appropriately have been entitled "Nietzsche as Educator."[45]

Philosophers and artists are paramount in the Nietzschean pantheon. Yet he also speaks of saints in this same context. Saints are included among the extraordinary individuals, here spoken of as "Schopenhauer's men," who are both the highest product of culture and the goal of nature. They are the natural educators, possessing the ability for uplifting others above a bestial existence of merely pursuing pleasure. Nietzsche's conception of the saint is obscure in this writing, yet his reference in this context to "those true men who are no longer animal, the philosophers, artists, and saints" is testimony to his belief that the practitioners of creative solitude have a significance that extends beyond their purely intellectual and aesthetic talents.[46] In the guise of a treatise on education Nietzsche was trying to articulate "a new concept of self-discipline (Selbst-Zucht)," one that deserves to be called spiritual because it encompassed the relation of the individual to nature, culture, history, self, and society—to the whole of life with which the creative person contends.[47] Like Pascal before him, Nietzsche recommends self-disciplined practices as part of a remedy for a problem whose magnitude and momentousness makes it spiritual. An undertaking of this sort requires extraordinary self-knowledge. For Nietzsche this means something more than quotidian self-consciousness and Socratic self-reflection. It demands rather a creative self-awareness sufficient to shape a unique character and destiny. To paraphrase Alexander Nehamas, it demands the artistry to transform one's own life into great literature.[48]

Even though Nietzsche conceived the locus of spirit to be entirely personal, the meaning he assigned the term is much indebted to Hegel. It is as if all of the complexity and contradiction embraced by Hegel's Absolute Spirit unfolding in cosmic history was concentrated by Nietzsche into the drama of individual destiny. One might then describe solitude as a moment in the dialectical development of the self—a moment born of strife and pregnant with overcoming. The precise nature of this conflict was first articulated by Nietzsche in his aphoristic writings of mid-career, in *Daybreak* and *The Gay Science*. There he begins his critique of traditional morality, introducing themes which eventually receive narrative embodiment in Zarathustra and discursive exposition in *On the Genealogy of Morals*.

The fifth book of *Daybreak* contains a series of aphoristic meditations on solitude; several reiterate themes advanced in the Schopenhauer essay, such as the importance of solitude for good education (443) and for original thinking (491). One succinctly reveals a new meaning of solitude in the course of a portrayal of morality as the stifling and spiteful force of social custom:

> It is, indeed, a fact that, in the midst of society and sociability every evil inclination has to place itself under such great restraint, don so many masks, lay itself so often on the Procrustean bed of virtue, that one could well speak of a martyrdom of the evil man. In solitude all this falls away. He who is evil is at his most evil in solitude: which is where he is also at his best—and thus to the eye of him who sees everywhere only a spectacle also at his most beautiful.[49]

If morality consists of the values posited by an unreflective consensus of society—the "herd instinct in the individual" he was later to call it—then a person who withdraws from the community for the purpose of gaining knowledge and mastery of self is immediately suspected of immorality.[50] Hence, solitude is a dangerous undertaking, as Nietzsche noted in the Schopenhauer essay. Yet in the above-quoted passage there is more than an acknowledgment of danger; there is a celebration of evil. Solitude is the occasion for deliberate moral conflict.

To understand why solitude advances from being dangerous to being evil some aspects of Nietzsche's developing philosophy must be recalled. Crucial to Nietzsche's mature philosophy is the claim that no system of values or body of truths has any absolute superiority, nor even a relative advantage that arises from factors intrinsic to the values or truths themselves. Truth, in all of its various forms, is as much an exercise of will as of inquiry. Nietzsche's essay, "On Truth and Lie in an Extra-Moral Sense," published posthumously, but written in 1873, shows that these ideas were present in Nietzsche's mind from an early date. *Daybreak*, the first book Nietzsche wrote after leaving the University of Basel in 1879, was written while he was living alone in Genoa. Traditional morality became the target of Nietzsche's invective at this time not simply because it was a single perspective which claimed absolute standing, but it was especially deserving of derision because the values promulgated, and their absolute status, were motivated by ill will. In morality he detected the ill will of the majority toward the individual and of the present generation to the bearers of new values. Solitude is the refuge of the individual and the womb of new values, and given Nietzsche's conception of morality, it is the home of "the evil one." By adopting this terminology, by identifying solitude with evil, Nietzsche adds defiance to danger as the hallmarks of this experience.

In his mature writings on morality the portrayal of the players in moral conflict becomes more carefully delineated: the individual/society conflict is refined as the master/slave dialectic, with the Jewish-Christian moral tradition being the voice of the slave mentality; the ill will toward exceptional individuals is specified as the feeling of *ressentiment*, a most vicious form of hatred because it breeds a "bad conscience" in its objects; and defiance is metaphysically grounded in the will to power and dramatically embodied in the self-overcoming of the Overman. The way in which the "campaign against morality" begun in early 1870s evolves into a trenchant diatribe against Christianity is also foreshadowed in Nietzsche's aphoristic writings. In the fifth book of *Daybreak* he wrote:

> To forego the world without knowing it, like a nun, that leads
> to a fruitless, perhaps melancholy solitude. It has nothing in
> common with the solitude of the *vita contemplativa* of the
> thinker: when he chooses that he is renouncing nothing.[51]

Solitude is a life-affirming experience for Nietzsche, being a restoration of the self through its removal from others, from society. The solitude of the convented nun—an ascetic solitude—has an entirely different motive, i.e. the renunciation of society and self in a quest for God. In *Daybreak* Nietzsche praises Luther for his destruction of the "Christian *vita contemplativa*" with all its castigations and mortifications; Luther, he says, makes a genuine *vita contemplativa* again possible in the Christian world. However, in *The Gay Science* he realized the need for a more radical cure for the spiritual malady of Europe. In was in this text that he first delivered his celebrated pronouncement that "God is dead." The meanings and consequences of this pronouncement are manifold, but for the present book it is sufficient to note that this divine passing makes genuine solitude possible: "For the pious there is as yet no solitude; this invention was made only by us, the godless."[52] Solitude is here portrayed as the spiritual discipline of the godless.

Danger, defiance, impiety—these are the realities that the solitary person embraces. They are what give style to a solitary character. Solitude is not recommended by Nietzsche as a religious or moral imperative but as a biological and aesthetic need—a strategy in the individual's contest with nature and society. This is true for all forms of self-mastery: "It will be the strong and domineering natures that enjoy their finest gaiety in constraint and perfection under a law of their own; the passion of their tremendous will relents in the face of all stylized nature, of all conquered and serving nature."[53] Walter Kaufmann contends that Nietzsche was the first author to use the word 'sublimation' to mean the redirection of fundamental human drives toward scientific and aesthetic ends.[54] Solitude, for Nietzsche, is an experience which effects this redirection.

In a previous quotation Nietzsche says solitude makes people evil and also beautiful. It is evil simply because it departs from the customary; it is beautiful because it forges an individual style. In his recent book on Nietzsche, Alexander Nehamas summarizes his major theme by saying that Nietzsche's "aestheticism is . . . the other side of his perspectivism."[55] In other words, Nietzsche's habit of resolving all philosophical justifications into aesthetic terms is intimately connected to his refusal to give any interpretation a singularly privileged status. Reflection on Nietzsche's understanding of solitude certainly corroborates this general insight.

So central is the notion of solitude to the dramatic structure of the *Thus Spoke Zarathustra* that Nietzsche in later years called it a "dithyramb on solitude."[56] A dithyramb is an ancient Greek choric hymn which recounts the adventures of Dionysus, the god of wine and fertility. It signifies precisely the paradoxical but creative combination of disciplined form and passionate feeling that Nietzsche associated with solitude itself. Although the structure of the Zarathustra narrative is more complex than can be accounted for by the dithyramb form, I believe that Zarathustra's experiences of and meditations upon solitude provide the dramatic framework of the first three parts of the text. The fourth part was originally intended as an intermezzo, leading to a second section comparable in scope to the first three parts collectively. This fact, along with an analysis that the internal structure of the text motivates me to accord an integral unity to the first three parts. More important than these purely textual points is that a review of solitude as theme and structural element of the *Zarathustra* reveals a new dimension to the drama of which solitude is a part, one which is insightful of the general notion of a spiritual discipline.

The prologue begins with Zarathustra's entry to solitude, and his subsequent egress:

> When Zarathustra was thirty years old he left his home and the lake of his home and went into the mountains. Here he enjoyed his spirit and his solitude, and for ten years did not tire of it. But at last a change came over his heart, and one morning he rose with the dawn, and stepped before the sun, and spoke to it thus:[57]

Note the parallel of spirit and solitude: the two are kindred notions in Nietzsche's mind. Note also that the silence of solitude is a prelude to speech to another self. This interdependence of self and other is announced in Zarathustra's first words to the sun:

> "You great star, what would your happiness be had you not those for whom you shine?"
> "For ten years you have climbed to my cave: you would have tired of your light and of the journey had it not been for me and my eagle and my serpent."
> "But we waited for you every morning, took your overflow from you, and blessed you for it."
> "Behold, I am weary of my wisdom, like a bee that has gathered too much honey; I need hands outstretched to receive it."[58]

A second relationship is evident here—the interplay of the full and the empty. In solitude Zarathustra has become full of wisdom, received from the overflow of the sun; he will empty himself by teaching:

"I would give away and distribute, until the wise among men find joy once again in their folly, and the poor in their riches."
"For that I must descended to the depths, as you do in the evening when you go behind the seas and still bring light to the underworld, your overrich star."
"Like you, I must *go under*—go down, as is said by man, to whom I want to descend."[59]

Here the more familiar Nietzschean theme of overcoming and undergoing parallels the fullness/emptiness pairing. Solitude is an experience of overcoming as of fullness. The first section of the prologue concludes with a repetition of these images:

"So bless me then, you quiet eye that can look even upon an all-too-great-happiness without envy!"
"Bless the cup that wants to overflow, that the water may flow from it golden and carry everywhere the reflection of your delight."
"Behold, this cup wants to become empty again, and Zarathustra wants to become man again."
Thus Zarathustra began to go under.[60]

Sexual and procreative imagery is rife here. Zarathustra is associated with the male symbols of the eagle and the serpent, and is expressly identified with the bee who has gathered honey for the sustenance of a queen and her progeny. Zarathustra wants to "become man (Mensch) again," to re-create himself and create the possibility of a new more vital humanity. This novel vision of humanity is revealed as the text progresses; it is shown to imply new truths, a new language, a new self, and, even, a new world.

The first part of the text not only begins with Zarathustra's experience of solitude, but it also contains explicit teaching on this theme. The section entitled "The Way of the Creator" begins with Zarathustra asking "Is it your wish my brother to go into solitude? Is it your wish to seek the way to yourself? Then linger a moment and listen to me."[61] The lesson Zarathustra teaches is that genuine solitude involves rejection of God, society, and all values except those one imposes on oneself. It is lawbreaking, self-mastery, abandonment. It is the will to truth creating truth:

> Can you give yourself your own evil and your own good and hang your own will over yourself as a law? Can you be your own judge and avenger of your law? Terrible it is to be alone with the judge and avenger of one's own law. Thus is a star thrown out into the void and into the icy breath of solitude.[62]

The passage ends with a series of apostrophes to the "lonely one," declaiming that the Overman is destined to die in order to live, to despise in order to love, and to destroy so that he might create. The truths born in solitude are paradoxical. They are rife with a negativity and a generality that makes them approximate the paradoxes born of semiotic self-reference.

The pattern of the first part is repeated in the two parts that follow. Zarathustra communes with himself in solitude and then embarks on a career of teaching. The second part begins:

> Then Zarathustra returned again to the mountains and to the solitude of his cave and withdrew from men, waiting like a sower who has scattered his seed. But his soul grew full of impatience and desire for those whom he loved, because he still had much to give them.[63]

Imagery of sexuality and fullness are again present. The motifs continue with it being said of Zarathustra that "his wisdom grew and caused him pain with its fullness"; and then he himself says, "My wild wisdom became pregnant on lonely (einsamen) mountains; on rough stones she gave birth to her young, her youngest."[64] In fact, what Zarathustra, or Nietzsche, creates is a an object of art, a work of language. Language is the medium in which Zarathustra appears, disappears, and reappears. "New ways I go, a new speech comes to me; weary I grow, like all creators, of the old tongues. My spirit no longer wants to walk on worn soles."[65] Solitude empowers Zarathustra to speak of himself and his world. It makes possible both the language of creation—in Nietzsche's case the doctrine of eternal recurrence— and the creation of language. Speech is the intricate juxtaposition of sounds and silence, and solitude guarantees the deepest silence; hence, it likewise makes possible the most articulate speech.

The teaching on solitude in the second part is contained in a section called "The Night Song." Like a musical composition shifting into a new key, solitude becomes identified with night and light imagery; and like a musical melody undergoing development by variation, Zarathustra speaks about solitude as giving birth to a teaching which both hurts and helps its pupils: "A hunger grows out of my beauty; I should like to hurt those for whom I shine. . . . Such revenge my fullness plots; such spite wells up out of my loneliness."[66] Revenge and spite are usually associated by Nietzsche with the slave morality of Judaism and Christianity. What prevents inconsistency here is that *ressentiment* is bred only if these feelings are not expressed directly. Zarathustra expresses such feelings in this song and so they receive the only justification possible, an aesthetic justification. Solitude is the prerequisite for the self being itself, even in its less noble manifestations. Hence Nietzsche's vision of a new humanity includes new truths, a new language for conveying those truths, and a new self who utters the fateful words.

The transition from the second part to the third is again accompanied by Zarathustra's retreat into solitude. Yet this time there is a difference because "the bear goes back to his cave without joy."[67] The symmetry of the text's structure is broken; Zarathustra's consummate creative act is foreshadowed. Zarathustra's consternation signals the central drama of the text: he is called to deliver a teaching he fears to utter. Zarathustra argues with his destiny: "Yes, I know it, but I do not want to say it. . . . It is beyond my strength," but his destiny responds harshly, "What do you matter, Zarathustra? Speak your word and break!"[68] The "word," of course, is the doctrine of the eternal recurrence, and eventually Zarathustra proclaims this teaching at the end of the third book. A number of sections precede and prepare for this dramatic culmination, including a third reflection upon solitude, this time taking the form of a dramatic apostrophe: "O solitude! O my *home*, solitude!"[69] Solitude is portrayed as a mother scolding, then comforting a wayward child who returns to her. Zarathustra finds among the multitude many who talk but few who listen; in solitude he is genuinely heard. Language and self are restored there, and truth is made possible. In this section Zarathustra dramatically realizes his own teaching on solitude, and he is empowered to undertake his greatest creation.

With the aid of his eagle and serpent Zarathustra eventually affirsm eternal recurrence. Images of fullness, language, pregnancy, and solitude abound in the first of seven such affirmations: "If I am a soothsayer and full of the soothsaying spirit . . . blessed is he who is thus pregnant!"[70] Mountain solitude empowers him to conceive this momentous word: "And verily, long must he hang on the mountains like a dark cloud who shall one day kindle the light of the future: O, how should I not lust after eternity and after the nuptial ring of rings, the ring of recurrence?"; and then, giving expression to this love, he repeatedly proclaims:

> Never yet have I found the woman from who I wanted children, unless it be this woman who I love: for I love you, O eternity.
> *For I love you, O eternity!*[71]

In his love for eternity Zarathustra confesses his willingness for all that has been to recur, and to recur eternally. Indeed, it is a strange word!

Like most of Nietzsche's more sympathetic interpreters, I do not construe the doctrine of eternal recurrence in any literal fashion. It is not an exception to his perspectivism, nor even is it a viable candidate for such a singular status as is, for instance, the doctrine of the will to power. I take it to be a radical expression of Nietzsche's demand for *amor fati*—for love of one's fate. It is an extreme celebration of life as it is, and a condemnation of all counterfactual attitudes—of hope, envy, regret, disappointment, nostalgia and messianism. Nietzsche only recommends change when it is part of the rhythmic vitality of life—when it is part of a dynamic of biological and phenomenological equilibration. He never sanctions flight from life.

The doctrine of eternal recurrence is radical in its being cosmological; its mythical and metaphysical sound should be attributed more to Nietzsche's fondness for hyperbole than to a literal reversion to archaic and traditional forms of discourse. He is playing the role of an "ironic mythmaker."[72] Nietzsche's new humanity would be neither entirely novel nor superlatively human if it did not command a strangely transformed cosmos as its audience. Eternal recurrence is an account of the new world which solitary persons inhabit. Nietzsche believed that you must "create the world before which you can kneel."[73] You may revere only worlds of your own creation. Solitude is the spiritual discipline of the godless, yet it is also the self-mastery of the creative ones who alone are capable of genuine feelings of reverence. Proclaiming the doctrine of eternal recurrence completes a sequence of creative acts that dramatically presents solitude as the spiritual discipline of godless creators.

By an analysis of the episodes of solitude and the teachings about it in *Thus Spoke Zarathustra*, I have indicated how solitude is shown to bring about the truth, language, and selfhood of the new humanity that Zarathustra heralds. I have also indicated that this godless variety of spiritual discipline exhibits some features of self-reference, symmetry, and equilibration I have made so central to my redescription of spiritual discipline. I have sought to learn from Nietzsche yet also to understand him in my own terms. This has been preparation for the next chapter in which I shall present a conception of spiritual discipline, if not for Nietzsche's new humanity, then at least for persons living in a contemporary context of radical pluralism. It will be a conception that, if not godless, then at least brackets (in the phenomenological sense) salvific considerations so that they do not obstruct embodied human flourishing in both its individual and (contra Nietzsche) its communal aspects.

CHAPTER 7

A Novel Response

A review of Nietzsche's thoughts on solitude has been useful for providing an example of a nonreligious conception of spiritual discipline. It has served a second purpose also. Language of emptiness and fullness was prominent in Nietzsche's discussion of solitude; its usage by him helped to give greater specificity to the thesis that spiritual forms of self-mastery promote a fullness of life which effectively answers the spiritual predicament associated here with Blaise Pascal. Fullness is identified by Nietzsche with feelings of power, and especially, with the experienced power to think, represent, and propagate new values. I subscribe to this meaning, but only insofar as it is qualified by other dimensions of fullness having a different character. This section will indicate these complementary meanings and conclude with a first formulation of a new conception of spiritual discipline that incorporates them.

One way to approach these complementary meanings of fullness is to investigate the relationship between solitude and religion. In *Beyond Good and Evil* Nietzsche admits that solitude, and also fasting and sexual abstinence, are practices that have historically been constant concomitants of religion.[1] Acknowledging this to be the case does not make solitude vulnerable to criticisms that Nietzsche levelled against religiously motivated ascetic ideals. Solitude is not born of *ressentiment*; quite to the contrary, in *The Gay Science* Nietzsche says that it is an antidote to feelings of excessive contempt for the multitude.[2] Nor is it an expression of the ascetic "will to nothingness." Instead, Zarathustra's example shows that solitude fosters a spiritual fullness, which, in turn, makes possible the most sublime of creations—new values. Nietzsche does not explicitly indicate why solitude and fullness are linked, nor does he elucidate the relationship between solitude and religion except insofar as the former is an expression of traditional ascetic ideals. I believe that a philosophical account of this relationship may be attained by investigating the interplay of emptiness and fullness common to Nietzschean solitude and at least some disciplined religious regimens. The presence of the empty/full dynamic on a plurality of levels of description—semio-logical, sociological, and cosmological—reveals a meaningful common nature shared by Nietzschean solitude and some traditional spiritual disciplines. It also points to important dimensions of a full human life.

Presumptive evidence for the presence of a dynamic of the empty and the full in religious behavior comes from the way in which formalized religious actions are classifiable in contrasting pairs: fasting and feasting, silence and singing, celibacy and sexual jesting are such pairs. Vigils and dreaming, and poverty and potlatch are others. Historians of religion locate the archaic contexts for many of these practices in the calendar of seasonal activities in which early agricultural communities engaged. I already intimated in the last chapter the importance I give to this aspect of the genealogy of religious practices. Some basic points bear repeating. The growing season of major crops marked off the most significant segment of the calendar. Dependence on these productive periods made life appear to be a series of leases in need of annual renewal. The drama of renewal was heightened by the regular intercession of fallow periods between growing seasons, periods often dictated by climatic, and ultimately astronomical, cycles. In cultures without sophisticated means for storing food, periods between harvests could be ones of restricted diet and relative want. Hence the seasonal calendar was governed by a dynamic of kenosis and plerosis, of emptying and filling. This dynamic was experienced as a natural phenomena, yet was also interpreted in more personal terms through the personification of natural forces as deities and through the visceral realization of human participation in natural processes.[3]

Many archaic myths and rituals were devoted to assuring the regular return of the natural preconditions of bountiful harvests: ample rain, warm weather, soil fertility, and so forth. Each season these natural realities need re-creation. In cultures of the ancient Near East regular constituents of the yearly ritual cycle can be identified. For instance, to insure a proper passing or emptying of the old year, rites of mortification were carried out. Fasting often occurred in this context, and the Christian tradition of fasting during Lent is probably a remnant of this archaic practice. Rites of purification also accompanied the close of a yearly cycle, with lustrations, exorcisms, and scapegoating being common practices. Priests or other figures representative of the community frequently isolated themselves at this time. Again, the Christian sacrament of baptism traditionally occurred immediately prior to Easter, and, as preparation for formal entrance into the Christian community, the baptismal candidate engaged in relative solitude of chastity and prayer.

The beginning of the new year was sympathetically experienced in cultic rites of invigoration and jubilation. Ritual combat and eroticism are the most vivid acts of invigoration. Celebrative practices like feasting, singing, and dancing are ways of signalling and magically effecting the resumption of a period of natural productivity. Such ritual actions, while undertaken with magical intent, may indirectly serve other purposes; references to Victor Turner's writings in the previous chapter touched on this point. Periods of extreme want place great strain on the system of ties and responsibilities which constitute human society. The recitation of myths and the enactment of rituals can promote social solidarity even if they do not directly change problematic natural conditions. Thus the rule-governed pattern of archaic social life had a rhythm of waxing and waning that parallelled seasonal cycles of change: the rules were generally relaxed during the interregnum between growing seasons and enforced most stringently during periods like harvest time when a maximum of social cooperation was needed. Ritual practices of celebration and austerity reflect and legitimate this social reality.

The Christian celebration of the Lord's Supper commemorates Christ's victory over death on the cross; it also celebrates proleptically life in the kingdom of heaven which Christ's saving work makes possible. Given the historical indebtedness of the Christian sacraments to Jewish and Canaanite rituals, it not surprising that in the Pauline literature Christ's passion is described by saying that he "emptied himself" (Phil. 2.7), and Christian salvation is portrayed as an experience of being "filled with all the fullness of God" (Eph. 3.19). In the early Christian period as the liturgical calendar became established and elaborated, the retrieval of empty/full themes from the agricultural seasonal calendar was continued. In some Christian traditions, most especially Orthodox ones, a liturgical calendar chronicling the emptying and filling of Christ's presence in the church still constitutes the matrix in which spiritual disciplines such as fasting and feasting occur.

As early Christian thinkers adopted the language of emptiness and fullness to express theological insights, so did Greek thinkers modify similar themes from their mythological heritage to serve philosophical purposes. The Neoplatonic account of creation is an influential instance of this transformation. Quite self-consciously adapting Greek mythological traditions, Plotinus uses this idiom to describe Intellect's production of Soul in the fifth Ennead:

> As the mysteries and the stories about the gods hint, saying
> that Cronos, the wisest god, before Zeus appears, holds back
> within himself what he produces, so that he is full and
> Intellect in satiety. Afterwards, so they say, he produces Zeus
> when already sated; for Intellect produces Soul, since Intellect
> is perfect. Indeed, since it is perfect, it had to produce; such
> a great power could not be barren.[4]

The process of the Intellect begetting Soul occurs in accordance with
a general principle stipulating that what is completely perfect or full
necessarily overflows beyond itself to create something other than
itself. Plotinus summarizes the principle by saying "Everything which
is already perfect produces."[5] Hence in the Plotinian scheme of
creation this same dynamic accounts for the begetting of Intellect from
the One, except that while the Intellect needs and contemplates the
One, as Soul does the Intellect, the One needs and contemplates
nothing other than itself. Its "selfsameness" remains undisturbed,
or in more anthropomorphic terms, its solitude persists.

The analogy between the language of Zarathustra's Prologue and
the Plotinian account of creation is striking: images of fullness,
fertility, creativity, and solitude abound. Yet this does not justify
reading Nietzsche as a Neoplatonist—not at all! Rather, just as
Christian theology and Neoplatonic philosophy represent a transformation of an historically antecedent dynamic of the empty and the
full so too does Nietzsche's conception of solitude represent a
transformation of the Christian and Neoplatonic versions of this
theme. Christian theology transforms the kenosis and plerosis of the
archaic seasonal calendar into a Trinitarian theism whose economy
of salvation provides a matrix for disciplined religious practices.
Neoplatonic philosophy transforms a similar model of kenosis and
plerosis into a cosmological idealism whose account of creation
provides a rationale for a disciplined contemplative orientation.
Finally, Nietzsche transforms the dynamic interplay of the empty and
the full in Christianity and Neoplatonism into an experience of
solitude that is the discipline of realists, which means, above all else,
the discipline of the godless.

Nietzsche's writings on solitude reveal his version of the interplay
of the empty and the full. The Nietzschean solitary endures a world
empty of others for the sake of a spiritual fullness. The solitary aspires
towards fullness in the absence of others so that the fruits of this
fullness may be presented to them. The fruition of solitude is the
teaching of paradoxical truths—truths so momentous that they

approach the status of myths. Included among these truths is the necessity of solitude for teaching, for myth-making.[6] By such deliverances the teacher is emptied of spiritual vitality, and so requires restoration and refilling, a return to solitude. The cycle begins again, and, indeed, in a sense it eternally recurs. This is Nietzsche's myth, yet unlike Platonic Christian theology, it affirms present reality and embodied life, not heavenly substitutes.

Solitude, for Nietzsche, then, dwells at the center of life; it embraces birth, sex, conflict, and deliverance. Solitude encompasses the fullness of the mother who nurtures life inside of herself and the fullness of the male offspring who sows life outside himself. It includes the emptiness of the mother whose child has been delivered and the emptiness of the male offspring whose seed has been expended. It is part of the cycle of life and death lived within life, and is an agent of the creation of the world within the created world. Its adoption is an immune response of the creative individual, and its presence is a contagion within established communities. Solitude is deliverance of the godless from God, of the immoralist from morality. Like the will to power, eternal recurrence, and other central Nietzschean themes, solitude promotes a paradoxical and defiant celebration of life amidst what Nietzsche perceived to be a modern Western European culture of death.

In each of these contexts—archaic myth, Christian theology, Neoplatonic speculation, and Nietzschean philosophy—one can see a somewhat different way of interpreting the meaning of the rhythmical interplay of the empty and the full. In each case the interpretation is given in order to resolve the spiritual predicament of how one acts to secure a good life, a full life. Too often the interplay of empty and the full has been rigidified so as to contribute to some simplistic moral dualism. For instance, Clement quickly has the kenotic Christ filled with a moral authority that becomes manifest in commandments that faithful Christians are enjoined to obey uncritically. Nietzsche resists such dualisms. He insists upon the historically contextual nature of all human phenomena, including the rhythmical experiences of emptiness and fullness. Zarathustra's example is an invitation to dramatic action and not to actions sanctioned by invariable rules. Nietzsche's application of the theme of the empty and the full retains its dynamic character. Only as such did he believe that it would be helpful to the human spiritual predicament as he understood it; only as such can regimens of abstention and invigoration break the force of socially promulgated habit and allow for the disciplined efforts which make for human excellence in its manifold forms.

Nietzsche believed that Christian ascetic ideals were elements in a strategy to find meaning in human suffering. He rejected this strategy because he felt the cost of pursuing it was too high, that it involved forsaking the discovery of meaning in human joy, creation, strife, and overcoming. I have argued that Nietzsche's treatment of ascetic ideals was one-sided because he abstracts ascetic practices from their celebratory counterparts. I have claimed that his own conception of solitude is a form of spiritual discipline bearing resemblance to traditional forms by its reinterpretation of the theme of the empty and the full. Hence I am more optimistic than he about the possibility of formulating a strategy for spiritual meaning that renders meaningful both human joy and human suffering, and that retains continuity with past traditions of spiritual discipline. I am also fortunate in being able to draw upon the writings of twentieth-century philosophers who have engaged anew at the ancient theme of the interplay of the empty and the full. Edmund Husserl's employment of empty and filled intentions as constitutive elements in a phenomenological theory of meaning has already been cited in this book. I shall invoke this resource again because it is helpful for articulating the strategy for spiritual meaning which is the central concern of this section.

Nietzsche never provided a general definition of spiritual discipline. Thus the one I shall offer here, though drawing upon Nietzsche's views and the tradition he transformed, will be my own formulation. I have argued above that the Nietzschean practice of solitude shares some important traits with traditional forms of spiritual discipline, yet I have just as emphatically noted that it lacks their soteriological orientation. For Nietzsche, life is not something from which one needs to be saved, and even suffering is a condition less to be transcended than to be rendered meaningful. On this point he differed strongly with Schopenhauer who gave a philosophically atheistic account of asceticism, but who retained a consistently salvific orientation. Nietzsche commended traditional ascetic ideals only insofar as they give meaning to human suffering, but condemned them for including in their meaning a denial of embodied, willing, joyful life. From this contrast emerges the requisite features of a Nietzschean definition of spiritual discipline: it must be semiological and life-affirming rather than soteriological and life-negating. Furthermore, neither signs nor life can be portrayed as static and unchanging: they must partake of the emptying and filling which Nietzsche understood to be best exemplified by the flux of solitariness and sociability evident in the lives of creative individuals.

I offer the following definition. Spiritual discipline is that type of meaningful, embodied action which engenders an interplay of emptiness and fullness that is both semiotic and physical. It consists of practical regimens of action which delineate, then erase, a picture of the self in the world, thereby symbolizing—at once indicating and exemplifying—an intense, creative vitality. Stated in a linguistic idiom, spiritual discipline involves a naming of one's most vital self, in celebration of human particularity, and then a self-forgetting of one's name in deference to some maximally inclusive totality. For Nietzsche this greater totality is not God or anything transcendental: it is rather the totality of active, creative life. It is that which eternally recurs, and that which is loved by the most sublime personalities.

Certainly naming and forgetting are typically Nietzschean exertions of will. In *The Gay Science* he speaks of fashioning new names as emblematic of creating new things; in *On the Genealogy of Morals* he praises "active forgetfulness" for clearing psychic space for new things.[7] Also, Zarathustra endures solitude and other austerities for the sake of teaching the reality of the Overman and eternal recurrence—a portrayal of new human selfhood and a concomitant cosmic vision. Hence the definition has continuity with Nietzsche's thought. It is also draws upon the account of the spiritual dimension of human existence presented in this book's introduction, and, indirectly, it involves the dynamic of self-referencing and self-vanquishing that I previously introduced in advocating the descriptive utility of the theme of semiotic self-reference.

Pictures and names are signs, and at least since the Stoics, signs have been understood as vehicles for presenting things which are absent. Since Edmund Husserl they have also been said to yield meaning by filling intentional acts of consciousness formerly empty.[8] Thus a spiritually disciplined practice resembles signification itself, presenting to the self a self which is absent, and also absenting the self from this form of self-presence. In more Nietzschean terms, spiritual discipline consists of undergoing self-dissection and over-coming self-conceptions through regimens of significant, embodied actions. It is a drama of embodied signs because the naming and forgetting, and the undergoing and overcoming, are never achieved without conflict. For Nietzsche, spiritually disciplined actions partake of the struggle to affirm one's unique destiny, even unto eternal recurrence.

My assessment of Nietzsche's version of spiritual discipline leads me to conclude, as others have, that Nietzsche celebrates above all else feats of imaginative creativity that effect a revaluation of values.

Yet this aesthetic emphasis, characteristic of Nehamas, Megill, and other contemporary interpreters, should not depreciate Nietzsche's insistence upon the inevitability of existential strife and the urgency of self-overcoming. Attributing to Nietzsche an advocacy of spiritual discipline as a drama of embodied signs integrates the aesthetic and existential dimensions of his philosophy. Like traditional ascetics Nietzsche struggles mightily to give meaning to human suffering; yet he does not flee it, but embraces and enfolds it with a joyful life of *amor fati*. For Nietzsche, his practice of solitude is an embodied expression of this defiant praise of Dionysus. For others—and especially for the followers of traditional religious paths to well-being—it is a provocation for rethinking the very idea of spiritual discipline, this time without any despising of the body, grovelling for salvation, or any of the other habitual behaviors which Nietzsche deemed decadent.

A cogent conception of spiritual discipline must have rational coherence, empirical applicability, and imaginative appeal. This book has least directly addressed the criterion of empirical applicability, though the example of Nietzschean solitude mentioned above, and the practices adverted to in its second part, have been designed to give some measure of empirical applicability to its central themes. The choice of Nietzsche as a partial exemplar of a new variety of spiritual discipline does much to insure that the proposal has imaginative appeal (at least, to a certain sort of human imagination). Extending his aesthetic emphasis by insisting that ascetic practices be conjoined with celebrative counterparts has more directly fostered the imaginative appeal of my own proposal.

The rational coherence of conceptions of spiritual discipline is, of course, the criterion that has been given most attention in this philosophical essay. It has been discussed by evaluating the presupposed beliefs of spiritual adepts which are thought by them to make their favored conception of spiritual discipline more rationally compelling. Clement's categoreal themes of suprasensual vision, unencumbered causality, and static hierarchy were employed in this fashion. For instance, the claim that the individual's saving encounter with God occurs as a vision of a deity that transcends normal eyesight may be regarded as a crucial presupposition for a second claim that the control of sensual impulses is a mark of the spiritually perfect person. In my view, a way of describing spiritual discipline requires presuppositions quite different from the ones present in Clement and other religious Platonists. Indeed, I have chosen to understand spiritual discipline in semiological rather than soteriological terms, as an activity directed toward signifying the sacred rather than establishing some more definitive relation with it. A consequence of this choice is that the paradoxical aspect of the spiritual life is associated less with an extraordinary sort of vision than with the peculiarity of language that strives to be unusually inclusive in its descriptive scope.

The elucidation of several further consequences of these basic choices will, I hope, augment its cogency and amplify differences between my proposal and those offered by Nietzsche and others. Nietzsche thought that his path to spiritual discipline and well-being was completely antithetical to religion. Schopenhauer before him thought that his philosophical rendering of asceticism had abstracted the essential truth from pessimistic religions like Hinduism, Buddhism, and Christianity. I have disagreed with Nietzsche's irreligiousness and with Schopenhauer's abstractionism. Instead I believe that a semiotic conception of spiritual discipline has relevance to diverse examples of spiritual discipline—be they religious or not— because it specifies an embodied dynamic of meaning that may be presupposed by these different practices. For this reason, I believe that such a philosophical rethinking of spiritual discipline is especially appropriate for persons seeking spiritual well-being in today's context of religious and cultural pluralism. Yet, even in its provisional formulations, this new conception has some substantive import. It has been shown to favor some spiritually disciplined practices over others; indeed, it gives the beginnings of a rationale for adopting them. When spiritual discipline is understood to be a drama of embodied signs—a summary formula for the views presented above— then surely it will also favor different dramatic scenarios. It is especially compatible with conceptions of spiritual discipline that are not subsumed within an other-worldly scheme of salvation. It has this much in common with Nietzsche's project of spiritual self-mastery.

Unlike Nietzsche, I am offering a conception of spiritual discipline that is meant to be applicable to traditionally salvific religious practices, though it is clearly less suited to spiritual practices that occur as preparations for a mystical encounter with God than as gestures of thanksgiving for divine favor already received. If 'maximally inclusive totality' is conceived theistically, the conception of spiritual discipline offered here may be applied to traditional Christian forms of spiritual discipline. As an embodied symbolic act, fasting and feasting, for example, may be construed as a means for witnessing to God's Son that becomes possible after having become joined to that life by the indwelling of the Holy Spirit. Since signs can never entirely be identified with what they signify, such spiritually disciplined practices are undertaken by persons who, though "not the light, . . . bear witness to the light" (John 1.8). To be part of a spiritual drama that involves all of reality is a momentous prospect; to imagine oneself a central player in the drama risks spiritual presumption. Christians mindful of Christ's own humility will likely be wary of ambitious spiritual aspirations. The Johannine office of the witness is humbly deferential to the work of Christ; even so it is quite dramatic, and not a little momentous to be an active sign of the God whose gracious initiative assures that love will reign over hatred and peace over strife. Religious varieties of spiritual discipline I regard as acts of bearing witness to what their practitioners believe is sacred.

In traditional theological terms the understanding of spiritual discipline advocated here is more continuous with a conception of the spiritual life as activity intended to "glorify God in one's body" (I Cor. 6.20) than as activity preparatory to an "assimilation to God" (*Theaetetus*, 176b). Signification requires differentiation of sign and thing signified; hence a semiotic conception of spiritual discipline is ultimately incompatible with mystical aspirations toward fundamental union with a transcendent God. It is, however, compatible with a more naturalistic form of mysticism wherein God is experienced as an immanent totality; this is so because spiritual practices may then be construed as a case of parts signifying a whole to which it belongs. This interpretation helps counter Nietzsche's claim that ascetic practices necessarily involve a disparagement of what is real and natural. An individual figure need not be overshadowed, but may be highlighted, by being placed before a sublime background. Different interpretations of the same action are possible according to one's perspective, a point that Nietzsche would have been unlikely to contend.

The severance of spiritual discipline from personal salvation is not meant to deny that spiritual discipline may be conjoined with saving grace; it merely is noncommittal about there being a causal connection between the engagement of the former and the bestowal of the latter. This agnostic obviation of a "works righteousness" mentality serves philosophically as a rejoinder to Nietzsche's claim that religious leaders use perfectionistic ascetic ideals to manipulate people's pious fear of God. The priest as master of ascetic ideals is denied the most strenuous form of manipulative power if realization of those ideals no longer is the key to winning God's blessing and heavenly bliss. Nietzsche himself remarked in *Daybreak* that Luther's rejection of the medieval model of the contemplative life had the liberating effect of making a new contemplative option possible. Luther was certainly a great enemy of all attempts to merit salvation. A similar liberating influence can be accorded to the impact on social ethics of Luther's novel understanding of the freedom of the Christian. By separating people's spiritual standing before God from their relationships with their neighbor, he freed the impulse to serve to neighbor and society from the taint of a selfish but disguised servility to God. Nietzsche was opposed neither to individual selfishness nor spiritual perfectionism; however, he was opposed to any form of duplicity. In *The Anti-Christ* he denounced Christian virtue as Christian shrewdness.[9] Yet so great had his hostility to religion become by this late date that he could not appreciate Luther's or any other theologian's resistance to forms of spiritual disingenuousness.

A further consequence of thinking of spiritual discipline in semiological terms is that it thereby becomes an ineluctably social phenomenon because language is itself social. As activities signifying a common sacred reality and cultivating a common emotional attitude towards it, spiritual practices can promote social cohesiveness, and in some circumstances, social transformation. Even the pursuit of solitude, if it is a spiritual witness rather than a spiritual work, cannot be understand as an transaction solely involving a solitary person and God. It is an action within a communal context of shared spiritual meanings and values. Anchorites may reinforce or challenge these communal meanings, but they cannot claim to have singly created them or to have fashioned comparable alternatives. Nietzsche's own godless perfectionism is evident when he attributes a capacity for myth-making to extraordinary individuals like himself. The social aspect of language was certainly acknowledged by Nietzsche; he even featured it in his celebrated definition of truth as "a mobile army of metaphors, metonyms, and anthropomorphisms—in short, a sum of human relations. . . ."[10] Yet he seems to have forgotten this principle when he talked of the creation of new spiritual meanings. This work he attributed to the *Übermensch*, to extraordinary individuals like Zarathustra, and in some of his later boasts in *Ecce Homo*, to himself. Explanations of this departure from his own perspectivism and historicism must be speculative. It may be related to Nietzsche's disenchantment with his early teachers, Schopenhauer and Wagner, and his refusal to be part of their community of disciples. It may be related to his inability to attract and appreciate admirers of his own work. Whatever the reason may be, there is in Nietzsche's conception of a life well lived a certain aura of spiritual titanism which combines perfectionism with an extreme individualism. It compromises the integrity of Nietzsche's insights by projecting a persona that did not accord with his real personality. *Ecce Homo* is a record of this late tendency of self-aggrandizement and is a preview of the fragmentation of selfhood that occurred when Nietzsche later succumbed to madness. A strategy for personal integrity is needed which addresses this danger. The outlines of such a strategy is the subject of this chapter's next section.

A STRATEGY FOR PERSONAL INTEGRITY

The conception of spiritual discipline advocated here is opposed to any exaggeration of the transformative power of particular spiritual regimens. Specifically, claims for a radical discontinuity between personalities before and after the adoption of some spiritual practice threaten to compromise the integrity of both the practice and its practitioners. If the claim is true, then psychological preconditions, or perhaps divine grace, should be accorded at least equal credit as the practice itself. If it is not true, then there is an undesirable discrepancy between the practitioners' self-portrayal and their image in the eyes of others who know them. In the first instance there is an excessive confidence in technique—a spiritual methodism. In the second there is an immodest estimate of one's own achievement—a spiritual titanism. Nietzsche's *Ecce Homo* provides a stunning exemplification of the latter phenomenon.

Spiritual titanism compromises the integrity of those who presume it. It fractures them into discordant private and public selves; it thereby engenders duplicity, and perhaps, even conscious deceit. Such spiritual titanism is an especially great flaw in conceptions of spiritual discipline which are themselves offered as a remedies to certain conditions of disintegration. The contemporary spiritual predicament prefigured by Pascal and diagnosed by Nietzsche was engendered by such conditions. When powerful institutions control individuals by the inculcation of addictive habits of behavior and thought, they promulgate at the same time discordant self-conceptions and world views. This is so because the habits encouraged are not advertised honestly, but rather are associated with products, services, and values that are supposed to make their consumers attractive, accomplished, and autonomous. Shoe merchants tout products of fine leather that severely strain their wearer's back; public relations agents recommend popular projects that subordinate excellence to success; and politicians promise peace and freedom from weapons of mass destruction. To succumb to these appeals is to become afflicted with a conflict of values, a condition, which, like a cancer, is most threatening when its presence is unsuspected.

A conception of spiritual discipline which has its practitioners point to the sacred, but not become identical with it, militates against the severest form of spiritual titanism. It is similarly cautionary because the signification process involved is more referential than expressive. For instance, daily prayer has not been described above as self-expression in the sense that German romanticism has given to the phrase 'Selbst-Ausdruck'. It is not the externalization of some ideal meaning about self and deity which finds its complete realization only in the act of expression itself. It is rather conversation with God; it consists words addressed to a divine personality with whom it establishes relationship but not unity, though the pervasive presence of this personality implies that prayerful words effect its correlation with the widest horizon of its world. That prayer occurs in regularized forms and at periodic times accentuates the way in which this practice helps to break harmful habitual behaviors more than transcend the human condition itself.

In this section I shall primarily be concerned with the threat to personal integrity posed by spiritual titanism. A traditional figure like Clement is vulnerable to the charge of spiritual titanism because of his use of the theme of unencumbered causality. A disciplined spiritual life, says Clement, engenders in the Christian believer, by the aid of God's grace but also as a result of free choice, both a divine potency and divine immutability. Clement says that "the Christian gnostic" becomes a passionless agent who in subordination to Christ is effective in bringing about a new creation. One shares in the power of Christ by disciplined regimens of self-denial which effect the absorption of one's personal identity into Christ's divine being. This is a Christian version of the Platonic ideal of deification. The transformation is unidirectional and ontological; it is not the alternating dynamic of self-referencing and self-vanquishing recommended in previous pages as a means for identifying the self analogously to how an object is constituted by its ways of being absent and present in language.

A particularly striking illustration of a simultaneous lack of personal integration and an excess of spiritual aspiration is evident in the first chapter of The Dialogue of Catherine of Siena, a thirteenth-century Christian mystic. Speaking of herself in the third person, she writes: "But there is no way she can so savor and be enlightened by this truth [i.e., God's goodness toward her] as in continual humble prayer, grounded in the knowledge of herself and of God. For by such prayer the soul is united with God, following in the footsteps of Christ crucified, and through desire and affection and the union of love he makes of her another himself."[11] The transition in Catherine's concluding phrase from a female worldly personality to a transcendent male identity is jarring to contemporary sensibilities shaped by feminism. Equally disturbing is the exaggerated self-portrayal that has her transformed by union with Christ from a person who is "the cause and instrument of every evil" into a person who "never ceases doing service for all the world."[12] It is difficult to imagine a single personality encompassing such extreme variations.

Nietzsche might seem to bear little comparison to Clement and Catherine at this point. The climactic event in the Zarathustra story is not prayer but the protagonist's pronouncement of the doctrine of eternal recurrence. This act is shown to be the epitome of self-overcoming, and self-overcoming is portrayed as the characteristic activity of the Overman. It exemplifies the paradoxical theme of the loss of self for the sake of gaining a spiritually higher self. Thus self-overcoming is at once the mark of a higher selfhood, yet it is also something less than an enduring identity that Clement claimed to have found in Christ because it is constantly being overcome. Here the loss of selfhood is part of a dynamic process of self-affirmation; also, it is not undertaken for the sake of obedience to any extrinsic authority. Nietzsche's titanism is of the nihilistic rather than the authoritarian sort. Where he agrees with more traditional figures is in according spiritually disciplined individuals immense status and power, approaching the exalted personas of the Son of God and the Overman respectively. They also agree that a person's failure to achieve spiritual perfection is a recommendation for more of the same. Clement enjoins further contrition and self-denial. Nietzsche calls for more "work," more self-overcoming. This is the task that Zarathustra sets for himself at the end of the fourth book, after he has failed to gather and maintain a band of disciples, ironically spoken of there as the "higher men" (höheren Menschen).[13]

The disparity between spiritual rhetoric and human reality sometimes, but not always, bespeaks a personal as well as an intellectual lack of integration. Catherine of Siena, despite her extreme language, was portrayed by contemporaries as having a talent for personal pacification and political mediation.[14] In an opposite manner, Nietzsche became increasingly intemperate in both his philosophy and life. *Ecce Homo* is a vivid account of the author's inflated estimation of his own personality and achievements. As much as I appreciate *Thus Spoke Zarathustra* I would hardly deem it, as Nietzsche does, "the greatest present that has ever been made to it (mankind) so far."[15] Many more such quotations could be cited. Alexander Nehamas has acknowledged that if Nietzsche's work is interpreted as a philosophical system it suffers from banality as well as from vagueness and inconsistency. He seems also to believe that if Nietzsche is read as using his own life and writing as the stuff of a literary creation he avoids these flaws.[16] Yet the tone of desperate self-importance that typifies *Ecce Homo* renders the work banal either as philosophy or literature. As the writings of Clement and Athanasius show, conceptions of a spiritually disciplined life—the aspect of Nietzsche's work of most concern here—can be communicated in either narrative or discursive forms; hence Nietzsche's aspirations to a higher spirituality in either genre make spirituality itself vulnerable to charges of pretension and insipidity.

Nehamas is correct, though, in saying that Nietzsche's banality is partially mitigated by his creativity, both in the sense of the uniqueness of his achievement and its fruitfulness for the imaginative projects of later generations. Commentators on the spiritual life as different as Clement and Nietzsche stress the importance of creativity because they seek a self-transformation that renders them more vital and whole. Clement's portrayal of spiritual perfection presupposes that creativity is identifiable with transcendent causal power. Such power is operative in the Christian doctrine of *creatio ex nihilo* in which a transcendent God creates the world without the aid of a preexistent material substrate.[17] This paradigmatic demonstration of creative power has neither a material agent nor a material medium: genuine power and gross materiality are judged antithetical. This opposition provided support for a second claim to the effect that progress toward a mystical vision of God is correlated with progress in becoming a spiritual agent free from the influence of the visible, material world. The soul advances as the body declines. The disciple learns from the master by becoming less himself or herself, and more a reflection of the master's values, beliefs, and practices. For Christians like Clement this means being a "new creation" in Christ (2 Cor.5.17). Nietzsche professed to reject such conformity to norms, as he did any flight from materiality or reliance upon divine grace; yet his later megalomaniacal writings seem to allow for no other path toward spiritual excellence than his own strategy of effecting a creative "revaluation of all values."

In an earlier chapter the notion of symmetrical structure was offered as an alternative to causal power as the primary means for describing regularities in nature. Also, the spontaneous breaking of achieved symmetries was used to describe creative discontinuities in a sequence of physical developments. It was intended to be an alternative to the idea of exceptional interventions in a causal nexus of phenomena. In antiquity the notion of symmetry was used to bridge the realm of fact and value: it described the regularity of the human form and also provided an explanation of its beauty. Neither symmetry nor any other concept can serve this same function today: nature cannot be said to be replete with intrinsic value now that teleological modes of explanation are no longer necessary for the natural sciences. Yet symmetry remains, I think, a suggestive categoreal theme with which to conceive anew the meaning of spiritual discipline because such discipline is intended to structure one's activities in a way that realizes an optimum of value—a good life. The thesis offered here is that spiritually disciplined behavior is recommended not because it complies with ancient religious models or conforms to unvarying natural norms, but because it provides a structure of behavior in which important values are conjoined, contested, and, at best, integrated into a life of personal integrity. A further recommendation for this approach is that it allows for the achievement of self-transformation without rank immodesty.

Nietzsche's spiritual titanism is at no time more evident than when he speaks about actions and values. Actions, but also objects or persons, are good or bad when they are so named by a strong and vital personality. In affirming this Nietzsche is a conventionalist in the sense that he acknowledges no intrinsic values; however, he departs from most thinkers of this type when he refuses to make society or tradition the agent of valuation. Only extraordinary individuals really make values, he says. Also, there is no property or trait that makes these individuals extraordinary; if there were, then values would be traceable to something intrinsic. What makes these individuals extraordinary is their ability to command fear and admiration, and, in effect, to have their valuations adopted by others. There is circularity in this account, but Nietzsche regards it as a virtuous circularity: it allows nothing to detract from what he thinks is crucial about values and that is the creative personality who makes them.

Nietzsche concludes that all spiritually disciplined practices are subservient to experiences of vitality and revaluation. Solitude, celibacy, and fasting are sanctioned only if they serve these ends. In *On the Genealogy of Morals* Nietzsche cites the example of the athlete's austerities on the eve of a competition. For Nietzsche, the most momentous conflict in life occurs between individuals proposing new values and societies defending old ones. So momentous is this struggle that it has a spiritual complexion. To create new values is a spiritual destiny: it constitutes the core of what it means to be a vital human being, and in Nietzsche's characteristic media of valuation—philosophy, literature, ironic myth—it includes a new understanding of the world in its greatest expanse and complexity. Nietzsche's *Thus Spoke Zarathustra* is mythic because its narrative action purports to convey the archetypical truth that all things eternally recur; it is ironic because it adopts mythic dimensions only as a strategic ploy in its battle to preserve personal integrity against religion's life-denying rationalizers—the theologians and like-minded philosophers.

Action and valuation occur quite differently in the archaic religious mentality that Nietzsche opposes. Mircea Eliade writes:

> If we observe the general behavior of archaic man, we are struck by the following fact: neither the objects of the external world nor human acts, properly speaking, have any autonomous value. Objects or acts acquire a value, and in so doing become real, because they participate, after one fashion or another, in a reality that transcends them.[18]

He continues by summarizing the life of an archaic individual as a repetition of archetypes: "What he does has been done before. His life is the ceaseless repetition of gestures initiated by others."[19] Clearly Eliade's own Platonist cast of mind is evident in these characterizations. In the present context this is not so objectionable because I believe that the Platonic tradition of philosophy itself represents a rationalization of the view that objects possess their reality, and actions their value, by conforming to authoritative prototypes. In the last section's discussion of the empty and the full, I argued in some detail that Nietzsche's philosophy contains a radical transformation of that archaic theme as it occurred in Christianity and Neoplatonism. Regarding actions and values Nietzsche similarly writes with conscious attention to the Christian and Neoplatonic transformation of archaic religious ideas. Yet on this topic he is more irreverently antithetical and less subtly transformative. Since the archaic sensibility requires exact repetition of archetypical acts, then Nietzsche irreverently requires complete nonconformity to traditional models of behavior. I think that Nietzsche's deliberate antinomianism is less interesting and persuasive than was his transformation of the emptiness and fullness theme. The pragmatic view of actions and

values to which I subscribe is a less extreme but still critical response
to the classical rationalization of the archaic view.

In *The Great Chain of Being* Arthur Lovejoy well describes the
conception of action and value that occupies a position intermediate
between the archaic example and Nietzsche's negation of it.[20] He
traces its sources to the philosophies of Plato and Aristotle; he
attributes its first formulation to the Neoplatonists; and he recounts
its elaboration in diverse cultural forms of the Christian West. Lovejoy
summarizes the "Great Chain of Being" with three principles: "a
principle of plentitude," which posits a primordial goodness which
overflows and creates things other than itself, i.e., it becomes the
source of all being and value; a "principle of continuity," which
requires a maximally diverse creation, and by implication, a plurality
of beings and values; and finally, a "principle of unilinear gradation,"
which stipulates that the variety of diversely valued being may be
arranged hierarchically. A consequence of this last principle is that
creatures capable of conscious, deliberative action are guided by the
very nature of their being to choose that which is highest in the
hierarchy of values.[21] For Neoplatonists like Plotinus and Proclus the
dynamics of creation are governed by a dialectical necessity; for
Christians it is empowered by the will of God—a will that is directly
exercised in acts of creation and redemption, and indirectly manifest
in Christians who imitate Christ and thereby do God's will.

To justify actions by appeal to the nature of things or the will
of God was regarded by Nietzsche as a symptom of alienation from
one's own willful nature. He advocated a reclamation of this basic
human will to power, and he regarded any unity of character and
purpose obtained by other means as specious. On this last point I
partially agree with him. In a cultural context where religion no
longer provides undisputed warrants for behavior, and where science
does not offer any empirically verifiable goal to life, human activity
which seeks commendation by direct invocations of religious or
scientific authority is capable of only abstract and superficial success.
John Dewey opined that the Greek ideal of a naturalistic theory of
value is retrievable only if nature and value are not metaphysically
merged—if genuine goodness is not identified with real being. In
Experience and Nature, he writes:

> Yet if we are to recur to the Greek conceptions, the return
> must be with a difference. It must surrender the identification
> of natural ends with good and perfection; recognizing that a
> natural end, apart from endeavor expressing choice, has no

intrinsic eulogistic quality, but is the boundary which writes 'Finis' to a chapter of history inscribed by a moving system of energies. . . . Again, the return must abandon the notion of a predetermined limited number of ends inherently arranged in order of increasing comprehensiveness and finality. It will have to recognize that natural termini are as infinitely numerous and varied as are the individual systems of action they delimit; and that since there is only relative, no absolute, impermeability and fixity of structure, new individuals with novel ends emerge in irregular procession.[22]

Clearly Dewey is here repudiating the "Great Chain of Being" schema articulated by Lovejoy. A consequence of Dewey's pluralistic account is that the theory of values devolves into a theory of criticism—into a method of discriminating between values on the basis of their conditions and consequences.[23]

In the case of the particular actions that comprise spiritually disciplined practices, a rejection of the traditional theories of value implies that such practices cannot rely on obedience for their justification, and, in particular, cannot use obedience as the sole path to personal integrity. Nietzsche abandons obedience for creativity, and Dewey for criticism. Nietzsche unambiguously aligns religion with decadent values; Dewey subtly makes it peripheral to the process of valuation. In *A Common Faith*, he generalizes: "Any activity pursued on behalf of an ideal and against obstacles and in spite of threats of personal loss because of conviction of its genuine and enduring value is religious in quality."[24] This statement implies that religion is a matter of how values are held, but not what they are. This latter and more substantive determination is made by methods of criticism independent of religion, and so Dewey's pragmatism makes adoption of a religious state of mind a tactic for achieving naturalistically conceived ends of individual well-being and social progress.

Spiritual discipline is recommended here as a means for attaining personal integrity. In advocating its rethinking I have departed from many traditional teachings, and I share with Nietzsche and Dewey an antipathy to relating values and action by means of obedience to established authority. Yet I differ from them both by claiming that religion is neither peripheral nor antagonistic to the quest for personal integrity. Consequently, I prefer to replace obedience with the notion of contestation instead of with the themes chosen by Nietzsche and Dewey. Specifically, I postulate spiritual discipline to be a structure of contested values. It can be creative in the sense that individual practitioners may adopt novel behavioral structures, such as, for instance, the nature and length of prohibitions in a fasting regimen or the movements and occasions of a liturgical dance. It also can be critical in a practical way because individuals may engage in this special type of structured behavior as a means to oppose and overcome certain socially induced destructive habits. In a more reflective fashion, these decisions regarding what to do and not do are undertaken with specific values in mind, e.g., service to God or fullness of life. Most importantly, it is the character of spiritually disciplined practices, I contend, that they engender vivid, embodied experiences of how disparate values contest with one another in the determination of even the simplest of actions. The experience of fasting brings forcefully to mind how every act of eating is a decision that involves considerations of physical health, personal taste, social custom, and practical convenience. Quotidian habits of consumption mask this diversity of competing values, often leaving them in a state of irresolute conflict. Spiritually disciplined practices seek to break these unconscious habits and thereby intentionally engage the welter of relevant values. Also, by engaging them in the context of newly wrought habits of a spiritual regimen, they seek to transform a commitment to multiple values from a destructive conflict into a structured contest. Here again is evidence of the noxious effects of enduring habits and the tonic effect of brief ones.

The idea of contestation was invoked previously when I described the master/disciple relationship. In this relationship the master's authority is first heeded, and then challenged by the talented tyro. Like a good sprinter or a great chess player the spiritual novice seeks to overcome his or her master, not in the objective sense allowed in formal competitions, but in a more elusive sense of accommodating a practice to personal and historical circumstances better than one can be explicitly instructed to do. It is hallmark of revolutionary spiritual figures that their achievement of personally transforming a tradition of teaching and practice attains historical importance: it is found attractive by large number of people because it effectively responds to broad social and cultural changes. Erik Erikson has interpreted the lives of Martin Luther and Mohandas Gandhi in this way.[25]

There are many other examples, though. The life of the Buddha, as recounted by Aśhvaghosa, provides illustrations of the sort of contestation to which I am alluding.[26] Upon renouncing the privileges of his royal upbringing, the young Siddhartha Gautama is said to have sought guidance from two yogins. Both were teachers of a discipline for attaining trance states (*dhyāna*). Gautama was said to have mastered these disciplines and to have been recognized as an equal by his teachers. Yet even so, he did not find peace; he left his teachers, and continued a search for a better path. In the sense that Gautama was unsatisfied with the spiritual accomplishments of his teachers—accomplishments which he himself was said to have attained—he contested their authority and he broke away from their example.

Dhyāna was one of the eight components in the traditional Indian discipline of yoga as represented in the *Yoga Sūtras* of Patañjali; two others were *āsana* and *prāṇāyāma*, respectively concerning the adoption of bodily postures and the rhythmical regulation of breath. Of course, teaching such bodily techniques requires demonstration by the master and imitation by the student. The student seeks to adopt a reflectively symmetrical mirror-image posture to that of the master, and he tries to regulate his or her respiration in accordance with the rhythms set by the master. In yogic practice generally the attainment of trance states presupposed a bodily state of harmony and quiescence, and Buddhist traditions of meditation, while differing on points of theory and practice with Patañjali's synthesis, retained these elements. These elements were very probably part of the practices that Gautama's teachers taught. They were part of what the Buddha found insufficient.

Immediately after leaving these teachers Gautama commenced a program of great austerity, including much fasting and extreme breath retention. He tried to surpass previous yogins in reducing the vitality of the body so as to promote the singular concentration of the mind. His first step on the path to enlightenment occurred when he recalled a state of happiness he experienced as a child—an embodied and vital state, but one free from sensual cravings and immoral thoughts. This led him to forsake the strategy of attaining enlightenment by means of ascetic discipline, and to locate enlightenment in insights, associated with, but not logically dependent upon such discipline. The Buddha's Middle Way rejects both bodily sensuality and bodily mortification, and proceeds on a level of meaning as much psychological as physiological. The *Dhammapada*, an early collection of Buddhist aphorisms, begins with the saying "Our life is the creation of our mind."[27] Hence the Buddha not only questioned the efficacy of particular yogic practices, but he also challenged the great value his teachers placed on ascetic practices. His Middle Way differently contended with the psychological processes of craving, suffering, and their cessation. His contest with his spiritual teachers included a contest of values—a deliberation regarding what is important for attaining spiritual well-being. Adopting the spiritual disciplines of yoga and like austerities provided the behavioral structure in which this contest of values was experienced and resolved.

A characteristic feature of Buddhist meditation is the injunction to concentrate the mind on images and ideas of foul things. Informed by young Gautama's first experience of a dead body, this concentration is often directly to the various conditions and appearances of a human corpse. For instance, in the *Visuddhimagga* of Buddhaghosa, a "swollen thing" is the first in the series of foul objects prescribed for meditation, the phrase referring to the condition of a corpse as inflated by the chemical reactions of decay. The purpose of this practice is to make vividly evident the nature of reality as painful, impermanent, and nonessential, and thereby to rid the practitioner of cravings which are the cause of suffering and continual rebirth. In the later Mahāyāna writings of figures like Nāgārjuna, the Buddhist marks of reality are supplemented, or summarized, by the notion of emptiness (*śūnyāta*). It is interesting that this Sanskrit word literally denotes an inflated or swollen object that appears to be a solid volume, but is actually hollow. Buddhist meditation, then, as a physical and mental discipline is designed to concentrate one's full attention to certain sensible realities so as to make possible a insight into their spiritual emptiness. Sensible realities are thus encountered neither as objects for control nor as incentives for flight, but rather as occasions for the exercise of a sublime equanimity that is the hallmark of Buddhist enlightenment. Cultivation of this unique equanimity is possible by adopting of the Four Noble Truths, and specifically, by following the Eightfold Path, which is the last of the four truths and a practical strategy for integrating the diverse impulses to control or flee sensible reality. The prescriptions for belief, behavior, and self-discipline constitute a strategy for personal integrity that seeks to mollify the conflict that arises when one value judgement seeks happiness in worldly activity and a second seeks peace in radical renunciation of the world. Mahāyāna Buddhists like Nāgārjuna assiduously refrain from choosing either one or the other, but instead they pursue physical and psychological regimens which make relative the differences, and which they hope will deprive them and their discordance of the capacity to cause suffering. In language that I have used, such persons adopt a spiritual discipline which embodies a structure of contested values, and they experience a tranquility, which is portrayed not as a condition of stasis, but as rhythmical movement within articulated bounds.

The meaning of spiritual contestation can also be gleaned from imaginative illustrations. Hermann Hesse, a student of both Nietzsche and Buddhism, provides fictional exploration of this theme in his last novel, *The Glass Bead Game*. It is the story of Joseph Knecht, a legendary master of the game of the book's title. Its setting is Europe a few centuries hence; there then exists a nonreligious but quasimonastic community devoted to preserving knowledge by means of expertise at playing a profound new game. The Glass Bead Game combines disparate features: of chess competition and mathematical calculation, of musical improvisation and encyclopedic learning. Especially relevant for present purposes is that the game is said to resemble traditional spiritual disciplines. The author describes the devotee's study of the Game as "a new, monastically austere intellectual discipline," and he sees their play of the Game as "virtually equivalent to worship."[29] Hesse is careful to describe the Glass Bead Game only indirectly, by alluding, for instance, to precursor versions such as "chess games in which the pieces and squares had secret meanings in addition to their usual functions," and by describing a physical implement for representing musical themes "modeled on a child's abacus."[30] Knecht is portrayed as saying: "The Game as I conceive it...encompasses the player after the completion of meditation as the surface of a sphere encompasses its center, and leaves him with the feeling that he has extracted from the universe of accident and confusion a totally symmetrical and harmonious cosmos, and absorbed it into himself."[31]

Knecht invokes the ideal of symmetry in his description of the Game's alluring structure. Hesse also makes the breaking of symmetry symbolic of a creativity in game play. The plot of the novel concerns the persons and realities which challenge the ideals symbolized by the Game and which imperil the continued existence of the Game community. As leader of the Game community, the Magister Ludi, Knecht contends with these various forces. One of the most serious challenges comes from a young Game player whose Games convey a personality and style unsettling to the Magister; Knecht records this impression of them:

> These Games were little dramas, in structure almost pure monologues, reflecting the imperiled but brilliant life of the author's mind like a perfect self-portrait. The various themes and groups of themes on which the Games were based, and their sequences and confrontations, were brilliantly conceived, dialectically orchestrated and counterpoised. But

beyond that, the synthesis and harmonization of the opposing voices was not carried to the ultimate conclusion in the usual classical manner; rather this harmonization underwent a whole series of refractions, of splintering into overtones, and paused each time, as if wearied and despairing, just on the point of dissolution, finally fading out in questioning and doubt. As a result, those Games possessed a stirring chromatics, of a kind never before ventured as far as I know. Moreover, the Games as a whole expressed a tragic doubt and renunciation; they became figurative statements of the dubiousness of all intellectual endeavor. At the same time, in their intellectual structure as well as in their calligraphic technique and perfection, they were so extraordinarily beautiful that they brought tears to one's eyes.[32]

Knecht recognizes in these games a beauty and originality which is achieved, not despite of, but because of their departure from the classical forms that he himself has taught and exemplified. Yet Knecht also sees tragedy there. Eventually he becomes convinced that life in the Game community, however aesthetically satisfying, is artificial and sterile if it fails to more fully and practically enrich the larger community in which it resides. Hesse, an admirer of Nietzsche, has Knecht say that "My life ought to be a perpetual transcending."[33] Knecht then leaves the Game community to tutor a young man destined for a position of power and influence in the wider world. Early on in this tutelage he goes swimming in a mountain lake with the young man, and he dies. In his demise the reader is free to read either quiet tragedy or ironic promise. Hesse's portrait of Joseph Knecht well dramatizes the dangers that spiritual titanism holds for the personal integrity of spiritual aspirants; it also illustrates the theme of the breaking of symmetry as a emblem of creativity; and finally it prefigures the topic of the next section in its suggestion that personal integrity requires service to a broader community than is defined by the interests and talents of a spiritually disciplined elite. From this point of view a strategy for promoting vital community life is the requisite complement of a quest for spiritual meaning and personal integrity.

A STRATEGY FOR COMMUNAL VITALITY

It was somewhat risky to conclude the last section with discussion of a work of speculative fiction. This choice of material risks persuading readers that the human predicament fictionally dramatized by Hesse and historically exemplified by Pascal reveals a possible future and a distant past, but, in fact, remains remote from contemporary social realities. The disenchantment of intellectuals and artists with societies whose public life they find banal, and the decision of such persons to retire from the larger social arena for the sake of cultivating more private vocations, may pose a recurring predicament for the culturally privileged, but their experience is not necessarily symptomatic of a larger societal crisis.

In his controversial book, *After Virtue*, Alasdair MacIntyre has argued that just this sort of implication holds in contemporary Western culture. One of the unique achievements of the book is its demonstration of how the disorder and inefficacy of public discourse today—and especially in public moral discourse—is emergent from a similarly chaotic social context. Since there are social reasons for public irrationality, individuals are limited in how they can effectively respond to it. This conclusion gives MacIntyre's essay a flavor of resignation. His own partial remedy is given with a familiar historical analogy that compounds the book's dispirited tone:

> What matters at this stage is the construction of local forms of community within which civility and the intellectual and moral life can be sustained through the new dark ages which are already upon us. And if the tradition of the virtues was able to survive the horrors of the last dark ages, we are not entirely without grounds for hope. This time however the barbarians are not waiting beyond the frontiers; they have already been governing us for quite some time. And it is our lack of consciousness of this that constitutes part of our predicament. We are waiting not for a Godot, but for another—doubtless very different—St. Benedict.[34]

Presupposed in this passage is MacIntyre's belief that an Aristotelian ethics of virtue remains the most intellectually viable form of moral discourse. He believes that the liberal individualism of Kant and Mill, with their respective emphases on laws and consequences instead of character, has failed to subvert the Aristotelian moral paradigm irretrievably, even though it has identified weaknesses in its original pagan and its Christianized medieval forms. Furthermore, says MacIntyre, it has been philosophically demonstrated, especially by Nietzsche, that liberal individualism is itself unable to sustain a coherent tradition of moral inquiry and practical reason. While MacIntyre's readings of the history of philosophy are themselves not an issue here, his way of posing this contemporary moral predicament as a choice between Aristotle or Nietzsche is instructive because it parallels alternatives posed in the last section between classical and Nietzschean accounts of valuation. Yet even given this parallel, and the author's disinclination, which I share, to affirm either disjunct wholly, MacIntyre's remedy for the ills he perceives has a different emphasis than does the strategy it is the task of this section to identify.

MacIntyre finds Nietzsche's "campaign against morality" to be a convincing critique of the Enlightenment tradition of liberal individualism; he also judges the doctrines of the Overman and the will to power to be that tradition's pathological fruition. As previous chapters attest, I share MacIntyre's appreciation of Nietzsche's critical talents, especially as he exercised them in decrying the Christian version of ascetic ideals, and I likewise withhold credence or enthusiasm for Nietzsche's Zarathustran fantasies. Yet, more than MacIntyre perhaps, I believe that Nietzsche is correct in insisting upon a conception of the human predicament that confounds traditional moral categories and requires unusual spiritual creativity. At least this spiritual dimension is what is of interest presently.

MacIntyre defines virtue in relation to "goods which are internal to practices," i.e., in relation to an updated version of the Aristotelian conception of praxis. Internal goods are specific to some individual practices and are obtainable only be engaging in them; they are more fully realized when such practices are done well. Such goods are distinguishable from the external goods of celebrity, wealth, or power which may accrue to persons with exceptional talents. To exemplify his definition of virtue MacIntyre cites some of the same practices I have cited: playing games like chess, pursuing arts like painting, and undertaking humanistic or scientific studies.[35] He emphasizes practices more immediately social and less individually embodied than the ones I have mentioned. He is also less ready to mention practices like prayer, yoga, and religious worship. Why these omissions are regrettable I shall seek to explain.

I agree with MacIntyre that Aristotle's ethics continues to be a valuable intellectual resource. In his conceptions of practical wisdom and action relative to a mean he provided philosophical themes that Clement and other early Christians would have been well advised to adopt in preference to severe Platonic and Stoic alternatives. More than MacIntyre, though, I have emphasized Aristotle's conviction that habits, as dispositions to act in certain ways, play a crucial role in promoting and hindering human happiness. Indeed, a high estimation of the tenacity and virulence of bad habits accounts for my conviction that a disciplined remedy for them must take on spiritual urgency. Also, a keen appreciation of how powerful institutions exert social control today by the inculcation of addictive behaviors requires, I think, a new criterion of virtue. It requires that in order for persons to be virtuous, i.e., to possesses qualities that promote practices whose goods are internal to themselves, they must endeavor to ensure that these practices are not recruited to the service of powerful, privileged interests. Hence they must resist established social norms in ways that Aristotle did not anticipate and that MacIntyre does not countenance.

Many books were prompted by MacIntyre's *After Virtue*: I find Jeffrey Stout's *Ethics After Babel* especially incisive and presently relevant. Though critical of MacIntyre's talk of a new dark ages of radical moral incoherence, Stout is very appreciative of his definition of virtue in terms of social practices. He uses this idiom to identify a contemporary moral peril as "the tendency of the capitalist marketplace and large-scale bureaucracies to provide material conditions that permit social practices to flourish, while at the same time they undermine the moral conditions needed to achieve goods internal to such practices."[36] Stout cites baseball as an instance in which the commercialization of a social practice increasingly makes money and power central concerns at the expense of excellence of play. Pete Rose's habit of gambling and George Steinbrenner's crass style of management exemplify the relevant personal vices. Yet larger economic and political forces are at work here, transforming internal goods into external goods, and doing so, I would add, in a not disinterested way. External goods can be granted or withheld by powerful institutions; they can be instruments of social control, especially when people become habituated to them. Corporations profit when the players' and fans' love of baseball becomes an obsession with winning and its rewards. In a context where such social forces are active, a preeminently virtuous person, I think, should not only personally realize goods internal to specific practices, but they also should resist the general trend toward a cynical transformation of internal goods into external goods. Where internal goods are so threatened, virtue must be civic virtue in this sense.

A noteworthy trend that Stout lists along with the above cited tendency is "the inability of religious practices to serve as a unifying ideological center around which whole societies could order various goods, practices, and institutions."[37] Stout, like MacIntyre, notes this fact but declines to suggest a new function for religious practices which might replace the traditional one now lost. I suggest that their new role might be as a sort of prophetic resistance to the transformation of internal goods into external ones. If religious practices are not reduced to means for attaining supernatural salvation—the sort of external good powerful religious institutions are tempted to bestow—and if they are not undertaken for frankly self-interested purposes—as when businessmen meditate to sell more stocks and bonds—that is, if they are appraised as spiritually disciplined practices in the sense proposed here, then they are practices whose goods are preeminently internal to themselves. As spiritual—as oriented to the world as a maximally inclusive whole and as projects of one's truest self—practices like prayer, yoga, T'ai Chi Ch'üan, or spiritual solitude not only promote the realization of internal goods but signal within a secular culture a resistance to a crudely utilitarian ethos. Pascal said that disciplined Christian behavior serves as a fixed point by which the decline of secular morals can be measured. In a more activist fashion the careers of twentieth-century religious leaders like Mohandas Gandhi and Martin Luther King, Jr. have combined elements of spiritual and political resistance: their examples illustrate, I think, how spiritually disciplined practices can contribute both symbolically and substantially to a strategy for vital community life.

MacIntyre is not oblivious to the political issues I have just interjected. He is critical of Aristotle for an elitism that led the Greek philosopher to deny virtue to slaves and barbarians (non-Greeks). He attributes this elitism to an impoverished historical sensibility among other things. I concur, but think that MacIntyre errs by not more consistently resisting Aristotle's political prejudices. The cultivation of small communities of moral and intellectual virtue to which most persons in contemporary society are not eligible, for want of civility or education, is a proposal not entirely free of Aristotelian hauteur. The hope of approximating the achievement of Benedictine monasteries in being repositories of learning and friendship during a period of cultural decline, while offered by MacIntyre only as a concluding programmatic suggestion, is, nevertheless, politically presumptuous and historically naive.

Benedictine monasteries increasing became institutions operating under the authority of the Roman Curia, and in later centuries, especially during the reign of Carolingian emperors, they were supported and encouraged by secular rulers. They were not motivated by a spirit of haughty flight from the world, but by a vocation to obedient service to ecclesiastical authority, and less directly, but just as surely, to the secular powers with which the medieval Church quarrelled but was essentially allied. What moral virtue the monks typified was of a quite unreflective sort. Their communities uniquely embodied the idea that stability is achieved by a rigid and hierarchical system of authority such as Clement thought to be the social ideal of the spiritual life. The Benedictine abbot is the epitome of Nietzsche's "ascetic priest" who exerts his will to power by getting others to adopt an ethos of humility, and in doing so, not only dominates his ascetic followers, but undermines the self-assertive persons who prize excellence above all else. While not entirely sharing Nietzsche's views at this point I do believe that the exercise of power chiefly through relations of hierarchical dominance is neither commendable as a way of treating other human beings nor efficacious as a way of achieving vital community life.

An elitism that seeks and achieves moral and intellectual excellence is laudable, and certainly MacIntyre cannot be faulted for upholding such ideals in his reconstruction of Aristotle's ethics of virtue; however, persons pursuing high standards so classically conceived risk either explicitly or implicitly translating this valuation of excellence into a rationale for privileged political interests. Aristotle does this explicitly, and MacIntyre does it less directly when he advises retreat from public life until virtuous persons of the sort he admires can effectively provide leadership. Forsaking a wider community in hopes of preserving what is best in that community's culture is a strategic decision. It posits that such action is the most likely way to insure the eventual flourishing of human good. Or, in a less consequentialist way, one might argue that a successful engagement in social discourse and action in a corrupted environment compromises precisely the human virtues that such action is intended to preserve. For instance, it is not consistent to mislead people into adopting social arrangements designed to allow for honest public discourse. Still, a social remedy that offers nothing immediately to effect a revitalized community fails to be fully compassionate; it may recommend hope but it offers little. Thus if the Biblical dispositions of love and hope are appended to the list of classical virtues, then a reconstruction of Aristotle's conception of virtue must include a different social ethic.

Medieval Benedictine communities understood themselves as compassionately working on behalf of the people from whom they had removed themselves. Their practices of worship and labor (including intellectual labor), and their fidelity to vows of obedience, poverty, and celibacy—all had a common theological purpose which was the accumulation of merit. This merit was not only thought to promote their own salvation, but also to yield a surplus that might benefit repentant sinners who look for God's mercy but who could not entirely change their secular callings so as to avoid sin. Luther and other Reformers vehemently rejected this whole economy of merit and I am not inclined to defend it theologically. Yet it reveals the lives of Benedictine monks to be ones of compassionate disengagement: they sought to serve their society by removing themselves from it in certain respects. Specifically, in order to accumulate merit for secular Christians they thought it necessary to remove themselves from secular callings. It is this Benedictine quality of compassionate disengagement that makes MacIntyre's allusion to St. Benedict something more profound than an superficial "dark ages" analogy. That he does not more precisely distinguish this quality from other less laudable aspects of the monastic ideal is reflective of his relative disinterest in specific religious practices.

MacIntyre does not restrict his account of virtue to the qualities of physical and intellectual practices. In its broadest sense he understands virtue to consist of those human qualities that make possible the realization of a common good possessed and developed within social traditions, and especially within traditions of moral philosophy. In a companion volume to *After Virtue*, entitled *Whose Justice? Which Rationality?*, MacIntyre articulates a notion of "tradition-constituted and tradition-constitutive enquiry" which he believes identifies the social contexts in which moral discourse is meaningful and effective.[38] He there discusses several traditions which inform contemporary intellectual life, including the Aristotelian-Thomistic tradition which he advocates and the tradition of liberal individualism he opposes. Intervening between an account of virtue as a set of qualities promoting practices and as a set of qualities constituting traditions is a second stage. Here virtue contributes to the good of a person's whole life. MacIntyre says that a teleological conception of human life is a necessary presupposition of virtue ethics, and judging that the goal-oriented cosmologies of Aristotelian biology and Christian eschatology do not well serve his philosophical purpose, he offers in their stead a narrative conception of meaningful human action. He says that people act in ways intended to give their lives a narrative wholeness. This involves a narrative linking of specific practices to social traditions. It involves stories of how the good realized in individual practices contribute to a common good realizable only through the agency of social traditions—of how intentional individual actions attain objective social significance. I will emphasize this linkage even yet more strongly.

In the human sciences equilibration processes are often invoked as a way to account for apparently purposeful behavior. In a previous chapter I articulated several notions of phenomenological equilibration and then employed them in describing stages of spiritual development. There is some analogy between these stages of spiritual development and the stages in MacIntyre's account of virtue. With reference to Merleau-Ponty a process of equilibration in bodily phenomenon was sketched and with reference to Piaget an equilibration process for intellectual phenomenon was identified. Their application to individual bodily and intellectual practices parallels MacIntyre's discussion of virtue in its first stage. Corresponding to MacIntyre's account of virtue in the context of social tradition was a social conception of phenomenological equilibration inspired by Dilthey's hermeneutical conception of the human sciences. What is absent from my own schema of spiritual development is anything that attends to narrative wholeness—to the special sort of well-being manifest in a life well lived. This I shall describe in the remainder of this section.

Two sociological processes of equilibration will be important to the narrative schema of spiritual development: Herbert Simon's account of "the equilibrium of an organization," or how organizations maintain an equilibrium between members leaving and entering, and Talcott Parsons's reflections on "the religious-secular balance in American society," or how differentiated social substructures with some measure of mutual antagonism, such as religious communities and secular institutions, maintain an operative integrity through self-corrective social mechanisms.[39] So long as it is remembered that equilibration process can be productive of novel and more complex systems of social relations I believe that such notions can be helpful for understanding not only how individuals pursue of sense of wholeness in their behavior, but also how communities remain vital in the presence of enervating forces. This type of description is not incompatible with narrative accounts of purposeful human action, either in MacIntyre's secular version or in versions advanced by contemporary Christian theologians. Instead it seeks to complement narrative accounts of the political dimension of spiritually disciplined practices with discursive counterparts.

In the following pages this complementary approach will be directed toward spiritual discipline insofar as it is part of a strategy for communal vitality. Specifically, attention will be given to the life stories of figures who have recently attained excellence by actions having both political and spiritual meaning. These persons were effective at revitalizing their respective communities in two ways. First, they attracted others to them, especially the socially marginalized and the culturally disenchanted who suffer most acutely today. In this way they promote the equilibration that Simon stresses and a social vitality understandable in terms of community membership and activity. Second, they productively transform relations between the religious and secular communities in their respective societies. In this way they foster the equilibration that Parsons describes and they foster a social vitality consisting of effective response to competing social forces. Both of these accomplishments were parts of an intentional effort to lead the societies in which they occurred toward a more just, compassionate, and enlightened social order. Persons who I believe meet this description are Leo Tolstoy, Mohandas Ghandi, Dorothy Day, Dietrich Bonhoeffer, and Martin Luther King, Jr. Certainly others could be mentioned in this context, but these names are sufficient to elucidate the thesis that spiritual discipline is a life of compassionate disengagement capable of promoting the vitality of community life. The spiritual narrative structure to be outlined will consist of a half dozen constitutive elements. They are not to be thought of as rigidly discrete episodes, though they do purport to have a more fluid temporal order. Not every element will have direct application to the lives of all of the persons listed above, but the elements are meant to be generally typical of this group and of persons like them. Finally, the narrative structure is characterized in terms not always reducible to the conscious intentions of its protagonists; it assumes a broader narrative setting which is the product of the reflective behavior of subsequent interacting agents. These caveats are important for the proper interpretation of narrative structure proffered here. It has six constitutive elements which I shall name with the following titles: Religious Training and Tutelage; Secular Vocation; Conflict and Uncertainty; Spiritual Turning Point; Simplification and Synthesis; and Reconciliation and Reclamation. Brief descriptions and exemplifications of them follow immediately.

Religious Training and Tutelage:

All of the exemplary figures had some early schooling in the religious beliefs and practices of their parents. King and Bonhoeffer, of course, had formal theological educations culminating in the receipt of advanced theological degrees. Tolstoy received formal religious training in Russian Orthodox theological doctrine until he left university studies in his second year and took up a military career;

however, he admits in the *Confession* that "my rejection of the doctrine became conscious at a very early age."[40] Gandhi received legal training in England but had some informal schooling in the Vaishnavite faith of his parents; he also absorbed Jainist influences, such as an abhorrence to meat-eating and injury of life, because his Indian birthplace, Gujarat, was populated by many Jains. Hence his religious eclecticism began early, though at first he felt "a sort of dislike" for Christianity because of the intolerance of some missionaries in his hometown.[41] Dorothy Day had the least early religious nurturing; neither parent regularly attended church even though her mother had been baptized an Episcopalian. In her autobiography, *The Long Loneliness*, she does recall attending Sunday school with the Methodist children who lived next door to her family in Oakland, and she remembers her mother's Christlike, but not overtly Christian, ministry to victims of the California earthquake of 1906.[42]

Personal tutelage supplemented religious instruction in the lives of most of these figures. This frequently included a struggle for personal identity and integrity of the sort mentioned in the last section. Certainly King learned much more about preaching from many years of observing his father in the pulpit at the Ebenezer Baptist Church in Atlanta than he did in his homiletics classes at the Boston University School of Theology. Also, King struggled with his father's strong personality and his often stated views that his son should pursue a safer and more conventional ministry. Dorothy Day spoke especially respectfully of Peter Maurin, with whom she founded *The Catholic Worker*, and Gandhi spoke of the Indian poet Raychandbhai as his "guide and helper," though at the time he wrote his autobiography he refrained from identifying anyone as his "guru."[43] Bonhoeffer had his teachers, Adolf von Harnack and Rheinhold Seeberg as models, and struggled continually with the theology and personality of Karl Barth. Only Tolstoy seemed to have acquired an original and forceful personality without proximate exemplars. In other respects, too, he will be the figure whose life is most resistant to the narrative structure proposed here. Yet for that reason his life is helpful for emphasizing the limitations of any such proposal.

Secular Vocation:

Traditionally, vocations to a life of service were religious, usually occurring in the context of some ecclesiastical institution. Yet with the development of reformist and revolutionary political movements in the nineteenth century a life devoted to the betterment of humankind took on a variety of secular forms, and each of these spiritual figures had a calling to one of them. They moved outside traditional religious institutions into a pluralistic arena of public action, but they did so for purposes and with methods often very consonant with their religious training, or, at least, with their mature interpretations of what was most valuable in their religious heritage. So Dorothy Day says that upon reading Upton Sinclair's *The Jungle*, which portrayed lives of urban poverty and exploitation, she "had received a call, a vocation, a direction to my life."[44] King was always quick to admit that he was enlisted in the Montgomery bus boycott through the initiative of the Montgomery Women's Political Council and other secular activists. Also, Bonhoeffer became involved in the conspiracy against Hitler through his brother-in-law, Hans von Dohnanyi, a lawyer. Gandhi began his activities on behalf of Indian and black South Africans in his capacity as a lawyer. Finally, even Tolstoy conforms to the model in this regard. His earliest educational activities on behalf of Russian serfs were inspired by political campaigns for the emancipation of the serfs led by people like Aleksandr Herzen. Twentieth-century saints—the most admired spiritual leaders of this century—seem to be very much shaped by this experience of a secular political vocation. Bonhoeffer gave the most sustained theological expression to this sensibility in his call for a "religionless Christianity" and a personal discipleship to Christ in a "world that has come of age."[45]

Conflict and Uncertainty:

By becoming involved in secular political controversies these figures also became engaged in conflict with conservative forces both secular and religious. Even preparatory steps toward such actions could earn reproach; for instance, Gandhi was excommunicated by his Bania caste leaders simply for leaving India to study in England. Tolstoy was rebuked by the Minister of the Interior in the Tsarist government for his educational writings: they were accused of being contrary to "the fundamental rules of religion and morality."[46] Years later, in 1901, Tolstoy was formally excommunicated by the Russian Orthodox Church on grounds of heresy. Bonhoeffer was widely known in his lifetime and after as a leader of opposition to the Nazi-dominated German Christian Church. Yet it is less well-known that after the war Bonhoeffer's own church leaders in Berlin-Brandenburg refused to acknowledge him as a Christian martyr because of his activities in the conspiracy against Hitler: Bonhoeffer's spiritual path led him into conflict with almost every official Christian institution in Germany. In each case these figures were led to disengage from active participation in established religious and secular institutions. This break was frequently signalled by a change in religious practice. At one juncture Gandhi made himself eat meat to signal his commitment to the reform of Indian ways, and Tolstoy desisted from taking Holy Communion at an early age. They made their breaks with traditional institutions, however, not because of disinterest or dislike of those who populated them, but because their compassion was of a sort that could be expressed only in novel ways and only once they had solidified new identities in relative isolation from their home communities.

Such conflict was a matter of private conscience as well as public dispute. The uncertainty concerned less the basic integrity of the struggle in which they engaged, than it did the tactics for reaching the desired ends and their own capacity to provide the leadership that was requested of them. King especially felt the burden of his calling: from the earliest days of the Montgomery bus boycott he was criticized by allies over questions of tactics and leadership, and he was abjured, threatened, and physically attacked by adversaries. King's middle-class background and his impressive formal education did not provide directly relevant resources for dealing with this dimension of his personal vocation. He was thereby led to take strength from the non-Christian example of Gandhi's practice of nonviolence! For Dorothy Day, Bible verses were a great comfort during her first experience of jail, when she was imprisoned following a suffragist picketing of the White House. Yet since Christian faith was not yet integrated into a life of political struggle, her resort to religious resources seemed later to be an unhealthy dependency and she tried to be rid of it. She felt the need to define and discipline herself in contradistinction to the accepted practices of the society she felt obliged to oppose.

Spiritual Turning Point:

If external conflicts and inner uncertainties grow continually more intense there will come a point when people reach their limit. Physical or psychological disability will force them to desist in the activity which is the cause of these tensions. Perseverance requires that a measure of spiritual equanimity be attained, and specifically, a peace that is consonant with their unconventional vocation. Very different events may be constitutive of this turning. In *Stride Toward Freedom*

King recounts a midnight locution from which he drew inspiration. It was during the Montgomery bus boycott: much courage was expected of him by black friends, and much hate was directed toward him by white adversaries. He sat at his kitchen table one sleepless night, pained and self-doubting, but then he heard words spoken to him: "Stand up for righteousness. Stand up for justice. Stand up for truth. And I will be with you."[47] God was now no longer remote or impersonal, but shared King's personal destiny. Tolstoy recounts in his *Confession* a similarly transformative moment of spiritual insight. His uncertainty concerned whether the artistic and intellectual elite who shared his progressive political views, regarding the plight and rights of the serfs, for instance, were the bearers of what is real and true. They seemed to think so, but Tolstoy had more respect than they for persons of simple and unassuming faith. The deep realization of this conviction was his spiritual turning point. "I understood that if I wish to understand life and its meaning, I must not live the life of a parasite, but must live a real life, and—taking the meaning given to life by real humanity and merging myself in that life—verify it."[48] Tolstoy says that he was saved from suicide by the realization that God was one with this "real life." Both Gandhi and Dorothy Day identified their spiritual turning points with experiences of new practical resolve: Gandhi when he seriously took the *brahmacarya* vow of sexual abstinence, and Day when she took the vows involved in having her daughter baptized and then in having herself "baptized conditionally" by a Roman Catholic priest.[49]

Simplification and Synthesis:

The results of transforming spiritual experiences are often to effect, or at least promote, a new synthesis of theological and philosophical ideas. This clarification of thought includes a new ranking of what is essential and what is not; this, in turn, allows for simplification of life in the sense of eliminating certain less important activities. Practices that help to maintain this proper ordering of one's life acquire a heightened significance. Gandhi and Day made decisions that demoted the prominence of sexual relationships in their lives and made possible a deeper commitment to the communities they sought to serve. Tolstoy, upon realizing that God was most manifest in the life of Russian peasants, pledged himself to adopt a simplicity of lifestyle that included voluntary abstention from the benefits of his title and wealth. As a result of his trip to India, the young King pledged never to benefit financially from the celebrity he acquired through leadership of civil rights causes. This discipline, unlike Gandhi's sexual self-discipline, was one that King maintained consistently.

Pecuniary and sexual austerity are, of course, traditional spiritual disciplines. It this is stage of the spiritual narrative in which such practices play a very prominent role, both in witnessing to God and also as testimony to the dignity and correctness of the political cause their practitioners serve. What is uniquely contemporary in the life stories of the spiritual figures grouped here is the way their disciplined spiritual lives testify to secular as well as religious visions of human well-being. All were writers throughout their lives: journalists, theologians, novelists. They communicated also by the spoken word, with King's gifts as a thinker and leader especially manifest in his preaching. They communicated a new synthesis of traditional religious teachings with contemporary political realities, and even more, they dramatized their teachings by enlisting spiritually disciplined practices in their public struggles. All were consistently nonviolent in practice; even though Bonhoeffer was engaged in conspiracies that contemplated violence, he himself had a consistently gentle and pacific demeanor. All of this group were persons given to prayer and meditation; the recollections of many survivors of German prisons and concentration camps who knew Bonhoeffer there include mention of his intensity and regularity in prayer.

Spiritual discipline was exercised in less conventional ways by these extraordinary persons. In many celebrated instances Gandhi employed fasting as a means for effecting change and enforcing nonviolence. He has made this practice, formerly an almost exclusively religious regimen, an enduring element of political resistance movements in subsequent decades. In a quite opposite way, Day and King made protest marching into something of a Christian ritual act: a new form of witness, not only to injustice, but to a God that is intolerant of injustice and wills something quite different for humankind. By giving secular practices new spiritual meaning and by giving religious practices a new secular arena of application, these figures extend their personal equanimity and intellectual synthesis to a wider social realm. Sadly, sometimes this last stage in the narrative occurred only after their death at the hands of the forces they opposed.

Reconcilation and Reclamation:

Of the figures mentioned here only Dorothy Day was effectively reconciled to the institutional representatives of her religious tradition, and, in turn, was reclaimed by them as one of their own.

When she died in 1980 the theological changes wrought by Vatican II and the sociological realities signalled by the emergence of liberation theology made her nonviolent Christian radicalism appear less extreme than it had at an earlier date. Tolstoy also lived a long life, and while on his death bed, representatives of the Russian Orthodox Church made overtures to restore him to good ecclesiastical standing, but he would have none of it. He died in 1910 without formal religious rites at his death or burial. However, he died a follower of Jesus Christ and many in the larger Christian tradition honor him as a genuine if irascible exemplar of the faith. Of course, Bonhoeffer, Gandhi, and King all died violent deaths at the hands of adversaries. They had anticipated this possibility and could be said to have extended a proleptic forgiveness to their misguided assailants. Each has been honored by their home communities and by others after their death. This is perhaps best attested by the celebration of Martin Luther King's birthday in the United States with a work holiday and religious commemorations.

These figures may be said to have promoted social well-being in another sense. They helped to make their religious communities vital in ways that promoted the vitality of the larger society. By their writings and lives, their thoughts and practices, these figures made participation in religious communities more attractive to many persons who perceived organized religion as dull, conservative, and antiquarian. They provided incentives for participation by the quality of life they led and by the challenge they presented. Giving traditional religious practices new meanings in the context of political struggles is an example of this sort of incentive. Also, by making political practices, like protest marching, take on a spiritual depth of meaning, they demonstrated how religious commitments can advance political causes, specifically, by reinforcing the civic virtue of caring deeply and acting conscientiously for the sake of the common good. They resisted social stasis and enervation, and a too rigid separation of spiritual and worldly concerns. Their disengagements from society was not quietistic, but served as opportunities for gaining the peace of mind and sense of direction that informed their public ministries. Also, their emergence from spiritual retreat into secular realms of public action was not merely disruptive; rather they helped to insure that the interaction between these two social spheres was dynamic but equilibrating, tending toward a more just variety of relative social stability. They were spiritually disciplined practitioners of a strategy for communal vitality which included both political activism and compassionate disengagement.

That spiritual discipline may be profitably thought of as a multiform strategy for achieving an optimum of human well-being, a fullness of life, has now been argued. Some summation is in order. Nietzsche's conception of solitude was helpful in showing that spiritually disciplined practices are ways for attaining a sense of life's spiritual meaning, a sense of how individuals stand in relation to all that is. It was also instructive in indicating how certain dangers are avoided by thinking of this relationship in semiological and aesthetic terms rather than in the traditional language of theology and soteriology. Spiritual discipline was said in this context to be constituted by practices which picture the self in its most encompassing world, and then effect the erasure of this picture; or in an alternative idiom, of they named the self as a resident of the world and then engender the forgetting that name. In a paradoxical way both the presenting and absenting of self—both self-referencing and self-vanquishing—become actions that witness to what is deemed most profound and constitute the life and death drama of the self as an embodied sign.

Yet a meaning that is attained by way of relationships of the self to the whole of reality remains abstract unless it is tied to more tangible human relationships. Hence the drama of spiritually disciplined witness is predicated upon a spiritual identity wrought from interaction with others, and especially, with a spiritual guide and teacher. Spiritual discipline in this context is comprised of those practices whose undertaking represent an inherent human good and whose proper understanding includes the recognition that they fulfill two criteria: that they be the result of the imitation and repetition of a model, and the proleptic realization of a distinctive and novel form of excellence. They are practices that conform to a classical canon of symmetry and yet break that symmetry in a way the exemplifies human creativity as it is the spontaneous reorganization of a complex system of elements. Indeed, spiritual discipline is a form of structured behavior that experiences, and, in a way, celebrates, the reality of contesting values.

Finally, neither human meaning nor human creativity can be profitably abstracted from the forms of community in which they occur. So in this last section spiritual discipline has been presented as a socially transformative set of practices which promotes a more vital human community, and in doing this, makes aspirations for meaningful and creative life concretely possible. Such practices as Gandhi's fasts or King's marches serve this end by directly promoting political ideas of social justice, but they also do it by revitalizing the religious communities from which they come and by transforming traditional ways in which religious and secular communities interact in a single social whole. In these two ways they promote the stability—the forces of social equilibration—needed for human cooperation in the economic, social, and cultural realms. Thus, spiritually disciplined practices constitute a political praxis in the sense of being socially transformative human action marked by a quality of compassionate disengagement. Clearly, Marx's metaphysics of history is not involved here, and neither were commitments made to Aristotle's hylomorphism nor Nietzsche's perspectivism when insights about spiritual practice were sought in their writings. The conception of spiritually disciplined praxis offered here shows the influence of these disparate philosophical thinkers, risking a certain heterogeneity, because, in my view, the predicament descendent from Pascal requires for its resolution a strategy of response as multiform as the predicament itself.

Conclusion: Beyond Diversion and Decadence

At the beginning of *Swann's Way*, the first of his novels collectively entitled *Remembrance of Things Past*, Marcel Proust has the story's protagonist make the following observation:

> The fault I find with our journalism is that it forces us to take an interest in some fresh triviality or other every day, whereas only three or four books in a lifetime give us anything that is of real importance. Suppose that, every morning, when we tore the wrapper off our paper with fevered hands, a transmutation were to take place, and we were to find inside it—oh, I don't know; shall we say Pascal's *Pensées*?[1]

Swann's remarks bespeak much confidence in the power of a great book to free its reader from the spell of what Pascal called "divertissement." Nietzsche similarly promised a transformed life to the readers of *Thus Spoke Zarathustra*. I am considerably less sanguine about the ameliorative effects of reading the *Pensées* or *Zarathustra*, masterpieces though they be, and I give no assurance at all that the mere reading this essay will transport its readers "Beyond Diversion and Decadence." Yet like Swann, I believe that one must begin this journey by making discriminations between what is more and less important. The thesis of this book is that spiritual discipline is important, and I have tried in its many pages to sketch the most prominent features of a new conception of spiritual discipline. I begin my conclusion, then, with a summary of these major points.

A basic presupposition of this essays insists that to talk about something spiritual is to talk about something human. What is spiritual is a specific aspect of human existence, one that has been hypothesized here to have an outer and inner complexion. Facing outward, human existence has been deemed spiritual insofar as it intentionally engages reality as a maximally inclusive whole. Facing inward, life has been accorded a spiritual dimension to the extent

273

that it is experienced as the project of one's most vital and enduring self. An integration of these inner and outer characterizations is achieved by equating the spiritual dimension of life with the existential task of discovering one's truest self in the context of reality apprehended as a cosmic totality. It is the quest for attaining an optimal relationship between what one truly is and everything that is. This spiritual quest has the character of a discipline when it adopts regimens of embodied behavior which are the results of instruction and the objects of criticism. These points were made in the book's introduction.

Spiritual discipline was recommended for its ability to solve spiritual problems. A problem is something proposed for examination and solution. A problem that elicits an urgency of feeling in addition to a playfulness of intellect I have called a predicament, and when the predicament includes consideration of the whole of reality and one's truest self I have called it a spiritual predicament. Pascal's life and writings were treated in a previous chapter as exemplary of an enduring spiritual predicament. From the vantage point of the late twentieth century Pascal's predicament appears multiform: he was a mathematical physicist whose knowledge of the natural world seemed to alienate him from nature; he was prose stylist whose most public communications seemed to prompt his retirement to a life of relative solitude; and he was a philosopher whose self-knowledge seemed to depreciate his sense of worth as a human being. For Pascal modern achievements became distinctly modern entrapments. Consequently, a radical depreciation of nature, society, and self came to inform Pascal's deliberations about what one should do when bemired by sin, beset be ignorance, and confronted by death. Supernatural revelation, submission to external authority, and self-mortification were the hallmarks of his conception of a spiritually disciplined response to this situation.

Pascal's predicament may have been modern but his remedy for it was quite traditional. Examination of Pascal's *Memorial*—the written account of his conversion experience—shows themes that received articulation very early in the Christian tradition. I chose Clement of Alexandria to be representative of this tradition because his essay on Christian spiritual life in the *Stromata* is a succinct and representative example of a philosophical rationale for spiritual discipline. Central to this rationale were the themes of suprasensual vision, unencumbered causality, and static hierarchy. Briefly stated, the experience of God was likened to a vision that transcended the physical senses and mobilized the loving will. Its prerequisite was a mastery of the body by the soul that enabled the Christian to be unencumbered by sensual impulses or distractions. Also, prerequisite for this encounter with God was the adoption of a secure place in a hierarchy of social relationships. Actually constitutive of "spiritual perfection" was the experiences of being an instrument of divine causality and of being a resident in a spiritual hierarchy with the Triune God at its apex.

In the second chapter the classical rationale culled from Clement's writings was found wanting on scientific, philosophical, and ethical grounds. Ancient Greek speculation provided Clement with his understandings of cosmology and anthropology. These accounts are no longer empirically adequate. Christian philosophers were attracted to Platonism's dogmatic idealism. In a quite different fashion, contemporary styles of doing philosophy recommend a more herme- neutic and phenomenological orientation. Finally, several recent intellectual movements, perhaps feminism most pointedly, have made people aware of the moral implications of devaluing human embodi- ment: it is not healthful, and it is often a pretext for injustice.

Two broad criteria for spiritually disciplined practices emerged from my criticism of Clement. They were that no spiritual practice should bring physiological or psychological harm to oneself or others, nor should it directly or indirectly foster the coercive and oppressive use of power. When interpreted generously, as I subsequently sought to do, the themes that comprised Clement's rationale yielded other positive insights. They revealed crucial aspects of how a practitioner of spiritual discipline seeks to respond to the human spiritual predicament. Directing attention to the function, as opposed to the substance of Clement's categoreal themes, I argued that enlightened spiritual practices should be a creatively self-transformative response to paradoxicality and complexity, especially as these are properties of the world experienced as a maximally inclusive whole by one truest self.

Pascal similarly suggested new directions despite his traditional piety. When his psychological insights, especially regarding habit, were combined with his philosophical appreciation of paradox they suggested a way of reformulating the human spiritual predicament. Pascal helps one to see that a regimen of spiritual discipline can provide practical means for resisting the acquisition of bad habits and for opposing those persons and institutions who promote them. Spiritual practices should be enlisted for these tasks both for the sake of one's own spiritual well-being, but also on ethical grounds:

solidarity with persons afflicted or oppressed is a moral obligation as well as a social prerequisite for attaining the fullest measure of spiritual well-being. Moving beyond Pascal's own views, I further argued that in social contexts where governments, corporations, professions, and churches use sophisticated techniques of persuasion to promote habitual behaviors, and thereby control putatively free populations, spiritual discipline should be understood to be a form of political resistance. Such resistance is most effective when the enduring habits inculcated by dominant social institutions are undercut by multiple and adaptable regimens of spiritual discipline— by what I epigrammatically called the practice of paradox.

The second and more speculative part of this book anticipated the main features of a new conception of spiritual discipline. In the third chapter spiritual discipline was identified with practical modes of cultivating self-awareness via semiotic self-reference. Illustrative practices of meditation, prayer, and fasting were discussed. Given the phenomenological interplay of presence and absence in perception and signification it was concluded that an emphasis on self-presence alone is one-sided. Spiritual discipline also involves the cultivation of practical modes for realizing self-absence. Christians may seek the righteousness of faith—the right relation of the soul to God, but Buddhists seek the cure for suffering—the vanquishment of the phenomenological self. Yet Christian and Buddhist spiritual practices are not simply polar opposites. Self-presence and self-absence are correlative terms and pertain respectively in this context to processes one might call self-referencing and self-vanquishing—to the representation of the self to the self and then the overcoming of that representation in deference to a totality which embraces but transcends it.

In the fourth chapter I contended that the most valuable spiritual disciplines contain an element of contestation. They share in the agonistic spirit of ancient Greek festivals of Olympic athletics and Athenian drama, though, as spiritual disciplines, they are usually enacted in the more intimate context of interaction between a master and the master's spiritual student. Given the presence of this element of spiritual discipline I argued that describing practices like Hesychast prayer, T'ai Chi Ch'üan and Hatha Yoga in terms of symmetry—a concept with artistic origins—is quite appropriate. The way in which the notion of symmetry has been developed in the mathematical and natural sciences of this century enables talk of symmetry to convey the accent on transformation and wholeness which marks the spiritual dimension of human existence. The second speculative chapter, in effect, attempted a retrieval of symmetry as a spiritual ideal.

When spiritual disciplines are practiced so as to include elements of contestation and novelty they take on an aesthetic character. In this same fourth chapter creative activities of both a strictly aesthetic and a traditionally religious sort were described in terms of a process of making and breaking symmetry. String quartet music, Zen conversation, and creative chess play were offered as exemplary phenomena describable in this manner. Regimens of prayerful devotion or yogic austerity, it was argued, can bring a quality of excellence to the lives of practitioners in a similar way as playing music enriches the lives of musicians. This aesthetic character of spiritual discipline becomes especially prominent when the salvific meanings of spiritually disciplined practices are de-emphasized as I have done. There is, though, a danger of too strongly stressing the aesthetic character of a spiritual disciplined practice. It risks making that practice a mere entertainment—a diversion in the Pascalian sense of something that occupies one's attention just enough to avoid really serious matters. The rejoinder given to this potential criticism was the claim that spiritual discipline as advocated in this book promotes personal integrity, both in the sense of urging a process of continual intellectual self-criticism, and also, by including a emphasis on physical well-being.

In the fifth chapter the notion of biological equilibration was used to describe how spiritually disciplined practices promote growth and vitality in their practitioners. A disciplined embodied practice was more sharply defined as one that maintains a sense of personal unity amidst an experience of intense bodily self-consciousness required by some formally prescribed regimen of behavior. This integration is often achieved relative to an external flow of experience, such as the music which helps shape the dancer's performance or the course of conversation which constitutes an interpreter's cultural tradition. If a spiritually disciplined practice is to be undertaken in a way that both attains excellence and yet remains responsible, then a socially educative process of equilibration is requisite for that discipline to be thoroughly learned, and an intellectually critical process is needed for it to be maintained with integrity. This is the case because of the unique promise and danger of life in community. Such a context makes possible the highest levels of individual development—biologically, psychologically, and spiritually. It provides the nurture which aids growth, the cooperation which allows differentiation, and the power which effects correction. Yet, as Nietzsche never ceased to point out, a community of unexceptional persons often conspires against extraordinary individuals in order to censure and stifle their disturbing creativity. When it does so the community becomes an collective agent of moral decadence which not only opposes extraordinary individuals but often infects them with its own decadent values.

At the beginning of the sixth chapter, it was noted that Nietzsche's conception of moral decadence has a twofold nature. It is either a slow and relatively unconscious ebbing of physiological vitality that militates against the satisfaction of basic instincts, or it is a deliberate strategy by which a pattern of activity, either privative or consumptive, serves to extirpate instinctive drives instead of satisfying them or sublimating them. The first kind of decadence is associated by Nietzsche with circumstances of cultural fatigue in which religions like Christianity and Buddhism thrive. More deliberate types of decadence are respectively associated with religious and lay asceticism. Monks and nuns consciously seek to eradicate their instinctive desires by making lifelong vows of abstinence. The consumptive form of decadence is less direct, but no less pernicious. It is also more germane to contemporary life.

Pious lay persons whose success is indebted to an inner-worldly ascetic ethos rarely give away all of their surplus income—monies not needed for a modest but healthy style of living. Their wealth increases and their level of consumption rises. Yet they cannot revel in the satiation of their needs and desires lest they feel sinful. Hence they develop a pattern of consumption which, while sating one form of desire, destroys another. Excessive eating and drinking, for instance, suppress sexual appetite. Nietzsche claimed that Christian ascetic ideals and Teutonic alcohol poisoning were the two great destroyers of the health of Western Europeans! He now seems like a prophetic visionary of today's consumerist apocalypse of diet fads, designer drugs, and sports cults. By including biological equilibration as a constitutive theme of a refashioned account of spiritual discipline I have tried to prevent such practices having the decadent implications that Nietzsche so eschewed. I also tried to meet Nietzsche's criticisms by borrowing elements of his own portrayal of solitude as a godless spiritual discipline. My contention that spiritually disciplined practices bear witness to what is most valuable in life was inspired by Nietzsche's high estimate of all activities that effect the creation of new values and the attainment of enhanced vitality.

In the seventh chapter I presented a conception of spiritual discipline as a multiform strategy for achieving spiritual meaning, personal integrity, and communal vitality. I did so by describing spiritual discipline as a drama of embodied signs, a structure of contesting values, and a life of compassionate disengagement. Having so recently made these proposals I will not now reiterate them. However, there is some need to clarify the relation of these strategic recommendations to the categoreal themes of the essay's second part. Are the categoreal themes to be construed as general truths of science, philosophy, and ethics which have these strategic recommendations as their practical implications? Not at all. To present them in this way would effectively revive the dogmatism and foundationalism I criticized in the Platonic rationale exemplified by Clement. The priorities are opposite. Practical strategies for achieving fullness of life have been my primary interest. The categoreal themes have been invoked to advance this practical agenda. Of course, a certain compatibility between descriptive themes and practical prescriptions is desirable. Specifically, the fullness of life which it is the aim of the spiritual disciplined practices to achieve can most credibly be claimed if their description and justification is informed by the secular learning in science, philosophy, and ethics. Also, if the spiritual dimension of existence is most manifest in encounters with the world as a maximally inclusive whole, then it is fitting that they borrow descriptive terminology from that area of human inquiry that provides the most systematically coherent and socially disseminated explanations of the world, and these, I think, are provided by the natural sciences. The practical strategies recommended here are claimed to have an imaginative congruity with the categorecal themes employed in the book's second part, and the rational justification for the spiritually disciplined practices they were used to describe is likewise offered as a case that is plausible, but by no means compelling.

In the foregoing paragraph I have tried to underscore the modesty of my claims. Now I wish to acknowledge the particularity of the context from which they have emerged. I have sought to maintain compatibility of a philosophical conception of spiritual discipline with more self-consciously religious conceptions. I have done so partly because of personal conviction. With fellow pragmatist and former colleague Cornel West, I confess that Christianity has been something that has helped keep me sane. Like West I also have pragmatic and political reasons for maintaining this openness to religion.[2] With a characteristic suspicion of triumphant religion Kierkegarrd wrote that "the deification of the established order is the secularization of everything."[3] I suspect that the converse is also true: in a culture where scientific research and practical utility are highly, and rightly valued, it is important to appreciate how religion can be socially subversive and imaginatively dissident. Of the individuals portrayed as twentieth-century saints in the last chapter it is Dietrich Bonhoeffer who reflects most directly my own religious tradition and theological views. I believe that there is a compatibility between the broad features of my conception of spiritual discipline with Bonhoeffer's vision of "religionless Christianity" in a "world come of age." Indeed, Bonhoeffer, like Nietzsche, has been a major inspiration for my proposal, and in the two thinker's views on spiritual life I find considerable similarities. I believe that Nietzsche, from outside the Christian community, and Bonhoeffer, from within it, were prophetic advocates of pluralistic and provisional conceptions of spiritual discipline.[4]

The intention to make my conception of spiritual discipline compatible both with elements of scientific learning and religious tradition reveals again my vocation as a philosopher of religion. Such reconciliations comprise one of the most constant themes of this species of philosophy. Yet I have undertaken this traditional project in an unusual way by making spiritually disciplined practices the focus of reflection rather than science and religion themselves. The question that has been most vigorously pursued here is how one might live so as to be most spiritually vital. Only provisional indications have been offered; only glimpses of such a life have been limned. I have ventured to say that it is a life beyond diversion and decadence, where traditional antagonists like science and religion, like excellence and peace, are reconciled, though never entirely, and not without conflict. This book has sought to exemplify this ideal by exploring alternative conceptions of spiritual life and by recording my reflective evaluations of them. In writing it I have tried show that urgent tasks are not best met with certain beliefs. The examples of Pascal's wagering and Nietzsche's overcoming teach something else. They teach that resolute and disciplined spirits are best served by critical and playful intellects.

NOTES

NOTES TO INTRODUCTION

1. Especially relevant is Brown's recent book, *The Body and Society: Men, Women, and Sexual Renunciation in Early Christianity* (New York: Columbia University Press, 1988). See also: Margaret R. Miles, *Fullness of Life: Historical Foundations for a New Asceticism* (Philadelphia: Westminster Press, 1981); and *Practicing Christianity: Critical Perspectives for an Embodied Spirituality* (New York: Crossroad Publishing, 1988).

2. Volumes of the *Theological Investigations* dealing with the "theology of the spiritual life" are especially relevant: Karl Rahner, *Theological Investigations,* vols. 3, 7, and 8 (London: Dartman, Longman, & Todd, 1967–1971).

   Gustavo Gutiérrez, *A Theology of Liberation: History, Politics and Salvation,* trans. and ed. Caridad Inda and John Eagleson (Maryknoll, N.Y.: Orbis Books, 1973); for subsequent developments of the theme of the spirituality of liberation, see: Jon Sobrino, *Spirituality of Liberation: Toward Political Holiness,* trans. Robert R. Barr (Maryknoll, N.Y.: Orbis Books, 1988), and Aloysius Pieris, *An Asian Theology of Liberation* (Maryknoll, N.Y.: Orbis Books, 1988).

3. Søren Kierkegaard, *The Sickness Unto Death: A Christian Psychological Exposition for Upbuilding and Awakening,* ed. and trans. Howard V. Hong and Edna H. Hong (Princeton: Princeton University Press, 1980), p. 103. (My quotation slightly revises the translation for grammatical purposes.)

4. Shunryu Suzuki, *Zen Mind, Beginner's Mind,* ed. Trudy Dixon (New York: Weatherhill, 1970), p. 118.

5. Thomas Merton, *Contemplative Prayer* (Garden City, N.Y.: Doubleday & Company, 1971), pp. 69 and 85ff.

6. David Ray Griffin, "Spiritual Discipline in the Medieval, Modern, and Postmodern Worlds," *God and Religion in the Postmodern World: Essays in Postmodern Theology* (Albany: State University of New York Press, 1989), p. 109.)

7. Albinus, *Didaskalikos* 2.2. The text quoted is from an unpublished English translation by Richard A. Norris, Jr.

8. *Marx-Engels Werke,* 42 vols. (Berlin: Institut für Marxismus und Leninismus, 1957–1985) 3:6.

9. English quotations from the Bible are from the Revised Standard Version unless otherwise noted.

10. Irenaeus, *Adversus haereses* (1.18.1) in J.P. Migne, ed. *Patrologiae cursus completus, Series Graeca,* 161 vols. (Paris: 1857–1866), 7:643–44; the translation is my own.

11. Elisabeth Schüssler Fiorenza, *In Memory of Her: A Feminist Theological Reconstruction of Christian Origins* (New York: Crossroad Books, 1985), especially pp. 3–91.

12. Merold Westphal, *God, Guilt, and Death: An Existential Phenomenology of Religion* (Bloomington, Ind.: Indiana University Press, 1984), pp. 1–23.

13. Alfred North Whitehead, *Process and Reality: An Essay in Cosmology,* ed. David Ray Griffin and Donald W. Sherburne, corrected ed. (New York: Macmillan Publishing, Free Press, 1978), p. 5.

14. Niels Bohr, "Discussion with Einstein on Epistemological Problems in Atomic Physics" (1949), *The Philosophical Writings of Niels Bohr,* 3 vols. (Woodbridge, Conn.: Ox Bow Press, 1987), 2:47.

15. Hermann Weyl, *Symmetry* (Princeton: Princeton University Press, 1952.)

16. No one has been more influential in shaping spirituality as a domain and discipline of academic study than has Ewert H. Cousins, Professor and Director of Spirituality in the Graduate Program at Fordham University. He is currently providing editorial supervision for two projects which attest the resurgence of interest in this area: they are the Paulist Press series of primary source materials gathered in *The Classics of Western Spirituality: A Library of the Great Spiritual Masters,* and the Crossroad Publishing Company series of secondary source materials entitled *World Spirituality: An Encyclopedic History of the Religious Quest.* The definition of spirituality offered here is indebted to Cousins's preface to the latter series.

17. Robert C. Neville, *Soldier, Sage, Saint* (New York: Fordham University Press, 1978), p. ix.

18. Ibid., p. 10.

19. Paul Ricoeur, *The Symbolism of Evil,* trans. Emerson Buchanan (Boston: Beacon Press, 1967), p. 167.

20. Immanuel Kant, *Critique of Pure Reason,* trans. Norman Kemp Smith (New York: St. Martin's Press, 1965), p. 297ff.

21. Ibid., p. 300.

22. Bertrand Russell, "Mathematical Logic as Based On the Theory of Types" (1908), *Logic and Knowledge: Essays 1901—1950,* ed. Robert C. Marsh (New York: Capricorn Books, 1971), pp. 59–102, especially p. 63.

23. Hence the specific attributes which this conception of selfhood shares with Peirce's conception are: the potentiality of the self as a member of a community, and specifically, of a maximally inclusive community; the irreducibility of the self to the status of a thing, and specifically, to a thing capable of exhaustive description; and the interpretability of the self as a process of becoming a self, and specifically, a semiotic process of self-dialogue and self-naming. For the Peirce citations, see: *Collected Papers of Charles Sanders Peirce,* 8 vols., ed. Charles Hartshorne, Paul Weiss, and Arthur W. Burks (Cambridge, Mass.: Harvard University Press, 1931–1958), respectively 5:402; 7:591; 5:313–14 and 6:157; for an argument for the general coherence of Peirce's semiotic idea of selfhood with an Aristotelian view of ethics, see: Vincent Michael Colapietro, *Peirce's Approach to the Self: A Semiotic Perspective on Human Subjectivity* (Albany: State University of New York Press, 1989), pp. 61–98.

NOTES TO CHAPTER 1

1. Alfred North Whitehead, *Adventures of Ideas* (New York: Macmillan Company, Free Press, 1967), especially pp. 160–72; for Russell on puzzles, see: "On Denoting," *Logic and Knowledge,* p. 47.

2. Blaise Pascal, *Pensées,* trans. A.J. Krailsheimer (London: Penguin Books, 1966), p. 61 (122). Pascal used male locutions to speak of human beings generally and English translations will reflect that fact; other authors will be similarly translated.

3. Krailsheimer's translation follows the order of the Lafuma edition and all references to Pascal's original French texts will be to the Lafuma editions; Blaise Pascal, *Oeuvres Complètes,* présentation par Louis Lafuma (Paris: Éditions du Seuil, 1963).

4. Lucien Goldmann, *The Hidden God: A Study of Tragic Vision in the "Pensées" of Pascal and the Tragedies of Racine,* trans. Philip Thody (New York: Humanities Press, 1964), pp. 171, 194–95.

5. Charles Baudouin, *Blaise Pascal ou l'Order du Coeur* (Paris: Plon, 1962), pp. iv and 13. Translations from this text and other texts cited in the original French are my own.

6. Louis Marin, *La Critique du Discours: Sur la "Logique de Port-Royal" et les "Pensées" de Pascal* (Paris: Éditions de Minuit, 1975), p. 117.

7. Blaise Pascal, "Pascal's Conversation with Monsieur De Saci on Epictetus and Montaigne (Excerpt from Fontaine's memoirs), *Great Shorter Works of Pascal,* trans. Emile Cailliet and John C. Blankenagel (Philadelphia: Westminster Press, 1948), p. 121.

8. Pascal, *Pensées,* trans. A.J. Krailsheimer, p. 33 (6).

9. Ibid., p. 59 (114).

10. Ibid., p. 163 (429).

11. Ibid., p. 152 (418).

12. Ibid., p. 245 (687).

13. Ibid., p. 85 (183).

14. Ibid., p. 309 (913).

15. Ibid., p. 315 (919).

16. Ibid., p. 310 (913).

17. Jean Mesnard, *Pascal: His Life and Works,* trans. G.S. Fraser (London: Harville Press, 1952), pp. 59–65.

18. Mesnard contends that, as with the story regarding the Neuilly Bridge, if the event recorded actually occurred at all, it probably occurred much later than in 1654; see *Pascal,* p. 61.

19. Ibid., p. 98 (216).

20. Ibid., pp. 108 (260), 164 (433), and 235 (621).

21. Ibid., p. 229 (597).

22. Pascal, "Excerpt from a Letter by Blaise Pascal to Monsieur and Mlle. de Rouannez," *Great Shorter Works of Pascal,* p. 151.

23. Friedrich Nietzsche, *Ecce Homo* (bound with *On the Genealogy of Morals*), trans. and ed. Walter Kaufmann (New York: Random House, 1969), p. 234 (2.3).

24. Friedrich Nietzsche, *Beyond Good and Evil* in *Basic Writings of Friedrich Nietzsche* (New York: Random House, Modern Library, 1968), p. 250 (46).

25. Friedrich Nietzsche, *The Will to Power,* trans. Walter Kaufmann and R.J. Hollingdale (New York: Random House; Vintage Books, 1967), p. 209 (388). For an extensive list of Nietzsche's remarks about Pascal, see: James Robert Dionne, *Pascal et Nietzsche: Étude Historique et Comparée* (New York: Burt Franklin, 1965), pp. 81–94.

26. Pascal, *Pensées,* trans. A.J. Krailsheimer, p. 82 (166).

27. For readers not familiar with the Wager argument its major thrust is evident in the following excerpts:

> "Either God is or he is not." But to which view shall we be inclined? Reason cannot decide this question. Infinite chaos separates us. At the far end of this infinite distance a coin is being spun which will come down heads or tails. How will you wager? Reason cannot make you choose either, reason cannot prove either wrong.... Yes, but you must wager. There is no choice, you are already committed. Which will you choose then? Let us see: since a choice must be made, let us see which offers you the least interest.... Let us assess the two cases: if you win you win everything, if you lose you lose nothing. Do no hesitate then; wager that he does exist.... Here there is an infinity of infinitely happy life to be won, one chance of winning against a finite number of chances of losing, and what you are staking is finite.

Ibid., pp. 150–51 (418).

28. Nicholas Rescher, *Pascal's Wager* (Notre Dame, Ind.: University of Notre Dame Press, 1985), pp. 22 and 30.

29. Pascal, *Pensées,* trans. A.J. Krailsheimer, p. 152 (418).

30. Ibid., p. 274 (821).

31. For a more elaborate description of how Pascal says reason, habit, and inspiration work together in the formation of belief, see: Hugh M. Davidson, *The Origins of Certainty: Means and Meanings in Pascal's "Pensées,"* (Chicago: University of Chicago Press, 1979), especially pp. 71–100.

32. Pascal, *Pensées,* trans. A.J. Krailsheimer, p. 247 (699).

33. Ibid., p. 68 (136).

34. Ibid., p. 66 (133).

35. "Letter from Pascal to Fermat (From Bienassis, 10 August 1660)," *Great Shorter Works of Pascal,* p. 216.

36. The influence of the Ignatian *Spiritual Exercises* on Descartes *Meditations* has often been claimed, leading philosophers like Zeno Vendler to characterize the the aim of the latter text as being to promote an intellectual conversion that commits the agent to a new life of the mind—a life of scientific rationalism. See: Zeno Vendler, "Descartes' Exercises," *Canadian Journal of Philosophy* 19.2 (June 1989): 193–224.

37. For more on this point, and for a general assessment of Pascal's place in the history of mathematics, see: Carl B. Boyer, *A History of Mathematics* (Princeton: Princeton University Press, 1985), pp. 395–401.

38. Pascal, *Pensées*, trans. A.J. Krailsheimer, p. 90 (199).

39. Ibid.

40. The English translation of the seventh chapter of Clement's *Stromata* is Henry Chadwick's revision of J.B. Mayor's translation in *Alexandrian Christianity*, ed. Henry Chadwick, Library of Christian Classics (Philadelphia: Westminster Press, 1954), p. 93 (7.1 (1); Chadwick consistently uses 'gnostic' with a lowercase 'g' to denote orthodox Christian knowers and I shall follow the same convention. The Greek text cited is the one which accompanies the original Mayor translation: Clement of Alexandria, *Miscellanies Book VII*, trans., intro., and notes by Fenton John Anthony Hort and Joseph B. Mayor (New York: Macmillan Company, 1902).

41. Plato, *Theaetetus*, trans. Harold North Fowler, in *Plato*, 12 vols., Loeb Classical Library (Cambridge, Mass.: Harvard University Press, 1914–1935), 7:130 (176b).

42. Charles Bigg, *The Christian Platonists of Alexandria* (Oxford: Oxford University Press, 1913); and Salvatore R.C. Lilla, *Clement of Alexandria: A Study in Christian Platonism and Gnosticism* (Oxford: Oxford University Press, 1971).

43. Harry Wolfson, *The Philosophy of the Church Fathers* (Cambridge, Mass.: Harvard University Press, 1956), pp. v–x.

44. Philo of Alexandria, *De vita contemplativa* in *Philo*, 10 vols., trans. F.H. Colson, Loeb Classical Library (Cambridge, Mass.: Harvard University Press, 1967), 9:119 (2).

45. Ibid., 9:161 (10).

46. Clement, *Stromateis VII*, in *Alexandrian Christianity*, p. 100 (7.3 (13)).

47. Ibid., p. 141 (7.12 (76)).

48. Plato, *The Republic*, trans. Paul Shorey, in *Plato*, 12 vols., 5:112–13 (510E).

49. Ibid., 5:114–15 (511C).

50. For an excellent summary of Clement's views on marriage and sex, see: Brown, *Body and Society*, pp. 122–39.

51. Clement, *Stromateis*, p. 103 (7.3 (17)).

52. Henry Chadwick, *Early Christian Thought and the Classical Tradition* (New York: Oxford University Press, 1966), p. 57ff.

53. Clement, *Stromateis,* pp. 112 (7.6 (30) and 121 (7.7 (44).

54. Ibid., p. 100 (7.3 (13)).

55. Marcus Aurelius, *Meditations,* trans. Maxwell Staniforth (London: Penguin Books, 1964), p. 51 (2.17).

56. Ibid., p. 57 (3.5).

57. *Clement of Alexandria,* trans G.W. Butterworth, Loeb Classical Library (Cambridge, Mass.: Harvard University Press, 1919), pp. 291–93 (11).

58. Aristotle, *The Metaphysics,* trans. Hugh Tredennick, in *Aristotle,* 23 vols., Loeb Classical Library (Cambridge, Mass.: Harvard University Press, 1926–1970), 18:152–53 (1073a).

59. Clement, *Stromateis,* p. 96 (7.2 (6)).

60. Ibid., p. 98 (7.2 (9)).

61. Clement did not actually use a variant of the word 'hierarchy' in describing this matter; the word was yet to be coined. He does speak of Christ as the High Priest who orders sacred reality and he uses the same Greek word as did the author of the letter to the Hebrews (4.14). The Greek word for 'hierarchy' (ἱεραρχία) was coined by transposing the component parts of the word for 'high priest'. Its technical theological meaning was specified by Pseudo-Dionysius in *De caelesti hierarchia* 3.1 and Clement's ideas quoted here anticipate this meaning.

62. Ibid., p. 129 (7.10 (57)).

63. Ibid.

64. For this social data, see: W.K. Lacey, *The Family in Classical Greece* (Ithaca, N.Y.: Cornell University Press, 1984), and Gerda Lerner, *The Creation of Patriarchy,* (Oxford: Oxford University Press, 1986).

65. Plato, *Laws,* trans. R.G. Bury, in *Plato,* 12 vols., 10:286–87 (713E).

66. Aristotle, *Politics,* trans. H. Rackham, in *Aristotle,* 23 vols., 21:18–19 (1254a).

NOTES TO CHAPTER 2

1. Niels Bohr, *The Philosophical Writings of Niels Bohr,* 3 vols. (Woodbridge, Conn.: Ox Bow Press, 1987), 1:108.

2. Ibid., 1:114.

3. Werner Heisenberg, *Physics and Philosophy: The Revolution in Modern Science* (New York: Harper & Row, 1958), pp. 201–02.

4. Alfred Tarski, "The Concept of Truth in Formalized Languages," *Logic, Semantics, Metamathematics,* trans. J.H. Woodger, ed. and intro. John Corcoran, 2nd ed. (Indianapolis, Ind.: Hackett Publishing Co., 1983).

5. John Dewey, *The Quest for Certainty: A Study of the Relation of Knowledge and Action* (New York: Minton, Balch, & Co., 1929), p. 23.

6. Richard Rorty, *Philosophy and the Mirror of Nature* (Princeton: Princeton University Press, 1979), especially pp. 131–64.

7. Athanasius, *The Life of Antony (and the Letter to Marcellinus),* trans. Robert C. Gregg, The Classics of Western Spirituality (New York: Paulist Press, 1980), p. 34 (5).

8. Ibid., pp. 34 (6) and 39 (9).

9. Aristotle, *The Metaphysics,* trans. Hugh Tredennick, 17:17 (983a).

10. Richard Feynman, *The Character of Physical Law* (Cambridge, Mass.: M.I.T. Press, 1967), p. 59.

11. Ibid.

12. Ibid., p. 84.

13. B.F. Skinner, *Verbal Behavior* (New York: Appleton-Century-Crofts, 1957), and Willard Van Orman Quine, *Word and Object* (Cambridge, Mass.: M.I.T. Press, 1960).

14. Noam Chomsky, "Review of B.F. Skinner's *Verbal Behavior.*" In *The Structure of Language: Readings in the Philosophy of Language,* J.A. Fodor and J.J. Katz, eds. (Englewood Cliffs, N.J.: Prentice-Hall, 1964), pp. 547–78.

15. William James, "The Idea of Consciousness." *Essays in Radical Empiricism (and A Pluralistic Universe),* ed. Ralph Barton Perry (New York: E.P. Dutton & Co., 1971), p. 120.

16. James, "The Experience of Activity." *Essays in Radical Empiricism,* p. 85.

17. Aristotle, *The Metaphysics,* 17:10–11 (982a).

18. Herbert Simon, *The Sciences of the Artificial,* 2nd ed. (Cambridge, Mass.: M.I.T. Press, 1981), p. 196.

19. Ibid., p. 209.

20. Herbert Simon, *Administrative Behavior,* 3rd ed. (New York: Macmillan Publishing, Free Press, 1976).

21. John Dewey, *Democracy and Education: An Introduction to the Philosophy of Education* (New York: Macmillan Company, 1922), pp. 81–116.

22. Pascal, *Pensées*, trans. A.J. Krailsheimer, p. 106 (257).

23. *The Principal Upaniṣads*, ed., trans., and intro. by S. Radhakrishnan (New York: Humanities Press, 1953), p. 64; for *brāhman* as immanent and transcendent compare *Śvetāśvatara Upanisad* 2.16–17 and 6.7–8.

24. Daisetz Teitaro Suzuki, *Outlines of Mahayana Buddhism* (New York: Schocken Books, 1963), p. 279; for a relevant Mahāyāna text, see Nāgārjuna's *Treatise on the Transcendentality of Bodhicitta*.

25. Westphal, *God, Guilt, and Death*, pp. 24–45.

26. Søren Kierkegaard, *Philosophical Fragments* (bound with *Johannes Climacus*, trans. and ed. Howard V. Hong and Edna H. Hong (Princeton: Princeton University Press, 1985), especially pp. 37–54. It is not only Jansenists and Lutherans who employ paradox as a theme of spiritual life; for a more traditional Roman Catholic variation, see: Henry De Lubac, *Paradoxes of Faith*, trans. Paule Simon et al. (San Francisco: Ignatius Press, 1986).

27. See: John Caputo, *The Mystical Element in Heidegger's Thought* (New York: Fordham University Press, 1986).

28. A popular, though flawed, spiritual manual that puts divind and human creativity at the center of the spiritual quest, see: Matthew Fox, *Original Blessing: A Primer of Creation Spirituality* (Santa Fe: Bear & Company, 1983).

29. Friedrich Engels, *The Peasant War In Germany* in *The German Revolutions*, ed. Leonard Krieger (Chicago: University of Chicago Press, 1967), p. 38.

30. Whitehead, *Process and Reality*, p. 21.

31. Daisetz T. Suzuki, *Zen and Japanese Culture*, (Princeton: Princeton University Press, 1959), pp. 219–20.

32. Chang Chung-yuan, *Creativity and Taoism: A Study of Chinese Philosophy, Art, and Poetry* (New York: Harper & Row, 1970), p. 55.

33. Suzuki, *Zen and Japanese Culture*, p. 27.

34. Clement of Alexandria, *The Instructor* in *The Ante-Nicene Fathers* 10 vols., eds. Alexander Roberts and James Donaldson (Grand Rapids, Mi.: Wm.B. Eerdmans Publishing, 1986), 2:237 (2.1) and 2:270 (2.13).

35. Pascal, *Pensées*, trans. A.J. Krailsheimer, p. 138 (380).

36. Ibid., p. 67 (136).

37. Ralph Waldo Emerson, *Selected Prose and Poetry,* 2nd ed. Reginal L. Cook (New York: Holt, Rinehart, and Winston, 1969), p. 106; for historical and pastoral treatments of this theme, see respectively: David E. Shi, *The Simple Life: Plain Living and High Thinking in American Culture* (Oxford: Oxford University Press, 1988), Richard J. Foster, *Freedom of Simplicity* (San Francisco: Harper & Row, 1989).

38. Henry David Thoreau, *Walden, or Life in the Woods* (New York: New American Library, Signet Classics, 1960), p. 66.

39. Mohandas Gandhi, *All Men are Brothers,* (New York: Columbia University Press & Unesco, 1958), p. 59.

40. Dewey, *Democracy and Education,* p. 27.

41. George Eliot, *Adam Bede* (New York: New American Library, 1961), p. 299.

42. Henry James, *Washington Square* (New York: New American Library, 1980), p. 11.

43. Saint Augustine, *Confessions,* p. 164 (8.5).

44. Pascal, *Pensées,* p. 152 (418).

45. Ibid., p. 274 (821).

46. For a more traditional reading, see: F.T.H. Fletcher, *Pascal and the Mystical Tradition* (Oxford: Basil Blackwell, 1954), pp. 112–22.

47. "The only habit a child should be allowed is to contract none." Jean-Jacques Rousseau, *Emile or On Education,* trans. Allan Bloom (New York: Basic Books, 1979), p. 63.

48. Friedrich Nietzsche, *The Gay Science,* trans. Walter Kaufmann (New York: Random House, 1974), p. 236–37 (295).

49. Blaise Pascal, *The Provincial Letters,* trans. A.J. Krailsheimer (Harmondsworth, England: Penguin Books, 1967), p. 149.

50. Friedrich Nietzsche, *Aus der Zeit der Morgenrröthe (1880–1881)* in *Gesammelte Werke,* Bandes 23 (Munich: Musarion Verlag, 1922–29), 9:71–72.2.

51. Pascal, *Pensées,* p. 61 (126).

52. Ibid., p. 135 (364).

53. Sigmund Freud, "Obsessive Actions and Religious Practices" (1907). *Standard Edition of the Complete Psychological Works of Sigmund Freud,* 24 vols., trans. and ed. James Strachey (London: Hogarth Press, 1953–74), 9:117–27.

54. Arthur Rimbaud, "Letter to George Izambard, 13 May 1871." *Rimbaud: Complete Works, Selected Letters,* English and French ed., trans. and ed. Wallace Fowlie (Chicago: University of Chicago Press, 1966), p. 303.

55. Enid Starkie, *Arthur Rimbaud* (New York: New Directions, 1961), pp. 95–103.

56. Pascal, *Pensées,* p. 45–47 (60).

NOTES TO CHAPTER 3

1. For the diverse meanings and applications of self-reference as a prominent rubric of contemporary intellectual life, see: *Self-Reference: Reflections on Reflexivity,* ed. Steven J. Bartlett and Peter Suber (Boston: Kluwer Academic Publishers, 1987).

2. This phrase is quoted in William and Martha Kneale's *The Development of Ligic* (Oxford: Oxford University Press, 1962), p. 228.

3. Russell first addressed these issues in the *Principles of Mathematics* of 1903, but he gave the more general treatment of them in the 1908 article in which he coined the phrase self-reference; see, "Mathematical Logic as Based on the Theory of Types" in *Logic and Knowledge,* p. 61ff.

4. Aristotle, *The Metaphysics,* 17:200–201 (1011b).

5. For the less technical exposition of Tarski's work on truth, see: Alfred Tarski, "The Semantic Conception of Truth and the Foundations of Semantics," *Philosophy and Phenomenological Research,* no. 4 (1944):341–76.

6. Sextus Empiricus, *Against the Logicians,* in *Sextus Empiricus,* trans. R.G. Bury, 4 vols., Loeb Classical Library (Cambridge, Mass.: Harvard University Press, 1933–49), 2:244–45 (2.11).

7. The English translation is my own; for the Latin text, see: Ancius Manlius Sererinus Boethius, *In Categorias Aristotelis* in *Patrologiae cursus completus: series Latina,* ed. J. P. Migne, 221 vols. (Paris: 1841–1877) 64:159–60.

8. For the probable sources of Augustine's knowledge of logic, see: B. Darrell Jackson, "The Theory of Signs in St. Augustine's *De doctrina Christiana.*" *Augustine: A Collection of Critical Essays,* ed. R.A. Markus (Garden City, N.Y.: Doubleday & Company, 1972), pp. 92–147.

9. Sancti Aureli Augustini, *De magistro* in *Corpus Scriptorum Ecclesiasticorum Latinorum,* vol. 77, recensuit et praefatus est Guenther Weigel (Vindobonae: Hoelder-Pichler-Tempsky, 1961), pp. 15–16 (10). Augustine

also alludes to the Liar paradox in his *Confessiones* (10.3); he does so to recommend divinely aided confession as the only truly reliable form of self-knowledge.

10. Saint Augustine, *Concerning the Teacher,* trans. George C. Leckie, in *Basic Writings of Saint Augustine,* ed. Whitney J. Oates, 2 vols. (New York: Random House, 1948), 1:372 (5.14).

11. For a more detailed account of the role of Christ in this context, see: R.A. Markus, "St. Augustine on Signs," *Augustine: A Collection of Critical Essays,* ed. R.A. Markus, p. 71ff.

12. Comparison of Russell's essay "On Denoting" with Heidegger's "The Age of the World Picture" manifests the relevant contrast. See: Russell, "On Denoting," *Logic and Knowledge,* pp. 39–56; and, Martin Heidegger, "The Age of the World Picture," *The Question Concerning Technology and Other Essays,* trans. William Lovitt (New York: Harper & Row, 1977), pp. 115–54.

13. In writing of this conception of philosophy Danto has spoken of it as "spiritual" and even "redemptive" for the fact that it brings to consciousness this peculiar way in which human beings, like their language and art objects, are a part of the world yet also apart from it. See: Arthur C. Danto, *What Philosophy Is: A Guide to the Elements* (New York: Harper & Row, 1971), p. 148; and *Analytical Philosophy of Knowledge* (Cambridge: Cambridge University Press, 1968), pp. 264–65.

14. *Chuang Tzu: Basic Writings,* trans. Burton Watson (New York: Columbia University Press, 1964), pp. 39–40 (2).

15. For more information about cosmographic constructions, see: Mircea Eliade, *Patterns in Comparative Religion,* trans. Rosemary Sheed (New York: New American Library, 1974), pp. 367–87.

16. For representative material of this sort, see: *The Chinese on the Art of Painting,* trans. and ed. Osvald Siren (New York: Schocken Books, 1963).

17. For more detailed information about how specific types of mandalas contribute to specific meditation techniques, see: Giuseppe Tucci, *The Theory and Practice of the Mandala,* trans. Alan Houghton Brodrick (New York: S. Weiser, 1970).

18. For Jung's major writings on this topic, see: *Collected Works,* eds. Herbert Read, Michael Fordham, and Gerhard Adler, 18 vols. (New York: Pantheon Books, 1953–73), 9.1:355–90.

19. Gottlob Frege, "On Sense and Reference." *Translations from the Philosophical Writings of Gottlob Frege,* trans. and ed. Peter Geach and Max Black (Oxford: Basil Blackwell, 1960), pp. 56–78.

20. Peter Brown, *The Cult of the Saints: Its Rise and Function in Latin Christianity* (Chicago: University of Chicago Press, 1981), pp. 88–89.

21. For a classic text on the veneration of remains of the Buddha, see: Edward J. Thomas, *The Life of Buddha as Legend and History,* 3rd ed., (London: Routledge & Kegan Paul, 1975).

22. Robert Nozick, *Philosophical Explanations* (Cambridge, Mass.: Harvard University Press, 1981), p. 78.

23. For the representation of self-reference in formal languages, see: Kurt Gödel, "On Formally Undecidable Propositions of *Principia Mathematica* and Related Systems I," *From Frege to Gödel: A Source Book in Mathematical Logic, 1879–1931,* ed. Jean van Heijenoort (Cambridge, Mass.: Harvard University Press, 1967), pp. 596–616; and Ernest Nagel and James R. Newman, "Gödel's Proof," *Contemporary Readings in Logical Theory,* ed. Irving M. Copi and James A. Gould (New York: Macmillan Company, 1967), pp. 51–71.

24. Ibid.

25. *The Koran Interpreted,* trans. Arthur J. Arberry, 2 vols. (New York: Macmillan Publishing Co., 1955), 2:29.

26. Saint Augustine, *Confessions,* trans. R.S. Pine-Coffin, p. 21 (1.1)

27. Ibid., p. 23 (1.4)

28. *Kena Upaniṣad,* trans. S. Radhakrishnan, p. 582 (1.3).

29. Augustine makes this predication and realization in *De doctrina Christiana* 1.6.

30. *Kena Upaniṣad,* trans. S. Radhakrishnan, p. 582 (1.5).

31. Ibid., p. 585 (2.3).

32. Ibid., p. 592 (4.8).

33. Edmund Husserl, *Logical Investigations,* trans. J.N. Findlay, 2 vols. (London: Routledge & Kegan Paul, 1970), especially Investigations 3 and 6.

34. Robert Sokolowski, *Husserlian Meditations: How Words Present Things* (Evanston, Ill.: Northwestern University Press, 1974), pp. 252–53 (9.88).

35. Raymund Smullyan has shown how self-quotation is one of the simplest ways of deriving formal versions of the Liar paradox; see: Raymund Smullyan, "Languages in which Self-Reference is Possible," *The Philosophy of Mathematics,* ed. Jaakko Hintikka (London: Oxford University Press, 1969), pp. 64–77.

36. Paul Ricoeur, *The Symbolism of Evil,* trans. Emerson Buchanan.

37. Jacques Derrida, *On Grammatology,* trans. Gayatri Chakravorty Spivak (Baltimore: Johns Hopkins University press, 1976), pp. 1–93.

38. St. John of Damascus, *On the Divine Images: Three Apologies against those who attack the Divine Images,* trans. David Anderson (Crestwood, N.Y.: St. Vladimir's Seminary Press, 1980).

39. Leonid Ouspensky and Vladimir Lossky, *The Meaning of Icons,* trans. G.E.H. Palmer and E. Kadloubovsky (Boston: Boston Book and Art Shop, 1952), pp. 53–55.

40. Ernst Kitzinger, "Byzantine Art in the Period Between Justinian and Iconoclasm." *The Art of Byzantium and the Medieval West: Selected Studies* (Bloomington, Ind.: Indian University Press, 1976), p. 201ff.

NOTES TO CHAPTER 4

1. For the diverse ways in which the notion of symmetry is used by contemporary mathematicians, natural scientists and humanistic scholars, see: *Symmetry: Unifying Human Understanding,* ed. Istvan Hargittai (New York: Pergamon Press, 1986).

2. Willard Van Orman Quine, "On What There Is," *From a Logical Point of View,* 2nd ed. (New York: Harper & Row, 1961), p. 15.

3. For references to the Canon by ancient writers, see: *Select Passages From Ancient Writers Illustrative of the History of Greek Sculpture,* ed. and trans. H. Stuart Jones (Chicago: Argonaut, 1946), pp. 124–31.

4. For an account of musical enjoyment in these terms, see: Eduard Hanslick, *The Beautiful in Music,* trans. Gustav Cohen (Indianapolis, In.: Bobbs-Merrill Company, 1957), p. 98ff.

5. For a comparison of the two composers, see: Paul Griffiths, *The String Quartet: A History* (New York: Thames and Hudson, 1983), pp. 104–05; and for a analysis of Bartok's chamber music in terms of symmetrical structure, see: Elliott Antokoletz, *The Music of Bela Bartok: A Study of Tonality and Progression in Twentieth Century Music* (Berkeley: University of California Press, 1984).

6. Saint Augustine, *Divine Providence and the Problem of Evil* trans. Robert Russell (New York: Cosmopolitan Science & Art Service, 1942), p. 9 (1.1.2).

7. For the Latin text, see: *De ordine* in *Corpus Christianorum, Series Latina,* vol. 29 (Turnholti: Typograph Brepols Editores Pontificii, 1970), pp.89–90 (1.12.2).

8. Ibid, p. 53 (1.9.27).

9. Ibid. pp. 67–85 (2.1–2) and 23–27 (1.4.10–11).

10. Ibid., p. 167 (2.19.51).

11. Jonathan Edwards, *Religious Affections*, ed. John E. Smith (New Haven: Yale University Press, 1959), 365ff.

12. For an informative but informal treatment of symmetry as a property of animals, see: Martin Gardner, *The Ambidextrous Universe: Left, Right, and the Fall of Parity*, rev. ed. (New York: New American Library, Mentor Books, 1969).

13. G.W.F. Hegel, *Phenomenology of Spirit*, trans, A.V. Miller (Oxford: Clarendon Press, 1977), pp. 111–18 (B.4.A); from this same philosophical tradition, see also: Erwin W. Strauss, "The Upright Posture," *Phenomenological Psychology*, trans. Erling Eng, (New York: Basic Books, 1966), pp. 137–65.

14. Baron Friedrich von Hugel, *Essays and Address on the Philosophy of Religion*, quoted from *Writings on Spiritual Direction by Great Christian Masters*, edited by Jerome M. Neufelder and Mary C. Coelho (New York: Seabury Press, 1982), p. 8.

15. Denise L. Carmody and John T. Carmody, *Shamans, Prophets, and Sages: A Concise Introduction to World Religions* Belmont, Cal.: Wadsworth Publishing Company, 1985).

16. Neville, *Soldier, Sage, Saint*, p. 117ff.

17. Thomas à Kempis, *The Imitation of Christ*, trans. Harold C. Gardner (Garden City,: Doubleday and Co., 1955), p. 31 (1.1).

18. Ibid., pp. 217–18 (4.8).

19. Ibid., pp. 223–24 (4.11).

20. Ibid., p. 87 (2.9).

21. Ibid., p. 32 (1.1).

22. For a general survey of this material, see: Joseph de Guibert, *The Jesuits, Their Spiritual Doctrine, and Practice*, ed. George A. Ganno, trans. William Y. Young (Chicago: Loyola University Press, 1964), especially pp. 527–43.

23. *The Spiritual Exercises of St. Ignatius*. trans. Anthony Mottola (Garden City, N.Y.: Doubleday and Co., 1964), p.37.

24. Ibid., pp. 40–41.

25. *The Rule of Saint Benedict,* in *Western Asceticism,* trans. and ed. Owen Chadwick, The Library of Christian Classics (Philadelphia: Westminster Press, 1958), pp. 294 and 299 (2 and 5).

26. Ibid. p. 294 (2).

27. Ignatius makes the sensuous imagination a central part of his process of guided spiritual discernment; this fact alone resists prejudices against the body and bodily perception. Although more a Platonist than I, Antonio T. De Nicolas, has philosophically explored this topic and has correctly called for a hermeneutics of spiritual texts attentive to the relation between interpretation and embodied habits: *Powers of Imagining-Ignatius de Loyola* (Albany: State University of New York Press, 1986) p. 93.

28. *Spiritual Exercises,* p. 85.

29. Neville, *Soldier, Sage, Saint,* p. 122.

30. Ibid., p. 121.

31. For the details of this process of pattern generation, see: Peter S. Stevens, *Handbook of Regular Patterns: An Introduction to Symmetry in Two Dimensions* (Cambridge, Mass., M.I.T. Press, 1984).

32. For further information, see: Garrett Birkhoff and Saunders MacLane, *A Survey of Modern Algebra,* rev. ed. (New York: Macmillan Company, 1953), p. 117ff.

33. Unlike Newton's formulation of the differential calculus, group theory was not originally investigated by Galois in the context of physical investigations; instead, it emerged from work in the theory of equations. See: Boyer, *History of Mathematics,* pp. 638–43.

34. Linus Pauling, *General Chemistry* (New York: Dover Publications, 1970), p.871.

35. Michael Polanyi, *Personal Knowledge: Towards a Post-Critical Philosophy,* corrected ed. (Chicago: University of Chicago Press, 1962, p. 48.

36. This statement requires some qulaifications; they are not important for this context, see: Feynman, *Physical Law,* pp. 84–87.

37. Diogenes Laertius, *Lives of Eminent Philosophers,* trans. R.D. Hicks, 2 vols. (Cambridge, Mass.: Harvard University Press, 1966) pp. 194–97 (7.87–88).

38. Gregory Palamas, *The Triads,* ed. John Meyendorff, trans. Nicholas Gendle, The Classics of Western Spirituality (New York: Paulist Press, 1983), p. 80; Meyendorff has been a source for my summary of Hesychasm, for instance, see: *St. Gregory Palamas and Orthodox Spirituality,* trans. Adele Fiske (Crestwood, N.Y.: St. Vladimir's Seminary Press, 1974).

39. Hegel, *Phenomenology of Spirit*, p. 59 (92).

40. *Yoga Philosophy of Patanjali*, trans. P.N. Murkerji, intro. and notes Swami Hariharananda Aranya (Albany: State University of New York Press, 1983), p. 6 (1.2).

41. Heinrich Zimmer, *Philosophies of India*, ed. Joseph Campbell (Princeton: Princeton University Press, 1969), p. 295.

42. Mircea Eliade, *Yoga: Immortality and Freedom*, trans. Willard R. Trask (Princeton, Princeton University Press, 1969), pp. 26–30.

43. *Yoga Philosophy*, p. 89 (1.41).

44. Heinz Pagels, *Perfect Symmetry: The Search for the Beginning of Time* (New York: Bantam Books, 1986), p. xvii.

45. Ibid., pp. 284–89 and 380–91; and Feynman, *The Character of Physical Law*, pp. 167–73.

46. Quoted in Hermann Weyl, *Symmetry* (Princeton: Princeton University Press, 1982), p. 31.

47. Julian Jaynes, *The Origin of Consciousness in the Breakdown of the Bicameral Mind*(Boston: Houghton Mifflin Company, 1977).

48. Hegel, *Phenomenology of Spirit*, pp. 479–93 (7).

49. For the history of chess, see: H.J.R. Murray's *The History of Chess* (Oxford: Oxford University Press, 1913); for a brief modern history, see: Richard Eales, *Chess: The History of a Game* New York: Facts on File Publications, 1985).

50. For historical information and speculation about the religious origins of chess and other board games, see: Nigel Pennick, *Games of the Gods: The Origin of Board Games in Magic and Divination* (New York: Weiser Books, 1989).

51. For example, see: Nuel D. Belnap, Jr. and Thomas B. Steel, Jr., *The Logic of Questions and Answers* (New Haven: Yale University Press, 1976), p. 16ff.

52. *The Zen Teaching of Huang Po on the Transmission of Mind*, trans. John Blofeld (New York: Grove Press, 1959), pp. 94–96 (27–29).

53. Yawunari Kawabata, *The Master of Go*, trans. Edward G. Seidensticker (New York: G.P. Putnam's Sons, 1981), p. 164.

NOTES TO CHAPTER 5

1. Walter B. Cannon, *The Wisdom of the Body*, 2nd ed. (New York: W.W. Norton & Company, 1939).

2. In his autobiography Cannon relates how James discouraged him from abandoning medical research for philosophy: *The Way of an Investigator: A Scientist's Experiences in Medical Research* (New York: W.W. Norton & Company, 1945), p. 19.

3. J.B.S. Haldane, "What is Life," *Adventures of A Biologist* (New York: Harper & Row, 1940), p. 59.

4. Norbert Wiener, *Cybernetics: or Control and Communication in the Animal and Machine.* 2nd ed. (Cambridge, Mass.: M.I.T. Press, 1961), especially pp. 1ff. and 95–115.

5. Cannon, *Wisdom of the Body*, p. 24.

6. Claude Bernard, *Leçons sur les Phénomènes de la Vie*, 2 tomes (Paris: Ballilére, 1878), pp. 111–14; Robert Boyle, *New Experiments Physico-Mechanicall*, 1662, 1.36.

7. Erwin Schrödinger, *What is Life & Mind and Matter* Cambridge: Cambridge University Press, 1967), pp. 72–80.

8. For the major writings attributed to Hippocrates, see *Hippocrates*, trans. W.H.S. Jones, 4 vols., Loeb Classical Library (Cambridge, Mass.: Harvard University Press, 1923–31).

9. For provocative remarks on this aspect of ancient Greek medicine, see: Michel Foucault, *The Use of Pleasure*, trans. Robert Hurley (New York: Randon House, 1986), pp. 95–139.

10. *Hippocrates*, 1: 34–37.

11. *Hippocrates*, 4:10–11.

12. This principle is attributed to Alcmaeon by both Aetius and Galen; for the full quotation see *Hippocrates*, 1:xlvii. That ἰσονομία was translated as 'aequilibrium' in Latin antiquity, see Cicero's *De natura deorum*, 1.109.

13. Saint Augustine, *Soliloquies*, trans. Thomas F. Gilligan, in *The Writings of Augustine*, Fathers of the Church (New York: Cima Publishing Co., 1948), p. 375 (1.14.24). In his *Retractiones* 4.3, Augustine described this denunciation of the body as too harsh.

14. For support for this thesis, see: Margaret R. Miles, *Augustine on the Body* (Missoula, Montana: Scholars Press, 1979).

15. *Ennarrationes in Psalmos* (121.6) in *Corpus Christianorum, Series Latina* 40: 1806–07; the translation is my own.

16. *Sermones* (155.15) in J.P. Migne, ed., *Patrologia Latina*, 38:849; the translation is my own.

17. C.H. Waddington, *The Nature of Life* (London: George Allen & Unwin, Ltd. 1961), p. 27.

18. Bernard, *Leçons sur les Phénomènes de la Vie*, 1:67; the translation is my own.

19. Isadora Duncan, *The Art of the Dance*, ed. Sheldon Cheney (New York: Theater Arts Books, 1928), p. 52.

20. Ibid., p. 68.

21. M. Merleau-Ponty, *Phenomenology of Perception*, trans. Colin Smith (London: Routledge & Kegan Paul, 1962), p. 148 (1.4).

22. Ibid. p. 92 (1.2).

23. Ibid. p. 153 (1.4).

24. Mihaly Csikszentmihalyi gives detailed accounts of this aspect of disciplined practices in his book, *Flow: The Psychology of Optimal Experience* (New York: Harper & Row, 1990).

25. Eugen Herrigel, *Zen in the Art of Archery*, trans. R. Hull, intro. D.T. Suzuki (New York: Random House, 1971).

26. Edward D. Andrews, *The Gift to be Simple: Songs, Dances, and Rituals of the American Shakers* (New York: J.J. Augustin Publisher, 1940), p. 103.

27. For an elaboration of the meaning of this phrase, see: Wang Yang-ming, "Inquiry on the Great Learning," *Source Book in Chinese Philosophy*, ed. Wing-tsit Chan (Princeton: Princeton University Press, 1963), pp. 659–67.

28. Lao Tzu, *Tao Te Ching*, trans. D.C. Lao (Harmondsworth, England: Penguin Books, 1963) p. 59 (3).

29. J.E. Lovelock, *Gaia: A New Look At Life on Earth* (Oxford: Oxford University Press, 1987), p. 11. In a subsequent book Lovelock has modified his claims, speaking less directly, for instance, of Gaia as an optimizing organism; however, the stress on homeostatic self-regulation remains: *The Ages of Gaia: A Biography of Our Living Earth* (New York: W.W. Norton & Company, 1988).

30. Niles Eldredge and Stephen Jay Gould, "Punctuated Equilibria: An Alternative to Phyletic Gradualism," *Models in Paleobiology*, ed., Thomas J.M. Schopf (San Francisco: Freeman, Cooper, & Co., 1972), p. 84.

31. Ibid.

32. Stephen Jay Gould, "Is a New and General Theory of Evolution Emerging?" *Paleobiology*, 6:119–30.

33. Such "allopatric" speciation was first studied by the zoologist Ernst Mayr, see: *Animal Species and Evolution* (Cambridge, Mass.: Harvard University Press, 1963).

34. A different and more controversial mechanism of evolutionary biological equilibration—called by some 'genetic homeostasis'—is defended by Ernst Mayr in *Toward a New Philosophy of Biology: Observations of an Evolutionist* (Cambridge, Mass.:, Harvard University Press, 1988), pp. 439–56.

35. Teilhard de Chardin, *The Phenomenon of Man*, trans. Bernard Wall (New York: Harper & Row, 1959), pp. 191–212; Gregory Bateson, *Steps Toward and Ecology of Mind* (New York: Random House, 1972), pp. 469–505.; Richard Dawkins, *The Selfist Gene* (New York: Oxford University Press, 1976), pp. 203–16.

36. Karl Popper, *Objective Knowledge: An Evolutionary Approach* (Oxford: Oxford University Press, 1971), p. 261.

37. Karl Popper, *The Logic of Scientific Discovery* (New York: Harper & Row, 1968), pp. 251–81; see also p. 108 for a sketch of his later views on knowledge and natural selection.

38. Popper, *Objective Knowledge*, p. 261.

39. Stephen Toulmin, "The Evolutionary Development of Natural Science," *American Scientist* 57:470–75; and *Human Understanding* (Oxford: Oxford University Press, 1972).

40. Popper, *Objective Knowledge*, pp. 183–86.

41. For development of this criticism, see: Michael Ruse, *Taking Darwin Seriously: A Naturalistic Approach to Philosophy* (Oxford: Basil Blackwell, Ltd. 1986), p. 53ff.

42. See "Evolutionary Love," in *The Collected Papers of Charles Sanders Peirce*, 6 vols., eds. Charles Hartshorne and Paul Weiss, (Cambridge: Harvard University Press, 1931–35) 6:287–317.

43. Thomas S. Kuhn, *The Structure of Scientific Revolutions* 2nd ed. (Chicago: University of Chicago Press, 1970, pp. 23–43, and for Kuhn's appeal to the model of Darwinian evolution, see pp. 172–73.

44. Emile Durkheim, *The Elementary Forms of Religious Life*, trans. Joseph Ward Swain (New York: Macmillan Company, Free Press, 1965), p. 22; for a biologist who invokes Durkheim in his reflections on religion, see: Edward O. Wilson, *On Human Nature* (New York: Bantam Books, 1979), p. 196.

45. John Henry Newman, *An Essay on the Development of Doctrine*, 1845 ed. (Harmondsworth, England: Penguin Books, 1974), p. 149. For Baur, doctrinal development was the outward expression of the idea of reconciliation immanent in the Christian doctrine of the Trinity construed with the help of Hegelian dialectics. For Newman the history of Christian ideas was unique among religions because its "progressive development" was assured by a "Divine Spirit" in a manner quite similar to how progress was guaranteed in pre-Darwinian accounts of natural evolution. For the characterization of Newman, see: Owen Chadwick, *From Bossuet to Newman: The Idea of Doctrinal Development* (Cambridge: Cambridge University Press, 1957); for Baur, see: Peter C. Hodgson, *The Formation of Historical Theology: A Study of Ferdinand Christian Baur* (New York: Harper & Row, 1966), 58ff.

46. Such secular influence is well represented by the Social Darwinist and dialectical Marxist, Karl Kautsky; see: *The Foundations of Christianity*, trans. H.F. Mins (New York: 1953).

47. Walter Bauer, *Orthodoxy and Heresy in Earliest Christianity*, ed. Robert A. Kraft and Gerhard Krodel (Philadelphia: Fortress Press, 1971), pp. 61–69.

48. Gerd Theissen, *Sociology of Early Palestian Christianity*, trans. John Bowden (Philadelphia: Fortress Press, 1978); and *The Social Setting of Pauline Christianity: Essays on Corinth*, ed. and trans. John H. Schutz (Philadelphia: Fortress Press, 1982).

49. Parsons is relevant here because his structural/functional approach explicity treats the stabilizing capacity of social systems as a process of equilibration and because his pragmatic temperament places social systems within the context of individual action theory. Disciplined spiritual practices in his view generally foster social equilibration by enjoining actions more conformist than deviant, and by enacting compensatory belief systems. See: Talcott Parsons, *The Social System* (New York: The Free Press, 1951), especially pp. 367–78.

50. In subsequent work Theissen has described the Biblical faith of early Christians as a means of cultural adaptation distinct from, but complementary to, Greek scientific rationality; furthermore he has sought to understand the development of the expressions of both faith and reason in terms of the social processes of an evolutionary epistemology; see: Gerd Theissen, *Biblical Faith: An Evolutionary Perspective*, trans. John Bowden (Philadelphia: Fortress Press, 1985).

51. For the origins of the relationship between rabbis and the Jewish community, see: E.E. Urbach, *The Sages—Their Concepts and Beliefs*, trans. Israel Abrahams (Jerusalem: Magnes Press, 1975), especially pp. 524–648; for an account of halakhic interpretation in terms of

Whiteheadian organismic conceptions of the relation between selves, beliefs, and societies, see: Max Kadushin, *The Rabbinic Mind*, 3rd ed. (New York: Bloch Publishing, 1972).

52. *Midrash and Literature*, eds. Geoffrey H. Hartman and Sanford Budick (New Haven: Yale University Press, 1986); note especially the articles by Jacques Derrida and Edmund Jabes.

53. Wilhelm Dilthey, "Der Aufbau der Geschichtlichen Welt in den Geisteswissenschaften, "*Gesammelte Schriften*, 7 vols. (Gottingen: Vandenhoeck & Ruprecht, 1913–67) 7:141.

54. Søren Kierkegaard, *Purity of Heart is to Will One Thing*, trans. Douglas V. Steere (New York: Harper & Row, 1956).

55. Friedrich Nietzsche, *The Anti-Christ* (bound with *Twilight of the Idols*, trans. R.J. Hollingdale (Harmonsworth, England: Penquin Books, 1968), p. 117 (6); the second phrase is from the subtitle of Nietzsche's literary autobiography *Ecce Homo*.

56. Marshall was aware of the limitations of his labors in mathematical economics, specifically lamenting the difficulty of formally representing economic "change and progress" with sufficiently "dynamical—or rather biological—conceptions"; see: Alfred Marshall, *Principles of Economics*, 2 vols. (New York: Macmillan Company, 1961), 2:xv.

57. Waddington coined the phrase 'homeorhesis' to identify this distinctly developmental process of biological equilibration; see: *The Strategy of the Genes: A Discussion of some Aspects of Theoretical Biology* (New York: Macmillan Company, 1957), p. 32.

58. D'Arcy Wentworth Thompson, *On Growth and Form*, ed. John Tyler Bonner, (Cambridge: Cambridge University Press, 1966); for "a law of similitude" stated in equilibration language, see p. 18.

59. Jean Piaget, *Biology and Knowledge: As Essay on the Relations Between Organic Regulations and Cognitive Process*, trans. Beatrice Walsh (Chicago: University of Chicago Press, 1971), p., 26.

60. For a summary presentation of this work, see: Jean Piaget, *The Origins of Intelligence in Children* (New York: W.W. Norton & Company, 1963).

61. Jean Piaget, *Genetic Epistemology*, trans. Eleanor Duckworth (New York: Columbia University Press, 1970, p. 15.

62. Lawrence Kohlberg (with Clark Power), "Moral Development, Religious Thinking, and the Question of a Seventh Stage," in *The Philosophy of Moral Development: Moral Stages and the Idea of Justice* (New York: Harper & Row, 1981), pp. 311–72.

63. By concentrating on faith as a dispositional orientation rather than on embodied practices and intellectual operations, Fowler's work loses relevance to the project here undertaken; for instance, there remains no substantive notion of equilibration in Fowler's account of the various stages. See: James W. Fowler, *Stages of Faith: The Psychology of Human Development and the Quest for Meaning* (New York: Harper & Row, 1981).

For the most part this also is the case for Kierkegaard's famous account of the aesthetic, ethical, and religious stages of life. Even when he adopts a non-Lutheran idiom in *Works of Love* his emphasis is more on love as a disposition than on works as concretely embodied practices; and while his account of the stages does invoke a notion of equilibrium (*Ligevaegt* in Danish), it is a fairly static one characteristic of the ethical stage of life. For an exposition of this difficult material, see: Stephen N. Dunning, *Kierkegaard's Dialectic of Inwardness: A Structural Analysis of the Theory of Stages* (Princeton: Princeton University Press, 1985), especially pp. 74–91.

64. Carol Gilligan, *In a Different Voice: Psychological Theory and Women's Development* (Cambridge, Mass.: Harvard University Press, 1982).

65. For this assessment of Piaget's work, see: Howard Gardner, *The Mind's New Science: A History of the Cognitive Revolution* (New York: Basic Books, 1985), p. 118.

66. For recent scientific work in this area, see: *The Mind's Eye: Readings from Scientific American*, intro. Jeremy M. Wolfe (New York: W.H. Freeman and Company, 1986), especially the articles by Gilman (chapter 9) and Hoffman (chapter 10).

67. Kant, *Critique of Pure Reason*, p. 297.

68. Texts in which the theme of mystical communion is developed include Gregory of Nyssa's formative *De vita Moysis* and the popular English tractate *The Cloud of Unknowing*.

69. For the sources for Greek terminology cited in this passage, see: Cheslyn Jones et al., eds., *The Study of Spirituality* (Oxford, Oxford University Press, 1986), pp. 184–89 and 168–73.

70. John Rawls, *A Theory of Justice* (Cambridge, Mass.: Harvard University Press, 1972), pp. 48–49.

NOTES TO CHAPTER 6

1. Friedrich Nietzsche, *On the Genealogy of Morals* (bound with *Ecce Homo*), trans. Walter Kaufmann and R. J. Hollingdale (New York: Random House, 1969), p. 37 (1.10). Generally I shall cite translations of Nietzsche's writings by Kaufmann and Hollingdale; when I cite words or phrases in the original German the edition used will be the *Gesammelte Werke*, 23 Bände (Munich: Musarion Verlag, 1922–29).

2. Ibid., pp. 162–63 (3.28).

3. Miles uses the phrase as an epigram for both the introduction to *Fullness of Life* and for the fifth chapter on asceticism in *Practicing Christianity.*

4. Arthur Schopenhauer, *The World as Will and Representation,* trans. E.F. Payne, 2 vols. (New York: Dover Publications, 1969), 1:379 (68).

5. Ibid., 1:383 (68).

6. Schopenhauer acknowledged the continuity of his philosophy with Christian ascetic thinkers, especially recommending to his readers the life and thought of Pascal; he discusses Clement of Alexandria at more length than Pascal, but finds in him an inconsistent combination of Judaic optimism and Christian pessimism. See: Schopenhauer, *World as Will and Representation,* 2:615 and 620ff (48).

7. Nietzsche, *Genealogy of Morals,* p. 39 (1.10).

8. Ibid., p. 116 (3.10).

9. Ibid., p. 120 (3.13).

10. Ibid., pp. 129–41 (3.17–20).

11. Ibid., pp. 135 and 139 (3.18 and 20).

12. Ibid., p. 121 (3.13).

13. Friedrich Nietzsche, *The Anti-Christ* (bound with *Twilight of the Idols*), intro. and trans. R.J. Hollingdale (Harmondsworth, England: Penguin Books, 1968), p. 16.

14. Ibid., p. 117 (5).

15. Ibid., p. 151 (39).

16. Ibid., pp. 146–47 (34).

17. Nietzsche, *Genealogy of Morals,* p. 38 (1.10).

18. Nietzsche, *Anti-Christ,* p. 149 (37).

19. Friedrich Nietzsche, *The Will to Power,* ed. Walter Kaufmann, trans. Walter Kaufmann and R.J. Hollingdale (New York: Random House, 1968), pp. 85–86 (135) and 183 (335).

20. Ibid., p. 170 (304).

21. For a representative text showing Nietzsche's attitudes towards women, see: Friedrich Nietzsche, *The Gay Science,* trans. Walter Kaufmann (New York: Random House, 1974), pp. 123–30 (60–75).

22. Jacques Derrida, *Of Spirit: Heidegger and the Question,* trans. Geoffrey Bennington and Rachel Bowlby (Chicago: University of Chicago Press, 1989).
Derrida has also written appreciatively about some of Nietzsche's remarks about women in *The Gay Science*; see: Jacques Derrida, *Spurs: Nietzsche's Styles,* trans. Barbara Harlow, English-French ed. (Chicago: University of Chicago Press, 1979).

23. Martin Heidegger, *Nietzsche,* trans. David Krell, 4 vols. (London: Routledge & Kegan Paul, 1981–87), 2:228.

24. Gerardus Van Der Leeuw, *Religion in Essence and Manifestation,* trans. J.E. Turner (New York: Harper & Row, 1963), p. 24 (1.3).

25. Ibid., p. 142 (32.1).

26. Nietzsche, *Gay Science,* p. 175 (116).

27. Joachim Wach, *Sociology of Religion* (Chicago: University of Chicago Press, 1944), pp. 55–108.

28. Ibid., p. 57.

29. Arnold van Gennep, *The Rites of Passage,* trans. Monika B. Vizedom and Gabrielle L. Caffee (London: Routledge and Kegan Paul, 1909); also, Victor Turner, *The Ritual Process: Structure and Anti-Structure* (Ithaca, N.Y.: Cornell University Press, 1977).

30. Max Weber, *The Sociology of Religion,* trans. Ephraim Fischoff (Boston: Beacon Press, 1963), pp. 166–84.

31. Max Weber, *The Protestant Ethic and the Spirit of Capitalism,* trans. Talcott Parsons (New York: Charles Scribner's Sons, 1958), p. 163ff.

32. Nietzsche, *Genealogy of Morals,* p. 143 (3.21).

33. Ibid., p. 111 (3.8).

34. Weber, *Protestant Ethic,* pp. 175–76.

35. Nietzsche, *Genealogy of Morals,* p. 102 (3.5).

36. Ibid., p. 97 (3.1).

37. Ibid., p. 107 (3.7).

38. Ibid., p. 109 (3.8).

39. Ibid.

40. Friedrich Nietzsche, *Ecce Homo* (bound with *On the Genealogy of Morals,* trans. Walter Kaufmann (New York: Random House, 1967), p. 326 (4.1).

41. Ibid., p. 224 (1.2).

42. Ibid., p. 233 (1.8).

43. Friedrich Nietzsche, *Untimely Meditations,* trans. R.J. Hollingdale (Cambridge: Cambridge University Press, 1983), p. 139 (3).

44. ibid., p. 140–43 (3).

45. Nietzsche, *Ecce Homo,* p. 281 (3.U.3).

46. Nietzsche, *Untimely Meditations,* p. 159 (5).

47. Nietzsche, *Ecce Homo,* p. 280 (3.U.3).

48. Alexander Nehamas, *Nietzsche: Life as Literature* (Cambridge, Mass.: Harvard University Press, 1985). Nehamas subscribes to the school of thought that understands Nietzsche apart from traditional intellectual pursuits, including academic philosophy; see: Gilles Deleuze, *Nietzsche and Philosophy,* trans. by Hugh Tomlinson (New York: Columbia University Press, 1983).

49. Friedrich Nietzsche, *Daybreak,* trans. R.J. Hollingdale (Cambridge: Cambridge University Press, 1982), p. 203 (499).

50. Nietzsche, *Gay Science,* p. 175 (116).

51. Nietzsche, *Daybreak,* p. 187 (440).

52. Nietzsche, *Gay Science,* p. 324 (367).

53. Ibid., p. 232 (290).

54. Walter Kaufmann, *Nietzsche: Philosopher, Psychologist, AntiChrist,* 4th ed. (Princeton: Princeton University Press, 1974), pp. 211–56.

55. Nehamas, *Nietzsche,* p. 8.

56. Nietzsche, *Ecce Homo,* p. 238 (2.1).

57. Friedrich Nietzsche, *Thus Spoke Zarathustra,* trans. Walter Kaufmann, in *The Portable Nietzsche* (Harmondsworth, England: Penguin Books, 1976), p. 121 (P.1).

58. Ibid., pp. 121–22 (P.1).

59. Ibid., p. 122 (P.1)).

60. Ibid.

61. Ibid., p. 174 (1.17).

62. Ibid., p. 175 (1.17).

63. Ibid., p. 195 (2.1).

64. Ibid., pp. 195–197 (2.1).

65. Ibid., p. 196 (2.1)

66. Ibid., p. 218 (2.9).

67. Ibid., p. 257 (2.22).

68. Ibid., pp. 257–58 (2.22).

69. Ibid., p. 295 (3.9).

70. Ibid., p. 340 (3.16).

71. Ibid.

72. For Nietzsche as an ironic mythmaker, see: Allan Megill, *Prophets of Extremity: Nietzsche, Heidegger, Foucault, Derrida* (Berkeley: University of California Press, 1985), p. 333ff.

73. Ibid., p. 225 (2.12).

NOTES TO CHAPTER 7

1. Friedrich Nietzsche, *Beyond Good and Evil*, in *Basic Writings of Nietzsche*, trans. Walter Kaufmann (New York: Modern Library, 1968), p. 251 (47).

2. Nietzsche, *Gay Science*, pp. 32–33 (P.1).

3. For more on the phenomenon of archaic religious ritual, see: Theodore H. Gaster, *Thespis: Myth, Ritual and Drama in the Ancient Near East* (New York: W.W. Norton & Co., 1971).

4. *Plotinus: Ennead V.1: On the Three Principal Hypostases*, trans. Michael Atkinson (Oxford: Oxford University Press, 1983), p. lxi (5.1.7).

5. Ibid., p. lvix. For a version of this same thought with 'full ($\pi\lambda\acute{\eta}\varrho\eta s$)' used as an alternative for 'perfect ($\tau\acute{\epsilon}\lambda\epsilon\iota os$),' see: *Ennead* 3.8.5.6.

6. Megill, *Prophets of Extremity*, pp. 65–102.

7. Nietzsche, *Gay Science*, p. 122 (58); Nietzsche, *Genealogy of Morals*, pp. 57–58 (2.1).

8. This parenthetical remark does not imply that Husserl consciously retrieves and transforms the religious usage of this pairing as Nietzsche does; see: Edmund Husserl, *Logical Investigations*, trans. J.N. Findlay (New York: Humanities Press, 1970), pp. 665–770.

9. Nietzsche, *Anti-Christ*, p. 133 (23).

10. Friedrich Nietzsche, "On Truth and Lie in an Extra-Moral Sense," *The Portable Nietzsche*, trans. and ed. Walter Kaufmann (New York: Penguin Books, 1976), p.47.

11. Catherine of Siena, *The Dialogue*, trans. Suzanne Noffke (New York: Paulist Press, 1980), p. 25 (1).

12. Ibid., p. 49 (13) and p. 37 (7).

13. Nietzsche, *Zarathustra*, p. 439 (4.20).

14. See, for instance, Noffke's introductory biographical remarks: Catherine of Siena, *Dialogue*, pp. 3–7.

15. Nietzsche, *Ecce Homo*, p. 219 (P.4).

16. Nehamas, *Nietzsche*, p. 232ff.

17. Scholars disagree about whether Clement was a forerunner of the doctrine of *creatio ex nihilio* or a subscriber to Platonic accounts of creation. E.F. Osborn has written that "Clement is the first person to state and give reasons for the doctrine of creation *ex nihilo*." See: Eric Francis Osborn, *The Philosophy of Clement of Alexandria* (Cambridge: Cambridge University Press, 1957), p. 33ff.

18. Mircea Eliade, *The Myth of the Eternal Return*, trans. Willard R. Trask (Princeton: Princeton University Press, 1971), pp. 3–4.

19. Ibid. p. 5.

20. Arthur O. Lovejoy, *The Great Chain of Being* (Cambridge, Mass.: Harvard University Press, 1964).

21. Ibid., pp. 24–66; for Lovejoy's denomination of the three principles, see pp. 52, 58, and 59.

22. John Dewey, *Experience and Nature* (New York: Dover Publications, 1958), p. 395.

23. Ibid., p. 396.

24. John Dewy, *A Common Faith* (New Haven: Yale University Press, 1934), p. 27.

25. Erik H. Erikson, *Young Man Luther: A Study in Psychoanalysis and History* (New York: W.W. Norton & Company, 1958); and *Gandhi's Truth: On the Origins of Militant Nonviolence* (New York: W.W. Norton & Company, 1970).

26. Aśvaghosa, *The Buddhacarita, or Acts of the Buddha*, ed. and trans. E.H. Johnson, reprint ed. (Philadelphia: Coronet Books, 1936).

27. *The Dhammapada*, trans. Juan Mascaro (New York: Penguin Books, 1973), p. 35 (2).

28. *The Path of Purity (Being a Translation of Buddhaghosa's Visuddhimagga)*, trans. Pe Maung Tin, Pali Text Society (London: Luzac & Company, 1971), p. 205ff.

29. Hermann Hesse, *The Glass Bead Game (Magister Ludi)*, trans. Richard and Clara Winston (New York: Bantam Books, 1979), pp. 24 and 31.

30. Ibid., pp. 9 and 22.

31. Ibid., p. 178.

32. Ibid., p. 132.

33. Ibid., p. 368.

34. Alasdair MacIntyre, *After Virtue: A Study in Moral Theory*, 2nd ed. (Notre Dame University Press, 1984), p. 245.

35. Ibid., p. 191.

36. Jeffrey Stout, *Ethics After Babel: The Languages of Morals and Their Discontents* (Boston: Beacon Press, 1988), p. 289.

37. Ibid.

38. Alasdair MacIntyre, *Whose Justice? Which Rationality?* (Notre Dame: Notre Dame University Press, 1988), p. 9.

39. Herbert A. Simon, *Administrative Behavior: A Study of Decision-Making Processes in Administration Organization*, 2nd ed. (New York: Macmillan Company, 1961), pp. 110–22, specifically p. 110; and Talcott Parsons, *Structure and Process in Modern Societies* (New York: Free Press, 1961), pp. 295–321, specifically p. 316.

40. Leo Tolstoy, *A Confession* (bound with *The Gospel in Brief* and *What I Believe*), trans. Aylmer Maude (London: Oxford University Press, 1940), p. 6 (1); for the most recent biography of Tolstoy, and the one reflected in my comments, see: A.N. Wilson, *Tolstoy*, (New York: Random House, 1989).

41. Mohandas K. Gandhi, *Autobiography: The Story of My Experiments with Truth*, trans. Mahadev Desai (New York: Dover Publications, 1983), pp. 18 and 29–30; the biography of Gandhi reflected in this section is by Louis Fischer, *The Life of Mahatama Gandhi* (New York: Harper & Row, 1983).

42. Dorothy Day, *The Long Loneliness: An Autobiography of Dorothy Day* (San Francisco: Harper & Row, 1981), pp. 20–22; for amplification of these points, see: William D. Miller, *Dorothy Day: A Biography* (San Francisco: Harper & Row, 1982).

43. Gandhi, *Autobiography*, p. 77.

44. Day, *Long Loneliness*, p. 38.

45. Dietrich Bonhoeffer, *Letters and Papers From Prison*, ed. Eberhard Bethge, enlarged ed. (New York: Macmillan Publishing Company, 1972), pp. 282 and 327; Bethge has also written the best biography of Bonhoeffer: *Dietrich Bonhoeffer: Man of Vision, Man of Courage*, trans. Eric Mosbacher et al. (New York: Harper & Row, 1977).

46. This document is quoted in: Aylmer Maude, *The Life of Tolstoy*, 2 vols. bound as one (Oxford: Oxford University Press, 1987), 1:290.

47. Martin Luther King, Jr., *Stride Toward Freedom: The Montgomery Story* (San Francisco: Harper & Row, 1986), p. 135; the biography most relevant here is by David J. Garrow, *Bearing the Cross: Martin Luther King, Jr. and the Southern Christian Leadership Conference* (New York: Random House, 1988).

48. Tolstoy, *Confession*, p. 61 (12).

49. Day, *Long Loneliness*, p. 148.

NOTES TO CONCLUSION

1. Marcel Proust, *Swann's Way*, trans. C.K. Scott Moncrieff (New York: Random House, 1970), p. 20.

2. Cornel West, *The American Evasion of Philosophy: A Genealogy of Pragmatism* (Madison, Wis.: University of Wisconsin Press, 1989), p. 233.

3. Søren Kierkegaard, *Training in Christianity*, trans. Walter Lowrie (Princeton: Princeton University press, 1967), p. 92.

4. I have made this case in some detail elsewhere; see: "Bonhoeffer, Nietzsche, and Secular Spirituality, *Encounter* 52.4 (Autumn 1991).

SELECT BIBLIOGRAPHY

à Kempis, Thomas. *The Imitation of Christ*. Translated by Harold C. Gardiner. Garden City, New York: Doubleday and Co., 1955.

*Albinus. *Didaskalikos*. 2.2. Translated by Richard A. Norris, Jr.

Andrews, Edward D. *The Gift to be Simple: Songs, Dances, and Rituals of the American Shakers*. New York: J.J. Augustin Publisher, 1940.

Antokoletz, Elliott. *The Music of Bela Bartok: A Study of Tonality and Progression in Twentieth Century Music*. Berkeley: University of California Press, 1984.

Aśvaghosa. *The Buddhacarita, or Acts of the Buddha*. Edited and Translated by E.H. Johnson. Reprinted edition. Philadelphia: Coronet Books, 1936.

Athanasius. *The Life of Antony (and the Letter to Marcellinus)*. Translated by Robert C. Gregg. Classics of Western Spirituality. New York: Paulist Press, 1980.

Aristotle. *Metaphysics*. Translated by Hugh Tredennick. In *Aristotle*: Vol. 18. Loeb Classical Library. Cambridge, Mass.: Harvard University Press, 1933.

_____. *Politics*. Translated by H. Rackham. In *Aristotle*: Vol 21. Loeb Classical Library. Cambridge, Massachusetts: Harvard University Press, 1932.

Augustine, Saint. *Concerning the Teacher*. Translated by George C. Leckie. In *Basic Writings of Saint Augustine*. Edited by Whitney J. Oates. Vol. 1. New York: Random House, 1948.

_____. *Confessions*. Translated by R.S. Pine-Coffin. London: Penguin Books, 1961.

_____. *De magistro*. Recensuit et praefatus est Guenther Weigel. In *Corpus Scriptorum Ecclesiasticorum Latinourm*. Vol. 77. Vindobonae: Hoelder-Pichler-Tempsky, 1961.

311

―――. *Divine Providence and the Problem of Evil.* Translated by Robert Russell. New York: Cosmopolitan Science & Art Service Co., 1942.

―――. *Ennarrationes in Psalmos.* In *Corpus Christianorum, Series Latina.* Vol. 40. Turnholti: Typograph Brepols Editores Pontificii, 1956.

―――. *De ordine.* In *Corpus Christianorum, Series Latina.* Vol. 29. Turnholti: Typograph Brepols Editores Pontificii, 1970.

―――. *Sermones.* In *Patrologia Latina* (See Migne, J.P.).

―――. *Solliloquies.* Translated by Thomas G. Gilligan. In *The Writings of Augustine.* Fathers of the Church. New York: Cima Publishing Company, 1948.

Aurelius, Marcus. *Meditations.* Translated by Maxwell Staniforth. London: Penguin Books, 1964.

Barth, Karl. *Church Dogmatics 3.2.* Translated by G.W. Bromiley et al. Edited by G.W. Bromiley and T.F. Torrance. Edinburgh: T. & T. Clark, 1960.

Bartlett, Steven J., and Peter Suber, eds. *Self-Reference: Reflections on Reflexivity.* Boston: Kluwer Academic Publishers, 1987.

Bateson, Gregory. *Steps Toward an Ecology of Mind.* New York: Random House, 1972.

Baudouin, Charles. *Blaise Pascal ou L'Ordre du Coeur.* Paris: Plon, 1962.

Bauer, Walter. *Orthodoxy and Heresy in Earliest Christianity.* Edited by Robert A. Kraft and Gerhard Krodel. Philadelphia: Fortress Press, 1971.

Beardsley, Tim. "Gaia: The Smile Remains, but the Lady Vanishes." *Scientific American* 261.6:35–36.

Belnap, Nuel D., Jr., and Thomas B. Steel, Jr. *The Logic of Questions and Answers.* New Haven: Yale University Press, 1976.

Benedict, Saint. *The Rule of Saint Benedict.* In *Western Asceticism.* Translated and edited by Owen Chadwick. Library of Christian Classics. Philadelphia: Westminster Press, 1958.

Bernard, Claude. *Leçons sur les Phénomènes de la Vie.* 2 tomes. Paris: Ballilère, 1878.

Bethge, Eberhard. *Dietrich Bonhoeffer: Man of Vision, Man of Courage.* Translated by Eric Mosbacher et al. New York: Harper & Row, 1977.

Bigg, Charles. *The Christian Platonists of Alexandria.* Oxford: University Press, 1913.

Birkhoff, Garrett, and Saunders MacLane. *A Survey of Modern Algebra.* Revised edition. New York: Macmillan Company, 1953.

Boethius, Ancius Manlius Severinus. *In Categorias Aristotelis.* In *Patrologia Latina* (see Migne, J. P.).

Bonhoeffer, Dietrich. *The Cost of Discipleship.* Revised edition. New York: Macmillan Company, 1963.

_____. *Letters and Papers from Prison.* Edited by Eberhard Bethge. Enlarged edition. New York: Macmillan Publishing Company, 1972.

Bohr, Niels. *The Philosophical Writings of Niels Bohr.* 3 vols. Woodbridge, Connecticut: Ox Bow Press, 1987.

Boyer, Carl B. *A History of Mathematics.* Princeton: Princeton University Press, 1985.

Boyle, Robert. *New Experiments Physico-Mechanical,* 1662.

Brown, Peter. *The Body and Society: Men, Women, and Sexual Renunciation in Early Christianity.* New York: Columbia University Press, 1988.

_____. *The Cult of the Saints: Its Rise and Function in Latin Christianity.* Chicago: University of Chicago Press, 1981.

Cannon, Walter B. *The Way of an Investigator: A Scientist's Experiences in Medical Research.* New York: W.W. Norton & Company, 1945.

———. *The Wisdom of the Body.* 2nd edition. New York: W.W. Norton & Company, 1939.

Caputo, John. *The Mystical Element in Heidegger's Thought.* New York: Fordham University Press, 1986.

Carmody, Denise L., and Carmody, John T. *Shamans, Prophets, and Sages: A Concise Introduction to World Religions.* Belmont, Cal.: Wadsworth Publishing Company, 1985.

Catherine of Siena. *The Dialogue.* Translated by Suzanne Noffke. Classics of Western Spirituality. New York: Paulist Press, 1980.

Chadwick, Henry. *Early Christian Thought and the Classical Tradition.* New York: Oxford University Press, 1966.

Chadwick, Owen. *From Bossuet to Newman: The Idea of Doctrinal Development.* Cambridge: Cambridge University Press, 1957.

Chang Chung-yuan. *Creativity and Taoism: A Study of Chinese Philosophy, Art, and Poetry.* New York: Harper and Row, 1970.

The Chinese on the Art of Painting. Translated and edited by Osvald Siren. New York: Schocken Books, 1963.

Chomsky, Noam. "Review Of B.F. Skinner's *Verbal Behavior.*" *The Structure of Language: Readings in the Philosophy of Language.* Edited by J.A. Fodor and J.J. Katz. Englewood Cliffs, N.J.: Prentice-Hall, 1964.

Chuang Tzu: Basic Writings. Translated by Burton Watson. New York: Columbia University Press, 1964.

Cicero. *De natura deorum* bound with *Academica.* Translated by H. Rackham. Loeb Classical Library. Cambridge, Mass.: Harvard University Press, 1933.

Clement of Alexandria. Translated by G.W. Butterworth. Loeb Classical Library. Cambridge, Mass.: Harvard University Press, 1919.

_____. *The Instructor.* In *The Ante-Nicene Fathers*, eds. Alexander Roberts and James Donaldson. Vol. 2. Grand Rapids, Mich.: Wm.B. Eerdmans Publishing, 1986.

_____. *Miscellanies Book VII.* Translation, introduction, and notes by Fenton John Anthony Hort and Joseph B. Mayor. New York: Macmillan Company, 1902.

_____. *Stromateis VII.* In *Alexandrian Christianity.* Edited by Henry Chadwick. Library of Christian Classics. Philadelphia: Westminster Press, 1954.

Colapietro, Vincent Michael. *Peirce's Approach to the Self: A Semiotic Perspective on Human Subjectivity.* Albany: State University of New York Press, 1989.

Courant, Richard, and Herbert Robbins, *What is Mathematics? An Elementary Approach to Ideas and Methods.* 4th edition. Oxford: Oxford University Press, 1949.

*Cousins, Ewert H., gen. ed. *The Classics of Western Spirituality: A Library of the Great Spiritual Masters.* New York: Paulist Press series.

*_____., gen. ed. *World Spirituality: An Encyclopedic History of the Religious Quest.* New York: Crossroad Publishing series.

Csikszentmihalyi, Mihaly. *Flow: The Psychology of Optimal Experience.* New York: Harper & Row, 1990.

Danto, Arthur. *Analytical Philosophy of Knowledge.* Cambridge: Cambridge University Press, 1968.

_____. *What Philosophy Is: A Guide to the Elements.* New York: Harper & Row, 1971.

Davidson, Hugh M. *The Origins of Certainty; Means and Meanings in Pascal's "Pensées."* Chicago: University of Chicago Press, 1979

Dawkins, Richard. *The Selfish Gene.* New York: Oxford University Press, 1976.

Day, Dorothy. *The Long Loneliness: An Autobiography of Dorothy Day.* San Francisco: Harper & Row, 1981.

de Chardin, Teilhard. *The Phenomenon of Man.* Translated by Bernard Wall. New York: Harper & Row, 1959.

de Guibert, Joseph. *The Jesuits, Their Spiritual Doctrine, and Practice.* Edited by George A. Ganno. Translated by William Y. Young. Chicago: Loyola University Press, 1964.

Deleuze, Gilles. *Nietzsche and Philosophy.* Translated by Hugh Tomlinson. New York: Columbia University Press, 1983.

De Lubac, Henry. *Paradoxes of Faith.* Translated by Paule Simon et al. San Francisco: Ignatius Press, 1986.

De Nicolas, Antonio T. *Powers of Imagining—Ignatius de Loyola.* Albany: State University of New York Press, 1986.

Derrida, Jacques. *Of Spirit: Heidegger and the Question.* Translated by Geoffrey Bennington and Rachel Bowlby. Chicago: University of Chicago Press, 1989.

_____. *On Grammatology.* Translated by Gayatri Chakravorty Spivak. Baltimore: Johns Hopkins University Press, 1976.

_____. *Spurs: Nietzsche's Styles.* Translated by Barbara Harlow. English-French edition. Chicago: University of Chicago Press, 1975.

Dewey, John. *A Common Faith.* New Haven: Yale University Press, 1934.

_____. *Democracy and Education: An Introduction to the Philosophy of Education.* New York: Macmillan Company, 1922.

_____. *Experience and Nature.* New York: Dover Publications, 1958.

_____. *The Quest for Certainty: A Study of the Relation of Knowledge and Action.* New York: Minton, Balch, & Co., 1929.

The Dhammapada. Translated by Juan Mascaró. New York: Penguin Books, 1973.

Dilthey, Wilhelm. "Der Aufbau der Geschichtlichen Welt in Den Geisteswissenschaften." In *Gesammelte Schriften*: Band 7. Gottingen: Vandenhoeck & Ruprecht, 1927.

Dionne, James Robert. *Pascal et Nietzsche: Étude Historique et Comparée*. New York: Burt Franklin, 1965.

Duncan, Isadora. *The Art of the Dance*. Edited by Sheldon Cheney. New York: Theater Arts Books, 1928.

Dunning, Stephen N. *Kierkegaard's Dialectic of Inwardness: A Structural Analysis of the Theory of Stages*. Princeton: Princeton University Press, 1985.

Durkheim, Emile. *The Elementary Forms of Religious Life*. Translated by Joseph Ward Swain. New York: Macmillan Company, Free Press, 1965.

Eales, Richard. *Chess: The History of A Game*. New York: Facts on File Publications, 1986.

Edwards, Jonathan. *Religious Affections*. Edited by John E. Smith. New Haven: Yale University Press, 1959.

Eldredge, Niles, and Stephen Jay Gould. "Punctuated Equilibria: An Alternative to Phyletic Gradualism." *Models in Paleobiology*. Edited by Thomas J.M. Schopf. San Francisco: Freeman, Cooper, & Company, 1972.

Eliade, Mircea. *The Myth of the Eternal Return*. Translated by Willard R. Trask. Princeton: Princeton University Press, 1971.

_____. *Patterns in Comparative Religion*. Translated by Rosemary Sheed. New York: New American Library, 1974.

_____. *Yoga: Immortality and Freedom*. Translated by Willard R. Trask. Princeton: Princeton University Press, 1969.

Eliot, George. *Adam Bede*. New York: New American Library, 1961.

Emerson, Ralph Waldo. *Selected Prose and Poetry*. Edited by Reginald L. Cook. 2nd edition. New York: Holt, Rinehart, and Winston, 1969.

Engels, Friedrich. *The Peasant War In Germany.* In *The German Revolutions.* Edited by Leonard Krieger. Chicago: University of Chicago Press, 1967.

Erikson, Erik H. *Gandhi's Truth: On the Origins of Militant Nonviolence.* New York: W.W. Norton & Company, 1970.

———. *Young Man Luther: A Study in Psychoanalysis and History.* New York: W.W. Norton & Company, 1958.

Feynman, Richard. *The Feynman Lectures on Physics.* 3 vols. With contributions by Robert B. Leighton and Matthew Sands. Reading, Mass.: Addison-Wesley Publishing, 1963.

———. *The Character of Physical Law.* Cambridge, Mass.: M.I.T. Press, 1967.

Fiorenza, Elisabeth Schüssler. *In Memory of Her: A Feminist Theological Reconstruction of Christian Origins.* New York: Crossroad Publishing, 1985.

Fischer, Louis. *The Life of Mahatma Gandhi.* New York: Harper & Row, 1983.

Fletcher, F.T.H. *Pascal and the Mystical Tradition.* Oxford: Basil Blackwell, 1954.

Foster, Richard J. *Freedom of Simplicity.* San Francisco: Harper & Row, 1989.

Foucault, Michel, *The Use of Pleasure.* Translated by Robert Hurley. New York: Random House, 1986.

Fowler, James W. *Stages of Faith: The Psychology of Human Development and the Quest for Meaning.* New York: Harper & Row, 1981.

Fox, Matthew. *Original Blessing: A Primer of Creation Spirituality.* Santa Fe: Bear & Company, 1983.

Frege, Gottlob. *Translations from the Philosophical Writings of Gottlob Frege.* Translated and edited by Peter Geach and Max Black. Oxford: Basil Blackwell, 1960.

Freud, Sigmund. *Standard Edition of the Complete Psychological Works of Sigmund Freud*. Translated and Edited by James Strachey. Vol 9. London: Hogarth Press, 1953–74.

Gandhi, Mohandas. *All Men are Brothers*. New York: Columbia University Press & Unesco, 1958.

_____. *Autobiography: The Story of My Experiments with Truth*. Translated by Mahadev Desai. New York: Dover Publications, 1983.

Gardner, Howard. *The Mind's New Science: A History of the Cognitive Revolution*. New York: Basic Books, 1985.

Gardner, Martin. *The Ambidextrous Universe: Left, Right, and the Fall of Parity*. Revised edition. New York: New American Library, 1969.

Garrow, David J. *Bearing the Cross: Martin Luther King, Jr. and the Southern Christian Leadership Conference*. New York: Random House, 1988.

Gaster, Theodor H. *Thespis: Myth, Ritual and Drama in the Ancient Near East*. New York: W.W. Norton & Company, 1971.

Gilligan, Carol. *In a Different Voice: Psychological Theory and Women's Development*. Cambridge, Mass.: Harvard University Press, 1982

Gödel, Kurt. "On Formally Undecidable Propositions of *Principia Mathematica* and Related Systems I." *From Frege to Godel: A Source Book in Mathematical Logic, 1879–1913*. Edited by Jean van Heijenoort. Cambridge, Mass.: Harvard University Press, 1967.

Goldmann, Lucien. *The Hidden God: A Study of Tragic Vision in the "Pensées" of Pascal and the Tragedies of Racine*. Translated by Philip Thody. New York: Humanities Press, 1964

Gould, Stephen Jay. "Is a New and General Theory of Evolution Emerging." *Paleobiology* 6:119–30.

Griffin, David Ray. "Spiritual Discipline in the Medieval, Modern, and Postmodern Worlds." *God and Religion in the Postmodern World: Essays in Postmodern Theology.* Albany: State University of New York Press, 1989.

Griffiths, Paul. *The String Quartet: A History.* New York: Thames and Hudson, 1983.

Gutiérrez, Gustavo. *A Theology of Liberation: History, Politics and Salvation.* Translated and edited by Caridad Inda and John Eagleson. Maryknoll, N.Y.: Orbis Books, 1973.

Haldane, J.B.S. *Adventures of a Biologist.* New York: Harper & Row, 1940.

Hanslick, Eduard. *The Beautiful in Music.* Translated by Gustav Cohen. Indianapolis, Ind. Bobbs-Merrill Company, 1957.

Hartman, Geoffrey H., and Sandford Budick, eds. *Midrash and Literature.* New Haven: Yale University Press, 1986.

Hegel, G.W.F. *Phenomenology of Spirit.* Translated by A.V. Miller. Oxford: Clarendon Press, 1977.

Heidegger, Martin. *The Question Concerning Technology and Other Essays.* Translated by William Lovitt. New York: Harper & Row, 1977.

―――. *Nietzsche.* Translated by David Krell. 4 vols. London: Routledge & Kegan Paul, 1981–1987.

Heisenberg, Werner. *Physics and Philosophy: The Revolution in Modern Science.* New York: Harper and Row, 1958.

Herrigel, Eugen. *Zen in the Art of Archery.* Translated by R. Hull. Introduced by D.T. Suzuki. New York: Random House, 1971.

Hesse, Hermann. *The Glass Bead Game (Magister Ludi).* Translated by Richard and Clara Winston. New York: Bantam Books, 1979.

Hippocrates. Translated by W.H.S. Jones. 4 vols. Loeb Classical Library. Cambridge, Mass.: Harvard University Press, 1923–31.

Hodgson, Peter, C. *The Formation of Historical Theology: A Study of Ferdinand Christian Baur.* New York: Harper & Row, 1966.

Husserl, Edmund. *Logical Investigations.* Translated by J.N. Findlay. 2 vols. London: Routledge & Kegan Paul, 1970.

Irenaeus. *Adversus Haereses* in *Patrologia Graeca.*(see: Migre, J.P.).

James, Henry. *Washington Square.* New York: New American Library, 1980.

James, William. *Essays in Radical Empiricism and A Pluralistic Universe.* New York: E.P. Dutton & Co., 1971.

_____. *Pragmatism and Other Essays.* New York: Washington Square Press, 1963.

Jaynes, Julian. *The Origin of Consciousness in the Breakdown of the Bicameral Mind.* Boston: Houghton Mifflin Company, 1977.

John of Damascus, Saint. *On the Divine Images: Three Apologies against those who attack the Divine Images.* Translated by David Anderson. Crestwood, New York: St. Vladimir's Seminary Press, 1980.

Jones, Cheslyn, et al., eds. *The Study of Spirituality.* Oxford: Oxford University Press, 1986.

Jung, C.G. *Collected Works.* Edited by Herbert Read, Michael Fordham, and Gerhard Adler. Vol. 9. New York: Pantheon Books, 1953–73.

Kadushin, Max. *The Rabbinic Mind.* 3rd edition. New York: Bloch Publishing, 1972.

Kant, Immanuel. *Critique of Pure Reason.* Translated by Norman Kemp Smith. New York: St. Martin's Press, 1965.

Kaufmann, Walter. *Nietzsche: Philosopher, Psychologist, AntiChrist.* 4th ed. Princeton: Princeton University Press, 1974.

Kautsky, Karl. *The Foundations of Christianity.* Translated by H.F. Mins. New York: 1953.

Kawabata, Yasunari. *The Master of Go*. Translated by Edward G. Seidensticker. New York: G.P. Putnam's Sons, 1981.

Kierkegaard, Søren. *Philosophical Fragments* bound with *Johannes Climacus*. Translated and edited by Howard V. Hong and Edna H. Hong. Princeton: Princeton University Press, 1985.

_____. *Purity of Heart is to Will One Thing*. Translated by Douglas V. Steere. New York: Harper & Row, 1956.

_____. *The Sickness Unto Death: A Christian Psychological Exposition for Upbuilding and Awakening*. Translated and edited by Howard V. Hong and Edna H. Hong. Princeton: Princeton University Press, 1980.

_____. *Training in Christianity*. Translated by Walter Lowrie. Princeton: Princeton University Press, 1967.

King, Martin Luther Jr. *Stride Toward Freedom: The Montgomery Story*. San Francisco: Harper & Row, 1986.

Kitzinger, Ernst. "Byzantine Art in the Period Between Justinian and Iconoclasm." *The Art of Byzantium and the Medieval West: Selected Studies*. Bloomington, Ind. Indiana University Press, 1976.

Kneale, William and Martha. *The Development of Logic*. Oxford: Clarendon Press, 1962.

Kohlberg, Lawrence, with Clark Power. "Moral Development, Religious Thinking, and the Question of a Seventh Stage." *The Philosophy of Moral Development: Moral Stages and the Idea of Justice*. New York: Harper & Row, 1981.

The Koran Interpreted. Translated by Arthur J. Arberry. 2 vols. New York: Macmillan Publishing Co., 1955.

Kuhn, Thomas S. *The Structure of Scientific Revolutions*. 2nd edition. Chicago: University of Chicago Press, 1970.

Lacey, W.K. *The Family in Classical Greece*. Ithaca, N.Y.: Cornell University Press, 1984.

Laertius, Diogenes. *Lives of Eminent Philosophers*. Translated by R.D. Hicks. 2 vols. Loeb Classical Library. Cambridge,Mass.: Harvard University Press, 1966.

Lao Tzu. *Tao Te Ching*. Translated by D.C. Lao. Harmondsworth, England: Penguin Books, 1963.

Lerner, Gerda. *The Creation of Patriarchy*. Oxford: Oxford University Press, 1986.

Lilla, Salvatore R. C. *Clement of Alexandria: A Study in Christian Platonism and Gnosticism*. Oxford: Oxford University Press, 1971.

Lovejoy, Arthur O. *The Great Chain of Being*. Cambridge, Mass.: Harvard University Press, 1964.

Lovelock, J.E. *The Ages of Gaia: A Biography of Our Living Earth*. New York: W.W. Norton & Company, 1988.

_____. *Gaia: A New Look at Life on Earth*. Oxford: Oxford University Press, 1987.

MacIntyre, Alasdair. *After Virtue: A Study in Moral Theory*. 2nd edition. Notre Dame, Ind.: Notre Dame University Press, 1984.

_____. *Whose Justice? Which Rationality?* Notre Dame, Ind.: Notre Dame University Press, 1988.

Marin, Louis. *La Critique du Discours: Sur la "Logique de Port-Royal" et les "Pensées" de Pascal*. Paris: Éditions de Minuit, 1975.

Markus, R.A. *Augustine: A Collection of Critical Essays*. Edited by R.A. Markus. Garden City, New York: Doubleday & Company, 1972.

Marshall, Alfred. *Principles of Economics*. 2 vols. New York: Macmillan Company, 1961.

Marx-Engels Werke: Vol. 3. Berlin: Institut für Marxismus und Leninismus, 1957–85.

Maude, Aylmer. *The Life of Tolstoy.* 2 vols. bound as one. Oxford: Oxford University Press, 1987.

Mayr, Ernst. *Animal Species and Evolution.* Cambridge, Mass.: Harvard University Press, 1963.

_____. *Toward a New Philosophy of Biology: Observations of an Evolutionist.* Cambridge, Mass.: Harvard University Press, 1988.

Megill, Allan. *Prophets of Extremity: Nietzsche, Heidegger, Foucault, Derrida.* Berkeley: University of California Press, 1985.

Merleau-Ponty, M. *Phenomenology of Perception.* Translated by Colin Smith. London: Roultledge & Kegan Paul, 1962.

Merton, Thomas. *Contemplative Prayer.* Garden City, N.Y. Doubleday & Company, 1971.

Meyendorff, John. *St. Gregory Palamas and Orthodox Spirituality.* Translated by Adele Fiske. Crestwood, N.Y. St. Vladimir's Seminary Press, 1974.

Mesnard, Jean. *Pascal: His Life and Works.* Translated by G.S. Fraser. London: Harville Press, 1952.

Migne, J.P., ed. *Patrologiae cursus completus: Series Graeca.* 161 vols. Paris: 1857–66.

Migne, J.P., ed. *Patrolgiae cursus completus: Series Latina.* 221 vols. Paris: 1878–90.

Miles, Margaret R. *Augustine on the Body.* Missoula, Mont.: Scholars Press, 1979.

_____. *Fullness of life: Historical Foundations for a New Asceticism.* Philadelphia: Westminster Press, 1981.

_____. *Practicing Christianity: Critical Perspectives for an Embodied Spirituality.* New York: Crossroad Publishing, 1988.

Miller, William D. *Dorothy Day: A Biography.* San Francisco: Harper & Row, 1982.

The Mind's Eye: Readings From Scientific American. Introduction by Jeremy M. Wolfe. New York: W.H. Freeman and Company, 1986.

Monod, Jacques. *Chance and Necessity: An Essay on the Natural Philosophy of Modern Biology*. Translated by Austryn Wainhouse. New York: Random House, 1971.

Murray, H.J.R. *The History of Chess*. Oxford Press: Oxford University Press, 1913.

Nagel, Ernest, and Newman, James R. "Gödel's Proof." *Contemporary Readings in Logical Theory*. Edited by Irving M. Copi and James A. Gould. New York: Macmillan Company, 1967.

Nehamas, Alexander. *Nietzsche: Life as Literature*. Cambridge, Mass.: Harvard University Press, 1985.

Neville, Robert C. *Soldier, Sage, Saint*. New York: Fordham University Press, 1978.

Newman, John Henry. *An Essay on the Development of Doctrine*. 1845 edition. Harmondsworth, England: Penguin Books, 1974.

Nietzsche, Friedrich. *The Anti-Christ* bound with *Twilight of the Idols*. Translated by R.J. Hollingdale. Harmondsworth, England: Penguin Books, 1968.

_____. *Beyond Good and Evil*. In *Basic Writings of Friedrich Nietzsche*. New York: Random House, Modern Library, 1968.

_____. *Daybreak*. Translated by R.J. Hollingdale. Cambridge: Cambridge University Press, 1982.

_____. *Ecce Homo* bound with *On the Genealogy of Morals*. Translated and edited by Walter Kaufmann. New York: Random House, 1969.

_____. *The Gay Science*. Translated by Walter Kaufmann. New York: Random House, 1974.

_____. *Gesammelte Werke*. 23 vols. Munich: Musarion Verlag, 1922–29.

_____. *On the Genealogy of Morals* bound with *Ecce Homo*. Translated by Walter Kaufmann and R.J. Hollingdale. New York: Random House, 1969.

_____. "On Truth and Lie in an Extra-Moral Sense." *The Portable Nietzsche*. Translated and edited by Walter Kaufmann. New York: Penguin Books, 1976.

_____. *Thus Spoke Zarathustra*. Translated by Walter Kaufmann. In *The Portable Nietzsche*. Harmondsworth, New York: Penguin Books, 1976.

_____. *Untimely Meditations*. Translated by R.J. Hollingdale. Cambridge: Cambridge University Press, 1983.

_____. *The Will to Power*. Translated by Walter Kaufmann and R.J. Hollingdale. New York: Random House, 1967.

Nozick, Robert. *Philosophical Explanations*. Cambridge, Mass.: Harvard University Press, 1981.

Osborn, Eric Francis. *The Philosophy of Clement of Alexandria*. Cambridge: Cambridge University Press, 1957.

Ouspensky, Leonid, and Vladimir Lossky. *The Meanings of Icons*. Translated by G.E.H. Palmer and E. Kadloubovsky. Boston: Boston Book and Art Shop, 1952.

Pagels, Heinz. *Perfect Symmetry: The Search for the Beginning of Time*. New York: Bantam Books, 1986.

Palamas, Gregory. *The Triads*. Edited by John Meyendorff. Translated by Nicholas Gendle. Classics of Western Spirituality. New York: Paulist Press, 1983.

Parsons, Talcott. *The Social System*. New York: The Free Press, 1951.

_____. *Structure and Process in Modern Societies*. New York: Free Press, 1961.

Pascal, Blaise. *Great Shorter Works of Pascal*. Translated by Emile Cailliet and John C. Blankenagel. Philadelphia: Westminster Press, 1948.

_____. *Oeuvres Complètes*. Présentation par Louis Lafuma. Paris: Éditions du Seuil, 1963.

_____. *Penseés*. Translated by A.J. Krailsheimer. London: Penguin Books, 1966.

_____. *The Provincial Letters*. Translated by A.J. Krailsheimer. Harmondsworth, England: Penguin Books, 1967.

The Path of Purity (Being a Translation of Buddhaghosa's Visuddhimagga). Translated by Pe Maung Tin. Pali Text Society. London: Luzac & Company, 1971.

Pauling, Linus. *General Chemistry*. New York: Dover Publications, 1970.

Pennick, Nigel. *Games of the Gods: The Origin of Board Games in Magic and Divination*. New York: Weiser Books, 1989.

Philo of Alexandria. *De vita contemplativa*. Translated by F.H. Colson. In *Philo*: Vol. 9. Loeb Classical Library. Cambridge, Mass.: Harvard University Press, 1967.

Piaget, Jean. *Biology and Knowledge: An Essay on the Relations Between Organic Regulations and Cognitive Process*. Translated Beatrice Walsh. Chicago: University of Chicago Press, 1971.

_____. *Genetic Epistemology*. Translated Eleanor Duckworth. New York: Columbia University Press, 1970.

_____. *The Origins of Intelligence in Children*. New York: W.W. Norton & Company, 1963.

Peirce, Charles Sanders. *Collected Papers of Charles Sanders Peirce*. 8 vols. Edited by Charles Hartshorne, Paul Weiss, and Arthur W. Burks. Cambridge, Mass.: Harvard University Press, 1931–58.

Pieris, Aloysius. *An Asian Theology of Liberation*. Maryknoll, N.Y.: Orbis Books, 1988.

Plato. *Laws*. Translated by R. G. Bury. In *Plato*: Vol. 10. Loeb Classical Library. Cambridge, Mass.: Harvard University Press, 1926.

_____. *The Republic*. Translated by Paul Shorey. In *Plato*: Vol. 5. Loeb Classical Library. Cambridge, Mass.: Harvard University Press, 1930.

_____. *Theaetetus*. Translated by Harold North Fowler. In *Plato*: Vol. 7. Loeb Classical Library. Cambridge, Mass.: Harvard University Press, 1921.

Plotinus: Ennead V.1: On the Three Principal Hypostases. Translated by Michael Atkinson. Oxford: Oxford University Press, 1983.

Polanyi, Michael. *Personal Knowledge: Towards a Post-Critical Philosophy*. Corrected edition. Chicago: University of Chicago Press, 1962.

Popper, Karl. *The Logic of Scientific Discovery*. New York: Harper & Row, 1968.

_____. *Objective Knowledge: An Evolutionary Approach*. Oxford: Oxford University Press, 1971.

The Principal Upaniṣads. Edited, translated, and introduced by S. Radhakrishnan. New York: Humanities Press, 1953.

Proust, Marcel. *Swann's Way*. Translated by C.K. Scott Moncrieff. New York: Random House, 1970.

Pseudo-Dionysius. *De caelesti hierarchia*. In *Patrologia Graeca*. (see Migne, J.P.)

Quine, Willard Van Orman. *From a Logical Point of View*. 2nd edition. New York: Harper & Row, 1961.

_____. *Word and Object*. Cambridge, Mass.: M.I.T. Press, 1960.

Radnitzky, Gerard, and W.W.Bartley, III, eds. *Evolutionary Epistemology, Theory of Knowledge, and the Sociology of Knowledge*. La Salle, Ill.: Open Court Publishing Company, 1987.

Rahner, Karl. *Theological Investigations*. Vols. 3, 7, and 8. London: Dartman, Longman, & Todd, 1967–71.

Rawls, John. *A Theory of Justice*. Cambridge, Mass.: Harvard University Press, 1972.

Rescher, Nicholas. *Pascal's Wager*. Notre Dame, Ind. University of Notre Dame Press, 1985.

Ricoeur, Paul. *The Symbolism of Evil*. Translated by Emerson Buchanan. Boston: Beacon Press, 1967.

_____. *Time and Narrative*. Vol. 1. Translated by Kathleen McLaughlin and David Pellauer. Chicago: University of Chicago Press, 1984.

Rimbaud, Arthur. *Rimbaud: Complete Works, Selected Letters*. English-French edition. Translated and edited by Wallace Fowlie. Chicago: University of Chicago Press, 1966.

Rorty, Richard. *Contingency, Irony, and Solidarity*. Cambridge: Cambridge University Press, 1989.

_____. *Philosophy and the Mirror of Nature*. Princeton: Princeton University Press, 1979.

Rousseau, Jean-Jacques. *Emile or On Education*. Translated by Allan Bloom. New York: Basic Books, 1979.

Ruse, Michael. *Taking Darwin Seriously: A Naturalistic Approach to Philosophy*. Oxford: Basil Blackwell, Ltd., 1986.

Russell, Bertrand. *Logic and Knowledge: Essays 1901–50*. Edited by Robert C. Marsh. New York: Capricorn Books, 1971.

_____. *Principles of Mathematics*. 2nd edition. New York: W.W. Norton & Co., 1938.

Schopenhauer, Arthur. *The World as Will and Representation*. Translated by E.F. Payne. 2 vols. New York: Dover Publications, 1969.

Schrödinger, Erwin. *Mind and Matter*. Cambridge: Cambridge University Press, 1967.

_____. *What is Life*. Cambridge: Cambridge University Press, 1967.

Select Passages From Ancient Writers Illustrative of the History of Greek Sculpture. Edited and translated by H. Stuart Jones. Chicago: Argonaut, Inc., 1946.

Sextus Empiricus. *Against the Logicians.* Translated by R.G. Bury. In *Sextus Empiricus*: Vol. 2. Loeb Classical Library. Cambridge, Mass.: Harvard University Press, 1933–49.

Shi, David E. *The Simple Life: Plain Living and High Thinking in American Culture.* Oxford: Oxford University Press, 1988.

Simon, Herbert. *Administrative Behavior.* 3rd edition. New York: Macmillan Publishing, 1976.

_____. *The Sciences of the Artificial.* 2nd edition. Cambridge, Mass.: M.I.T. Press, 1981.

Skinner, B.F. *Verbal Behavior.* New York: Appleton-Century-Crofts, 1957.

Smullyan, Raymund. "Languages in which Self-Reference is Possible." *The Philosophy of Mathematics.* Edited by Jaakko Hintikka. London: Oxford University Press, 1969.

Sobrino, Jon. *Spirituality of Liberation: Toward Political Holiness.* Translated by Robert R. Barr. Maryknoll, N.Y.: Orbis Books, 1988.

Sokolowski, Robert. *Husserlian Meditations: How Words Present Things.* Evanston, Ill.: Northwestern University Press, 1974.

The Spiritual Exercises of St. Ignatius. Translated by Anthony Mottola. Garden City, N.Y.: Doubleday and Co., 1964.

Starkie, Enik. *Arthur Rimbaud.* New York: New Directions, 1961.

Stevens, Peter S. *Handbook of Regular Patterns: An Introduction to Symmetry in Two Dimensions.* Cambridge, Mass.: M.I.T. Press 1984.

Stout, Jeffrey. *Ethics After Babel: The Language of Morals and Their Discontents.* Boston: Beacon Press, 1988.

Strauss, Erwin W. *Phenomenological Psychology.* Translated by Erling Eng. New York: Basic Books, 1966.

Suzuki, Daisetz Teitaro. *Outlines of Mahayana Buddhism*. New York: Schocken Books, 1963.

_____. *Zen and Japanese Culture*. Princeton: Princeton University Press, 1959.

Suzuki, Shunryu. *Zen Mind, Beginner's Mind*. Edited by Trudy Dixon. New York: Weatherhill, 1970.

Symmetry: Unifying Human Understanding. Edited by Istvan Hargittai. New York: Pergamon Press, 1986.

Tarski, Alfred. "The Concept of Truth in Formalized Languages." *Logic, Semantics, Metamathematics*. Translated by J.H. Woodger. Edited and introduced by John Corcoran. 2nd edition. Indianapolis, Ind.: Hackett Publishing Co., 1983.

_____. "The Semantic Conception of Truth and the Foundations of Semantics." *Philosophy and Phenomenological Research* no. 4 (1944):341-76.

Theissen, Gerd. *Biblical Faith: An Evolutionary Perspective*. Translated by John Bowden. Philadelphia: Fortress Press, 1985.

_____. *The Social Setting of Pauline Christianity: Essays on Corinth*. Edited and translated by John H. Schütz. Philadelphia: Fortress Press, 1982.

_____. *Sociology of Early Palestinian Christianity*. Translated by John Bowden. Philadelphia: Fortress Press, 1978.

Thomas, Edward J. *The Life of Buddha as Legend and History*. 3rd edition. London: Routledge & Kegan Paul, 1975.

Thompson, D'Arcy Wentworth. *On Growth and Form*. Edited by John Tyler Bonner. Abridged edition. Cambridge: Cambridge University Press, 1966.

Thoreau, Henry David. *Walden, or Life in the Woods*. New York: New American Library, 1960.

Tolstoy, Leo. *A Confession* bound with *The Gospel in Brief* and *What I Believe*. Translated by Aylmer Maude. London: Oxford University Press, 1940.

Toulmin, Stephen. "The Evolutionary Development of Natural Science." *American Scientist* 57:470–75.

_____. *Human Understanding.* Oxford: Oxford University Press, 1972.

Tucci, Giuseppe. *The Theory and Practice of the Mandala.* Translated by Alan Houghton Brodrick. New York: S. Weiser, 1970.

Turner, Victor. *The Ritual Process: Structure and Anti-Structure.* Ithaca, N.Y.: Cornell University Press, 1977.

Urbach, E.E. *The Sages—Their Concepts and Beliefs.* Translated by Israel Abrahams. Jerusalem: Magnes Press, 1975.

Van Der Leeuw, Gerardus. *Religion in Essence and Manifestation.* Translated by J.E. Turner. New York: Harper & Row, 1963.

van Gennep, Arnold. *The Rites of Passage.* Translated by Monika B. Vizedom and Gabriella L. Caffee. London: Routledge and Kegan Paul, 1909.

Vendler, Zeno, "Descartes' Exercises." *Canadian Journal of Philosophy*, 19.2. June 1989.

Wach, Joachim. *Sociology of Religion.* Chicago: University of Chicago Press, 1944.

Waddington, C.H. *The Nature of Life.* London: George Allen & Unwin, Ltd., 1961.

_____. *The Strategy of the Genes: A Discussion of Some Aspects of Theoretical Biology.* New York: Macmillan Company, 1957.

Wang Yang-ming. "Inquiry on the Great Learning." *Source Book in Chinese Philosophy.* Edited by Wing-tsit Chan. Princeton: Princeton University Press, 1963.

Weber, Max. *The Protestant Ethic and the Spirit of Capitalism.* Translated by Talcott Parsons. New York: Charles Scribner's Sons, 1958.

_____. *The Sociology of Religion.* Translated by Ephraim Fischoff. Boston: Beacon Press, 1963.

West, Cornel. *The American Evasion of Philosophy: A Genealogy of Pragmatism.* Madison, Wis.: University of Wisconsin Press, 1989.

Westphal, Merold. *God, Guilt, and Death: An Existential Phenomenology of Religion.* Bloomington: Ind. University Press, 1984.

Weyl, Hermann. *Symmetry.* Princeton: Princeton University Press, 1952.

Whitehead, Alfred North, *Process and Reality: An Essay in Cosmology.* Edited by David Ray Griffin and Donald W. Sherburne. Corrected edition. New York: Macmillan Publishing, 1978.

_____. *Adventures of Ideas.* New York: Macmillan Company, 1967.

Wiener, Norbert. *Cybernetics: or Control and Communication in the Animal and Machine.* 2nd edition. Cambridge, Mass.: M.I.T. Press, 1961.

Wilson, A.N. *Tolstoy.* New York: Random House, 1989.

Wilson, Edward O. et al. *Life On Earth.* 2nd edition. Sunderland, Mass.: Sinauer Associates, Inc., 1978.

_____. *On Human Nature.* New York, Bantam Books, 1979.

Wolfson, Harry. *The Philosophy of the Church Fathers.* Cambridge, Mass.: Harvard University Press, 1956.

Writings on Spiritual Direction By Great Christian Masters. Edited by Jerome M. Neufelder and Mary C. Coelho. New York: Seabury Press, 1982.

Yoga Philosophy of Patañjali. Translated by P.N. Murkerji. Introduction and notes by Swāmi Hariharānanda Āranya. Albany: State University of New York Press, 1983.

The Zen Teaching of Huang Po on the Transmission of Mind. Translated by John Blofeld. New York: Grove Press, 1959.

Zimmer, Heinrich. *Philosophies of India.* Edited by Joseph Campbell. Princeton: Princeton University Press, 1969.

INDEX

Aaron, Hank, 111
Abbot, monastic, 136–137
Abstractionism, 205–206
Adaptation, 192–193, 194, 195
Addiction and addictive habits, 88, 90, 244–245, 259
Advertising, ix, 89, 244–245
Agape and agapism, 190, 215
AIDS, 90
Albinus, 4, 53
Alcmaeon of Croton, 165–166
Alcoholism, 218
Americans, Native, 87
Anaximenes, 141
Anchorites, 189, 243
Apology and Apologetics, 6–7, 8–9, 10
Apprenticeship, spiritual. *See* Masters, spiritual, and their disciples
Aquinas, Thomas, 10, 81; *Summa Theologiae,* 47
Archimedes, 164
Architecture, classical Greek, 61–62
Architecture, church, 104–105
Aristotle, 9, 51, 101, 261; on God, 41, 42, 55, 67; on habits, 81, 258; and praxis, 4, 258; on slavery, justification of, and static hierarchy, 45; on soul as cause, 55–56; on truth and semiotic self-reference, 97; "Wise men give orders," and totalitarianism, 60–61; *Metaphysics,* 9, 41, 55; *Nicomachean Ethics,* 4, 68; *Posterior Analytics,* 61
Art, modern, 124
Artists, 74, 220
āsana, 253
Ascetic: creativity, 75; ideals, 9, 31, 88, 189, 207, 220, 238

Ascetic Ideals, The Perils of: countering Nietzsche's critique of religious practices, 203–219
Ascetic: life, 34; practices, 219, 242; priest, 161, 206–207, 208, 210, 216, 219, 221, 242, 261; self-discipline, 34
Asceticism, 206, 208, 217, 221; Nietzsche's criticism of, 203–206; Schopenhauerian rationale for, 203, 205, 238. *See also* "Will to nothingness;" Practices, ascetic; Sex, abstinence from; Fasting; Poverty
Athanasius: *Vita Antonii,* 54
Athletics, 169
Augustine, 47, 81, 97, 114, 115, 129; doctrine of election, 32; on God, 32, 117; on signs, 99, 100; on spiritual discipline, 166–167; on spiritual life, 130; *Confessiones,* 114; *Contra Academicos,* 99; *De doctrina Christiana,* 117; *De libero arbitrio,* 130; *De Ordine,* 129–130; *Soliloquia,* 47, 166
Autarky (self-sufficiency), 39, 42
Authoritarianism, 61, 68
Axioms, geometrical, 29

Balance, 169–170, 176
Baptism, 36, 234, 268
Barth, Karl, 6
Baseball, 259
Baudouin, Charles, 20
Bauer, Walter, *Orthodoxy and Heresy in Earliest Christianity,* 183–184
Beethoven, Ludwig van, 127–128
Behavior, religious. *See* Practices, spiritually disciplined

335